A GATEWAY FROM THE EASTERN MEDITERRANEAN TO INDIA

The Red Sea in Antiquity

A GATEWAY FROM THE EASTERN MEDITERRANEAN TO INDIA

The Red Sea in Antiquity

Edited by

Marie-Françoise BOUSSAC
Jean-François SALLES

MANOHAR
2005

MAISON DE L'ORIENT MEDITERRANEEN
JEAN POUILLOUX

First published 2005

ISBN 81-7304-570-4

Published by
Ajay Kumar Jain for
Manohar Publishers & Distributors
4753/23 Ansari Road, Daryaganj
New Delhi 110 002

Printed at
Lordson Publishers Pvt Ltd
Delhi 110 007

Distributed in South Asia by
FOUNDATION
BOOKS
4381/4, Ansari Road
Daryaganj, New Delhi 110 002
and its branches at Mumbai, Hyderabad,
Bangalore, Chennai, Kolkata

CONTENTS

Trade patterns in the Red Sea

Literary sources and ancient navigations

Miscellanea

PREFACE

After the favourable reception of collections of essays such as *Athens, Aden, Arikamedu. Essays on the interrelations between India, Arabia and the Eastern Mediterranean*, 1995 (ed. by M.-F. Boussac and J.-F. Salles, Manohar - Centre for Human Sciences, New Delhi), *Crossings. Early Mediterranean Contacts with India*, 1997 (ed. by F. De Romanis and A. Tchernia, A Manohar - CSH Publication in association with the Italian Embassy Cultural Centre, New Delhi), or more recently *Archaeology of Seafaring. The Indian Ocean in the Ancient Period*, 1999 (ed. by H. Prabha Ray, Pragati Publications, Delhi), it has seemed appropriate to present here a new *florilegium* of contributions specifically devoted to the Red Sea and its ancient relations with India.

Most of the papers were delivered on the occasion of a seminar held in Lyon (Institut Fernand-Courby - Maison de l'Orient Méditerranéen) late 1995: the meeting was intended to present and discuss a pre-print version of the book by F. De Romanis, *Cassia, cinnamomo, Mediterraneo ed Erythra thalassa da Nero ad Augusto*, which the author kindly provided the participants with before the official publication of the volume (*Cassia, cinnamomo, ossidiana : uomini e merci tra Oceano Indiano e Mediterraneo*, L'Erma di Bretschneider, Roma), in 1996. The seminar was published as a "dossier" of the journal *Topoi* (Lyon), vol. 6/2, 1996, pp. 649-941, and a selection of the papers was translated in order to be submitted to an Indian editor. It also sounded useful to include in the present compendium two papers by F. De Romanis written "answers" to the *Topoi* dossier, as well as a couple of book reviews related to the main topic (see *Miscellanea*) which might be of interest for English-speaking readers. More importantly, Prof. H. Cuvigny kindly prepared an updated review (2000) of current researches in the Eastern Desert of Egypt, which constitutes a major contribution to the theme of the book.

Studies about the interconnexions between the Indian world and the Mediterranean countries in Antiquity have been blooming in the past decades in the West and in India. Researches have variedly focussed on archaeological, historical, economic or intellectual matters, although more anthropological approaches were also proposed, through the ethnography of maritime India for example, or through the elucidation of the impacts of religious or cultural changes on the ancient societies, their structures, their economy and their own perception of the antique world.

Among this literature, a frequent weak point might be encountered in the form of a linear reasoning, taking into consideration the total amount of the available sources from the both sides of the topic (*i.e.* India and the West), but ignoring the reality of the numerous stages on the way of any voyage from the Mediterranean to India or vice-versa. On the contrary, it becomes gradually evident that more regional studies would allow a much better understanding of the trade interconnexions between these two distant regions: what has emerged, for instance, in recent writings on the *Periplus of the Erythraean Sea*, is a dynamic segmentation or sectorisation of trade exchanges, which gives the sub-regions and their populations a central role, far away from the irrealistic (?), at least atypical, "non-stop" navigation from any harbour of the Red Sea to any far-flung port of Southern India.

The Red Sea certainly appears as a nice case study in this perspective. The region is well documented by a large amount of Classical sources, and epigraphical researches have provided numerous finds in different languages. Moreover, archaeological excavations and surveys have been flourishing throughout the region in the past few years, with outstanding results, for example at Berenike. As a "counter-part", the themes developed by F. De Romanis, a distinguished Classical philologist also specialised in Tamil language, are groundbreaking when confronting, in a regional perspective, two totally different streams of historical information. Then, a meeting of Egyptologists, Classical scholars and Indianists, from various disciplines, historians, archaeologists and philologists could only bring a comprehensive and innovative approach of the subject, a selection of which is tentatively presented in this volume.

The English version of the French contributions was prepared by Mrs L. Sahgal under the supervision of the *Bureau du livre*, Cultural Section of the French Embassy in New Delhi, which kindly provided the financing of the translation from French to English (F. De Romanis' papers in Italian were translated into English by the author himself). After a preliminary revision of the texts by M.-F. Boussac, each author was given proofs in English for the last corrections. The setting and final preparation of the volume was prepared by F.L. Lucarelli (Institut F.-Courby, Lyon), whom we want to thank for his tireless dedication to that enterprise.

Any responsibility for the delay of the final disclosure of the volume and for any mistake which this book still contains lie with the undersigned scientific editors.

Marie-Françoise BOUSSAC Jean-François SALLES

REMARKS ON F. DE ROMANIS' BOOK
THE EGYPTOLOGIST'S POINT OF VIEW

Though the first part of the book (Chapters I to IV and Appendix) makes fascinating reading, it is a subject of controversy because its arguments are based on ancient Egyptian philology. Its very basis is a hieroglyphical term whose meaning is not known and spelling uncertain. It changes constantly and is subject to phonetic variations difficult to demonstrate as when the author tries to establish the Egyptian origin of the archaic Greek term ΚΑΣΣΙΑ and also of the Hebrew equivalent *qsy'wt* (p. 43 and n. 43).

Besides, not being qualified to deal with the related issue of the Greek origin of ΚΙΝΝΑΜΩΜΟΝ derived from the Biblical Hebrew word *qnm(w)n* which competes in texts with the term *qnh*, although we have referred to it here in order to understand De Romanis' approach, we have no intention whatsoever of contesting the validity of the terms he uses in the linguistic field. Since he is quite emphatic that the Hebrew *qesyôt* is "evidently and without the slightest doubt the equivalent of the Greek κασία" (p. 43), we can only subscribe to what appears to be perfectly legitimate up to that point. But that is not the case with what follows.

Our observations will therefore concentrate mainly on the hieroglyphical sources and the problems they may create and on the botanical aspect which the author has dealt with only in passing.

1. Egyptian, phonetic and semantic sources

The author claims that the term κασία/*casia*/*cassia* or the French *casse* is derived from the Egyptian *šsꜣt/ẖsꜣyt*, following Edel's opinion (*SAK*, 11, 1984, 187-193) regarding the passage of the palato-alveolar fricative to the aspirate guttural. Phonetically, there is nothing unusual about it in old Egyptian, but it is more difficult to trace from *šsꜣt/ẖsꜣt* all the words starting with not *Š* or *H̱* (𓄡), but *Ḫ* (𓐍), because it is at least a term written as *ḫsꜣyt* almost certainly

A Gateway from the Eastern Mediterranean to India. The Red Sea in Antiquity
J.-C. GOYON, pp. 7-11

identifiable with dioecious bryony which has evidently no connection. It is moreover rather surprising to note that the word *Šsꜣt,* which occurs in this written form only in the Old Kingdom and became *ẖsꜣyt* in the medical texts of the Middle Kingdom, would later become so rare after the New Kingdom — and the text of Hatshepsut's expedition to Punt — when it was written as *ḫsꜣyt* or *ḫꜣsyt.* There is something even stranger: if, as the author believes, probably justifiably (p. 64), that it was towards the 7th or 6th century that the Greeks adopted the passage of *qasyôt* to κασία, how is it that one can find only two examples of this term in hieroglyphical documents belonging to the subsequent period: one belonging to the 30th dynasty (DARESSY, *ASAE*, 16, 1916, 223 [8]) and the other to the Ptolemaic period following 237 B.C. (CHASSINAT, *Edfou* VII, 131 [6]) relating to aromatic substances written as *ḫsyt* and *ḫsꜣy.w* (Edfou)? Of course, the argument is not very valid, but it appears paradoxical that this denomination, which the Egyptians who consorted with the Greeks from the Saitic pharaohs onwards were no more familiar with, should be just the one chosen by the Hellenes while their interlocutors, who sometimes had more than ten synonyms for *Boswellia* or *Commiphora* resins viz. olibanum, styrax or myrrh, used it but rarely. The answer perhaps is that *ẖsꜣyt / ḫsꜣyt / ḫꜣsyt* <*šsꜣt* is only the "old-fashioned" name of a "resin" or "oleo-resin" from the south and not a commonly used name in spoken Egyptian and that a more practical name hides in the vast semantic arsenal of medicine and sacred perfumery.

Another difficulty arises from the proposed equivalence, viz. phonetics. If the concerned word beginning with an aspirate guttural in its recent state had survived in the Coptic language (which does not seem to be the case), its initial letter could have behaved in only one of the three following ways:

– becoming a palato-alveolar fricative: ϣ
– changing into the recent variety of the aspirate guttural: ϧ
– becoming hard if need be and changing into *gu*- ϭ, but it would not have given a *k* likely to be understood as K in Greek.

Let us, however, set this problem aside as the study of ancient Egyptian phonetics is still in its infancy and is yet to be properly systematized.

2. The botanical problem

However, we must take up the botanical problem in all seriousness. In the Appendix (p. 109), the author lists the main critics of the theory that holds that cassia and cinnamon were obtained from Eritrea and Somalia/Ethiopia. But he does not clarify, except in a note or in parenthesis, that the "African barks" of the Ancients could be different from the modern species of "Chinese" aromatic barks (il nostro cinnamomo)! It should have been clarified at the very outset what modern apothecaries, perfumers, herbalists and druggists consider as CASSIA and CINNAMON.

CASSIA is produced by *Laurus Cassia* L / *Cinnamomum obtusifolium* Nees. What is called cinnamon in the spice trade comes from Ceylon and is obtained from the *Cinnamomum Zeylanicum* Nees and what is known as "casse" in France is "Chinese cinnamon". Another variety which has been somewhat neglected is "Malabar cinnamon" obtained from the *Malabathrum* tree which was used mainly by veterinarians (A. GUÉRILLOT-VINET and L. GUYOT, *Les Épices*, Que Sais-je? No. 1040, 1963, p. 52 sq.; F.A. FLÜCKIGER, *Pharmakognosie des Pflanzenreichs*, 3rd ed., Berlin, 1891, p. 592 sq.). It may be noted that while the rolled bark provides the spice called cinnamon (cannella or "small cane" in Italian), the roots provide camphor and the leaves an essential oil extracted by decoction.

The authors of works based on the botanical study of these "spices" are certain that cinnamon-producing trees never grew in Eastern Africa, although they concede that the spice may have been traded on the African and Arabian coasts (*Les Épices*, p. 54). It is also necessary to determine the date when this trade started. It is very doubtful if it was practised by the Pharaonic Egyptians even though as early as 1886, Flückiger (*Pharmakognosie*, pp. 49 & 594-595), together with Lieblein, supported the same theory as De Romanis. But it was firmly refuted by Chevalier de Jaucourt in 1751 in *l'Encyclopédie* II, p. 593. We may note with Chevalier de Jaucourt that the cinnamon-based anointing oil mentioned in Biblical literature could not have been perfumed with the "wood" or the "bark" of the Ceylonese or Chinese cinnamon because they would have to be distilled before use. Since the distillation process was still unknown, only a resin or an oleoresin could have impregnated an oil or an unguent with their perfume by a process of marination. We must also leave out cinnamon "wax", extracted by decoction from the fruits of this tree, which was used only for making perfumed candles in Europe.

But coming back to the medical uses mentioned in texts belonging to the end of the Middle Kingdom, without laying too much stress on them, we find that the editors of the *Wörterbuch der ägyptischen Drogennamen, Grundriß der Medizin* VI, Berlin, 1959, pp. 417-418, keeping in mind the ingredients mentioned in recipes and directions for use (plasters, unguents, application), proposed as an equivalent for *ḫsꜣyt* "Balsam oder Harz" without identifying it. They were quite right to do so because of the uncertainty about the nature of the product whose hieroglyphical symbol sometimes matches the sign for tree and more often the sign denoting grains or even the vessel used for unguents obtained from resins and oleoresins. If it were really "cinnamon", and that too in the form of a **bark**, the sign denoting a branch would have been used.

A conclusive argument is provided by one of the recipes in the Ebers medical papyrus No. 255 referring to the use of *gnn n ḫsꜣyt* "a soft extract of *Khesayt*". As Chassinat (*Mystères d'Osiris au mois de Khoïak* I, 1966, p. 219 and n. 1) has shown, the term *gnn / gꜣn* was used specially to describe the unctuous quality of resins impregnated with their natural oleoresin, before being processed. Further, *Edfou* VII, 130 (14 sq.) – 131 (1-6) specifies in line 6 that *Khesayt* is one of the "aromatic substances" and resins obtained from Punt or the "Land of God" used like olibanum as a sacred fumigant (title of the scene: "fumigation with olibanum" *kꜣp 'ntiw* 130, 14). This would eliminate *a priori* both cassia and cinnamon if *khesayt* is taken to be the semantic correspondent because the cinnamon oil used by perfumers is obtained through a chemical action whereas the bark when it is pounded and **distilled, which the ancient Egyptians did not do**, does not produce any "oil" and much less a "resin" (J. VON WIESNER, *Rohstoffe des Pflanzenreichs*, 4th ed., vol. I, Leipzig, 1927, p. 102). Finally, in traditional medicine as practised in the 18th and 19th centuries (see Chevalier de Jaucourt, article titled "Canelle" in Diderot-d'Alembert, *Encyclopédie*, tome II, Paris, 1751, pp. 594-595), when cinnamon was still in use, it was only used internally or orally (as a mouth wash) and not externally for applications as in the case of *khesayt* in Pharaonic times.

We must however take for granted, like the author (pp. 59 sq. and 150 to 156), that the substance called *khesayt* was considered to be a native of Southern Egypt and of Punt or Opus according to the earliest hieroglyphical sources. But the exact location of Opus, like that of the "Land of God" is still uncertain and a subject of controversy. Nevertheless, it is likely that the areas producing olibanum, myrrh and styrax in Eastern Africa, Somalia, Eritrea, lower Ethiopia or the western and southern coast of Arabia were all part of "Punt". The author (pp. 150-156) presents an interesting hypothesis that the term *wḏlṯt* in Pharaonic geographical lists may cover the place name Adulis occurring in Graeco-Roman sources and the idea is probably to be kept. On the contrary, his assimilation (p. 156) of the Biblical *wdn /'wzl* (p. 70) with *wtnt* found in the texts of Thutmosis III and the Ptolemies, if phonetically plausible, gives rise to scepticism as soon as one tries to show that it was the land that produced cassia and cinnamon. There is, however, a certain amount of unanimity among Egyptologists (S. AUFRÈRE, *Univers minéral* in IFAO *Bd'E* 105/2, Cairo, 1990, p. 757 and note a, below) that *wdn /wdnt* corresponds to the coastal region of the Gulf of Aden and that if one obtains *ḥmꜣgt* from there, the only thing certain about it is that it is red and can be used as a pigment, and that it is probably not hematite (the author provides the concerned references, pp. 61-63 and n. 102-104), amethyst or garnet nor is it a "resin" (Vercoutter). It is particularly as a producer of fresh OLIBANUM in the form of tears, meant for burning, that the region of *wdn / wdnt* is famous in all the "geographical" texts in hieroglyphics of the

Ptolemaic and Roman periods. It is not possible to mention all the sources and we give below a brief selection that should suffice:

— CHASSINAT, *Edfou* II, 200 (6), list of olibanums coming from Oudenou, showing that this olibanum was in the form of "tears" (the size of a swallow's egg, *ibid.*, 201, 15) which is the normal form of olibanum used for burning still called *ꜣwyšꜣ wꜣḏ*;

— CHASSINAT, *Dendara* II, 11 (14); 180 (9-10); 217 (12), among others for the use of this fresh *aouysha* olibanum in liturgical fumigation.

Thus, nothing in the available documents provided by hieroglyphical sources or by botanical data supports the thesis that the Egyptians' mythical land of Punt was the place from where the Hebrews and later the Greeks and Romans obtained cassia and cinnamon if they correspond to Chinese or Ceylonese cinnamon. In the Middle Ages, as the author himself points out (p. 116, n. 40) citing a Syriac text in support, it was styrax which was called cinnamon. So it is perhaps not necessary to look for the origin of casia, cassia or the French "casse" in Egypt as the Hebrew *qasyôt* fully justifies etymological requirements and *qnm (w)n*, which does not have an ancient Egyptian etymology (at least the author does not suggest any) is most probably "Ma'in cane" or *canna minea*. It appears to me that the author is quite right to link the two without going beyond the Semitic domain or sources that he has every right to use. But all said and done, the author should be thanked most heartily for his fine work and for the opportunity it provides for healthy debate and reflection.

Jean-Claude GOYON
Emeritus Professor of Egyptology
University of Lyon II

A FANTASMATIC CINNAMON

In a recent issue of *Topoi,*[1] A. Tchernia ends his article on "Rome and India" with a glowing tribute to the Italian historian Santo Mazzarino credited among other things with destroying the myth of Hippalos, "the inventor of the monsoon". He also includes in his praise Mazarino's pupil, Federico De Romanis, who, he claims, "is methodical and possesses exceptional philological gifts". Like A. Tchernia, I was looking forward to the publication of *Cassia, cinnamomo, ossidiana*, especially because the two products from the plant world find frequent mention in Theophrastus' treatise which I am in the process of editing.[2] Even at the risk of being called tactless for not joining in the chorus of praise, I must confess that I found the book disappointing. I had expected an exhaustive study of ancient texts concerning these spices, a detailed reference to the debate between the supporters and the opponents of their Indian origin and, in the absence of a fresh viewpoint, a well-founded and restrained judgement on each of the theories discussed. However, the botanical problem is dismissed right away as being insoluble[3] and the signifier is studied without any reference to the signified thereby entailing all the hazards involved in such a method. It is not for me to comment on the legitimacy of the parallel drawn between the Egyptian

1. *Topoi* 3/2, 1993, pp. 525-534. See in particular pp. 533-534.
2. Published in CUF, Paris (Les Belles Lettres), under the title *Recherches sur les plantes (HP=Historia plantarum* in references*).* Three volumes have already appeared in 1988, 1989 and 1993 and two are yet to be published of which volume V in which the controversial problem of the origin of *kas(s)ia* and *kin(n)amômon* (that I shall call "cassia" and "cinnamon" without any prejudice to their botanical identity) will be discussed.
3. P.33: "We do not know today which are the species with which we should identify κασία and κινάμωμον, both bushes with a highly valued aromatic bark."

A Gateway from the Eastern Mediterranean to India. The Red Sea in Antiquity
S. AMIGUES, pp. 13-20

šsꜣt/hsꜣt and the Hebrew *qṣy ᶜwt* (from which the Greek *kas[s]ia* is derived),[4] which induced the author to look for cassia's origin in East Africa and, therefore, also the origin of cinnamon which has always been associated with it from ancient times. Since these substances are aromatic barks[5] which cannot be ascribed to any of the species now found in Somalia, Ethiopia or their neighbouring countries, the only possibility is to link them to "a species which is extinct or which has not yet been identified" (p. 109). This difficulty does not deter the author from claiming without any hesitation (p. 97) that "the Greek word (κασία) is derived from an Egyptian term designating an African spice". Being very sure of himself, he does not bother about the proponents of "the widespread, but nevertheless untenable, theory that κασία and κινάμωμον correspond to the present-day cinnamon" (p. 33, n. 1). He displays his conceit in an even more distasteful manner on p. 109: "The common history of both terms, as we have demonstrated above, decisively eliminates any possibility of a Far-Eastern origin of these spices as also of the terms designating them. There is no need to repeat that such a belief is totally baseless and preposterous." The use of such strong language does not do credit to the author.

There is no question of dealing with the entire problem in this article. The following observations are only meant to complement the author's exposition of his thesis and rectify some mistakes in order to help the reader to form his/her own opinion.

There is no doubt that F. De Romanis has taken great pains over his study of the spice trade in ancient times in the Mediterranean and the "Erythraean Sea". The footnotes provide innumerable references to a wide variety of works on history and geography, from Egyptology to the economic history of the Mediterranean Basin and the Middle-East in ancient times, etc. with the deliberate exclusion of botany. The author does not venture into this field as he does not expect to find anything there after having categorically declared that the trees producing cassia and cinnamon have become extinct or have not been rediscovered. Nevertheless, even in the disciplines in which we may unreservedly admire his extensive knowledge, there are surprising omissions. Firstly, there is no mention of Olck's article *Casia* in the *Real Encyclopädie*[6] containing the most

4. The Semitic origin is generally accepted. Apart from E. MASSON, *Recherches sur les plus anciens emprunts sémitiques en grec*, Paris, 1967, pp. 48-49, quoted on p. 43, n. 38, see in particular CHANTRAINE, *DELG*, *s.v.* "κασία "; J. ANDRÉ, *Les noms des plantes dans la Rome antique*, Paris, 1985, *s.v.* "casia".

5. Cf. Theophrastus, *HP* IX, 5, 1 (on the subject of *kinamômon*): "it is the bark that is used and not the wood"; IX, 5, 3 (similarly about *kasia*) "the useful part is the bark".

6. *RE III* 2, 1899, c.1637-1651.

complete information about these spices together with references to Greek, Latin, Hebrew and Arabic texts in addition to etymological explanations of their names taken from Asian languages. I find it difficult to believe that F. De Romanis is unaware of the existence of this article and I am afraid that he has ignored it because the author's views are radically opposed to his own. As a matter of fact, Olck claims (c. 1637) that "*casia* or *cassia* and *cinnamomum* or *cinnamum* are species of cinnamon belonging to the genus *Cinnamomum*", and his etymological study of the Hebrew *kezî'ah* or the Greek κασία makes him conclude (c. 1640) that "it is not necessary that *kezî'ah* should be derived from the Egyptian *khisīt* (...); on the contrary, the word seems to come directly from *keï-schi*" (which means "twig of cinnamon" in Chinese). This point could have provided an interesting subject of discussion perhaps with the participation of specialists in Far-Eastern languages. It appears that for the same reason F. De Romanis has overlooked J. INNES MILLER's fundamental work, *The Spice Trade of the Roman Empire (29 B.C. to A.D. 641)*, Oxford, 1969, which deals in great detail with cassia and cinnamon (pp. 42-47; 74-77) and devotes a whole chapter (pp. 153-172 with a map) to the "cinnamon route". F. De Romanis undoubtedly has valid arguments against the hypothesis regarding the Indian or Far-Eastern origin of these spices which, as we have seen, he considers "preposterous". Then why has he not put forth these arguments?

Another problem which has not received enough attention is that of "travelling words" as they are called by M. Casevitz who has studied the journey of some of these words from India to Greece.[7] According to him, cassia and cinnamon, both species of the genus *Cinnamomum* (in other words, two species of cinnamon as we know it today) "came mainly from India and their name appears in the Semitic world as a borrowed term transmitted by traders". If we were to accept the following line of descent, viz. Egyptian *khisīt*—> Hebrew *kezî'ah*[8] *—>Greek* κασία that F. De Romanis takes for granted, it does not mean that the three terms have always designated one and the same spice. Transferring the name of a plant or a vegetable product to another which shares with it a characteristic that is of special significance to us is one of the main problems of phytonymy. Guesswork would naturally play a major role when the word is borrowed from a foreign language. For example, the Hebrew word *shôshan* for lily and the Arabic *sousan* are believed to originate from the Egyptian word for lotus *soushin*[9] owing to a certain similarity between the two flowers, both of which are pure white and have clean-cut lines. It is therefore quite conceivable that an Asian spice should have received a Greek name which itself was derived

7. "Sur les 'mots voyageurs' de l'Inde jusqu'en Grèce", *Topoi* 3/2, 1993, pp. 401-406.

8. I have adopted Olck's transcriptions here and in the following pages because they are more manageable for the lay reader.

9. See V. LORET, *La flore pharaonique*, 2nd ed., Paris, 1892, pp. 113-114.

from the Hebrew version of the Egyptian name of an African spice. It is also possible that there may have been an assimilation of similar sounding words. If we were to suppose that the term *keï-schi* accompanied Chinese cinnamon to Palestine where the Hebrew *kezî'ah* designated another aromatic substance (perhaps a gum resin exuded by one of the numerous species of East African trees or a species of sandal-wood as it has sometimes been suggested),[10] there could have been an amalgamation of these terms followed by the fading away of their original meaning not commonly used. In short, the linguistic ramifications are likely to be much more complicated than F. De Romanis could have ever imagined.

However, it is his treatment of ancient sources which gives rise to more misgivings in my mind. Quite naturally, there is a lengthy commentary on Herodotus, II, 110-111 (pp. 99-103) because it is the oldest document in Greek regarding cassia and cinnamon; but to my mind the study is incomplete and partial. As every one knows, Herodotus' statements are often suspect and the passage in question is confusing. As a matter of fact, it is the Arabs, Herodotus claims, who collect cassia from a swamp inhabited by enormous bats and steal cinnamon bearing "a name learnt from the Phoenicians" from birds who bring it to steep cliffs to build their nests. But this statement is immediately contradicted by the following remark (III, 111): "From where cinnamon comes and which land produces it, nobody can say; but some persons, whose assertions appear plausible, claim that it grows in the land where Dionysus was reared", in other words, Ethiopia[11] according to Herodotus. F. De Romanis quotes this tradition because it supports his thesis, but he fails to add that another version of the legend claims that Dionysus was born in Asia.[12] Theophrastus reports (*HP* IV, 4,1) that Alexander and his companions discovered ivy, the plant associated with Dionysus, "in India, on a mountain called Mount Meros,[13] from where, as everybody knows, the legend claims that Dionysus comes". Herodotus'

---

10. A hypothesis recently formulated with much circumspection by B. HERZHOFF, in U. EIGLER-G. WÖHRLE, *Theophrast. De odoribus*, Edition, Übersetzung, Kommentar, mit einem botanischen Anhang von B. Herzhoff, Stuttgart, 1993, pp. 84-85, with references to botanical literature on the sweet-smelling sandal, which should be taken into account when re-examining this question.

11. II, 146: "The Greeks say of Dionysus that as soon as he was born, Zeus sewed him up in his thigh (ἐς τὸν μηρόν) and carried him to Nysa, which is beyond Egypt, in Ethiopia".

12. Cf. P. GRIMAL, *Dictionnaire de la mythologie grecque et romaine*, 4th ed., Paris, 1969, p. 127, *s.v.* "Dionysos": "Zeus carried Dionysus (...) to the land called Nysa, which according to some is in Asia and to others in Ethiopia or in Africa".

13. Ἐν τῷ ὄρει τῷ Μηρῷ καλουμένῳ literally, "on the mountain said to be 'of the Thigh'". Arrian (*An.* V, 2, 5-7) and Quintus Curtius (VIII, 10, 13-17) describe in greater detail the bacchanalia of Mount Meros.

statements should not be taken literally because it seems that for him Arabia, which is (III, 107) "southwards the last inhabited country" and Ethiopia, the mythical birthplace of Dionysus, are both distant unknown lands. The fairy tales associated with the collection of spices confirm this impression. It is doubtful if the cassia swamps and cinnamon cliffs were "actually the swamps of the Nile and the Ethiopian highlands crossed by trade routes".[14] Analyzing these "stories capable of revealing the mythical significance of spices" from a different viewpoint, M. Detienne observes that they "can only be deciphered through the oppositions and categories mentioned in the wondrous tales about the Land of Spices".[15] M. Detienne's views may or may not be accepted but one must agree that in the passage from Herodotus, the imaginary is more evident than the real. One century after Herodotus, Theophrastus too narrates (*HP*, IX, 5, 2) a "wonderful story" of the same kind relating to cinnamon, but it is circumscribed by two sentences which clearly indicate that himself was sceptical about it.[16] Pliny (XII, 85), after summarising Herodotus' account, even goes so far as to declare that "it is tales like these that are used to raise the prices of things". These nonsensical stories were invented by traders who exaggerated the danger of obtaining these spices in order to justify the high price they charged for them and to discourage future competition.[17] From the moment when someone looks at them with a critical eye, one cannot take them seriously.

It is paradoxical that F. De Romanis should give so much weight to Herodotus' flimsy evidence and refrain from scrutinizing what Theophrastus, Antiquity's only true botanist, has to say on this matter. Contrary to Herodotus, Theophrastus had what we may call a scientific attitude and his information was obtained from the best available sources of his times. However, his claim (*HP* IX, 4, 2) that "frankincense, myrrh, cassia and cinnamon are found in the Arabian Peninsula near Saba, Hadramaut, Kitibaina and Mamali" should not be taken too literally. This is so because in the description (IX, 4 and 5) which follows this opening statement, the groups frankincense-myrrh and cassia-

---

14. J.I. MILLER, *o.c.*, p. 155.

15. *Les jardins d'Adonis*, Paris, 1972, pp. 36-43, particularly p. 39. Major oppositions between the collection of cassia and cinnamon: in the swamps/near inaccessible cliffs; chthonic winged creatures like bats/birds living on mountain tops; the former are driven away/the latter are lured.

16. "A legend (μῦθος) is related about it. It is in truth no more than a legend (μῦθος)".

17. This last point has been elaborated in the article by R. HENNIG, "Κιννάμωμον und κινναμωφόρος χώρα in der antike Literatur", *Klio*, 32, 1939, pp. 325-330; see pp. 325-326. Though the author is otherwise partial to the "African hypothesis", his judgement on the passage from Herodotus deserves to be quoted: "The fantastic tale vividly calls to mind a story from the Thousand and One Nights, viz. the Adventures of Sindbad the Sailor, and it is probably not an accident that in both cases the Arabs were the inventors of the story closely related to a tale of adventure."

cinnamon are treated differently. In the first case, Theophrastus reveals that his source of information was mainly sailors setting off from the Gulf of Heroes[18] who "landed to fetch water from the mountain and, while they were doing so, noticed the trees and the collection of their products." The information obtained from their account has the exactitude and precision of notes taken from nature. To this evidence that Theophrastus considers to be the most reliable, he adds, out of a sense of scrupulousness, the traders' rather doubtful testimony (IX, 4, 8). "Wood (from the myrrh-tree) was brought to Antigonus by Arabs who transported the frankincense to the coast; (...) however, these informants provided a further proof of their ignorance: they believed that frankincense and myrrh are produced by the same tree". Theophrastus probably owes his meagre information about cassia and cinnamon-trees (IX, 5, 1 and 3) to these traders and to them alone: "Both of them are bushes, not very tall, about the same height as the chaste-tree (*Vitex agnus-castus*), many-branched and woody. (...) It is said of the cassia that its young stems are thicker (than those of the cinnamon) and quite fibrous". It was enough to see the tubular fragments of bark that Dioscorides (I, 13, 1) calls συρίγγια or "small pipes"[19] to get an idea of the small size and the branchy appearance of the trees from which they had been taken. There is nothing in Theophrastus' text to prove that cassia and cinnamon were produced in Arabia which supplied them through one route or another to the Mediterranean trade.[20]

On the other hand, other passages in the *Historia plantarum* provide evidence that supports the Indian origin of these spices. To start with, in *HP*, IV, 4, 14, the author remarks on the peculiarity in the plant world of "aromatic plants from Arabia, Syria and India such as frankincense, myrrh, cassia, balsam, cinnamon and others of the same kind". It is natural that frankincense and myrrh should be linked with Arabia, and balsam with Syria (according to IX, 6, 1: "The balsam tree grows in the deep valley of Syria").[21] Similarly, it seems logical to associate India with cassia and cinnamon, especially because, after mentioning the aromatic plants of Syria, IX, 7, 2 says, "All the other sweet-smelling plants used as spices are imported partly from India, from where they are sent by sea (τὰ μὲν ἐξ Ἰνδῶν κομίζεται κἀκεῖθεν ἐπὶ θάλατταν καταπέμπεται), and partly

---

18. See my article "Anaxikrates' Expedition to Western Arabia" *in this volume*.

19. How can we not think of our own "cinnamon sticks"?

20. This confusion between the natural source and the commercial source is a very common occurrence at all times. See examples given by HENNIG, *o.c.*, p. 326, regarding *regio thurifera*.

21. In the Dead Sea depression around Jericho (cf. Strabo, XVI, 2, 41 = C 763). Among the accounts provided by travellers, see the detailed descriptions by Pierre Belon (in S. SAUNERON, *Le voyage en Égypte de Pierre Belon du Mans 1547,* Cairo, 1970, 110b-111b) and by Prosper Alpin, *Plantes d'Égypte*, edited by R. DE FENOYL, Cairo, 1980, pp. 48-59.

from Arabia; thus, apart from cinnamon and cassia, also *komakon*". We have here an irrefutable proof of the existence in the last quarter of the 4th century B.C. of a sea-trade in spices between India and the Mediterranean region. The same text tells us that spices were also sent by land: "Cardamom and amomum, according to some, come from Media; others say that they come from India, as also spikenard and other spices, or (at least) most of them".[22] Since cardamom (*Elettaria cardamomum* White & Maton) comes from the Malabar Coast and amomum (*Amomum subulatum* Roxb.) from the Eastern Himalayas, these substances may well have passed through Media, but they come from further east.[23] It is again quite paradoxical that F. De Romanis should take note (p. 182) of the mention in *Historia plantarum* (IX, 20, 1) of two types of pepper one of which appears to him to be the Indian *pippalī*, but that he should absolutely refuse to consider cassia and cinnamon as two species of the present-day cinnamon produced in tropical India, including Ceylon, and the Far-East. Even if we were to suppose that the precious information provided by Theophrastus escaped his attention, he could not have been ignorant of Arrian's observation (*Indica*, 32, 7) regarding ras Musandam: "Those who were in the know said that it was the promontory at the tip of Arabia and that it was called Cape Maketa; from there cinnamon and other such substances were transported to Assyria". Quoting this passage, J.-F. Salles[24] adds that "these commodities evidently came from India", to illustrate the more general claim that "in Alexander's time, the point at which goods from India arrived was situated in the region of ras Musandam". It is surprising that F. De Romanis did not consider these "data" as evidence.

Finally, a word on F. De Romanis's treatment (pp. 110-111) of Pliny's famous passage (XII, 86-88) on the transportation of cinnamon to the port of Ocilia on simple rafts that moved with the wind. His thesis regarding the African

---

22. No African region figures among the spice-producing countries mentioned by Theophrastus. If, as an exceptional case, two of these substances most sought after by the perfume industry, viz. cassia and cinnamon, came from Somalia or Ethiopia, it is difficult to imagine that our botanist, who is also the author of the treatise *Des odeurs* in which these substances are mentioned several times (§ 17; 28; 30; 32; 34; 35), should have been unaware of it or should not have found any occasion to mention it.

23. By the same logic, the Greeks call the citron tree (*Citrus medica* L.) the "Persian" or "Median apple-tree" (περσικὴ/μηδικὴ μηλέα) because it was brought from Persia by Alexander's army, although its natural birthplace is the Indo-Malaysian region. Similarly, the peach-tree (*Persica vulgaris* Miller), though a native of China, gets its Latin name *persica* (which became *pessica* and *pesca* in late Latin and *pêche* in French) from Persia.

24. "La circumnavigation de l'Arabie dans l'Antiquité classique", pp. 75-102 of *L'Arabie et ses mers bordières. I. Itinéraires et voisinages*, TMO No.16, Lyon, 1988. See p. 90 and n. 46.

origin of this spice is definitely strengthened in so far as Pliny places it "in the part of Ethiopia to which Troglodytes are joined by common marriages". But apart from the fact that in the works of ancient historians Ethiopia and India have a confusing resemblance,[25] such as the one pointed out earlier regarding Dionysus's birthplace, several points in Pliny's text, which F. De Romanis has chosen to ignore, suggest the existence of a much longer and more dangerous sea-route than the one round the Horn of Africa. Going from Ethiopia south of Cape Guardafui, to Ocelia, south-west of the Red Sea, was not a daring adventure on the open seas and the journey could not have taken five years.[26] This has given rise to the now widely accepted idea[27] that Pliny ascribed to the Troglodytes the first part of the journey across the Indian Ocean, and perhaps even further, undertaken by oriental sailors, "in all likelihood Malays".[28] That is the interpretation that F. De Romanis should have refuted point by point, had the need arisen, instead of basing himself on a truncated quotation. Hennig, who is more impartial, has clearly indicated what in his eyes was the real problem: such a trade between the Far-East and the land of Punt from where the Egyptians under the eleventh and twelfth dynasties obtained their *khisīt* is inconceivable at such an early date (c. 2000 B.C.).[29] But for the argument to be relevant, firstly the relation between *khisīt* and κασία should be ascertained and secondly, it should be demonstrated that these two terms designate the same substance constantly and without ambiguity, something which remains to be done.

The subject of his thesis provided F. De Romanis an excellent opportunity to treat cassia and cinnamon with the competence that is evident in other parts of his work. It is sad to say that he has missed this opportunity.

Suzanne AMIGUES
University of Montpellier

---

25. Studied in D. LENFANT's recent article "L'Inde de Ctésias. Des sources aux représentations", *Topoi* 5/2, 1995, pp. 308-336, especially pp. 313-314.

26. "The Troglodytes buy it (cinnamon) from their neighbours and transport it across the vast sea on rafts without a rudder to guide them, without oars to pull them or push them forward, without sails, without any means to assist them; man and his temerity make up for everything (...). It is said that those who carry on this trade take at least five years to come back and that many of them perish on the way" (transl. from A. Ernout, CUF, 1949).

27. This idea was particularly developed in MILLER, *o.c.*, pp. 156-159.

28. P. FOURNIER, n. 1 to Pliny, XII, 89 (p. 94 of Ernout's ed.)

29. *O.c.*, p. 327. On the land of Punt and its links with Egypt, consult in particular J. LECLANT, "L'exploration des côtes de la mer Rouge. À la quête de Pount et des secrets de la mer Érythré", *Annales d'Éthiopie* 11, 1978, pp. 69-73.

AN ANSWER TO J.-Cl. GOYON AND S. AMIGUES*

Amigues and Goyon would have liked me to identify (and immediately) the botanical species κασία and κινάμωμον. Apparently they are not satisfied when I say that κασία and κινάμωμον are shrubs with an aromatic bark and perhaps they also think that before giving the history of the word "obsidian" I should have devoted a chapter to the chemical composition of this mineral. However, my work is not a book about palaeobotany, nor is it about mineralogy. On the contrary, it is a book about economic and social history and considering its aims it would make absolutely no difference if I were to identify, provided such a thing was possible today, κασία and κινάμωμον with one plant or another.

But, as a matter of fact, what Amigues and Goyon pose as a "question of botany" does not intend to satisfy an innocent thirst for knowledge; rather, it is a pretext and a cover for the usual reversal of the methodologically correct procedure. *Recta methodos*, indeed, would want identification of the species to arise from a calm analysis of the sources. On the contrary, in the Amigues' and Goyon's approach, the *a priori* identification precedes and conditions the analysis — and leads it astray. The results turn out to be those often seen in the past: against the evidence from the most — and best — ancient sources, for whom κασία and κινάμωμον are East African shrubs, unquenchable faith is placed in the old identification with trees in China, Indochina, Sri Lanka, Malabar. We shall soon see how strained this is. However it is just as well to clarify the different starting point first.

According to Amigues, "le rapprochement de l'égyptien šs3t/ /h̲s3t et de l'hébreu qṣy'wt (d'où le grec kas(s)ia)[1] [...] conduit l'*a.* à chercher en Afrique

---

* *Topoi* 6/2, 1996, pp. 651-655 and 657-664.

1. Amigues and Goyon would have done well to explain — it's an important point — that I do not share the *communis opinio* according to which κασία would be a loan-

orientale la patrie de la cassia etc." No, it is not like that. It is not true that I am building upon that much to decide upon the geography of κασία and κινάμωμον; on the contrary I identify it by analysis and a critical discussion of Greek and Latin texts throughout a time-span stretching for about a thousand years, from Herodotus to Cosma.[2] This is what makes me certain — if Amigues and Goyon will excuse me — that κασία and κινάμωμον grew in an area around the Gulf of Aden.[3]

Rather than trusting the evidence of the sources, Amigues and Goyon prefer to rely on the authority of Olck and Miller in the case of Amigues and, in the case of Goyon, on the word of an unspecified group of "apothicaires, parfumeurs, herboristes ou droguistes modernes". Thus they assert, and this assumption becomes the corner-stone of their observation, that κασία and κινάμωμον are what we now call cassia and cinnamon and therefore they must have come from the Far East.

Κινάμωμον and *dārṣīnī*, ancient cinnamon and modern cinnamon, are often identified as the same plant on the base of three clues:

1) in both cases, the bark is the precious part of the plant;

2) by mediaeval times the ancient term κινάμωμον was often employed to mean *dārṣīnī*, our modern cinnamon;

3) the etymology — often repeated and as often wide of the mark — of κασία derived from *keï-shi* o *keï-shin*, transcriptions of Japanese words which, in fact, refer to *dārṣīnī.*

I showed in the book when and why the word κινάμωμον began to be understood as *dārṣīnī.* The insufficiency of the first element, the unfoundedness of the third, had already been proved by arguments that I considered (and still consider) convincing: therefore I did not feel obliged to repeat other people's observations but only, if anything, to refer. This struck Amigues as an act of

word from a Semitic language: on the contrary, both of them attributed to me an Egyptian > Hebrew > Greek derivation. I have explained clearly why I do not believe in the hypothesis attributed to me, I have explained clearly why a direct Egyptian > Greek derivation strikes me as very much more likely. But Amigues and Goyon seem to think that a Greek word corresponding to a Hebrew word in the Bible — it does not matter where or how — must of necessity be a Greek loan-word from the Hebrew. They are not even vaguely struck by the suspicion that it might be the contrary, as in the specific case. I think is much more likely, given the quality of Biblical attestation of *qṣy'wt* and its isolation within the context of Semitic languages.

2. Among them, as regards κασία, the *Periplus Maris Erythraei*, a text which is almost maniacally exact, as far as commercial geography is concerned.

3. The "rapprochement" to the Egyptian *šs3t/* > *ẖs3t* [> *ẖs3yt* / *ẖ3syt*?] and the Hebrew *qnh* (not *qṣy'wt*!) is useful for me, if anything, to give a historical explanation of characteristic oscillation between Africa and Arabia throughout the ancient tradition of κασία and κινάμωμον as well as the parallel semantic proximity of κασία and κινάμωμον.

"suffisance déplaisante", all the more serious since it is associated with an attitude that is, according to her, anything but coherent: further on, in fact, Amigues points out my "étrange paradoxe". Even admitting that one of the two kinds of pepper named by Theophrastus is the *pippalī* of North West India, why ever should I absolutely refuse to recognise in κασία and κινάμωμον "deux espèces de cannelle, produits de l'Inde tropicale, y compris Ceylan, et de l'Extrême-Orient"? Why ever should I refuse to believe that the Hebrew *qṣy'h* comes "directement de *keï-schi* (en chinois 'rameau de cannelle')"?[4]

I would say that the real paradox is that a scholar like Amigues should prove to be so disarming. Amigues would have found an answer to these questions if she had consulted the bibliography to which I refer. In any case, even if she had not read the bibliography, a calm spell of reflection should have induced her at least to avoid repeating age-old absurdities.

The word πέπερι, of Indian origin and referring to an Indian spice, enters the Greek vocabulary through Persian, not long before the composition of the Hippocratic Γυναικεῖα (IV century B.C., more likely the second half rather than the first). Within this chronological framework the introduction of a word and of a spice from North West India (I repeat, and stress: North West) into the Mediterranean world and the Greek language is easily explained. In this context I went back to Darius and the exploitation he promoted of the waterway between North West India and the Persian Gulf and I stressed the long-lasting consequences of his policy, even in the Eastern Mediterranean, much later.

The theory of a derivation of the Hebrew *qṣy'h* from the Chinese, however, belongs to a completely different story, because it forces one to admit a loan-word — pay attention! — from Chinese to Hebrew, going back to a period no later than the VII century B.C. A loan-word, moreover, which would be direct, according to Olck (and also according to Amigues who repeats it), almost as though Hebrews and Chinese spoke to one another in the VII century B.C.! Let us not take into account the fact that the Chinese word *gui* does not seem to have been applied to *Cinnamomum cassia* before the III century A.D. (about nine centuries later than Sappho's mention of κασία). Let us not take into account the fact that the oldest evidence relating to the medicinal use of *gui* bark (*gui pi*) goes back to the V-VI century A.D. (about nine centuries after the Hippocratic *corpus*). Let us not take into account the other serious objections which Laufer put forward together with these in 1919, opposing the etymology that Amigues accepts today[5] — objections that neither Amigues nor Miller's "ouvrage fonda-

---

4. The formulation, which Amigues claims, is Olck's.

5. "[...] the wild fantasies of a Schumann or Muss-Arnolt [Olck's sources, Miller's source in his turn], who lack the most elementary knowledge of East-Asiatic history": B. LAUFER, *Sino-Iranica*, Chicago, 1919, p. 543.

mental" (1969)[6] take into account. Let us not take into account the fact that the modern cinnamon is a tree,[7] while the ancient authors knew κασία and κινάμωμον as shrubs;[8] this is a point on which P. Crone (1987), whom I quoted, insisted. Let us leave any problem of phonetics out of it. How should we judge the theory of a loan-word, no later than the VII century B.C., from Chinese to Hebrew?

Unlike the modern age where the mass media makes it possible for the whole world to learn words like *perestrojka* in a few days, the transmigration of words from one language to another in the ancient world assumes important and wearisome processes, the more important and wearisome, the more "distant" are the languages involved. A distance which does not depend just on the physical distance, but also on its "density" — density of men, languages, cultures, states, economies etc. Perhaps an example will make it clearer: the first Greek author to mention Σῆρες, ethnonym behind which it is usual to glimpse the Chinese words for silk, is Apollodorus of Artemita, between the end of the II and the beginning of the I century B.C.[9] If silk took such a long time to transfer, in such a confused, indirect and tortuous way, a Chinese word in the Greek language when Greek culture had penetrated into the heart of Central Asia, is it likely that modern cinnamon would have done it six centuries earlier in such a straightforward way? Is it at all credible that in its wandering throughout Asia cinnamon would not have left some other trace apart from the relatively ancient one in Greek and a very feeble one, probably late in date, in Hebrew? In actual fact, when the Chinese cinnamon does move, in the late classical period or in the early Middle Ages, it leaves a clear-cut track, such as, for example, the Persian word *dārčīnī*, "wood from China" (< Middle Persian **dār i čēnīg*. The loan-words *daričenik* and *dārṣīnī*, respectively Armenian and Arabic, come from this). We may note: "wood from China" say the Persians, with words in their

---

6. Miller's book is one of those that sorely tests the Plinian motto *nullum esse librum tam malum ut non aliqua parte prodesset*. In any case, its *aliqua pars* is certainly not the one dedicated to κασία and κινάμωμον. I regret an old quotation: *Helikon* 22/27, 1982/1987, p. 170, ft. 84.

7. According to the species, it can grow up to more than ten metres. According to Flückiger quoted by Goyon the *Cinnamomum zeylanicum* is "bis etwa 10 Meter hoher".

8. Pliny knew that *cassia* and *cinnamomum* are small shrubs varying in height from a span to three cubits. Theophrastus mentions shrubs. Galenus saw a δένδρον ὅλον of κινάμωμον contained in a box of four and a half cubits.

9. *FGrHist* 779 F 7a, cfr. W.W. TARN, *The Greeks in Bactria and India*, Cambridge, 1951², p. 110; M.G. RASCHKE, *New studies in Roman Commerce with the East*, *ANRW* 9.2, Berlin-New York, 1978, p. 694, n. 89; wrongly, I think, F. ALTHEIM - R. STIEHL, *Geschichte des Mittelasiens im Altertum*, Berlin, 1970, p. 435, attribute to Nearchus the Σηρικά of Strab. XV 1, 20; reasonably Raschke supposes "one or more intermediary stages" between Chinese and Greek.

own language, and the sound is repeated by Armenians and Arabs. That is, they do not say *gui*, *gui pi*, *gui zhi* or anything similar. Not even Persians, Armenians or Arabs manage to do in Late Antiquity or in the Middle Ages what Amigues would have Hebrews do before the VII century B.C.: adopting the Chinese word for cinnamon.

There is more, yet more. About four centuries after the word πέπερι entered the Greek language, the Sanskrit *pippalī* is still found in North West India, at Barygaza (it is the πέπερι μακρόν of *PME* 49). If κασία were really to derive from Chinese, if κασία and κινάμωμον were really to be identified with the mediaeval *dārṣīnī*, we might expect that the sources relating to the one and the other would go back to the same geographical context. So how on earth do they come to be *toto caelo* different? How can we reconcile an importation of κασία — both the object and the word — from China in the VII century B.C. with what the Greek and Latin sources tell us, not even two centuries later, about the geography of κασία and κινάμωμον? I am well aware that at this point the *deus ex machina* of the "secret monopoly" is brought up, which would keep the real origin of κασία and κινάμωμον secret: the Greeks and Romans, poor devils, believed that κασία and κινάμωμον were plants from East Africa (or Arabia, anyway) but unknown to them the plants came from India, Sri Lanka, Indochina and China and their real origin had to be kept secret by the Arabs, owners of the monopoly. But how could they manage to do that? And if so, why was it that in all Ἐρυθρὰ θάλασσα there was only one secret monopoly, precisely that of κασία and κινάμωμον? And is it not a very peculiar red herring that offers a nearer origin rather a more distant one? And why ever should we find κασίας χύμα πλεῖστον only at Mosyllon and nowhere else? In actual fact, the theory of a "secret monopoly" must be taken for what it is: science fiction. The methodical approach on which it is based would also allow an extra-terrestrial origin for κασία and κινάμωμον.

Once you have accepted that reversal of the *recta methodos* mentioned above and stubbornly refuse to abandon yourself to fantasising about the "secret monopoly", you feel the overwhelming need to prove that the Greek and Latin sources make it possible to refer κασία and κινάμωμον to the Far East. Amigues, too, has thrown herself into this task, with the results that we shall now examine, point by point. In a way that is all her own, Amigues tries to prove that some ancient authors stress the Indian provenance[10] of κασία and κινάμωμον (God alone knows how to reconcile the product's Indian origin with the Chinese origin of the Greek name).

10. Strangely enough, Amigues omits to quote all the evidence that really points to India as the origin of κασία and/or κινάμωμον; I have quoted and evaluated it all in my book.

1) Herodotus states that according to some people the κινάμωμον grows in the place where Dionysus was brought up. In order to explain which place was intended by the readers/listeners of Herodotus at least, if not by the authors of such traditions, Amigues believes she can evoke the myths pertaining to Mount Μηρός in India, known to Theophrastus, rather than the traditions that Herodotus himself attributed to the Greeks (or, at this point, any one of the other thousand traditions). Would we expect too much if we say that she should prove that these myths go back to the V century B.C. or, at least, that a mountain called Μηρός in India was known to Herodotus and his contemporaries?

2) After having solemnly proclaimed Theophrastus the "seul véritable botaniste de l'antiquité", Amigues adds, only two or three lines later, that the only botanist of classical times must not be taken literally when he writes γίνεται μὲν οὖν ὁ λίβανος καὶ ἡ σμύρνα καὶ ἡ κασία καὶ ἔτι τὸ κινάμωμον ἐν τῇ τῶν Ἀράβων Χερρονήσῳ περί τε Σαβὰ καὶ Ἀδραμύτα καὶ Κιτίβαινα καὶ Μαμάλι.[11] Indeed, in Amigues' opinion, another passage from Theophrastus would offer proof of an Indian origin for κασία and κινάμωμον: I shall give the quotation in a note, leaving it to the reader to judge how well-founded this assertion might be.[12] Reference to the India of κασία and κινάμωμον would be necessary "d'autant plus qu'on lit en IX, 7, 2, après la mention des plantes aromatiques de Syrie: 'Tous les autres végétaux d'odeur agréable utilisés comme aromates sont importés pour partie de l'Inde d'où il s'ont expédiés par mer (τὰ μὲν ἐξ Ἰνδῶν κομίζεται κἀκεῖθεν ἐπὶ θάλατταν καταπέμπεται) et pour partie de l'Arabie; ainsi, outre le cinnamome et la cassia, également le *komakon*'". I have given Amigues' text with her translation of the passage from Theophrastus, the *ad verbum* quotation, when it strikes her as opportune, and her learned semicolon after "Arabie".[13] What Amigues wants Theophrastus to have said is that κινάμωμον, κασία and κώμακον come from India or Arabia, but she cannot make him say so, because οἷον κτλ. obviously refers to τὰ δ' ἐξ Ἀραβίας. If Theophrastus had wanted to say what Amigues would have liked, he would undoubtedly have written: τὰ δὲ ἄλλα πάντα τὰ εὔοσμα οἷς πρὸς τὰ ἀρώματα χρῶνται, οἷον πρὸς τῷ κιναμώμῳ καὶ τῇ κασίᾳ καὶ κώμακον, τὰ μὲν ἐξ Ἰνδῶν κομίζεται κἀκεῖθεν ἐπὶ θάλατταν καταπέμπεται, τὰ δ' ἐξ Ἀραβίας. But

11. Theophr., *h.p.* IX 4, 2.

12. *Ibid.* IV 4, 14: περιττότερα δὲ τῶν φυομένων καὶ πλεῖστον ἐξηλλαγμένα πρὸς τὰ ἄλλα τὰ εὔοσμα τὰ περὶ Ἀραβίαν καὶ Συρίαν καὶ Ἰνδούς, οἷον ὅ τε λιβανωτὸς καὶ ἡ σμύρνα καὶ ἡ κασία καὶ τὸ ὀποβάλσαμον καὶ τὸ κινάμωμον καὶ ὅσα ἄλλα τοιαῦτα.

13. I shall quote the whole sentence. Theophr., *h.p.* IX 7, 2: τὰ δὲ ἄλλα πάντα τὰ εὔοσμα οἷς πρὸς τὰ ἀρώματα χρῶνται, τὰ μὲν ἐξ Ἰνδῶν κομίζεται κἀκεῖθεν ἐπὶ θάλατταν καταπέμπεται, τὰ δ' ἐξ Ἀραβίας, οἷον πρὸς τῷ κιναμώμῳ καὶ τῇ κασίᾳ καὶ κώμακον.

Theophrastus did not write this and one should not try to translate as if he had. "Le seul véritable botaniste de l'antiquité" has one and one only opinion, as to the origin of κασία e κινάμωμον: they come from Arabia.

3) In the third place, Amigues calls upon evidence not so much of Arrianus (from Nearchus) as of J.-F. Salles, who expressed the opinion that the κινάμωμον distributed from the Arab promontory of Maketa came from India: I respect J.-F. Salles, but I would have liked his statements to be better explained, so as to be able to criticise or, if the case should arise, agree: in the form in which he has expressed it, I cannot do either. Amigues "s'étonne que cette 'évidence' ne se soit pas imposée comme telle à l'esprit de F. De Romanis". If it is the passage from Nearchus that is being alluded to, then I have considered it, judging it to be not too different from J.-F. Salles, with the exception, of course, of the origin of κινάμωμον.

4) Finally, Amigues examines Pliny the Elder. We get off to bad start here, too, because Pliny, writing the passage under consideration, states explicitly that κινάμωμον *nascitur in Aethiopia Trogodytis conubio permixta*. But Amigues is not the type to lose heart over trifles like this. First she calls upon "ressemblances troublantes" between India and Ethiopia in ancient times and then she brings out several points that I had craftily kept silent about: the *uasta maria* traversed by the *Troglodytae* before arriving at Ocilia; their *audacia* in crossing it with their rudimental *rates*; and finally, a voyage lasting five years, which would be discussed soon enough. Amigues' conclusion (taken from Miller and therefore become "idée couramment[14] admise": *ipse dixit*): "Pline rapporte aux Troglodytes la première partie d'un transport effectué en réalité à travers l'océan Indien et peut-être au-delà par des marins orientaux, 'vraisemblablement des Malais'". As regards the *uasta maria* and the *audacia*, the tones of this description fit into the framework of a *topos* recurrent in classical literature, where a sea voyage is always audacious (*e.g.* the famous Plin., *n.h.* XIX 3-6), the vessels are always small, the sea is always vast. True enough that in this case recourse to this *topos* seems justified by the primitiveness of the Troglodytes' *rates* — the σχεδίαι and σκάφαι of the βάρβαροι in *PME* 7 — may it also be suggested by an Ocean voyage from Malaysia to Arabia? That lasts for five years? In boats without rudders, oars or sails? The author of this passage was, or would be, a *praefectus classis*, an Imperial Admiral, he had a sufficiently good idea of the location of the *Troglodytae*, of *Aethiopia* and of Ocelis/Ocilia; is it at all conceivable that he would have wanted to say anything of the kind?

[...] illi [...] produnt [...] uix quinto anno reuerti negotiatores et multos interire. The *illi* are the Gebbanitae of the port of Ocilia. They say that the

---

14. And why not? Cfr., e. g., the enthusiastic agreements of E.W. GRAY, *JRS* 60 (1970), p. 222; and RASCHKE, *art. cit.*, p. 652: "rather bizarre theory".

negotiatores of κινάμωμον are lucky to return in the fifth year and many of them die. Return where? Evidently here Pliny is writing from the Gebbanitan point of view and therefore the return of the *Troglodytae* is a return to Ocilia. Which, of course, tells us nothing about the duration of the voyage from the country of the *Troglodytae* to Ocilia. If anything, it tells us about the difficulties (probably emphasised by the Gebbanitae, the κινάμωμον merchants) met with by the *Troglodytae* while finding the κινάμωμον in *Aethiopia* and transporting it (*multos interire*) to Ocelis. The passage is clear enough for anyone who does not need to send the *Troglodytae* all the way to Malaysia: once they had procured the κινάμωμον from their neighbours, the *Troglodytae* set sails at around the winter solstice (*circa brumam*), when the monsoon blows from the NE (*euri* and then *argestae* at Bab el-Mandeb) and they reached Ocelis from the Horn of Africa, very likely after only a few days' sailing. Pliny does not tell us how they tackled the return voyage, nor are we qualified to fantasise about it.

In Goyon's inferences, too, on one occasion the belief in the Far Eastern origin of κασία and κινάμωμον compromises a calm analysis of the sources and a careful historical evaluation of their implication. It was a pleasant surprise, I confess, to note Goyon's interest and even his hesitant approval of the comparison between the place-names *wḏlṯt* and Adulis: because of its historical implications, in fact, I consider this to be the most important conclusion of all the ones I have put forward. Moreover, Goyon also seems to recognise the phonetic plausibility of the comparison *wḏlṯt* ≈ *'wzl* and *wdnt* ≈ *wdn*. Except for the fact that at this point he realises that this could all lead to the conclusion that the *qnh* the prophets mention (sometimes translated as κινάμωμον by the Septuaginta) is imported from East Africa. So then he immediately makes haste to announce his scepticism, since I was on the point of making *wdn* and/or *wdnt* the homeland of κασία and κινάμωμον.[15]

I have little to object to about the first part of Goyon's *Remarques*, dedicated to phonetic and semantic problems, except for his belief in the identification of *ḫ3syt* proposed by Dawson, a belief which is perhaps excessive, I feel, and except for the fact he finds it paradoxical that a word used less and less by the Egyptians in the later period should be precisely the one that the Greeks borrowed. Indeed, it is true that there are only two pieces of evidence for its use between the Saite and the Ptolemaic Periods, but there were hardly hundreds of occurrences in earlier time, up to the III millennium B.C., not even a few dozen,

15. Let's rather say, "place of importation". And let us specify: strictly speaking Ez. 27, 19 does not make it possible to establish *qnh* comes from *wdn* or *'wzl*, but in the book I have let the connection between the presence of *ywn* at *'wzl* and the mention of κασία (to be identified with *qnh*) by Sappho appear.

and the fact that it is still in use in the Persian and Ptolemaic period testifies to its vitality in the Saite Period.

Furthermore, once a word enters another language it develops a new life in it, altogether independent of the original language. Ever since the early VI century B.C. at least, κασία is a Greek word to all intents and purposes and with regard to its derivation from *šs3t* > *ḫs3yt* / *ḫs3yt* / *ẖ3syt* it is not fair to object that the word does not survive in Coptic,[16] above all when we consider that in Greek, which, from this point of view, is a marginal language and therefore conservative, the words κασία has been subjected to the rivalry, strong in the commercial language of the Roman period, of a host of other, non-Greek, names for the infinite species of κασία and κινάμωμον. Nor is it fair to object that the phonetic results in Coptic would have been different; it is like saying that Νεκθερῶς could not be a transcription from *Nḫtf-jrw* since the Greek transcription from the Coptic is Νιστερῶς.

As for the second part of the *Remarques*, it goes without saying that Goyon finds me fully in agreement with him when he proves that the Egyptian word that I put as the origin of the Greek κασία does not mean our modern cinnamon. I also congratulate Goyon when he reminds us that the Chevalier de Jaucourt had deduced that the *qnmn* of the Book of Exodus "ne pouvait être parfumée avec du 'bois' ou de 'l'écorce' de cannelle de Chine ou de Ceylan, car il aurait fallu auparavant les distiller". But if this is true, would it not be necessary, even only on the basis of this, to re-open the debate about the identification of *qnmn* with "cannelle de Chine", accepted on the basis of the response of the "apothicaires" etc.? Or is one to deny — I really hope not — that κάρφεα of *qnmn* — κινάμωμον (or their products) were used to perfume the Biblical oil?

I find myself agreeing with Goyon much less when he attempts to prove that the word *ḫs3yt* cannot refer to aromatic barks. I shall start from the argument that he considers "décisif", i.e. from the expression *gnn n ḫs3yt*, for an explanation of which Goyon invokes a proof by Chassinat, which actually, however, relates to the term *g3*, not *gnn*. It is, of course, possible that the same word is lurking behind the two spellings, but it is not certain. In any case, even if Goyon has seized upon the truth, that is, even if *g3* and *gnn* do both happen to mean "resin" or something of the sort, the conclusions he has drawn would not be justified even then. In fact, I would reason as follows. If the expression *gnn n ḫs3yt* occurs only once in a medical recipe while only *ḫs3yt* occurs in nine others, we should not infer that *ḫs3yt* is always *gnn n ḫs3yt*, as if the two expressions were absolutely identical. We should rather conclude that *gnn n ḫs3yt* is a by-product from a *ḫs3yt* plant different from the one more commonly used which, precisely because it is more common, is called simply *ḫs3yt*. A

16. The Latin *tus*, a loan-word from Greek, continues to mean incense, even after the Greek language, not later than VII century B.C. replaced θύος by λίβανος/λιβανωτός.

Greek scholar would reason in the same way, faced with the words ξυλοκιννάμωμον and κιννάμωμον, in which he would recognise products that do indeed come from the same plant (κιννάμωμον), but are decidedly different: the first *lignum* ("wood"), less precious and less used, the second, *cortex* ("bark"), used more and infinitely more precious.[17] Thus it is the latter that has the same name as the plant. In short, the *gnn* may also be employed, but it is not the most frequently utilised part of the *ḫs3yt*. I couldn't say whether, in the expression *gnn n ḫs3yt*, *gnn* really means "resin" or something of that kind; but I do know that even if this were the case it would not furnish any elements contrary to the identification of that *ḫs3yt* with κασία / κινάμωμον, since even the *cinnamum* Pliny knew (or better its root) excretes a resin or something of the sort (Plin., *n.h.* XII 94).

Nor does the argument inferred from the determinatives seem any more solid. In the Greco-Roman period, the bark of κασία and κινάμωμον are ingredients for ointments and I do not see why they could not also have an ointment pot as a determinative. I do not see why the determinative for grains could not indicate barks in a worked form, since we know that in Theophrastus' time at least (and perhaps also in that of Pliny, who repeats it), the κασία was cut into small pieces, scarcely two inches long, only so as to separate the bark from the trunk. As for the tree branch that Goyon would like to find more frequently, it is true that it is rare in a far from infinite number of attestations, but it is there where we would expect it to be: the reliefs of Deir el-Bahari.

Goyon points out that in the Edfu text the *ḫs3yt* is part of the herbs that must be sprinkled on the flames for the sacred fumigations; I can remind him that the Greeks made a not dissimilar use of κασία (together with μύρρα and λίβανος) in the VII-VI century B.C., and so did the Hebrews of *qnh* (together with *lbnh*).

Will all this be sufficient to enable the problem of Sappho's mention of κασία to be set within a methodologically correct framework, solved in a plausible historical context? Will it be sufficient to discourage the proposal of Chinese etymologies for κασία again, with direct, awe-inspiring transmigration from Chinese to Hebrew? Or will the irresistible fascination of an almond-eyed Sappho continue to open enchanted horizons?

Federico DE ROMANIS

---

17. The price of the former is 10 *denarii*, while the second costs 1500 *denarii* per pound.

RESEARCHES IN THE EASTERN DESERT 1996-1999

Since the seminar on the Red Sea in Lyon in March 1995, of which the proceedings were published in *Topoi* 6/2 (1996), archaeological excavations have continued in the Eastern Desert. We will not concern ourselves with the two missions not interested in Erythraean trade, viz. the now completed excavations at Mons Porphyrites (1994-1998) carried out by the British team led by David Peacock and Valerie Maxfield and the survey of the Byzantine village of gold-miners at Bi'r Umm Fawâkhîr being carried out by Carol Meyer (University of Chicago) since 1992.

But on the other hand, we are concerned with the following projects: (1) the excavation at Berenike of Trogodytes started in 1994 under the joint supervision of Willemina Wendrich (CNWS, Leiden University) and Steven E. Sidebotham (University of Delaware); (2) the survey of the Berenike Desert (S.E. Sidebotham *et al.*); (3) the survey of *Via Hadriana* (S.E. Sidebotham and R.E. Zitterkopf); (4) the excavation of small Roman forts (*praesidia*) on the two roads joining Coptos to the Red Sea ports of Myos Hormos (Qusayr and/or Qusayr al-Qadim) and Berenike (under the supervision of H. Cuvigny, French Ministry of Foreign Affairs and IFAO).

1. Berenike

Provided with ample funds, the Dutch-American team is doing an excellent job. A general plan of the town has been drawn up and several soundings have provided information about its topographical development from the Ptolemaic period (not fully uncovered owing to the thickness of later sedimentary deposits) to the Byzantine period. The archaeological material has been handed over to a wide range of specialists, including even an expert on beads.[1] It is true that more than 2,000 pieces of jewellery (beads) were recovered coming not only from the

1. Peter Francis, Director of the Center for Bead Research in Lake Placid.

A Gateway from the Eastern Mediterranean to India. The Red Sea in Antiquity
H. CUVIGNY, pp. 31-42

Mediterranean region but also from Sri Lanka and Persia which sometimes bear testimony to their owners' religious beliefs. W. Wendrich, the head of the mission who is also a specialist in basketry and matting, has discovered significant craft traditions in cordage, mats and baskets. She has come to the conclusion that from the 4th century onward there was a strong Nubian influence which is evident in all types of archaeological finds. For example, in the levels dating back to the Early Empire, there is a predominance of pork followed later by goat and sheep meat which was also predominant during the pre-Roman period. In the 1st century, there was deep-sea fishing (tuna fishing) but from the 4th century onwards, the people of this region were content to fish in coastal waters. In any case, there was a significant fall in the consumption of fish during this period. This change in food-habits is probably due to a change in the population. The excavators suspect that the population of Berenike in the later period had a large proportion of people from Nubia and the desert areas. Their influence is also seen in the handmade and incised pottery and food habits characterised by the consumption of fruits from the desert (*Balanites aegyptiaca, Zizyphus spina Christi*) and sorghum,[2] a cereal which has not been found in the granaries of the Early Roman Empire. The excavators believe that these people were perhaps Blemmyes who, as we learn from Epiphanius of Constantia (*c.* 310/320-402) and Olympiodorus (who visited their kingdom around 402), worked the beryl mines of Mons Smaragdus to the north-west of Berenike during the lifetime of these writers.

The archaeologists of Berenike observed a new spurt of activity in this port, after a slack period, at the time the Blemmyes rose to power. In the report on their 1996 excavation, the authors conclude, "The early Roman era (Augustus to the second half of the first century A.D.) and the second half of the fourth century A.D. on witnessed robust commercial endeavours at Berenike. There is little evidence that the early Roman trade boom persisted into the second century, certainly not in the latter part of the century [...]. The early third century at the port may have been better economically than the latter part of the second century as seen from the dedications associated with the inscription of A.D. 215, but there is little evidence for much activity throughout the remainder of the third century or the early fourth". The later excavations (reports not yet published) have not disproved this impression.[3] Bringing to light this economic revival of the port during the Byzantine period, rarely mentioned till now in any of the written sources,[4] is undoubtedly one of the major accomplishments of the Berenike excavation.

---

2. Could it be κένχρος which, according to Strabo, was the staple food of the Ethiopians together with barley (17.2.2)?

3. S.E. SIDEBOTHAM, *per litt.*

4. There are three of them:

Bibliography 1[5]

S.E. SIDEBOTHAM, "Roman interests in the Red Sea and Indian Ocean" in J. READE (ed.), *The Indian Ocean in Antiquity*, London, 1996, pp. 287-308.

S.E. SIDEBOTHAM, W.Z. WENDRICH (eds), *Berenike 1995, Preliminary report of the 1995 excavations at Berenike (Egyptian Red Sea coast) and the survey of the Eastern Desert*, Leiden, 1996.

S.E. SIDEBOTHAM, W.Z. WENDRICH (eds), *Berenike 1996, Report of the 1996 excavations at Berenike (Egyptian Red Sea coast) and the survey of the Eastern Desert*, Leiden, 1998.

S.E. SIDEBOTHAM, W.Z. WENDRICH (eds), *Berenike 1997, Report of the 1997 excavations at Berenike (Egyptian Red Sea coast) and the survey of the Eastern Desert*, Leiden, 1999.

W. VAN NEER, "Archaeozoological data on the food provisioning of Roman settlements in the Eastern Desert of Egypt", *Archaeozoologia* 9, 1997, pp. 137-154.

R.T.J. CAPPERS, "Botanical contribution to the analysis of subsistence at Berenike" in O.E. KAPER (ed.), *Life on the fringe. Living in the Southern Egyptian deserts during the Roman and early Byzantine periods*, Leiden, 1998, pp. 75-86.

W.Z. WENDRICH, "Fringes are anchored in warp and weft: the relation between Berenike, Shenshef and the Nile Valley" in O.E. KAPER (ed.), *Life on the fringe*, pp. 243-251.

S.E. SIDEBOTHAM, "Berenike, trade and the military: investigations at a Red Sea port in Egypt" in N. GUDEA (ed.), *Roman frontier studies 1997. Proceedings of the XVIIth International Congress of Roman Frontier Studies*, to be published.

2. Survey of the Eastern Desert

At the same time as the excavations at Berenike, a survey of its immediate hinterland and the roads running through the Eastern Desert between the

(1) Epiphanius of Constantia writes about the second half of the 4th century. During his time, the Empire had three ports on the Red Sea which he mentions in the following order: Aila, Clysma and Berenike. Egeria (*apud* Pierre Diacre, *CSEL* XXXIX, p. 116), describing Clysma in the years around 380, writes that it was the only port of the Roman Empire from where ships set sail for India. Was she ill informed? Or was Berenike no longer under Roman control?

(2) According to the *Martyrium s. Arethae*, in 524 Byzantium sent some ships as reinforcements to the king of Aksum who was making preparations to attack Southern Arabia. These ships were moored as follows: 20 in Clysma, 15 in Aila, 7 in Iotabe and only 2 in Berenike (*Acta Sanctorum*, Octobris X, p. 747). The Byzantine participation in the Aksumite crusade is however subject to doubt: see J. BEAUCAMP, Fr. BRIQUEL-CHATONNET & Chr. ROBIN, "La persécution des chrétiens de Nagrân et la chronologie himyarite", to be published in *Aram* (I am grateful to Chr. Robin for having sent me the manuscript of this article). At least the *Martyrium* indicates that the Berenike port was moderately active in the early part of the 6th century.

(3) Inscriptions from the Byzantine period in the *paneion* of Wadi Minayh al-Hyr on the Coptos-Berenike road (F. DE ROMANIS, *Cassia, cinnamomo, ossidiana. Uomini e merci tra oceano Indiano e Mediterraneo*, Roma, 1996, pp. 214-215).

5. Articles meant for lay readers have not been included.

latitudes of Coptos and Syene is carried out. The sites are systematically inspected and dated with the help of pottery found on the surface. Thanks to the discovery of totally new sites, it has been possible to determine the route followed by the ancient road between Edfu and Duwayq (Phalakron)[6] and infer that there was an Edfu-Marsa Nakari (Nechesia?) road passing through Barramiyya (S.E. Sidebotham was to start excavations at Marsa Nakari in May 1999). It is now quite clear that the Edfu-Marsa Nakari road and the Edfu-Duwayq road were regularly used during the Ptolemaic period and the Early Roman Empire while the Coptos-Berenike road (which the Ptolemaic road from Edfu joins at Duwayq) was used towards the end of Augustus' rule[7] and continued to be used during the Byzantine period. The reason why travellers in the 1st century A.D. and later in the 4th to 6th century A.D. followed a route that took two days more than if they had taken the Ptolemaic Edfu-Berenike road is not yet clear.

Bibliography 2

R.S BAGNALL, J.G. MANNING, S.E. SIDEBOTHAM, R.E. ZITTERKOPF, "A Ptolemaic inscription from Bir 'Iayyan", *CdE* 71, 1996, pp. 317-330.[8]

S.E. SIDEBOTHAM, "Caravans across the Eastern Desert of Egypt: recent discoveries on the Berenike-Apollinopolis Magna-Coptos roads" in A. AVANZINI (ed.), *Profumi d'Arabia. Atti del Convegno, Pisa, 1995*, Firenze, 1997 (Saggi di Storia antica 11), pp. 385-393.

S.E. SIDEBOTHAM, W.Z. WENDRICH, "Fieldwork in Southeastern Egypt: excavations at Berenike and survey of the Eastern Desert 1994-1996", *Archaeological News* 21-22, 1996-1997, pp. 34-40.

S.E. SIDEBOTHAM, "The Roman Frontier in the Eastern Desert of Egypt" in W. GROENMAN-VAN WAATERINGE, B.L. VAN BEEK, W.J.H. WILLEMS, S.L.WYNIA (eds), *Roman Frontier Studies 1995, Proceedings of the XVIth International Congress of Roman Frontier Studies*, Oxford, 1997, pp. 503-509.

S.E. SIDEBOTHAM *et al.*, *Barrington Atlas of the Greek and Roman world* (R.J.A. Talbert ed.), Princeton, 2000, maps no. 78 & 80.

R.E. ZITTERKOPF, "Roman construction techniques in the Eastern Desert" in O.E. KAPER (ed.), *Life on the fringe*, pp. 271-286. The results of this survey are also recorded in the annual reports on the Berenike excavations (*supra*).

---

6. That is how the name is spelt in ostraca from the 2nd century A.D.

7. Regarding the date of the opening of the Coptos-Berenike road, see F. DE ROMANIS, *op. cit. supra* n. 4, p. 224.

8. It is a kind of milestone (but the distance from the Nile was of course indicated in stadia!)

3. Via Hadriana

Since 1996, S.E. Sidebotham and R. Zitterkopf have been carrying out a systematic survey[9] of the *Via Hadriana* with the intention of determining its exact route and of locating, describing, redrawing and dating all its landmarks such as cairns, wells, halting places, etc. with the help of pottery found on the surface. No section of the road seems to have been paved and no milestone has been found. The existence of this road joining Berenike to Antinooupolis is known through only one source, viz. its dedication dated 137 A.D. (*OGI 701* = A. BERNAND, *Pan du désert*, No. 80). It is not clear why it was built. It is difficult to imagine that it was built for economic reasons because it duplicates the two other already equipped roads linking Myos Hormos and Berenike with Coptos which were also much shorter. Sidebotham and Zitterkopf hope that their surveys will provide an explanation (see *infra* for possible lines of thinking). Nevertheless, some sections were frequently used until the 4th or 5th century, at least by pilgrims going to Saint Anthony, Saint Paul or Saint Catherine.

Bibliography 3

S.E. SIDEBOTHAM, R.E. ZITTERKOPF, "Survey of the Via Hadriana by the University of Delaware: the 1996 season", *BIFAO* 97, 1997, pp. 221-237.

S.E. SIDEBOTHAM, R.E. ZITTERKOPF, "Survey of the Via Hadriana: the 1997 season", *BIFAO* 98, 1998, pp. 353-365.

4. Praesidia

During the Lyon seminar, we were able to distribute copies of our newly-written article confirming the identification of Qusayr with Myos Hormos.[10] The six ostraca mentioning Myos Hormos, which we published in this article, were later followed by many others, also providing the name of the Coptos-Qusayr road. The Ancients indifferently referred to it as the "Myos Hormos road" or the "Myoshormitic road" although a recent article tries to prove on the basis of the *Periplus Maris Rubri* that Myos Hormos was actually situated in the Bay of Safaga.[11] As compared to our 1994 article, we have changed our position on one point. We find it necessary to assume that Ptolemaic Myos Hormos lies under modern Qusayr and that Qusayr al-Qadim is an extension of this port built at the end of Augustus' rule (unless it replaced it). But this conclusion — based on the meagre evidence provided by the Ptolemaic remains at Qusayr and

9. Except when it goes through mine-fields!

10. A. BÜLOW-JACOBSEN, H. CUVIGNY, J.-L. FOURNET, "Myos Hormos: New Papyrological Evidence", *BIFAO* 94, 1994, pp. 27-42.

11. The whole argument rests as a matter of fact on the misinterpretation of the word λίμην that Mrs. Fanfoni has interpreted as "bay", whence the Bay of Safaga…

particularly on the absence of pottery from the pre-Christian period at Qusayr al-Qadim — may perhaps be proved wrong by the excavations just started by David Peacock at Qusayr al-Qadim in the spring of 1999.

At the time of the Lyon seminar, we had already conducted two excavations at the small fort of Al-Zarqa' (Maximianon). Since then, we have excavated in the same manner — concentrating on refuse dumps and the search for texts —[12] the *praesidia* of Al-Muwayh (Krokodilo on the Myos Hormos road) and Khashm al-Minayh (Didymoi on the Berenike road). We have also drawn up maps of all the small forts that are still standing on the Myos Hormos road. This has led to a general rethinking of the chronology of the dual network of *praesidia*.

One thing that becomes apparent is that there is no relation between the *praesidia* and Erythraean trade. At the time of the trade-boom the *praesidia* had not yet been constructed and later, when it was revived, they did not exist any more. At the beginning of Augustus' rule when Myos Hormos was at its most prosperous, according to Strabo there were wells (ὑδρεῖα, *hydreia*) and water-tanks (δεξαμεναί, *dexamenai*) along the Coptos-Myos Hormos road and the wells were not fortified. Unlike the Mons Claudianus of Trajan's time, the Julio-Claudian village near the quarries of Wadi al-Hammamat, where according to the ostraca both civilian quarrymen and soldiers lived, was not fortified. The refuse dump at Al-Zarqa covered an establishment that was earlier than the *praesidium*. According to Jean-Pierre Brun, it probably dates back to the first half of the 1st century A.D. and is not fortified. Pliny, who describes the Berenike road in 50 A.D. when it carried the major portion of the caravan traffic at the cost of the Myos Hormos road, talks only of *hydreumata*. The term *praesidium* which is predominant in the 2nd century ostraca was not yet in use.[13] That is why I would like to make a distinction between the "time of the *hydreumata*" (i.e., unfortified wells) and the "time of the *praesidia*"[14] which according to J.-P. Brun's archaeological analyses seems to begin under the Flavians (or perhaps even earlier during Nero's rule?).

The time of the *praesidia* covers the whole of the 2nd century and ends during the first half of the 3rd century. We may note that this period corresponds

12. Number of listed ostraca: 1550 in Maximianon, 800 in Krokodilo and 730 in Didymoi.

13. Pliny uses the term but only to designate the garrison of the *hydreuma Trogodyticum*, a site located about 2 miles off the road (and not a caravanserai capable of accommodating 2000 travellers as claimed by some).

14. I shall deal at length with this distinction by referring to the evidence furnished by new ostraca in the paragraph "Des *hydreumata* aux *praesidia*" in CUVIGNY *et al.*, *La route de Myos Hormos*, to be published.

to a recession at the port of Berenike (cf. *supra*) and that the network was denser precisely on the Myos Hormos road which is assumed to be the least important.[15]

But there was a break between the time of the *hydreumata* and the time of the *praesidia*. What could possibly have happened? The answer is perhaps provided by the Krokodilo ostraca which contain a fairly large number of copies of the official correspondence between the heads of stations (*curatores praesidiorum*) and their superiors. Several letters refer to attacks on travellers and *praesidia* by "barbarians". It therefore appears that as early as Trajan's reign at least (the earliest mention of "barbarians" in a Krokodilo ostraca dates back to 108 A.D.), the Bedouins of Upper Egypt and Lower Nubia, described by Strabo as completely inoffensive, became aggressive and dangerous. Sulpicius Serenus' victory over the Agriophagi celebrated in an inscription coming from either Coptos or Thebes does not appear any more to be an isolated event (*Pan du désert*, No. 87, c. 122) but one of the episodes of the rising threat of nomads in the Eastern Desert.

The ostracological corpus of Didymoi covering a wider chronological spectrum than the ostraca of Krokodilo and Maximianon however suggests that finally a *modus vivendi* was established during the first quarter of the 3rd century between *praesidia* and the barbarians. I am referring in particular to an ostracon which mentions that a *dekanos* came with five barbarians and they were given rations of bread and wine. Did the army then come to an understanding with some of the Bedouins who offered their services as guides and escorts?

What else do the ostraca talk about? They consist to a large extent of letters exchanged by civilians and also by the military personnel of the various *praesidia*. As a matter of fact, the *praesidia* invalidate the traditional picture of the Roman camp (which has been questioned for some time now) as being practically barred to the civilian population. Side by side with the garrison, which rarely seems to have consisted of more than a score of soldiers, the *praesidia* had a large civilian population including women and children whose relationship with the soldiers is still beyond our ken. The correspondence throws light on the micro-economy of the world of *praesidia*: their sometimes unsuccessful attempts to raise pigs, the existence of prostitution, the export of vegetables from Persou[16] (Bi'r Umm Fawakhir) — an important vegetable-growing centre in the middle of the desert — to the neighbouring *praesidia* and the competition between civilian suppliers having agents in different garrisons.

---

15. Pliny and later the *Itinerarium Antonini* mention only the Berenike road.

16. Regarding this place-name, first the name of the *bekhen* stone quarries of Wadi al-Hammamat during the Ptolemaic period and at the beginning of the Early Empire, and then the name of the *praesidium* of Bi'r Umm Fawakhir, see H. CUVIGNY, "Le crépuscule d'un dieu" (cf. bibliography 4).

Our texts have confirmed the hypotheses of R.T.J. Cappers, paleobotanist associated with the Berenike excavation, regarding the presence of gardens in the desert. They also enable us to confirm or to question some of his assumptions about the species of plants cultivated in these gardens. The ostraca actually specify the nature of vegetables grown in Persou — mainly cabbages, leeks, salads and aromatic herbs — and sold by correspondence to the *praesidia*. Onions and garlic, like lentils, cereals, chaff and fodder came from the Nile valley. Only crops that could not survive the long journey from the Nile valley were grown in the desert. R. Cappers wonders if cereals were not grown around Berenike because he has found a large quantity of chaff in the sediments he has examined. As a matter of fact, the ostraca indicate that large quantities of chaff were imported from the valley for the sites in the desert. Several circulars issued by the Prefect of Berenike order the *curatores praesidiorum* to escort the donkeys loaded with wheat, barley and chaff to Myos Hormos (which indicates that the cereals imported in the desert were already dehusked). The chaff was used not only for making plaster and bricks[17] but it was also used as fuel (for heating ovens and baths), litter for animals (whole layers of chaff can be found in the dumping grounds of *praesidia* apparently as a result of the cleaning of stables), perhaps also as supplementary fodder for donkeys and horses[18] (barley and chaff are often mentioned together in our ostraca).

We have seen that one of the duties of the *curatores praesidiorum* was to provide armed escorts to caravans transporting food supplies. The diaries probably maintained by the *curator praesidii* which were curiously written on amphoras found in Krokodilo, enable us to understand how the *praesidia* network functioned. These documents recorded the daily and even hourly arrivals and departures of horsemen sometimes entrusted with escorting travellers and sometimes with carrying official mail. The main reason for the existence of these *praesidia* was to have a certain number of horsemen permanently on their rolls (perhaps not more than four per garrison) to escort travellers and carry mail. These horsemen went only as far as the next station where they were relieved by others. Their duty done, they returned to their post. This system made for a quick exchange of orders and information between the valley, posts in the desert and the Red Sea ports. That is how the news of an Arab raid in Lower Nubia reached the *praesidia* on the Myos Hormos road in a matter of days.[19]

---

17. R.T.J. CAPPERS, in SIDEBOTHAM, WENDRICH, *Berenike '96*, p. 323.

18. This is a common practice today but we do not have any evidence to show that it existed in the Roman cavalry (K.R. DIXON, P. SOUTHERN, *The Roman Cavalry*, London, 1992, p. 209).

19. I have dealt in detail with this subject in the chapter "Le fonctionnement du réseau" in the joint work to be published shortly under the title *La route de Myos Hormos* (cf. bibliography 4).

The excavation of refuse dumps led not only to the discovery of texts but of all sorts of "secondary products" derived from ostraca,[20] mainly pottery, animal remains (M. Leguilloux) and masses of textiles, some of which are surprisingly fine (D. Cardon, H. Granger-Taylor). This refinement which was not lacking in Berenike during the Byzantine period has also impressed the specialists studying the textiles discovered at this site who have remarked, "The inhabitants of late Roman Berenike did not lack textile comforts. Their cotton garments and woollen outer wear admirably suited the climate. In their homes spartan furniture and rough finished walls could have been disguised under an astonishing range of high-class coverlets, hangings and curtains. Berenikians, even in the fifth century AD, had high expectations".[21] The exact dates furnished by the ostraca help us to date certain types and Dominique Cardon has been able to show that several weaving techniques must been dated earlier than has hitherto been believed. There are marked differences in the textiles found in Berenike and in the *praesidia*. In the latter, we have not found any cotton but only woollen textiles while in Berenike there was a large proportion of cotton textiles under the Early Roman Empire as well as during the Byzantine period.

Bibliography 4

Fr. BRIQUEL-CHATONNET, L. NEHMÉ, "Graffiti nabatéens d'Al-Muwayh et de Bi'r al-Hammamat (Égypte)", *Semitica* 47, 1997, pp. 81-88.

H. CUVIGNY, "Le crépuscule d'un dieu: le déclin du culte de Pan dans le désert Oriental", *BIFAO* 97, 1997, pp. 139-147.

A. BÜLOW-JACOBSEN, "Prostitution in ørkenen", *Papyrus. Ægyptologisk tidsskrift* 17.2, 1997, pp. 46-48 (in Danish).

M. LEGUILLOUX, "Quelques aspects de l'approvisionnement en viande des *praesidia* du désert Oriental égyptien", *Archaezoologia* 9, 1997, pp. 73-82.

A. BÜLOW-JACOBSEN, "Traffic on the roads between Coptos and the Red Sea", in O.E. KAPER (ed.), *Life on the fringe. Living in the Southern Egyptian deserts during the Roman and early Byzantine periods*, Leiden, 1998, pp. 63-74.

Fr. COLIN, "Les *paneia* d'El-Buwayb et du ouadi Minayh sur la piste de Bérénice à Coptos: inscriptions égyptiennes", *BIFAO* 98, 1998, pp. 89-125.

D. CARDON, "Textiles archéologiques de Maximianon-Al Zarqa et Didymoi: exemples précoces de teinture par réserve sur laine", *CIETA-Bulletin* 75, 1998, pp. 14-20.

H. CUVIGNY, "Bouchons cachetés des fouilles d'Adolphe Reinach à Coptos", *Bulletin des Musées et des Monuments Lyonnais*, 1998/4, pp. 2-7.

H. CUVIGNY, A. BÜLOW-JACOBSEN, "Inscriptions rupestres vues et revues dans le désert de Bérénice", *BIFAO* 99, 1999, pp. 133-193.[22]

H. CUVIGNY, "*Procurator Montis*", in *Papyri in honorem Johannis Bingen octogenarii editae,* Leuven 2000, pp. 415-418.

---

20. The term has been used by Jean-Pierre Brun, in charge of the study of pottery, the most plentiful of all the "secondary products" together with textiles.

21. J.P. & F.C. WILD in *Berenike '96*, p. 236.

22. It is about the *addenda* and *corrigenda* of Greek and Latin inscriptions on the *paneia* found in Al-Buwayb, Wadi Minayh and the stopping place at Wadi Minayh al-Hyr.

J.-P. BRUN, A. BÜLOW-JACOBSEN, D. CARDON, H CUVIGNY (ed.), J.-L. FOURNET M. LEGUILLOUX, M.-A. MATELLY, M. REDDÉ, *La route de Myos Hormos*, being printed at IFAO.

H. CUVIGNY, "De Koptos à Myos Hormos", can be consulted on the Internet at the following address: <http:www.france.diplomatie.fr/culture/archeo>

See also our preliminary reports published annually since 1994 in *BIFAO* (under the heading "Travaux de l'IFAO").

Conclusion

In spite of their quantity, the texts on ostraca found in the refuse dumps of the *praesidia* on the Myos Hormos and Berenike roads are unusually silent about the Erythraean trade. We first blamed the nature of these texts. The ostraca were documents of a temporary nature, generally meant for private use. It is not therefore surprising that the correspondence of Philokles, grocer and pimp who was a central figure in the majority of our ostraca files, never mentions the caravans carrying exotic goods that must have passed through the *praesidia* where Philokles, his agents, his family and his prostitutes went about their business. But the copies of official documents found in Krokodilo are equally silent on this point. On the other hand, they talk about what became a constant worry for the military authorities during Trajan's rule, viz. the threat posed by "barbarians" to travellers and Roman outposts in the desert. These new data call into question the theory that during Trajan's rule Rome had affirmed its ascendancy over both sides of the Red Sea, since the eastern side had become the Roman province of Nabataea, and on the western side great quantities of inscriptions and buildings proclaimed Rome's control over resources and public highways across the Eastern Desert.[23] Also, it is necessary to prove wrong the still prevalent notion that the Berenike Desert, pacified by Sulpicius Serenus' victory over the Agriophagi[24] and penetrated after 137 A.D. by the *Via Hadriana*, had become a nome, the nome of Berenike. This notion was based on two arguments that have now become obsolete: (1) the last prefect of Berenike whose exact dates are known to us was for a long time Antistius Asiaticus (90/91), but *P. Turner 34* has since then pointed out the existence of another prefect of Berenike in 216; (2) *P. Hamb. 7*, has revealed that there was a "nome of Berenike" in 132. But an inscription found in Kôm Tukala in the western delta

23. J. DESANGES, "Les relations de l'empire romain avec l'Afrique nilotique et érythréenne, d'Auguste à Probus", *ANRW* 2.10.1, 1988, p. 20.

24. Hypothesis advanced by J. DESANGES, *o.l.*, p. 22.

after *P. Hamb. 7*, generally unknown to historians, shows that this Berenike is not the same as Berenike of the Trogodytes.[25]

F. De Romanis[26] believes there was a link between the belligerence of the Barbarians in the Eastern Desert (and Lower Nubia) and the building of the Trajan Canal which made the northern Red Sea ports (Clysma, Aila)[27] prosperous. If we were to draw conclusions from this hypothesis, it would seem that the setting up of *praesidia* along the Myos Hormos and Berenike roads during Trajan's reign (or perhaps even earlier in the time of the Flavians), far from being a sign of the total control of the desert or the consequence of a heavy caravan traffic which would have made the Roman authorities invest in the building of a denser network of wells and other amenities for commercial travellers, was their response to an increasing feeling of insecurity which provoked a slump in the ports of Myos Hormos and Berenike[28] and the setting up of a alternative route. As a matter of fact, during Pliny's time, which was also the time of the *floruit* of the Coptos-Berenike road, the caravans had to be satisfied with a few *hydreumata* where they stocked up on water. Otherwise, they camped in the open desert in natural stopping places which changed according to circumstances (weather conditions, the phase of the moon, time of departure...).[29] The same is true of the Myos Hormos road which was at its peak at the beginning of Augustus' reign when the *praesidia* that we see today had not yet made their appearance. Contrary to what was believed till now, the proliferation of *praesidia* in the Berenike desert is not an indication of the boom of commercial traffic in this area. The fortlets were not built to provide more comfort to the caravaneers but to protect them and perhaps also to assert the Roman presence in the Eastern Desert and even create a buffer zone to prevent

---

25. I shall deal in detail with this question in the section "Le nome fantôme de Bérénice" in the chapter on the working of the *praesidia* network in *La route de Myos Hormos* (see bibliography 4).

26. F. DE ROMANIS, " Τραϊανὸς ποταμός: Mediterraneo e Mar Rosso da Traiano a Maometto", to be published in: *Controllo degli stretti e insedimenti militari nel Mediterraneo. Atti del Convegno di Studi in occasione dell'Assemblea generale del Comitato internazionale de Scienze storiche, Spoleto 3-4 settembre 1997.* I am grateful to the author for having sent me the manuscript of this stimulating article.

27. It should be noted that the *Via Nova Traiana* linking Bostra to Aila was built at the same time as the Trajan Canal. The digging of the canal started in 112 while the milestones along the *Via* are dated from 111 to 117.

28. This seems to be confirmed by the Berenike excavations.

29. The most obvious examples are the *paneion* of Wadi Minayh and the halting place of Wadi Minayh al-Hyr situated about 5 km apart. See in this volume F. DE ROMANIS, "Greek graffiti found in the Wādi Menīḥ el-Ḥēr. A *vestorius* between Coptos and Berenike", pp. 43-57.

the Barbarians from advancing further north and disrupting work in the imperial quarries of Claudianus and Porphyrites as they were to do later.[30]

As for the *Via Hadriana*, F. De Romanis suggests that it was intended to serve as an alternative to the roads converging on Coptos which had become dangerous.[31] But why should the distant and desolate Red Sea coast have been safer from the attacks by Barbarians than the interior of the Eastern Desert? I personnally wonder if the *Via Hadriana* was not meant to enable the Roman army to keep a close watch on the coast, prevent undesirable attacks from the sea and protect coastal navigation from the depredations of wreckers. It may be recalled that an Aksumite king had to bring to heel the Kinaidokolpites living on the Arabian coast of the Red Sea. The latter were known to have boats and, unless there is an interpretation mistake on my side,[32] to engage in piracy. These events, narrated in the *Monumentum Adulitanum,* occurred before 220 A.D. and may even go back to the 2nd century. But they definitely belong to the "time of the *praesidia*" which was between the "time of the *hydreumata*" and the crisis in the 3rd century. By the way, this most unusual ethnic group of Kinaidokolpites finds mention in an ostracon discovered in Maximianon which can be stratigraphically dated to the middle of the 2nd century. This memorandum records that two soldiers (probably horsemen) "left with a *diplôma*[33] concerning the Kinaidokolpites". The ostraca found later by our team in Krokodilo show that warnings against "barbarians" are a recurrent feature in the *diplômata*. Therefore I am also tempted to think that the *diplôma* regarding the Kinaidokolpites also contained a warning, in this case against an attack by pirates from across the sea.

There is no doubt that these hypotheses need support from stronger documentary evidence, and I am aware that it is hazardous to assume, as I have done, a reconciliation between Romans and Barbarians in the Berenike Desert on the eve of the 3rd century crisis on the basis of a single terse note... Let us hope that our English, Dutch, American and French fund givers will understand this and make it possible for us to continue the work.

Hélène CUVIGNY
CNRS

---

30. As testified by some unpublished ostraca found in Mons Claudianus.

31. Article mentioned in n. 26.

32. See in this volume, H. CUVIGNY and Chr. ROBIN, pp. 59-82.

33. In this context an official circular.

GREEK GRAFFITI FOUND IN THE WĀDI MENĪḤ EL-ḤĒR A *VESTORIUS* BETWEEN COPTOS AND BERENIKE

The researchers' perseverance and diligence is well rewarded by the Eastern Desert of Egypt, as shown by the papers read in this seminar. And as research in the area is far from being completed, further relevant discoveries can be easily expected. Intensification and coordination of the inquiries are bound to integrate the data handed down by an unusually generous literary tradition on the history of trade in the Red Sea and in the Indian Ocean.

Partially known as yet, the epigraphic documentation along the caravan routes between the Nile and the Red Sea can remarkably contribute: a specimen, suggested by re-examination of H.A. Winkler's photographs and notes,[1] can be here discussed.

1. Greek Graffiti found in the Wādi Menīḥ el-Ḥēr

I have elsewhere argued for the identification of the first *mansio in monte* ("station in the desert") of the Coptos-Berenike caravan route described by Pliny[2] with the area including the site of the Wādi Menīḥ Paneion.[3] Here, after a

---

1. I wish to thank the Egypt Exploration Society Committee for permission to publish Winkler's photographs and drawings and Dr. P. Spencer, Secretary of the Egypt Exploration Society, for kindly facilitating my research.

2. Plin., *n.h.* VI 102: *a Copto camelis itur, aquationum ratione mansionibus dispositis: prima appellatur Hydreuma XXII (milia), secunda in monte diei itinere*. For the reading *XXII (milia)*, cf. F. DE ROMANIS, "Romanukharaṭṭha e Taprobane. Sui rapporti Roma-Ceylon nel I sec. d.C.", *Helikon* 28, 1988, pp. 13-14, n. 21.

3. F. DE ROMANIS, *Cassia, cinnamomo, ossidiana. Uomini e merci tra oceano Indiano e Mediterraneo*, Roma, 1996, pp. 206-209.

A Gateway from the Eastern Mediterranean to India. The Red Sea in Antiquity
F. DE ROMANIS, pp. 43-57

day's journey from the el-Laqeṭa oasis, caravans travelling to (or from) Berenike stopped for the first (or the last) time in a waterless spot: no wonder, therefore — also considering the sacred character of the site due to the image of Min — that the Wādi Menīḥ shelter is so rich in travellers' graffiti.[4] Nevertheless the area of the first *mansio in monte*, precisely because it was far from water-holes, was not confined to this sacred place, known to the camel-drivers: traces of merchants' halts are found elsewhere in the same area.

I do not refer only to the inscription of the Minaean merchant Yḏkr'l next to the Bīr Menīḥ,[5] which probably dates back to a time preceding the construction of the *lacci* (water tanks) along the Coptos-Berenike caravan route,[6] and is therefore older than the journey's perfectioned time-table as known by Pliny. I rather refer to the halts documented by the graffiti which Winkler photographed and/or copied in the Wādi Menīḥ el-Ḥēr, on the site marked in his map as 24N, quite near to the Paneion of Wādi Menīḥ.[7]

It may be too much to claim with Meredith that "we can take these two sites [...] as one";[8] nevertheless we can point out that the relative closeness of the two sites couples with significant similarities in their epigraphic documents: as in the Paneion of Wādi Menīḥ, in Wādi Menīḥ el-Ḥēr we find Nabataean[9] as well as Greek inscriptions, the latter dating back to the first decades of the Christian era.

In his book, Winkler describes the site as follows: "Wādi Menīḥ el-Ḥēr. Two huge boulders near the southern border of the wādi; rocks and shelter at this border. Enormous number of Blemyan signs. Some Greek, Nabataean, and Arabic inscriptions. Camel, asses, ibexes, and apparently of the same recent date, elephant and man. No drawings earlier than Graeco-Roman, few of later date".[10] Luckily, the photographs of the two "huge boulders" are kept in the

---

4. *Ibid.*, pp. 203-217.

5. *RES* 3571.

6. *ILS* 2483.

7. H.A. WINKLER, *Rock Drawings in Southern Upper Egypt*, I, London, 1938, map. A few years ago, I searched this spot unsuccesfully.

8. D. MEREDITH, "Classical notes", appendix to E. LITTMANN, "Nabataean Inscriptions from Egypt. II", *BSOAS* XVI, 1954, p. 239. Meredith thought that in the same place the *statio* of *Afrodito*, formerly visited by J.G. Wilkinson, should be found. It was instead recently spotted by S. Sidebotham in a place called Khawr ej-Jir, "several kilometers away" from Wādi Menīḥ el-Ḥēr. Three or four kilometres south of the *statio*, Sidebotham records "petroglyphs, recent Bedouin *wasum* [...], and other graffiti from different ages": S. SIDEBOTHAM, "Routes Through the Eastern Desert of Egypt", *Expedition* 37, 2, 1995, p. 51.

9. LITTMANN, *art. cit.*, n. 74-76 (Wādi Menīḥ); 77-79 (Wādi Menīḥ el-Ḥēr).

10. WINKLER, *op. cit.*, p. 7.

Egypt Exploration Society archives, which enabled E. Littmann's publication of the Nabataean inscriptions.[11]

Among the Greek graffiti inscribed on the two huge boulders, one is dated:

Π...αcμηφιc Κεφαλᾶτοc/ Π..ẹ.νcιc Ἐπωνύχου/ **L** δ Τιβερίου Φαῶφι ε.[12]

The dating 5 Phaophi of the fourth year of Tiberius (17 AD)[13] includes this inscription in the chronological interval between the earliest (4 BC) and the latest (44 AD) dated inscription of the Wādi Menīḥ Paneion.

On the other hand, its onomastics shows noteworthy affinities with that of the so-called Nikanor's archive: the anthroponym Ἐπώνυχοc in genitive in l. 2, following another anthroponym in nominative (for which I cannot suggest any certain restoration) couples with one Κάcτωρ Ἐπωνύχου staying in Berenike and in Apollonos Hydreuma in Tiberius' and Claudius' time;[14] with one Ἐπώνυχοc staying in Berenike in Caligula's years;[15] with one Ἐπώνυχοc Ἀχιλλέωc mentioned in documents ranging from 30 to 52 AD (in a not specified year the man is in Berenike).[16] Similarly the Πετεασμῆφιc (to be restored with all probability in l. 1) can find parallels in the onomastics of Coptos and of the Red Sea harbours.[17]

---

11. LITTMANN, *art. cit.*, pl. IV; V.

12. See *fig.* 1 (photograph; the inscription is more or less at the center of the rock, a little on the right) and *fig.* 2 (Winkler's transcription). Winkler's drawings of the site of Wādi Menīḥ el-Ḥēr are to be found on pages 86-93 of a Notebook, which is kept in the archives of the Egypt Exploration Society and marked Packet III book 4: the inscription we are examining is on p. 91. This is probably the inscription referred to in *BSOAS* XVI, 1954, pl. V: "Several Greek inscriptions, one dated October 2nd, AD 16": the reading **L** δ is however certain.

13. The date corresponds to October 2nd according to the Julian-Alexandrian calendar, and to September 22nd according to the revolving Egyptian year. About the persistence in Roman age of the latter calendar, cf. DE ROMANIS, "Romanukharaṭṭha e Taprobane", *cit.*, pp. 5-19; *id.*, "Ancora a proposito di *A.É.* 1954, n. 121a", *Helikon* XXIX-XXX, 1989-1990, pp. 369-371; *id.*, *Cassia, cinnamomo, ossidiana*, *cit.*, pp. 211-212.

14. *OPetr* 239; 245; 280; 285.

15. *OPetr* 258.

16. *OPetr* 235; 251; 279. We may as well note one Ἐπώνυχοc Πετεασμήφιοc in *OPetr* 203, of 3 AD from Coptos.

17. In *OPetr* 223 and in *OPetr* 208 one or two Πετεαcμῆφιc Ἡρακλήου, respectively in Myos Hormos in 6 AD and in Coptos in 44 AD.; one Πετεαcμῆφιc in *OPetr* 224; one Μω.τιc Πετεαcμήφιοc in Myos Hormos in 50 AD (*OPetr* 277); one Ὧροc Πετεαcμήφεωc in Myos Hormos in 61 AD (*OPetr* 288; 291). We may as well mention one Πετεαcμῆφιc Πακοίβιοc in 2 AD (*OPetr* 202, from Coptos); and one Ἐπώνυχοc Πετεαcμήφιοc in 3 AD (*OPetr* 203, da Coptos).

Another inscription, not photographed, but only copied by Winkler, dates back to Tiberius'age, maybe to the month of August, 21 AD:

Ψενοcῖρις Ψεμμίνιος/ πρεcβυτέρο τοῦ Γαλάτου/ L ζ Τιβερίου Μεcο‹ρ›ὴ ΠΟ/ Ἐπαγω(μένων).[18]

The name Ψενοcῖρις is also mentioned in Nikanor's archive, but its bearer, staying in Berenice in 34 AD, is evidently different from the graver of this inscription.[19]

Onomastic resemblances between the Wādi Menīḥ el-Ḥēr graffiti and Nikanor's archive are less trivial when they concern Roman family names (*gentilicia*). This is the case of the inscription Μαμιλίου Μαροῦ,[20] recalling one Πόπλιος Μαμίλιος 'Αμβρόcιος residing in Myos Hormos in 6 AD,[21] one Πόπλιος Μαμίλιος 'Ανδρόμαχος residing in Myos Hormos in 43-44 AD,[22] and earlier still one Ῥουφίων Μαμιλίου who in 18 BC receives, on behalf of Μαμίλιος Χρήcιμος and probably in a Red Sea harbour, 22 tin πλάκες.[23]

As yet, it is difficult to fully evaluate the majority of the remaining graffiti, as their texts appear to be vague.[24] One exception is an inscription copied by Winkler on the same page as the graffiti of one of the two huge boulders:

Τίτος Οὐεcτώριος Ἰάλυcος/ L η Τιβερίου Και [– – –] ΙΑΠΟΥ Ι.[25]

---

18. Notebook Packet III book 4, p. 93 (*fig.* 3). On l. 2 I think **L** ζ should be read. On l. 2 again I can't explain ΠΟ after Μεcο‹ρ›ή.

19. *OPetr* 239: Ψενοcῖρις Πετεαρποχράτου. The name is also attested at Abū Kū', cf. J.-L. FOURNET, "Les inscriptions grecques d'Abū Kū' et de la route de Quft-Quṣayr", *BIFAO* 95, 1995, p. 179.

20. *Fig.* 1 and 4 (Notebook Packet III book 4, p. 90): ΟCΑΜΟC / ΤΩ ΠΟΠΛΙΩΙ/ ΜΑΜΙΛΙΟΥ ΜΑΡΟΥ.

21. *OPetr* 223.

22. *OPetr* 271.

23. *OBodl* 1968. χρηcιμ seems to be the man's abbreviated *cognomen*.

24. Notebook Packet III book 4, p. 90 (*fig.* 4): Cεβηρῖνος. Χορζαῖος Cυμμάχου. *Fig.* 5: Ἡρακλῆι/ Πτολεμα..c/ καὶ οπρατρικις.

25. Notebook Packet III book 4, p. 90 (*fig.* 4). On l. 2, it is obvious to integrate Και[σαρος, which may be followed by Cεβαcτοῦ, but a vertical stroke immediately preceding the A in the transcription makes it difficult to read]ΒΑCΤΟΥ. At the end of the line, I is also enigmatic.

We are still in Tiberius' years,[26] precisely in 21-22 AD: the graver is a Roman citizen, with a Greek *cognomen* and a *gentilicium* belonging to one of the big merchant families from Puteoli, which on different evidence had already been inferred as active in Egypt.

2. The *gens Vestoria* from the Mediterranean Sea to the Ἐρυθρὰ θάλασσα

In fact, one Vestorius had imported from Alexandria to Puteoli the technique for production of *caeruli temperationes*, the "Egyptian blue":[27] and this, earlier than the publication of Vitruvius' *de architectura*.[28] As is well known, this information from Vitruvius received new light from the excavation of the wreck near the Planier island off Marseille:[29] together with amphorae bearing stamps *M. Tucci L. f. Tro./ Galeonis*, in the cargo of this merchant ship, sunk around the middle of the first century BC, balls of *caeruleum* have been found.[30]

Tchernia convincingly suggested that the man mentioned in the amphorae's stamps should be identified both with the Galeo from which Cicero inherits[31] at the beginning of 47 BC, and with the M. Tuccius who in 51 BC sued C. Sempronius Rufus,[32] a Roman senator well known among Puteoli's merchants.[33]

A supporter of M. Tuccius against C. Sempronius Rufus was C. Vestorius from Puteoli, a man who in Cicero's letters appears as an active broker, building

---

26. Incidentally, it may be worthwhile noting that in the Wādi Menīḥ Paneion most of the dated inscriptions date back to the Augustan age — 4 BC, 2 BC, 6 AD —, whereas in the nearby Wādi Menīḥ el-Ḥēr they mostly belong to the Tiberian age.

27. Vitr. VII 11, 1: *caeruli temperationes Alexandriae primum sunt inventae, postea item Vestorius Puteolis instituit faciundum*. On this material, cf., e.g., D. ULLRICH, "Egyptian Blue and Green Frit: Characterization, History and Occurrence, Synthesis", *Pact* 17, 1987, pp. 323-332.

28. On the chronology of the *de architectura*, cf., e.g., E. ROMANO, *La capanna e il tempio: Vitruvio o dell'architettura*, Palermo, 1987, pp. 15-45.

29. A. TCHERNIA, "Premiers résultats des fouilles de juin 1968 sur l'épave 3 de Planier", *Études classiques* 3, 1968, pp. 51-82.

30. *Ibid.*, p. 67. On other *caeruleum* findings, cf. *ibid.*, p. 75, n. 55; 56. A.J. PARKER, *Ancient Shipwrecks of the Mediterranean & the Roman Provinces*, Oxford, 1992, n. 616; 691; 755; 826; F.B. ATKINS, "Egyptian Blue", in A.C.C. BRODRIBB, A.R. HANDS, D.R. WALKER, *Excavations at Shakenoak Farm, near Wilcote, Oxfordshire*, II, Oxford, 1971, pp. 56-58 (I owe these references to A. Tchernia, whom I wish to thank).

31. Cic., *ad Att.* XI 12, 4.

32. *Id.*, *ad fam.* VIII 8, 1.

33. *Id.*, *ad Att.* V 2, 2.

contractor and businessman in general.[34] He probably was at odds with C. Sempronius Rufus[35] a few months before Tuccius' action against Rufus. It is today commonly accepted that, as Tchernia had suggested, the vitruvian Vestorius and the ciceronian C. Vestorius and M. Tuccius (Galeo) are to be identified as the sponsors of the commercial undertaking unluckily ended off Marseille.

In the factories established in Puteoli by Vestorius the so-called *Vestorianum*, a by-product of the *caeruleum Aegyptium,*[36] was also probably invented, either by C. Vestorius himself or by another man bearing the same family name, who might have continued his business, not later than the middle of the first century AD.[37]

Until now, that business in Egypt was not occasionally pursued by the *gens Vestoria*, was only indicated by a few weak clues. Beside the technique for production of *caeruli temperationes* imported from Alexandria to Puteoli by a Vestorius, one might have quoted the "Egyptizing" *cognomen* of T. Vestorius Arpocras minor, mentioned in a tablet, dated AD 21 July 38,[38] from the Puteolan "Sulpicii archive"; or else, one might have recalled the permanence in Egypt, but

---

34. Cf. V. SIRAGO, "La personalità di C. Vestorio", *Puteoli* 3, 1979, pp. 3-16; but especially J. ANDREAU, "À propos de la vie financière à Pouzzoles: Cluvius et Vestorius", in *Les "bourgeoisies" municipales italiennes aux IIe et Ier siècles av. J.-C. Centre Jean Bérard. Institut Français de Naples 7-10 décembre 1981*, Naples, 1983, pp. 9-20.

35. Cic., *ad Att.* V 2, 2.

36. Plin., *n.h.* XXXIII 162: *nuper accessit et Vestorianum, ab auctore appellatum. fit ex Aegyptii leuissima parte; pretium eius in libras (denarius) I. idem et Puteolani usus, praeterque ad fenestras; cylon uocant.* With regard to the reading concerning the price of *Vestorianum,* I don't think Broterius' emendation [(denarii) XI] is necessary; such an emendation is instead accepted by H. Zehnacker in the "Les Belles Lettres" edition.

37. In Plin., *n.h.* XXXIII 162, *nuper accessit* must not be meant absolutely, that is referring to the time of composition of the *Naturalis Historia,* (in which case the invention of the *Vestorianum* should be dated to the late Julio-Claudian period), but should be seen in opposition with *antiquitus* in Plin., *n.h.* XXXIII 161: the *tria genera* of *caeruleum* were already known to Theophr., περὶ λίθων 55, Pliny's source for this passage. It may be also noted that according to Pliny the *Vestorianum* was invented before the *Indicum* (known to Vitruvius: Vitr. VII 9, 6) began to be imported.

38. *TP* 98. Cf. G. CAMODECA, "Per una riedizione dell'archivio puteolano dei Sulpicii", *Puteoli* VII-VIII, 1983-1984, p. 11, n. 19, according to whom the man's *cognomen* "non può non richiamare, anche se forse per una semplice coincidenza, gli stretti legami alessandrini di C. Vestorius". Moreover Camodeca rightly infers from *minor* the existence of a *maior* bearing the same name: nevertheless that they were brothers and *conliberti* at the same time, as Camodeca dobtfully supposes, is the remotest among possibilities.

only in the second century AD, of one Τίτος Οὐεστώριος Λ..ολος.[39] Now the Wādi Menīḥ el-Ḥēr graffiti of T. Vestorius Ialysos confirms the trading function held in Egypt by his *gens*, extending it to the Ἐρυθρὰ θάλασσα. As the family name is relatively rare,[40] and as many of the people mentioned in the Wādi Menīḥ Paneion[41] graffiti also seem to have connections with Campania, no doubt is left in fact on T. Vestorius Ialysos belonging to the Puteolan milieu.[42] It may seem odd, but it is not accidental that one of Puteoli's quarters (*regio uici Vestoriani et Calpurniani*)[43] was named after the two family names who are graved on the rocks of the first *mansio in monte* of the Coptos-Berenice caravan route.[44]

---

39. *SB* VI 9254.

40. Outside Puteoli and Egypt it is attested in Rome: *CIL* VI 28637; 28637a; 28638; 29678; 33733; in Praeneste, in Republican age: *CIL* I^2 311; and finally in nearby Pompeii: cf. P. CASTRÉN, Ordo populusque pompeianus. *Polity and Society in Roman Pompeii*, Roma, 1983^2, pp. 238-239.

41. Cf. DE ROMANIS, *Cassia, cinnamomo, ossidiana, cit.*, pp. 241-259.

42. Besides T. Vestorius Arpocras minor (and the connected T. Vestorius Arpocras maior), one may mention T. Vestorius Phoenix in *TP* 98, T. Vestorius Zelotus in *CIL* X 1557, T. Vestorius Alexander, T. Vestorius Pelops and Vestoria Elpis in *CIL* X 3029. On february 2nd, 53 AD one C. Vestorius Felix is attested: *TP* 60.

43. *CIL* 1631.

44. I refer to the inscription of Laudanes, slave of Calpurnius Moschas, cf. DE ROMANIS, *Cassia, cinnamomo, ossidiana, cit.*, pp. 211; 252-253. Connection with the Calpurnii from Puteoli is also accepted by G. LACERENZA, "Laudanes schiavo di Calpurnius Moschas. Nota su un graffito greco dal Wādi Mānīḥ (Egitto)", in *Ostraka* 4.1, 1995, pp. 191-193, who traces the name Laudanes back to Semitic onomastics — to his list I would nevertheless add the Egyptian Λαυτᾶνις/Λαυδᾶνις in *BGU* II 589, 8 and *OTebtPad passim* (II-III cent. AD) and maybe also Λατᾶνις in *P. Par.* 9, 11, late Ptolemaic. According to Lacerenza, the name Λαυδάνης should suggest an "arabo del Ḥawrān, probabilmente di ceppo, più che nabateo, 'safaita'" (p. 192) bought from his master (himself maybe, according to Lacerenza, from Ḥawrān) in Ḥawrān or in an other emporion of the Mediterranean Sea: I wouldn't go further than connecting the name Laudanes with the old relationship between the emporion of Coptos and the opposite coast of the Red Sea, which is supported by the evidence of epigraphy in the East Egyptian desert and in Coptos, as well as by Strabo's description of that Egyptian emporion: πόλις κοινὴ Αἰγυπτίων τε καὶ Ἀράβων (Strab. XVII 1, 44), a "city common to Egyptians and Arabs". Strabo was in Coptos two decades before the date of Laudanes' inscription, when Aelius Gallus was praefect of Egypt. Besides other inaccuracies, as, e.g., the identification of the Wādi Menīḥ shelter with the *statio* of *Afrodito* allegedly mentioned by Pliny, or Euphemos being freedman and not slave (p. 191), it is surprising that Lacerenza (p. 191, n. 5) claims I changed my mind about the hypothesis on Annius Plocamus (Plin., *n.h.* VI 84) being freedman (whether he should be identified or not with P. Annius Plocamus in the Wādi Menīḥ inscription and with P. Annius Plocamus in Bacoli inscription): I have anyway reasserted and, as I

On the other hand, the connection between T. Vestorius Ialysos' business and the importation in Puteoli of the "Egyptian blue" production by Vestorius, a big trader between Alexandria, Puteoli and Marseille, should not be straightforward, as is shown both by the different *praenomina* (C. vs. T.) of the two businessmen and by the approximately 65 years' lapse of time between our graffiti and the last mention of C. Vestorius in Cicero's letters. Nevertheless this does not lessen our interest in such a connection; I would rather say it strengthens it, as it shows that the *gens Vestoria* held fast, but pliably, to its business.[45]

The halt of T. Vestorius Ialysos at Wādi Menīḥ el-Ḥēr in 21-22 AD must be considered not only in the light of the business trade widely spreading across the Mediterranean Sea as early as the middle of the first century BC, but also in the frame of the activity of Cicero's C. Vestorius as a broker. At about the same time as T. Vestorius Ialysos' journey between Coptos and Berenice, the emperor Tiberius deplored, if we are to give credit to his letter to the Senate, as reported by Tacitus,[46] the outflow of Roman coins, *lapidum causa, ad externas aut hostilis gentis.*[47] Southern India was the most frequent destination of Roman coins leaving the Roman empire[48] and Berenice was the harbour whence more often one sailed to southern India.[49] In the coin hoards found in southern India,[50]

---

believe, strengthened my argument in *Cassia, cinnamomo, ossidiana, cit.*, p. 249, n. 28.

45. For a single *gens*, a more than fifty years' long business in trade, at first only across the Mediterranean Sea, later in the Erythraean Sea as well, is not unparalleled: cf., as for the Annii, DE ROMANIS, *Cassia, cinnamomo, ossidiana, cit.*, pp. 249-250. Similarly, the lapse of time between the Mediterranean Sea business of the Peticius who picked up Pompey after the Pharsalos battle (Caes., *b.c.* III 96; Plut., *Pomp.* 73, 3) and the halt of C. Peticius, in Wādi Hammāmāt, on the road to Myos Hormos (cf. A. TCHERNIA, "Le dromadaire des Peticii et le commerce oriental", *MEFRA* 104, 1992, pp. 293-301), though not definable, must have been considerable.

46. Which we may in any case consider as rewritten according to Thucydides' principle on respecting the ξύμπασα γνώμη τῶν ἀλεθῶς λεχθέντων, as can be seen in Claudius' speech (Tac., *ann.* XI 23-24), compared with its original text (ILS 212), cf. lastly A. GIARDINA, "L'identità incompiuta dell'Italia romana", in *L'Italie d'Auguste à Dioclétien. Actes du colloque international...*, Rome, 1994, p. 2.

47. Tac., *ann.* III 53. For an even-minded commentary, taking into account numismatical evidence as well, cf. A. TCHERNIA, "Mousson et monnaies: les voies du commerce entre le monde gréco-romain et l'Inde", *Annales (HSS)* 1995, pp. 1001-1009.

48. Pliny estimates that the amount of money outflowing from the empire to southern India was roughly a half of that outflowing towards India, China and Arabia together: Plin., *n.h.* VI 101; XII 84.

49. DE ROMANIS, *Cassia, cinnamomo, ossidiana, cit.*, p. 171-183.

50. Cf. lastly P. TURNER, *Roman Coins from India*, London (1989); P. BERGHAUS, "Zu den römischen Fundmünzen aus Indien", *Revue Suisse de Numismatique* 1992,

the abundance of Augustus' and Tiberius' *denarii* and the scarcity of republican *denarii* as well as of those issued after the monetary reform by Nero in AD 64 show on the one hand that non-Egyptian merchants took part in trade with Southern India (as is well known, *denarii* did not circulate in Egypt), on the other hand that exported coins were carefully selected.[51] Obviously, such a selection implies the handling of considerable financial resources. The graffiti in the first *mansio in monte* of the Coptos-Berenike caravan route suggest that such a selection was possibly cared for by the business and merchant classes of Puteoli, who as early as in Republican times used to be given and to invest the

---

pp. 226-247; *id.*, "Roman coins from India and their imitations", in A.K. JHA (ed.), *Coinage, Trade and Economy, 3rd int. colloquium*, Nashik, 1991, pp. 108-121.

51. Such a selection is explained with a "contatto diretto e privilegiato con la fonte di emissione" by M. CRAWFORD, "Economia imperiale e commercio estero", in *Tecnologia, economia e società nel mondo romano. Atti del convegno di Como, 27-29 settembre 1979*, Como, 1980, p. 217, who suggests that some members of the imperial family possibly took part to trade with India (one Anicetus, *uicarius* of one Communis, himself slave of Tiberius, stayed in Berenice, in 33-35 AD, cf. *OPetr* 237; 238; 239; 242; one other slave of Tiberius is mentioned in *OPetr* 247); other *uicarii* of imperial slaves are in Berenice during the Julio-Claudian age: *OPetr* 280; 285; 292; one *uicarius* of a slave of Augustus is in Quṣūr al-Banāt: FOURNET, *art.cit.*, p. 201. D. MC DOWALL, "Indian Imports of Roman Silver Coins", A.K. JHA (ed.), *op. cit.*, pp. 145-163, suggests instead that *denarii* of the Julio-Claudian emperors were exported only after Vespasianus' debasement, in virtue of the Gresham Law (this is certainly true of the Augustus' *denarius* with countermark of Vespasianus, found in Budinatham: cf. Tchernia, *Mousson et monnaies*, *cit.*, p. 1004). Both explanations hold good only for marginal aspects of this phenomenon: as it is shown by the ostraka from Nikanor's archives and especially from the inscriptions along the caravan routes of the Eastern desert, trade with India was mostly carried on by people who cannot be immediately connected with the imperial family; besides, if members of the imperial family (with their slaves and freedmen) were uniquely or at least mainly responsible for the outflow of money, they would have been at the same time the target of Tiberius' rebuke in the *Annales*. On the other hand, it is almost impossible to disconnect the exportation of *denarii* towards southern India from the evidence — certainly earlier than Vespasianus' debasement — of *PME* 56: προχωρεῖ δὲ εἰς αὐτὴν προηγουμένως χρήματα πλεῖστα (these χρήματα are undoubtedly the δηνάριον χρυσοῦν καὶ ἀργυροῦν also exported to Barygaza, *PME* 49); and it is equally impossible to disconnect it from Tiberius' complains in the *Annales* (on the chronology of the *Periplus Maris Erythraei*, cf. lastly F. PAULI, "NAHAPĀNA/ MANBAN.Σ vor 78 n.Chr.? Ein epigraphischer Neufund aus Indien und seine Bedeutung für die antike Südasien-Chronologie", *Studien zur alte Geschichte S. Lauffer zum 70. Geburstag am 4 August 1981 dargebracht von Freunden, Kollegen und Schülern*, Roma, 1986, II, pp. 744-753; L. CASSON, *The* Periplus Maris Erythraei. *Text with Introduction, Translation, and Commentary*, Princeton, 1989, pp. 6-7; Chr. ROBIN, "L'Arabie du sud et la date du *Périple de la Mer Érythrée* (nouvelles données)", *JA* 279, 1991, pp. 1-30; for a more definite dating before 50 AD, cf. G. FUSSMAN, "Le *Périple* et l'histoire politique de l'Inde", *ibid.*, pp. 31-38. For the use of *denarii pari pondere* in the "erythraean" trade during the age of Claudius, cf. DE ROMANIS, "Romanukharaṭṭha e Taprobane", *cit.*, pp. 29-37).

Roman aristocrats' money, as is shown by the cases of M. Cluuius and, indeed, of C. Vestorius.

Federico DE ROMANIS

Fig. 1 (Copyright Egypt Exploration Society)

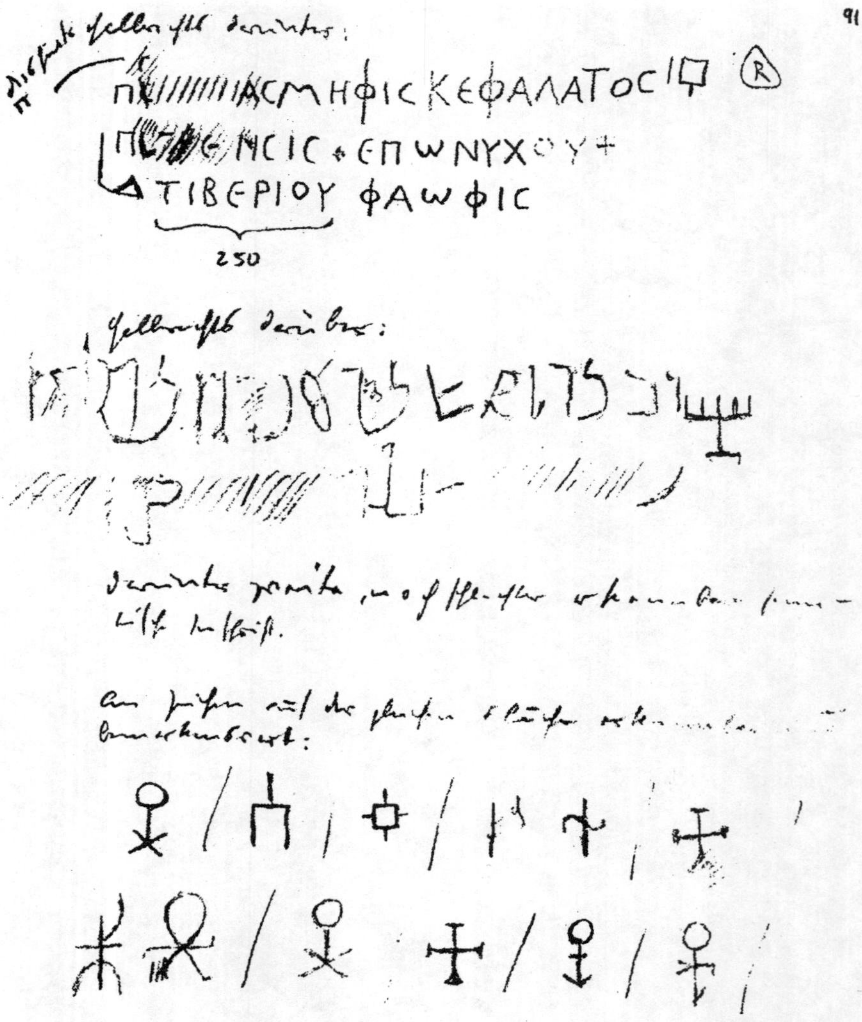

Fig. 2

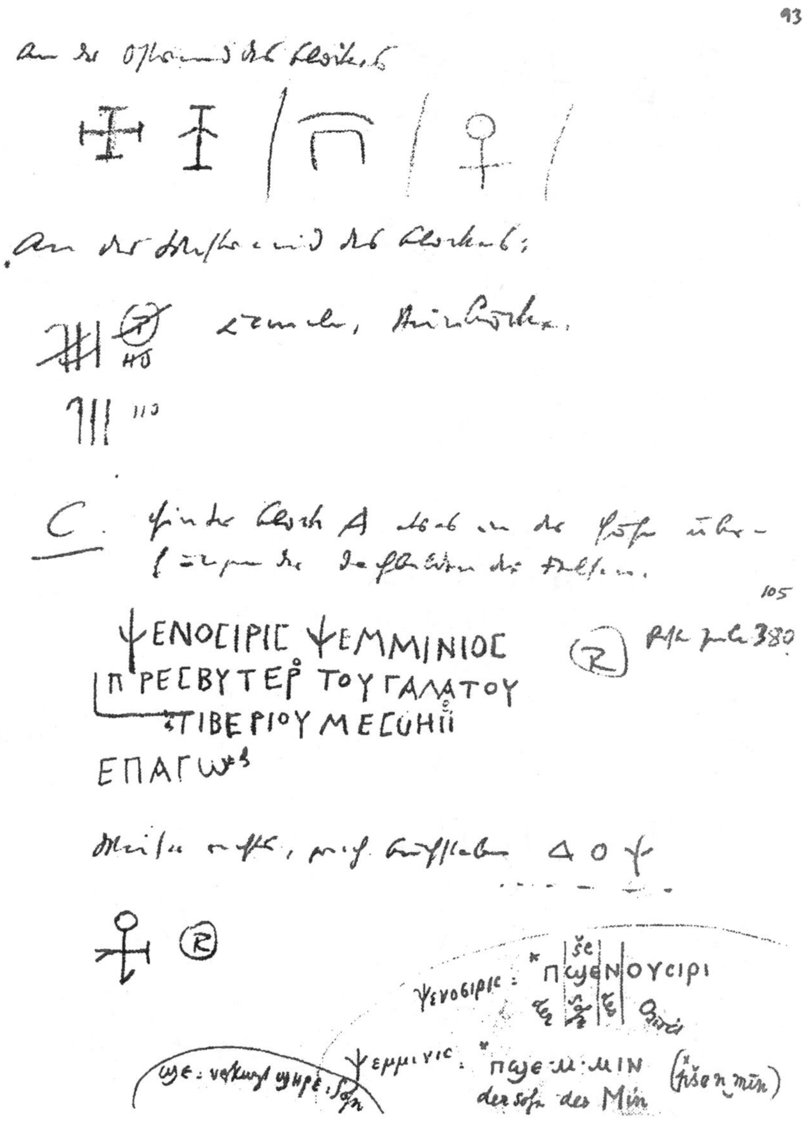

Fig. 3

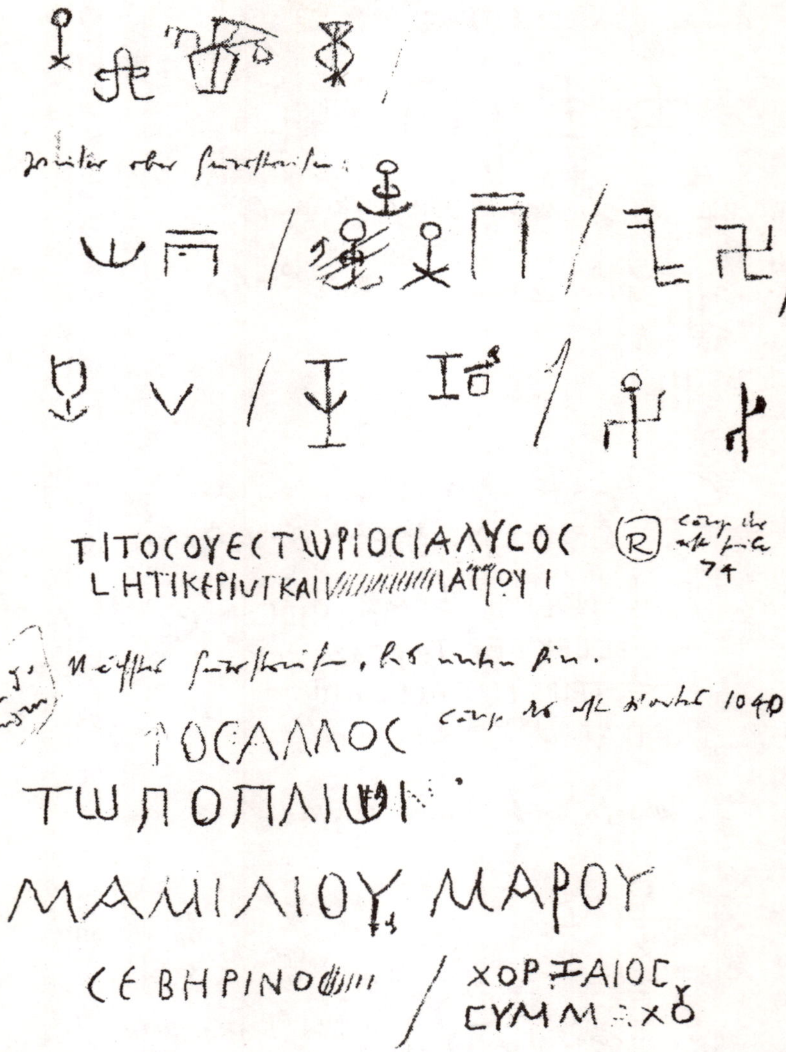

Fig. 4

Fig. 5 (Copyright Egypt Exploration Society)

KINAIDOKOLPITAI MENTIONED ON A GREEK OSTRACON FROM THE EASTERN DESERT*

The passage of caravans transporting import and export goods through Maximianon (az-Zarqā') had practically no effect on the written documentation found there. There are only four texts that can be added to this file: two Nabataean ostraca,[1] one dipinto on a pot which contained malabathron intended for Myos Hormos and a simple memorandum given below mentioning the Kinaidokolpitai.

I. The Ostracon[2]

O.Max. inv. 81	*c.* 150 A.D.
9 x 11.5 cm	*Fig.* 1

It belongs to a small group consisting of four pieces containing lists of names preceded by a date and on one occasion, as in this case, by a brief description of a mission. The present ostracon is a report about the departure of two soldiers. To our knowledge, this type of document has no parallel, but it may be assumed that the ostracon was used to compile reports on the activities of troops in the Maximianon garrison. We have not found such reports in Maximianon, but there are some in a slightly earlier collection of ostraca from Al-

* The ostracon was found in the course of the first archaeological mission to az-Zarqā' (January 1994) financed by the French Ministry of Foreign Affairs and IFAO.

1. Published by C. TOLL, *BIFAO* 94, 1994, pp. 381-382.

2. It was presented in a paper at the Berlin Papyrology Congress in August 1995.

A Gateway from the Eastern Mediterranean to India. The Red Sea in Antiquity
H. CUVIGNY & C. ROBIN, pp. 59-82

Muwayḥ (*O. Krok.*) which was discovered recently.[3] It lists daily and hourly arrivals and departures of riders carrying dispatches which were sometimes called ἐπιστολαί (*epistolai*) and sometimes διπλώματα (*diplômata*).

It was a *diplôma* which carried by the two soldiers, probably cavalrymen. Δίπλωμα may refer to any official document. Several possible meanings have been listed: letter of recommendation, subpoena, passport, "postal passport" authorising the bearer to use the facilities of the imperial post for his official journeys and for transporting his possessions against payment and within certain limits. The meaning "dispatch" is new (but probably that is how δίπλωμα was meant to be understood in another military ostracon, *SB* XIV 12040). *O. Krok.* Inv. 5, a collection of copies of *diplômata*, gives us an idea of the appearance and content of these documents which could be reports as well as instructions written by an officer and addressed to one or several persons, who happened to be in most cases "*curatores* of the *praesidia* on the Myos Hormos road". The texts of *diplômata* that have been preserved by *O. Krok.* Inv. 5, date back to 118 A.D. and refer to the insecurity in the desert (attacks by "barbarians", measures to be taken, etc.). We shall never know if our Kinaidokolpitai were brigands or inoffensive traders or slaves for sale. Because the object of the dispatch is known, it is either a report written in Maximianon or a circular which, after it was read and copied, was sent on to the next *praesidium*.

Τυβι κ̄
ἐξελταν μετὰ
δύπλομα
περὶ Χινεδο-
κολπιτῶν
Ἄρρις
Ἀρεώθης

1 κ *post corr.* 2. ἐξῆλθον 3. διπλώματος

"20 Tybi. Left with a dispatch concerning the Kinaidokolpitai: Arrius and Hareôthès".

3. δύπλομα. Under the influence of the Latin *dupl-*

4. περ written on [κα̣ι̣]

4-5. Χινεδο-. This is the only occurrence of this ethnicon with an initial *chi*; this transcription calls to mind the written form *Chindenoi* (Χινδηνοί) (transcribing *Kinda*) in Nonnosus (cf. note 79, *infra*).

6-7. The two names were added later.

---

3. The *praesidium* of Al-Muwayḥ is situated, like Maximianon, on the road from Koptos to Myos Hormos. The ancient name of this site was Krokodilô. Hence the abbreviation *O. Krok.* to designate the ostraca found in this site. A series of excavations financed by the French Ministry of Foreign Affairs and IFAO was carried out in January 1995.

Fig. 1 — Ostracon found in az-Zarqā'

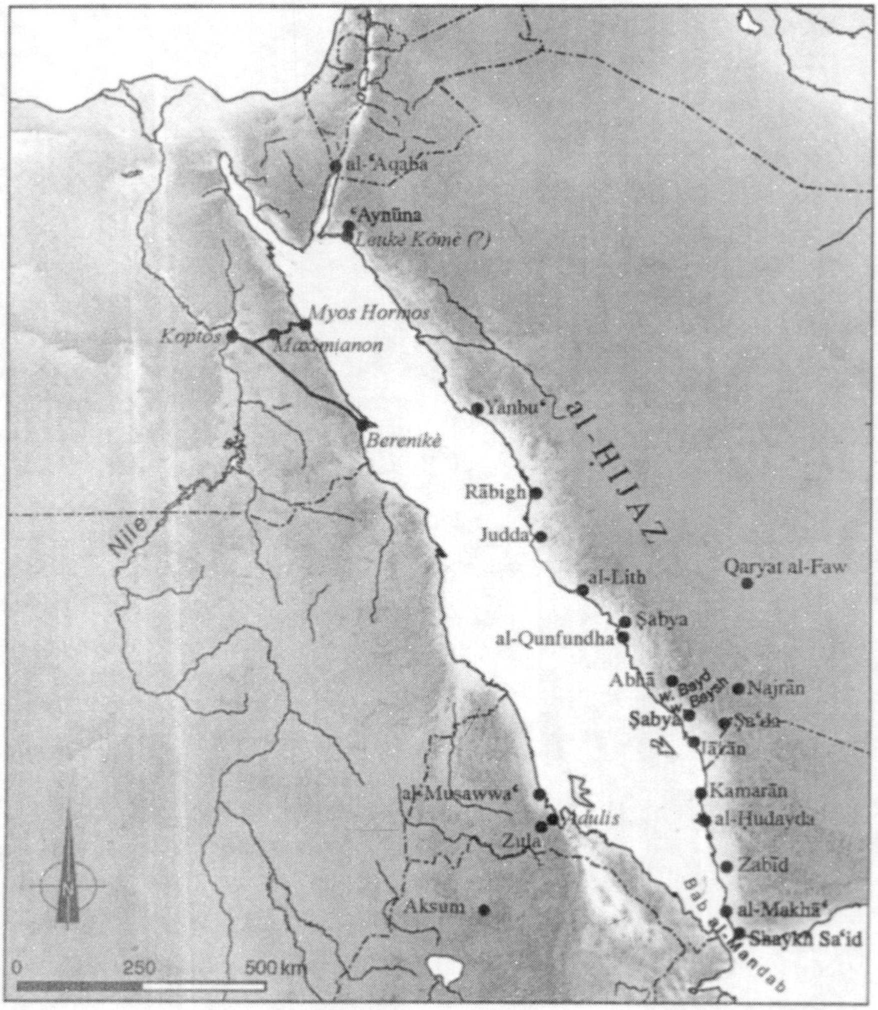

Fig. 2 — Map of the Red Sea

II. Is It Possible to Identify the Kinaidokolpitai?

a. Other Records

In all other cases, this ethnicon is written with an initial *kappa*. As a matter of fact, it is a compound of the words κίναιδος, *kinaidos* ("homosexual")[4] and κολπίτης, *kolpitês* ("who lives in the gulf", *i.e.* the Arabian Gulf[5] as we know from Ptolemy).

1. Ptolemy (*c.* 150 A.D.) gives the most precise information about their location (*Geography* 6, 7, 5 and 23). He locates them on the coastal strip in Western Arabia. The last village mentioned before the Kinaidokolpitai territory (therefore to the north) is Iambia (probably Yanbu',[6] situated 280 km to the north-north-west of Judda), and the last tribe is the Arsai. It is tempting to identify the Arsai with the Irāsha tribe, constituting an important part of the population of Balī, who lived and still lives in North Hijaz (CASKEL 1966 I, table 329, and II, p. 358; SPRENGER § 2, followed by GLASER, p. 104).[7]

The land of the Kinaidokolpitai included from north to south:

---

4. But with amusing, colourful and festive connotations. In some contexts, κίναιδος (*kinaidos*) has the value of a true technonym and it designates a dancer specialised in lewd dances. On this point, cf. LETRONNE, *Rev. Philol.* 1, 1845, pp. 161-164, commenting in detail on a graffito of Philae (*I. Philae* II 155) left by the *kinaidos* Strouthion — *i.e.* "the Sparrow", a very apposite stage name. Letronne reminds us that the diminutive κιναίδιον (*kinaidion*) is the name of a bird for which a scholium gives as equivalent σεισοπυγίς (*seisopygis*) "which shakes its rump". The French word *hoche-queue* (wagtail) evokes the same imagery. Regarding these dancers, see lastly Fr. PERPILLOU-THOMAS, "Artistes et athlètes dans les papyrus grecs d'Égypte", *ZPE* 108, 1995, pp. 228-229. This tradition was still alive in Egypt in the time of Flaubert who loved watching shows of κίναιδοι (*kinaidoi*) whom he called "male almehs" (cf. A.Y. NAAMAN, *Les Lettres d'Égypte de Gustave Flaubert*, Paris, 1965, letter VII: "citizens of dubious occupations dressed as women and who wiggle their hips attractively". We come across the ornithological metaphor again in letter X: "it is a *trilling of muscles*").

5. In other words, the Red Sea as we understand it today.

6. Identification suggested by SPRENGER, § 24. It is quite possible that Yanbu' is a pre-Islamic name. In any case, it is mentioned in Islamic sources in relation to events during Prophet Mohammed's lifetime.

7. However, in the early years of Islam, Yanbu' was not a part of Balī but of Juhayna (M.J. KISTER, "Ḳuḍā'a", *Encyclopaedia of Islam*, new edition, V, Leiden, 1986, pp. 314-318, cf. p. 315 A; Yāqūt, Mu'ǧam al-buldān, *s.v.*).

— **Kopar** (village).

SPRENGER, § 37, MORITZ, *RE* 11, 1360-1361, WISSMANN *apud* GROHMANN have identified Kopar with al-Jār, situated about 100 km to the south of Yanbu'. In addition, WISSMANN identifies Kopar with Pliny's Coboea (*HN* 6.150). But these are hypothetical propositions.

— **Arga** or **Agar**[8] (village).

Located by SPRENGER, § 38, according to indications given by Ptolemy, half way between Kopar and Zabram and identified with Rābigh, situated 150 km to the north of Judda. Sprenger draws our attention to a homonym in the area, viz. "al-'Arg" (probably read as al-'Irq), which, according to him, cannot be identified with Arga because it was situated in the interior.[9] For WISSMANN 1970, col. 915, Arga is 'Irq al-Ghurāb "at the entrance of the port of Judda".[10] None of these identifications is certain.

— **Zabram** or **Zambram**[11] or **Zadramè**[12] or **Zaaram**,[13] capital (βασίλειον, *basileion*) of the Kinaidokolpitai.

Although the palaeography favours the reading Zambram, SPRENGER, § 39, is quite certain that we should accept the vulgate reading Zaaram, in which he recognises Ẓahrān ("Tzahran"), the name of a fertile wādī (now known as Wādī Faṭīma, situated between Mecca and Judda). There is a village there which was called Marr Ẓahrān in the old days. Sprenger believes that Ptolemy gave the name of the town to the port. GLASER, p. 235, also identifies Zabram with Ẓahrān. WISSMANN, on the contrary, on the basis of the distribution of place-names mentioned by Ptolemy and of homophony,[14] proposes Marsa Ibrāhīm, close to Al-Līth, 190 km to the south-east of Judda (A. DIETRICH, *RE*, Reihe 2, Hbd 9 [II],

---

8. Agar: the reading of Vaticanus graecus 191 (=*X*), the only uncontaminated representative of the recension Ξ of the archetype, generally superior to the recension Ω (I. RONCA, *Ptolemaios. Geographie 6, 9-21. Ostiran und Zentralasien*, Teil 1, Rome, 1971, cf. *stemma* p. 10). Scholars who have made use of Ptolemy 6.7 have not had access to the reading of *X*.

9. The place-name al-'Irq, which designates various types of steep slopes, is frequently found in Saudi Arabia. Al-JĀSIR mentions dozens of them (pp. 804-807).

10. Al-JĀSIR, p. 806, mentions a 'Irq al-ghurāb but in the region of Ẓahrān al-Janūb (to the west of Najrān, not far from the border of Yemen). It has not been possible to find the one at Judda in modern maps.

11. Reading of *X* , probably more faithful to the archetype because the manuscript *C* of the Ω tradition proposes the reading *Zambra*.

12. This is how it is in Stephanus of Byzantium (*Ethnika* 293).

13. Old editions.

14. He bases himself on an argument advanced by A.K. Irvine that Zabram could represent the Guezian place-name "za-Abrāham" not known anywhere else.

1967, *s.v.* Ζααράμ). But this place-name which means "Ibrāhīm's (= Abraham's) Anchorage", is bound to belong to a later period following the spread of Judaism, Christianity and Islam,[15] so that this hypothesis seems quite weak.[16]

— **Kentos** or **Kentosi**[17] (village)

SPRENGER, § 40, seems to believe that in Greek Kentos means "horn" ("das Horn"). According to him, it is a free translation of the Arabic word *šu'ayba*, a diminutive of *šu'ba*, which means the gap between the two horns of an animal. But the word *κεντος (*kentos*) does not exist in Greek (was he thinking of κέντρον [*kentron*] which means "goad"?). The Arabic does not fit either since *šu 'ayba* rather means "small ravine" (diminutive of *ši'b*). In short, the supposed passage of the word from Arabic to Greek is quite speculative.

GLASER, p. 235, identifies Kentos with an obscure Qaryat Kinda ("Dorf der Kinda"), a little to the south of Judda. But as we shall see, in Greek the *k* in Kinda should become a *chi* and not a *kappa*.

WISSMANN 1970, col. 907, compares Kentos to al-Qanāt, which is supposed to be the ancient name of al-Qunfudha situated at the mouth of Wādī Qanawnā.

— **Thebai** (city, *polis*). *Thebai* (Θεβαι) is the reading of two interesting manuscripts, *X* and *U*,[18] belonging to two different traditions of the text. Other manuscripts generally have *Thêbai* (Θῆβαι). This spelling makes this city a homonym of Thebes in Boeotia.

MÜLLER, *GGM* I, pp. 183-184, does not express any opinion about the reading to be accepted, but he thinks that *Thebai/Thêbai* should be derived from the Debai tribe mentioned by Agatharchides (see *infra*). In addition to the phonetic resemblance,[19] there is the fact that the Debai were very hospitable to the Peloponesians and the Boeotians because of their legendary relationship with Herakles who was a native of Thebes.

According to SPRENGER, § 41, Thebai is an adaptation of Dhahabān (from the Arabic *ḏahab* or "gold") (followed by WISSMANN *apud* GROHMANN) and

---

15. The earliest definite indications of this spread go back to the 4th century A.D., long after Ptolemy's time.

16. We may add that if the Abyssinians conquered the West Arabian coast, it is not very likely that the metropolis of an Arabic tribe would have a Guezian name. Marsa Ibrāhīm is not mentioned in al-JĀSIR.

17. Reading of *X*; the ligature εν is ambiguous in the manuscript of *Geography*. We cannot exclude *Kantosi*.

18. *U* = Urbinas graecus 82, which is the earliest manuscript of *Geography*. It belongs to a different tradition derived from the recension Ω.

19. GIGNAC, *Grammar* I, pp. 96-97, points out some examples of alternation between θ/δ (*th/d*) in the Greek *koine* (this phenomenon, though not unheard of, is not very common).

corresponds to the Tabis of Stephanus of Byzantium[20] and to the Debai mentioned by Strabo and Agatharchides. Sprenger wrongly attributes to Müller the claim that the Debai must have been known earlier as the *Thêbaioi* (Thebans) and the city as *Thêbai*.

GLASER, pp. 30-31, does not think that it is necessary to identify Thebai with the Ṭabya (corrected to Ṭayba) of al-Hamdānī 120/17. However, he is sure that it is a city connected with the Debai situated to the north of Baitios; p. 235: Thebai is perhaps Al-Qunfudha, 310 km to the south-east of Judda.

RYCKMANS, p. 94, "easily recognises" in Thebai the name of the town Ṣabyā which "corresponds to the Debai" (*ibid*. n. 49).[21]

WISSMANN 1970, col. 916: Thebai is a transliteration of the Arabic Dhahabān. Many places in Southern Arabia go under this name and the one in question is in Wādī Ḍankān.

These various identifications are not very convincing because neither Dhahabān nor Ṣabyā are normally transliterated in Greek as *Thebai* or *Thêbai*.

— The river (*i.e.* wādi) **Baitios** which marks the southern boundary of their land. Modern scholars generally identify the Baitios with Wādi Baysh and its branch, Wādi Bayḍ (WISSMANN 1970, col. 917-918).

According to MÜLLER, *GGM I*, pp. 183-184, and GLASER, p. 31, it is the gold-bearing river flowing through the land of the Debais. According to SPRENGER, the Baitios gets its name from Wādī Bayḍ (§ 30) which is very small. As a matter of fact, Ptolemy attributes to it the features of Wādi Baysh (§ 49). GLASER, p. 217, admits that the word Baitios is close to Baysh or Bayḍ, two wādī about which there is uncertainty. Also, he prefers to rule out this identification and proposes that the Baitios probably corresponds to Wādi Kisān.

From the phonetic point of view, it appears that *tau* in the Greek Baitios is more easily transliterated as *ḍāḍ* (*in* Bayḍ) than as *shīn* (in Baysh). Maxime Rodinson has demonstrated that the *ḍāḍ* in Guezian could be transcribed as *tl* in Greek.[22] On the other hand, the Arabic letter *shīn* (South Arabic s^2) which is at the end of Baysh is transliterated as *sigma* in a name like S^2*bwt* (Σάβατα in Strabo 16.4.2; Σαυβαθά in *The Periplus of the Erythraean Sea* 27; Σάββαθα in

20. Τάβις is defined as a *polis* of Arabia mentioned by Hecataeus in his *Periegesis* of Egypt: shouldn't Arabia be understood there as the Arabic Desert to the west of the Nile Valley?

21. It must be noted that there are two Ṣabyās in Western Arabia. The first one is 30 km to the north of Jāzān and the second one is 30 km to the north of al-Qunfudha.

22. "Les nouvelles inscriptions d'Axoum et le lieu de déportation des Bedjas", in *Raydān* 4, 1981, pp. 97-116, cf. p. 101.

Ptolemy, *Geography* 6.7.38 and 8.22.14; the Latin Sabota and Sabbatha in Pliny *HN* 6.155, 12.52 and 6.154; presently Shabwa).[23]

— According to Ptolemy, the land of the **Kassanitai** stretches to the south of the land of the Kinaidokolpitai.

SPRENGER, § 43, identifies them with the great Ghassān tribe, a branch of the Azd[24] according to those who recorded the traditions of the Islamic period. Before the birth of Islam, the Ghassān tribe moved to the north while other Azd tribes stayed back. According to al-Hamdāni 54/16, they had a common border with the Kinānas.

§ 52: the Kassanitai were the Kasandreis or the Gasandoi that Agatharchides mentions as living to the south of the Debai (respectively *apud* Photius and Diodorus), Pliny's Casani (*HN* 6.150).

GLASSER, pp. 31 and 34: the Kassanitai (=Pliny's Casani) get their name from either Jāzān (a town) or Kisān (a wādī which he spells as Kasān and sometimes Kesān)[25] in the 'Asīr, but not from the Ghāssans.

RYCKMANS, p. 83: "(dhū-Sahrat) stretched towards the west of Ṣan'ā', in the land of the Akk tribe (Ry 539); it corresponded to the land of Ptolemy's Kassanites and stretched in the north up to Ğīzān (formerly Ğāzān from which the name Kassanites was derived)".

Ptolemy lists one after the other the lands of the Kinaidokolpitai, the Kassanitai, the Elisaroi, the Homeritai (Himyarites) lying from north to south along the Arabic coast beyond the strait of Bāb al-Mandab. The Elisaroi who controlled the ports of Muza (Arabic Mazwa' presently known as al-Makhā or Moka) and Okelis (presently Shaykh Sa'īd) on the strait are the al-Ash'ar (Sabaean Ash'arān, s^2r^n). The land of this tribe stretches from the north of al-Makhā to the strait, corresponding approximately to its location in the 6th century A.D. and in the early years of Islam.[26] The Kassanitai, who lived to the north of the Elisaroi, dominated the coast of North Yemen from the border of the Kinaidokolpitai up to Adedou kome, probably al-Ḥudayda.

The name Jāzān, originally that of a wādī, goes back at least to the beginning of Islam.[27] It was probably pronounced Gāzān in ancient times and it

23. Also see *infra* al-Ash'ar (Sabaean Ash'aran, $'s^2{}'r^n$) transliterated as Elisaroi in Ptolemy, *Geography* 6.7.7.

24. CASKEL I, Tabl. 176, pp. 193-195 & 207-208, and II, pp. 35-38 & 273.

25. al-JĀSIR, p. 1049.

26. Chr. ROBIN, "La Tihama yéménite avant l'Islam: notes d'histoire et de géographie historique", in *Arabian Archaeology and Epigraphy*, 6, 1995, pp. 225-235, cf. pp. 232-233.

27. *Encyclopaedia of Islam*, new edition, II, Leiden, 1977: G. RENTZ, "Djayzān", pp. 529-531, cf. p. 529 B.

may correspond phonetically to Kassan(itai) but the problem of its passage from a place-name to the name of a tribe persists.

The Ghassān tribe appears at first sight to be a better candidate for identification. It is difficult to prove if the Arabic letter *ghayn*, which is quite rare, is normally transliterated by a *kappa* in Greek, but that is not the real difficulty.[28] The main argument in support of this identification is found in the Arabic traditions. Ghassān is supposed to have been closely related to ʿAkk in very ancient times.[29] As Ryckmans (*supra*) observes, Ptolemy's Kassanitai were located in a region which later came to be known as the land of the ʿAkk.[30]

The South Arabic inscriptions do not give any indication about the geography of the Arab tribes in the 2nd century A.D. On the contrary, the location of Ghassān was established with some precision in the 4th century A.D. thanks to a text dated 470 Ḥim. (probably 360 A.D.)[31] according to which the Ḥimyarites faced the ʿAbdqaysān (*ʿbdqys^{1n}*, ʿAbd al-Qays in Arabic) tribe at "Siyyān near the Sigah well, between the land of the Nizār^{um} and the land of the Ghassān".[32] We actually know of a well and a mountain called Sijā (= Sigah) on the plain of as-Siyy (=Siyyān), 410 km to the north-east of Mecca. Since tradition considers Ghassān as South Arabian (in the Ḥimyarite circle of influence) and Nizār (=Nizār^{um}) as North Arabian (outside the Ḥimyarite sphere of influence), it is possible that the Ghassān territory extended to the south of Sayyān (a little to the south of the 24th parallel) and the Nizar^{um} territory to the north. But if we identify Ptolemy's Kassanitai with the Ghassāns, we have to assume that this tribe moved 500 to 1000 km towards the north between the 11th and 14th centuries.

---

28. A good example of the transliteration of *ghayn* by *kappa* was given by Walter W. Müller in a paper presented at the Congress of "Profumi d'Arabia" (Pisa, 9-21 October, 1995). The Greek μοκροτου (*mokrotou*) (*Periplus of the Erythraean Sea* 9 & 10), qualifying a quality of incense, probably comes from a South Arabic or Arabic word (not recorded) whose present form is *muǧ(u)r* (Arabic) or *meǧerāt*, *meǧirot* (modern South Arabic) signifying "incense-tree".

29. R. WILSON, "Some notes on the Arabic historiography of Tihama in the pre-Islamic and early Islamic periods", in *Arabian Archaeology and Epigraphy* 6, 1995, pp. 277-285, cf. p. 279, and n. 28 (p. 284).

30. The existence of a watering hole named Ghassān (al-Hamdāni 71/23-24) in the lower course of Wādī Rimaʿ, 60 km to the south of al-Ḥudayda (in a region that came under the al-Ashʿar rather than the ʿAkk), may also be mentioned, even though this argument is not conclusive.

31. The South Arabic dates depend on the beginning of the Ḥimyar^{um} era. We assume here that it started in 110 B.C., but it is not impossible that it may have started in 115 B.C.

32. ʿAbadān 1/29 (*b-S^{l}y^{n} ʿly mw b'r^{n} S^{l}gh bynn ʿrḍNzr^{m} w-'rḍ Ḡs^{ln}*): see Chr. ROBIN & I. GAJDA, "L'inscription du wādī ʿAbadān", in *Raydān* 6, 1994, pp. 113-137 & 193-204.

2. In his *Chronicle,* written in the year 234,[33] S. Hippolytus presents the Kinaidokolpitai as Madianite colonists: Μαδιηναίων δὲ ἄποικοι γεγόνασι οἱ Κιναιδοκολπῖται (*Chronicle,* § 207).[34] This passage is repeated in the *Liber Generationis, GLM,* p. 167: *Madianensium inhabitores Cinaedocolpitae.* Is this piece of information, which does not seem to have held the attention of specialists in pre-Islamic Arabia, of any value? It seems to us that the Kinaidokolpitai have been confused with the *Kinaioi* (Cinaeans) of the Old Testament. Regarding these people, cf. *Dictionnaire de la Bible, s.v.* Cinaeans (where the following spellings are given : Hebrew *qēnī,* variants in the LXX: Κεναῖος, Κιναῖος, Κενι, Κενεζι).[35] Several passages from the Old Testament referring to the Madianite Raguel, his sons Hobab and Jethro (sometimes identified with Raguel and sometimes with Hobab), reveal the relationship between the Madianites and the "Cinaeans". Haber the Cinaean "separated from the sons of Hobab" (LXX *Jud.* 4.11); Hobab (or Jethro according to the versions) is called "Cinaean" (LXX *Jud.* 1.16: Ιωβαβ / Ιοθορ τοῦ Κειναίου). Therefore the author of the article on "Cinaeans" concludes that "Jethro, whether he is identical to Hobab or different from him, also belongs to the Madianite tribe and performs sacerdotal functions. *Exod.* III.1. We must therefore conclude that the Cinaeans were a small group that originally belonged to the Madianite tribe". This ethnic group reappears in Josephus's *Jewish Antiquities* 5.207 in an uncertain form (*Kenetidai, Kenelidai* or *Keneaidai*): παρά τινα τῶν Κενελίδων γυναῖκα Ἰάλην ὄνομα (Κενελιδων, Niese's assumption according to the Latin *cenelidarum*; κενεαιδων mss. (very close to κιναιδ); κενετιδων (ed. pr.).

3. Stephanus of Byzantium (5th century A.D.) writes in his *Ethnika, s.v.* Ζαδράμη: Βασίλειον τῶν Κιναιδοκολπιτῶν, περὶ οὗ ἐροῦμεν ἐν τῷ κ̄. εἰσὶ δὲ ἔθνος τῆς εὐδαίμονος Ἀραβίας. Μαρκιανὸς ἐν περίπλῳ αὐτῆς "Ζαδραμιτῶν [καὶ] Κιναιδοκολπιτῶν". τὸ ἐθνικὸν Ζαδραμαῖος, "Zadramê, capital of the Kinaidokolpitai, about whom I shall write under the letter K. They are a people of Arabia Felix. Marcianus in his *Circumnavigation* of Arabia writes: 'of Zadramitai [and of] Kinaidokolpitai'. The ethnicon is *Zadramaios*". The occurrence of the Kinaidokolpitai in Stephanus of Byzantium does not mean that these people still existed in the times of this grammarian who was only concerned with collecting geographical names from literature and indicating accentuation and

33. *Dictionnaire d'archéologie chrétienne et de liturgie* VI.2.2457.

34. Remains of § 204-209 are preserved in the *P. Oxy.* 870 (where the name of the Kinaidokolpitai is missing).

35. *I Reg.* 30.29: ἐν ταῖς πόλεσιν τοῦ Κενεζει (var. ms. τοῦ Κειναίου). From the consonantal point of view, *Kenezi* is close to *Kinaido-*. We may note (what the *Dictionnaire de la Bible* does not point out although it refers to the passage) that *Gen.* 15.19 mentions τοὺς Κεναίους καὶ τοὺς Κενεζαίους (*tous Kenaious kai tous Kenezaious*).

derivations. He has taken many names from Herodian's books on grammar (2nd century A.D.) where the mention of the Kinaidokolpitai and their capital has been restored according to Stephanus of Byzantium.[36] We assume that Marcianus of Heraclea, quoted by Stephanus of Byzantium, lived around 400 A.D. But his *Periplus* is only a copy among others of Ptolemy (or even of one of Ptolemy's plagiarists)[37] and it cannot be used as an argument to support the existence of the Kinaidokolpitai during the later period. Some manuscripts of Stephanus of Byzantium place a copula between Ζαδραμιτῶν (*Zadramitôn*) and Κιναιδοκολπιτῶν (*Kinaidokolpitôn*), but two of them (of which the best) omit it. In the latter case, we understand it as "the Zadramitai (who were) Kinaidokolpitai" while in the other as, "the Zadramitai and the Kinaidokolpitai" as though they were two different peoples.

4. Finally, the Kinaidokolpitai are mentioned in the *Monumentum Adulitanum*, a Greek inscription that was subsequently lost. It is known to us today only through a transcription made in Adulis (now a ruin near Zula on the Erythraean coast, 40 km to the south of Masawwa) during the reign of Justin (518-27), by Cosmas Indicopleustes (*Christian Topography* II, 60-63; the last edition by E. BERNAND, in *Recueil des inscriptions de l'Éthiopie des périodes préaxoumite et axoumite*, Paris, 1991 = *RIÉth*, No. 277). This monument commemorates the exploits of a king, probably the king of Aksum whose name has not been preserved. Not only does he boast of his conquests on the African continent which have extended his empire up to Egypt, but also of making a successful inroad into the Arabian peninsula, defeating the Arabitai and the Kinaidokolpitai:

καὶ πέραν δὲ τῆς Ἐρυθρᾶς θαλάσσης οἰκοῦντας Ἀραβίτας καὶ Κιναιδοκολπίτας, στράτευμα ναυτικὸν καὶ πεζικὸν διαπεμψάμενος καὶ ὑποτάξας αὐτῶν τοὺς βασιλέας, φόρους τῆς γῆς τελεῖν ἐκέλευσα καὶ ὁδεύεσθαι μετ΄ εἰρήνης καὶ πλέεσθαι, ἀπό τε Λευκῆς κώμης ἕως τῶν Σαβαΐων χώρας ἐπολέμησα.

"... and the Arabitai and the Kinaidokolpitai, who live on the other shore of the Red Sea, having sent an army and a navy and subjugated their kings, I ordered them to pay a tribute for their land and allow the land and sea traffic to proceed peacefully and I made war from Leuke Kome to the land of the Sabaeans".

---

36. A. LENTZ, *Herodiani Technici Reliquiae* I, Leipzig, 1867, p. 325, l. 3.

37. J.O. THOMSON, *History of Ancient Geography*, Cambridge, 1948, p. 373.

Shortly after the passage about the Arabitai and the Kinaidokolpitai, the king says, "All these peoples, I was the first and the only one of the kings who preceded me to subjugate them".

Instinctively, we understand (and that is the currently accepted interpretation) ὁδεύεσθαι μετ´ εἰρήνης καὶ πλέεσθαι to mean "I ordered them to go in peace on land and sea". It signifies the return to normality after the war and peace granted in return for a tribute. But these verbs are not recorded as such[38] and it is better to consider them either as passive and impersonal, although it is quite rare in Greek except for declarative verbs ("I ordered them to travel in peace..."), or as passive and personal ("allow their territory to be crossed in peace...").[39] Even if Wissmann translates it as "I ordered them to go in peace",[40] he explains elsewhere that the Aksumite king attacked these tribes to put an end to their acts of piracy in the Red Sea.[41]

The inscription does not tell us anything precise about the location of the Kinaidokolpitai. It just indicates that their territory *and* also that of the Arabitai covered the area between Leuke Kome and Saba' but did not included the two cities. In addition, the position of Leuke Kome (left out by Ptolemy)[42] is not known for certain. According to some, Leuke Kome is just south of the entrance to the Gulf of Aqaba, at the mouth of Wādī'Aynuna,[43] but according to others it is at Yanbu' or in its immediate vicinity.[44]

As for the Arabitai, ancient writers do not mention any tribe having this name in the Arabian Peninsula. It is difficult to admit that Ἀραβῖται is a doublet of Ἄραβες and that it refers to Arabs in general. The ethnic group Arabitai exists in the literature and refers to an Indian community living on the banks of

38. There are no examples in H. Estienne's *Thesaurus*.

39. This option ("leave in peace" instead of "go in peace") is found only in CONTI ROSSINI p. 19, and perhaps also in KOBISHCHANOV, *Axum*, p. 39, who gives an ambiguous translation ("having commanded them to pay the tribute and conduct affairs peacefully on land and sea") and interprets the passage as an injunction to the Arabitai and the Kinaidokolpitai to give up piracy. The transliteration *Cynaido-kolpitae* found at this point and which gives a fanciful interpretation of the name is not based on anything concrete.

40. WISSMANN, HÖFNER, p. 119. Also W. WOLSKA-CONUS in his edition of Cosmas Indicopleustês, *Christian Topography* p. 376.

41. WISSMANN 1968, col. 1306.

42. Ptolemy probably moved Leuke Kome to the opposite shore of the Arabian Gulf where one finds this White Village having the ghostly name of Leukos Limen, "White Port" (A. BÜLOW-JACOBSEN, H. CUVIGNY, J.-L. FOURNET, "The Identification of Myos Hormos. New Papyrological Evidence", *BIFAO* 94, 1994, p. 28, n. 7).

43. CASSON 1989b, p. 188, quoting M. INGRAM *et alii, Atlal* 5, 1981, pp. 76-78.

44. Among them WISSMANN 1964, p. 65, n. 155.

the River Arabis.[45] RYCKMANS, pp. 94-95, identifies the Arabitai mentioned in the Adulis inscription with Ptolemy's Kassanitai.[46]

The date of these events has been discussed for a long time.[47] Mostly, they have been placed in the 3rd century A.D.[48] However, recent findings in South-Arabic epigraphy permit us to be more precise. It is necessary to take into account several features of the Adulis Monument:

1. It dates back to a time when the Abyssinian power was growing, as pointed out by the builder of the Monument. But this argument is difficult to handle because we have a very limited knowledge about the history of Abyssinia.

2. Abyssinia controls a significant part of the eastern coast of the Red Sea from a port in the north to the land of the Sabaeans.[49] Apart from this text, there is no other documentation about the Abyssinian occupation of the Arabic coast to the north of Yemen. In any case, the inscription precedes 260-270, when the lands adjoining Yemen came under Sabaean and then under Ḥimyarite[50] influence.

3. Abyssinia does not control the Yemenite coast as it did under the reign of Sha'r^{um} Awtar (*c.* 215-230) until *c.* 260-270.

4. The relations between Saba' and Abyssinia seem to have been quite good, which could correspond to the alliance between Saba' and Abyssinia mentioned in the South Arabic texts under the reign of 'Alhān Nahfān (*c.* 200-215) and on the Abyssinian side, the reign of "Gadarat, king of the Abyssinians" (*Gdrt mlk Ḥbs*^{2}*t*^{n}, *CIH* 308/11. See also Nāmī N'J 13+14[51] referring to the Abyssinians, Sabaeans and Hadramawtians allied against Ḥimyar^{um}). Diplomatic contacts between Saba' and Abyssinia continued during the reign of Sha'r^{um} Awtar, son of 'Alhān Nahfān (Ja

---

45. These forms have many variations. Side by side with *Arabitai*, we find *Arabes* and side by side with Arab-, we find Arb-, as Herodian observes (Hdn. Gr. 1.86.23 : Ἄρβις ποταμὸς Ἰνδικῆς καὶ ἔθνος. λέγεται δὲ καὶ Ἄραβις. The form Ἀραβῖται (*Arabitai*) of the ethnic group is found in Arr. *An.* 6.21.4., St. Byz. *s.v.* Ἄραβις (*Arabis*) and Ἄρβις (*Arbis*) and in some of Ptolemy's manuscripts, *Geogr.* 6.21. Ancient evidence about these peoples and other variants has been collected by C. MÜLLER, *CGM* I, p. 335, and I. RONCA, *Ptolemaios Geographie 6.9-21* (*Ostiran und Zentralasien*), Rome, 1971, p. 71.

46. The names of several Arabic tribes could be the source of the Greek *Arabitai*: see for example 'Arib, Harība or Ḥarb in the index of CASKEL II.

47. In any case, it is not possible to attribute this inscription to a Ptolemy as done by the author of *Christian Topography*.

48. DESANGES 1978, p. 345 and n. 234.

49. It is difficult to locate exactly the northern boundary of the Sabaean territory in the coastal area before the Abyssinian occupation of the Yemenite coast towards 220 A.D. (see *infra*). In the earlier period, Saba' stretched at least up to Ḥūth in the 2nd century A.D. and up to Ṣa'da after the beginning of the 3rd century A.D.

50. Chr. ROBIN, "La première intervention abyssine en Arabie méridionale (de 200 à 270 de l'ère chrétienne environ)", *Proceedings of the Eighth International Conference of Ethiopian Studies*, Adis Ababa, 1989, pp. 147-162, cf. p. 155.

51. J. RYCKMANS, "L'inscription sud-arabe Nami 13-14", in *Eretz-Israel 9*, 1969 (= W.F. Albright volume), pp. 102-108.

631; the king of Abyssinia was still *gdrt mlk Ḥbs*^{2}*t w-'ks*^{1}*m*^{n}, "Gadarat king of Abyssinia and the Aksumites", line 13). This episode could have taken place in the early years of Sha'r^{um}'s reign. Later, and until the expulsion of the Abyssinians from Arabia, their relations were hostile.

The Adulis monument is therefore certainly earlier than 220 A.D. It is tempting to attribute it to Gadarat, a king whose presence is recorded not only in Arabia but also in Ethiopia (see *RIÉth* 180: *Gdr ngšy 'ksm*, "Gadara king [negus] of Aksum". He is the first to our knowledge to hold the title "King of Aksum" or "King of Aksumites").[52] The reign of Gadarat/Gadara corresponds to the rebirth of writing and the beginning of the territorial expansion towards Yemen after a period of friendship with Saba'. It could very well have begun with the control of the Arabian coast to the north of Yemen. If the Adulis Monument was not built by Gadarat/Gadara, it must have been built by one of his immediate predecessors.

Is it possible that the campaign against the Kinaidokolpitai also preceded Abyssinia's resurgence as shown by the South Arabic and Abyssinian epigraphs and that it even went back to the early 2nd century? At least this is what Wissmann thinks. According to him, the Adulis inscription goes back almost to the time when Ptolemy was writing his *Geography*[53] or is even earlier. This dating is based on a passage from the Talmud mentioned by Conti-Rossini[54] which narrates the meeting in about 130 A.D. between a rabbi travelling in

52. We do not know the title of Zoskales, a king mentioned in the *Periplus of the Erythraean Sea* (*c.* 40-50 A.D., see *infra*, note 62) in the Adulis region and also the extent of his kingdom which did not necessarily include Aksum (CASSON 1989a, pp. 109-110).

53. WISSMANN 1964, p. 66: he bases his argument on the fact that the bounds of the Kinaidokolpitai's territory as defined by Ptolemy are the same as those mentioned in the Adulis inscription. However (1) this inscription does not categorically state that Leuke Kome marked the northern boundary of this land, but only that it was the northern limit of the operations (we must also take into account the "Arabitai" whose location is not known to us); (2) for the two texts to correspond, Leuke Kome should be identified with Yanbu' although this identification is not acceptable to all. According to Wissmann and others, the subjugation of the Kinaidokolpitai is evident even in Ptolemy's text. The geographer does not attribute to them a μητρόπολις (*mêtropolis*), but he simply points out a βασίλειον (*basileion*), a term which designates in his book the residence of a vassal prince, as opposed to μητρόπολις, capital of an independent state (RYCKMANS, p. 95; WISSMANN 1968, col. 1307). There is however no trace in Ptolemy's book of this expansion of the Aksumite kingdom as we are reminded by KOBISHCHANOV, *Axum*, p. 42. For a map of the southern part of the Arabian Peninsula during the time the Kinaidokolpitai were a part of the Aksum empire, see WISSMANN 1970, col. 919-920.

54. CONTI-ROSSINI, pp. 17-18. Argument approved by RYCKMANS, p. 95.

Southern Arabia and a local potentate of the Ethiopian race. But J. Desanges prefers to date it to the end of the 2nd century A.D.[55]

b. Who Does not Know the Kinaidokolpitai?

The descriptions of the western coast of the Arabian Peninsula prior to Ptolemy make no mention of the Kinaidokolpitai although the sound of the word is such as to rouse the imagination of a Hellenophone.

Agatharchides' descriptions in his book on the Erythraean Sea (recopied by Diodorus, Photius and Artemidorus of Ephesus *apud* Strabo), which can probably be traced to a source belonging to at least the 2nd century B.C., mentions the presence of the *Debai* (Δεβαι)[56] people in this region. This ethnic name is also to be found in the town of Θεβαι (*Thebai*) mentioned by Ptolemy as being in the land of the Kinaidokolpitai. The Debai led a nomadic life (associated with camel-breeding) and the sedentary life of farmers (γεοῦχοι, "land owners" according to Agatharchides, and γεωργοί or "peasants" according to Strabo). They were a belligerent people who fought on camel-back (Diodorus and Strabo). They were selective in their relations with the Greek world and welcomed only the Boeotians and Peloponnesians. They did not work the gold carried by the river that crossed their land. According to this threefold evidence, to the south of the Debai there was a gold-bearing region occupied by the Alilaioi and the Kasandreis (*apud* Photius) or Gasandoi (*apud* Diodorus), tribes who worked the gold mines. MÜLLER (*GGM*, 184), followed by WISSMANN 1970, col. 913, identifies the Alilaioi with the Banī Hilāl.

GLASER, p. 29, locates the Debai to the south of al-Qunfudha, at Āl Khatārish[57] to be precise, about five to six hours by road to the west of Maḥājil[58]

---

55. DESANGES 1984, pp. 257-258: "However, it is a little surprising that Aksum should have had as early as Trajan's reign the military capacity on land and sea to dominate a large part of Hedjaz and Asir. It would be historically easier to accept a date at the end of the 2nd century even while conceding the importance of these openly claimed conquests by the unnamed king of Aksum" (DESANGES 1984, p. 258). KOBISHCHANOV (*Axum*, pp. 42-48) does not express any opinion about the date of the inscription which he places between the 2nd century and the first half of the 4th century A.D. But this date is not acceptable since the Abyssinians came back to the Arabian Peninsula only in the 6th century A.D. On the other hand, the king who speaks here is a worshipper of Ares, while the Abyssinian kings converted to Christianity during the reign of Constantine (DESANGES 1984, p. 257).

56. Agatharchides, *De Mari Erythraeo*, ed. C. Müller, *Geographi Graeci Minores* I, pp. 183-184; Diod. Sic. 3.45.3-5; Strabo 16.4.18.

57. al-JĀSIR, p. 387, mentions a village named al-Khatārisa (with a *sīn*) but in the region of Jāzān.

58. Read Muḥāyil (al-JĀSIR, p. 1096), at a distance of 60 km to the north-west of Abhā.

and between Qunfudha and Marsà Ḥalj,[59] a region where the Bedouins often found gold in his time. Regarding the Debai, Glaser points out that al-Hamdānī 119/1 mentions a village called adh-Dhayba (ad-Dayba in the Spitta codex) near the town of Abhā.

Pliny makes no mention of the Debai. Instead, he speaks about the Clari and locates them between the Ichtyophagi and a gold-bearing region (*HN* 6.150, from north to south:...*Ichtyophagorum. Dein Clari, litus Mamaeum, ubi auri metalla, regio Canauna, gentes Apitami, Casani*...). In the Casani, we recognise the Kassanitai who, according to Ptolemy, were the southern neighbours of the Kinaidokolpitai. The *regio Canauna* derives its name from Wādī Qanawnā which flows into the Red Sea at al-Qunfudha (SPRENGER, § 52; WISSMANN 1970, col. 908).[60]

The *Periplus of the Erythraean Sea,* which updates the evidence provided by Pliny whose sources were often outdated,[61] gives a descriptive account of these places as they were between 40 and 50 A.D.[62] It does not mention the Kinaidokolpitai either. The descriptions of the coast of the Arabian Peninsula just to the south of Leuke Kome are rather gloomy (§ 20): the miserable shacks of the Ichtyophagi on the seashore where the bandits from the hinterland come to pillage the ships approaching the coast or capture the shipwrecked victims. The Arab states (τυράννων καὶ βασιλέων τῆς 'Αραβίας) take frequent but ineffective measures against these Κανραῖται (*Kanraitai*), bandits who speak two languages. The trading ships casting off from Leuke Kome keep to the high seas and approach the Arabian coast only to the far south of the peninsula, after the Burnt Island (probably the small island of Jabal aṭ-Ṭā'ir, 85 km to the north-north-west of Kamarān).[63] Anything pertaining to the Kinaidokolpitai's territory is inevitably included in this description.

GLASER corrects Κανραῖται to Καρναῖται (*Karnaitai*), "inhabitants of Karna".[64] SPRENGER, § 31, conjectures without the least hesitation *Kananitai, i.e.*

59. al-JĀSIR mentions only one al-Ḥalj in the region of al-Līth.

60. This identity corresponds to the rules governing the transliteration of Arabic into Greek and Latin drawn up by M. Rodinson, see *infra*.

61. RYCKMANS, p. 87.

62. For a justification of the earlier date (instead of the 3rd century A.D.), an hypothesis which is supported in particular by Jacqueline Pirenne), see C. ROBIN, "L'Arabie du Sud et la date du *Périple de la mer Érythrée* (nouvelles données)", *Journal Asiatique* 279, 1991, pp. 1-30, and G. FUSSMAN, "Le *Périple* et l'histoire politique de l'Inde", *ibid.*, pp. 31-38; N. GROOM, "The *Periplus*, Pliny and Arabia" in *Arabian Archaeology and Epigraphy* 6, 1995, pp. 180-195.

63. CASSON 1989a, p. 47.

64. GLASER, pp. 165-166: these Karnaitai were probably Bedouins, confused by classical writers with the Minaeans whose principal area was called Karna or Qarnaw (*Qrnw*) in South Arabic. Also see CASSON 1989a, p. 146. This hypothesis

members of the Kināna tribe. Wissmann accepts this conjecture. For Wissmann, who mistakenly dates the *Periplus* to the early 3rd century A.D.,[65] any mention of the Kananitai is an indication that the Kinaidokolpitai no longer existed at this time (*RE* Suppl.-Bd. 12, 1922). If, on the other hand, the *Periplus* is assigned to the 1st century A.D., as we have been doing, we are tempted to see a link between the reference to the shipwrecking Kanraitai (or whatever their name), who were in conflict with the neighbouring states, and the Aksumite intervention which was probably supported by the allied states[66] who supposedly asked Aksum for help against the pirates.[67]

c. A Short-lived Confederation

To summarise, the ethnic group Κιναιδοκολπίτης emerged from nowhere during the 2nd century and found mention in Ptolemy's work, in Maximianon's ostracon and in the Adulis inscription (*c.* 200). An important change could account for its sudden appearance. The Aksumite intervention could provide a ready explanation for this change. This makes Ryckmans' hypothesis quite attractive. According to him, the birth of this ethnic name, written in Greek as Κιναιδοκολπίτης, probably dates back to the subjugation by the powerful Aksumites[68] of the unruly and elusive tribes in the coastal area whose customs were as diverse as their names. The conquerors must have divided them into subordinate provinces. One of them must have been a federation of two major tribes that were perhaps already naturally related (cf. Debai who were simultaneously nomadic and sedentary or the bilingual Kanraitai). This new artificially created ethnic group was probably given an equally artificial and short-lived name of Kinaidokolpitai.[69]

---

does not have any historical basis because the small caravanner kingdom of Ma'īn (whose territory comprises three towns of Jawf in Yemen) disappeared in about 120 B.C. and was replaced by the Amir^{um} tribe in the caravan trade of Southern Arabia.

65. *RE* Suppl.-Bd. 12, 542 & 922: *c.* 210-220.

66. That is how the Aksumites, active in the south-western part of the Arabian Peninsula, practised diplomacy in the 3rd century by allying themselves at times with the Ḥimyarites and at times with the Sabaeans (DESANGES 1984, pp. 257-258).

67. CONTI-ROSSINI, p. 24, paints a similar picture but with different issues at stake.

68. RYCKMANS, p. 95: "Ptolemy's use of the curious compound name Kinaidokolpites can be explained quite easily as the geographer must have borrowed it from the official Ethiopian terminology that must have devised it".

69. This hypothesis is a little disturbing because the Adulis inscription gives the impression that the Kinaidokolpitai were known by this name even before their defeat.

d. Discussion of Identities Suggested Earlier

Our predecessors always believed that Κιναιδοκολπίτης was a tendentious transliteration of an Arabic word and they advanced two hypotheses on this subject. According to Sprenger, the element *Kinaido-*[70] corresponds to Kinana (§ 30) and *kolpitês* to Kalb (§ 32). Kinana is an Arab tribe living in the region around Mecca[71] and Sprenger remarks that the Kalb[72] are often associated with it (§ 32). He is not unaware that in the early years of Islam, the Kalb lived in the Syrian Desert, far from the Kinaidokolpitai. But he reminds us that according to al-Bakrī, their native place was Tihāma (the coastal area to the west of Mecca). It is true, as Sprenger himself admits, that this is what genealogists say of all Arab tribes. Sprenger would like to equate the Kalb with the *Clari* mentioned by Pliny while describing this area (*HN* 6, 150). He feels that their name should be corrected, because it does not have a morphological equivalent in the Arabic,[73] into *Clabi*[74] (Wissmann, who harks back to the Kinaidokolpitai time and again,[75] fully subscribes to this idea).[76]

GLASER, p. 232[77] is not opposed to the Kalb hypothesis. He proposes the alternative Aklub, the name of a clan belonging to the 10th century which he found in the *Register zu den geneal. Tab.*, p. 55.[78] However, he categorically rejects the identification with the Kināna: "Der älteren Ansicht dass der Name Kinda in Kinaidokolpitai enthalten ist, schloss sich 1863 Viv. de Saint Martin an; darnach wäre der Name aus Kunaida (Diminutif von Kinda)[79] und aus einem

70. Sprenger humorously remarks that the traders of Berenike deserved this name more than their Arab neighbours.

71. *Encyclopaedia of Islam*, new edition, V, Leiden, 1986; W.M. WATT, "Kināna b. Khuzayama", pp. 118-119; CASKEL I, Tabl. 36-48 & II, p. 6.

72. *Encyclopaedia of Islam*, new edition, IV, Leiden, 1978; J.W. FÜCK, "Kalb b. Wabara, I. Période anté-islamique", pp. 513-514; CASKEL, I, tabl. 280-296, & II, pp. 76-79.

73. The liquid consonants *l* and *r* are never found together in an Arabic root.

74. SPRENGER, § 52, n. 1. No manuscript reading supports this hypothesis whichever way you look at it.

75. See in particular WISSMANN 1970, col. 907. Also WISSMANN 1968, col. 1304-1307 and 1964, pp. 65-69. Also WISSMANN, HÖFNER, p. 119, & RYCKMANS, pp. 93-95 (the last two are quoted by DESANGES 1978, p. 345 and n. 235).

76. WISSMANN 1970, col. 907. He differs from Sprenger only in regard to the identity of the Kalb.

77. Followed by the old article *Kinaidokolpitai* in *RE* 11 (1922), 458-459 [MORITZ].

78. See CASKEL II, pp. 150-151 where you find al-Aklab, Aklab, Aklub and al-Aklūb.

79. See *Encyclopaedia of Islam*, new edition, V, Leiden, 1986 (I. SHAHID & A.F.L. BEESTON, "Kinda", pp. 121-123); CASKEL I, tabl. 233-243 & II pp. 47-53. This Arab tribe of Southern Arabia (first settled in the region of Qaryat al-Fāw, 250 km

andern Worte (Aklub, Kalb?) zusammengesetzt. Ich stehe nicht an, mich gleichfalls der älteren Ansicht anzuschliessen, indem ich den Namen als eine Aneinanderreihung von Kunaid und Aklub, also Kunaidaklub halte, voraus die Griechen Kinaidokolpitai gemacht haben".

What are these hypotheses worth?

In the beginning of the 3rd century, the Arab Kiddat[80]/Kinda tribe was centred in Qaryat al-Fāw (ancient *Qryt^m ḏt-khl^m*), 250 km to the north-north-west of Najrān.[81] It is quite possible that its influence extended to the area around Najran,[82] but there is nothing to suggest a domination of the coastal areas.

The Kināna tribe probably lived in the coastal areas near Mecca in the early years of Islam. But it is not mentioned in any of the pre-Islamic epigraphical texts so that we are not sure of its existence in the 2nd and 3rd centuries.

As for the Kalb, this tribe lived in the area bordering on Syria and is not mentioned in the inscriptions. It is therefore not a suitable candidate for identification.

Another argument, this time philological, opposes the identification of the Kinaidokolpitai with the tribes mentioned earlier. If the word Κιναιδοκολπῖται is derived from the name of an Arab tribe, it may be asked if there are any rules for the transliteration of Arabic phonemes (in Arabic and South Arabic languages) into Greek. Maxime Rodinson has shown that the *qāf* is usually transliterated as *kappa*. Cases where *kappa* is a transliteration of *kāf* are not

to the north-north-east of Najran, and later in Ḥaḍramawt) was the principal auxilliary of the Ḥimyarite kings in the 5th and 6th centuries in Central Arabia where many Kindite princes reigned over the Ma'add^{um} tribe. This tribe is found under the name Χινδηνοί in Nonnosus (*apud* Photius, *Bibl.* 3, Belles Lettres I, p. 4, l. 36). In the time of Nonnosus (6th century A.D.), two "Saracen" tribes, the Χινδηνοί and the Μααδηνοί (Sabaean Ma'add^{um} and Arab Ma'add^{um}), were under the rule of the same chief. The earliest reliable evidence regarding the *Kinda* (South-Arabic *Kdt*) is seen in the Sabaean inscriptions belonging to the first half of the 3rd century A.D. The diminutive "Kunayda" proposed by Glaser is not found anywhere.

80. Presumed to be the vocalisation of the South Arabic *Kdt* with the regular assimilation of *n*.

81. See Sabaean inscription Ja 635.

82. A king of Kiddat/Kinda belonging probably to the 5th century A.D., Ḥugr son of 'Amr^{um} (Ḥujr son of 'Amr, known as Ākil al-murār, "he who lives on bitter herbs", according to the Arab tradition) has carved his name on a rock about 120 km to the north of Najrān (G. RYCKMANS, "Graffites sabéens relevés en Arabie sa'udite" in *Rivista degli Studi Orientali* XXXII, 1957 [= Scritti in onore di Giuseppe Furlani], p. 561 : *Ḥgr bn 'mr^m mlk Kdt*).

many and often doubtful: *e.g.* Kamarān = Καμαρηνοί, Kinana/Kinda/Kalb = Κιναιδοκολπῖται, Makka =Μακοραβα.[83]

The rule laid down by Rodinson for words that he thinks are Arabic may be extended to regions to the south-west of the Arabian Peninsula where Semitic languages different from Arabic were used. There too, Arabic names whose indigenous form and Greek transliteration are known confirm that *kappa* usually — it may even be said systematically — corresponds to *qāf.* These are the place-names and the ethnic groups:

Ns²qᵐ → Ns^2q^m	Νασκος (Ptolemy, *Geogr.* 6.7.35)
Qn'	Κανη (*Periplus* 27; Ptolemy, *Geogr.* 6.7.10)
Qrnw	Καρνα (*e.g.* Strabo, 16.4.2)
Qtb^n	Καταβανία (*e.g.* Strabo, 16.4.4)
or the aromatic plant:	
qlm	κάλαμος, fragrant reed
It is *chi* that corresponds to *kāf*:	
$'k^m$	'Αχχῖται (Ptolemy, *Geogr.* 6.7.23)
Klyb	Χολαιβος (*Periplus* 23)
Krb'l	Χαριβαηλ (*Periplus* 26)
ms^lk	μόσχος, musk

Consequently the proposed identifications, all names beginning with *kāf* (Kinda, Kinānā, Kalb), are not very satisfactory from the transliteration point of view. There is however one small reservation: it must be remembered that in Maximianon's ostracon the word begins with a *chi.*

Conclusion

It seems that the Kinaidokolpitai dominated a large portion of the coastal area. No other ancient tribe controlled so vast a territory. It could have only been a loose federation of tribes probably held together by a common religion.

---

83. M. RODINSON, "Sur la prononciation ancienne du *qāf* arabe", in *Mélanges Marcel Cohen, Études de linguistique, ethnographie et sciences connexes offertes par ses amis et élèves à l'occasion de son 80ᵉ anniversaire*, avec des articles et études inédits de Marcel Cohen, réunis par David Cohen (Studies in linguistics, ethnography and allied sciences offered by his friends and students on his 80th birthday together with unpublished articles and studies by Marcel Cohen collected by David Cohen), The Hague-Paris, Mouton, 1970), pp. 298-319, cf. pp. 312-313. We may add as an exception the name of the spice *kmkm*, κάγκαμον, cancamum in Latin, or the place-name S^3krd, Διοσκουρίδου, modern Suquṭra (not significant because it is probably derived from an Indian name).

The South Arabian inscriptions mention the existence in the 3rd century of a grouping of this type called Daw'ắt (*Dw't*) which brought together a number of tribes whose territories were dispersed along the coast from Yemen to 250 km to the south-east of Mecca.[84] If the Daw'at extended further to the north-north-west, it would be a better candidate for identification with the Kinaidokolpitai. What remains then is to explain the difference in names. Kinaidokolpites could very well be a Greek nickname and not an adaptation. Agatharchides (*apud* Photius 250.60) provides an explicit example of this phenomenon where an African people were given a nickname by the Greeks. It was a compound and comical name inspired by their way of life (they were dog-breeders). It had nothing to do with the ethnic name by which they were known locally: "a people whom the Greeks called *Kynamolgoi* ("milkers of she-dogs/bitches"), but whose neighbours called them by a name meaning "Savages" (*Agrioi*) [Ἄγριοι]."

There may have been other groupings apart from the Daw'at and the Kinaidokolpitai may have derived their name from one of them, but to the best of our knowledge there is no known tribe in Arabia (except perhaps the Daw'at) which can be reasonably identified with the Kinaidokolpitai. So the mystery remains unsolved.

Anyhow, the Kinaidokolpitai cut a fine figure in the gallery of strange ethnic names with which the fanciful imagination of the Greeks enriched distant lands. As it happens, it was not a novel idea for do we not find a distant echo of this tendency in Aristophanes? In the *Birds*, the Hoopoe asks Euelpides and Pisthetairos with great solicitude what kind of city they would like to live in. "A city," Pisthetairos answers, "where the father of a handsome boy would say to me with indignation: "Fine things I hear of you [...]! You met my son returning from the baths and never kissed, or hugged, or fondled him, You, his paternal friend! "Poor Poppet!" the Hoopoe exclaimed, "You are in love with ills indeed! Well there's the sort of city (εὐδαίμων πόλις, *eudaimôn polis*) that ye want by the Red Sea.[85]

Hélène CUVIGNY (CNRS), Christian ROBIN (CNRS)

84. See Ja 616/23-26. The inscription lists 13 fractions of the Daw'at. Among those that have been identified, the northernmost tribe is probably the Ghāmid^{um} (*Gmd*^{m}) whose name Ghāmid has been preserved in a region of Saudi Arabia situated 350 km to the north-west of Najrān or 250 km to the south-west of Mecca.

85. *Birds,* 139-145 (Loeb Classical Libray, Transl. B.B. Rogers). It must be clarified, to be completely honest, that when the Ancients talk of the "Red Sea" (Ἐρυθρὰ θάλασσα, *Mare Rubrum*) they refer to all the seas washing the shores of the Arabian Peninsula and not the Red Sea as we know it today, so that this comparison with Aristophanes may be not quite as relevant as it appears to be.

Bibliographical Abbreviations

CASKEL 1966
W. CASKEL, *Ǧamharat an-nasab. Das genealogische Werk des Hisam ibn Muḥammad al-Kalbī*, 2 vol., Leiden.

CASSON 1989a
L. CASSON, *The* Periplus Maris Erythraei, Princeton.

CASSON1989b
L. CASSON, "South Arabia's Maritime Trade in the First Century A.D.", in T. FAHD, ed., *L'Arabie préislamique et son environnement historique et culturel*, Université des Sciences Humaines de Strasbourg, Travaux du Centre de recherche sur le Proche-Orient et la Grèce antiques 10, Leyde, pp. 187-194.

CIH
Corpus Inscriptionum Semiticarum, pars IV: *Inscriptiones himyariticas et sabaeas continens*, Paris, 1889-1932.

CONTI-ROSSINI
C. CONTI-ROSSINI, "Expéditions et possessions des Ḥabašāt en Arabie", *Journal Asiatique* 18, 1921, pp. 5-36.

DESANGES 1978
J. DESANGES, *Recherches sur l'activité des Méditerranéens aux confins de l'Afrique (VIe siècle avant J.-C.-IVe siècle après J.-C.)*, Collection de l'École Française de Rome 38.

DESANGES 1984
J. DESANGES, "Rome et les riverains de la Mer Rouge au IIIe siècle de notre ère. Aperçus récents et nouveaux problèmes", *Ktèma* 9, pp. 249-260.

GIGNAC, *Grammar*
F.T. GIGNAC, *A Grammar of the Greek Papyri of the Roman and Byzantine Periods*, Milan, 1976.

GLASER
E. GLASER, *Skizze der Geschichte und Geographie Arabiens von den ältesten Zeiten bis zum Propheten Muhammad*, II, Berlin, 1890.

GGM
C. MÜLLER ed., *Geographici Graeci minores*, Paris, 1882.

GLM
A. RIESE ed., *Geographi Latini Minores*, Hildesheim, 1964.

al-HAMDĀNĪ
David Heinrich MÜLLER, *al Hamdânî's Geographie der arabischen Halbinsel*, 2 vol., Leiden, 1884 & 1891.

Ja
A. JAMME, *Sabaean Inscriptions from Maḥram Bilqîs (Mârib)*, Publications of the American Foundation for the Study of Man III, Baltimore, 1962.

al-JĀSIR
Ḥāmid al-JĀSIR, *al-Mu'ǧam al-ǧuǧrāfi li-l-Bilād al-'arabiya as-sa'ūdiyya*, Nuṣūṣ wa-abḥāṯ ǧuǧrāfiyya wa-ta'riḫiyya 'an Ǧazīrat al-'Arab, 19, ar-Riyāḍ (1397 h/1977 m.), 2 vol.

KOBISHCHANOV 1979
Y.N. KOBISHCHANOV, *Axum*, University Park & London.

RYCKMANS
J. RYCKMANS, "Petits royaumes sud-arabes d'après les auteurs classiques", *Le Muséon* 70, 1957, pp. 75-96.

SPRENGER

A. SPRENGER, *Die alte Geographie Arabiens als Grundlage der Entwicklungsgeschichte des Semitismus*, Bern, 1875.

WISSMANN 1964

H. VON WISSMANN, *Zur Geschichte und Landeskunde von Alt-Südarabien*, Sammlung Eduard Glaser II, Österreichische Akademie der Wissenschaften, Philosophisch-historische Klasse, Sitzungsberichte 246, Vienna.

WISSMANN 1968

H. VON WISSMANN, Ζααβράμ, *RE*, Suppl.-Bd. 11, col. 1304-1312.

WISSMANN 1970

H. VON WISSMANN, *Ophir, RE*, Suppl.-Bd. 12, col. 906-980.

WISSMANN *apud* GROHMANN

H. VON WISSMANN, Map""Das vorislamische Arabien" in A. GROHMANN, *Arabien*, Handbuch der Altertumswissenschaft III, 1, 3, 3, 4, Münich, 1963.

WISSMANN, HÖFNER

H. VON WISSMANN & M. HÖFNER, *Beiträge zur historischen Geographie des vorislamischen Südarabien*, Akademie der Wissenschaften und der Literatur in Mainz, Abhandlungen der geistes- und sozialwissenschaftlichen Klasse 1952/4, Wiesbaden, 1952.

QUSEIR AL-QADIM
AND THE LOCATION OF MYOS HORMOS

There is more than a little irony in the present discussion of the archaeological remains at Quseir al-Qadim. The pronouncement of Couyat in 1910 that Quseir al-Qadim was only a medieval site carried much weight for subsequent explorers.[1] The excavations conducted by the author from 1978 to 1982 sought an Islamic port of the Abbasid period, as claimed in the *Encyclopaedia of Islam.*[2] While the medieval remains are there (and have much interest), most of the site is an early Roman settlement (1st and 2nd centuries A.D.). Apparently this Roman port may now be identified as Myos Hormos, an identification (and prestige) conferred on this site by others. While the location of Myos Hormos at Quseir (or Quseir al-Qadim) has had its proponents from early days, the site of Abu Sha'ar is thoroughly embedded in the literature as this ancient port. The excavations at Abu Sha'ar[3] have resulted in the collapse of this traditional identification and attracted renewed interest in Quseir al-Qadim.

---

1. " [...] Couyat rendered a real service in pointing out that Ḳusêr el-Ḳadîm is a mediaeval and not a classical site. I have examined the site and found there potsherds of Arab ware, fragments of matting, and date-stones of very recent appearance", G.W. MURRAY, "The Roman roads and stations in the eastern desert of Egypt", *JEA,* 11, 1925, p. 142; his reference is to J. COUYAT-BARTHOUX, "Ports gréco-romains de la Mer rouge et grandes routes du désert arabique", *CRAIBL,* 10, 1910, p. 526. At the same time, R. Weill suggested that Myos Hormos might be Quseir in the excavation report, Koptos: "Relation sommaire des travaux exécutés ... en 1910", *ASAE,* 11, 1911, p. 101.

2. M. PLESSNER, "Ḳusair", *EI,* 1, 1927, 1158.

3. S.E. SIDEBOTHAM, "Preliminary report on the 1990-1991 seasons of fieldwork at 'Abu Sha'ar (Red Sea coast)", *JARCE*, 31, 1994, pp. 133-58. (This article represents an advance for those following results of these excavations — the site plan now has the north at the page top.)

Myos Hormos and Berenice were "designated" or "restricted" ports (*apodedeigmenos hormos*), according to the *Periplus.* The traditional identification of Quseir al-Qadim with the ancient port of Leukos Limen led Sidebotham to comment, "the discovery of the import-export trade between South India, South Arabia and Egypt at Leukos Limen proves, however, that the Erythraean Sea trade was not confined to [Berenice and Myos Hormos]".[4] Alternatively, the *Periplus* could be used to argue that Quseir al-Qadim must be Myos Hormos and not Leukos Limen. Indeed, Reddé and Golvin have shown clearly that the distance between Berenice and Myos Hormos in the *Periplus* (1800 stades) is the exact distance from Ras Banas (Berenice) to Quseir al-Qadim.[5] The purpose of this paper is a reconsideration of the results of the archaeological excavations at Quseir al-Qadim in light of this suggested identification with Myos Hormos. As the following discussion will fully demonstrate, the process of archaeological research is not only one of discovery but one of interpretation.

Archaeological evidence from Quseir al-Qadim

A. Artifacts

The locational debate will not be resolved short of finding a dedicatory inscription firmly attached to an architectural monument. Lacking this, one may begin with documentary evidence as the category most acceptable to historians. Bagnall's reading of the papyri and ostraca suggested two apparent attestations of Leukos Limen, though this interpretation has been challenged.[6] There is, however, one ostracon with reference to Myos Hormos.[7] Further, internal documentation shows that Quseir supported a military detachment, a garrison under a

4. S.E. SIDEBOTHAM, *Roman economic policy in the Erythra Thalassa 30 BC - AD 217,* Leiden, 1986, pp. 96-97.

5. M. REDDÉ and J-C. GOLVIN, "Du Nil à la mer rouge: Documents anciens et nouveaux sur les routes du désert oriental d'Égypte", *Karthago,* 21, 1986-87, p. 63. L. CASSON, *The* Periplus Maris Erythraei, Princeton, 1989, p. 97, keeping the traditional identification of Myos Hormos with Abu Sha'ar, dismisses the distance as an underestimate (elsewhere he finds the distances given in the *Periplus* quite accurate).

6. R.S. BAGNALL, "Papyri and ostraka from Quseir al-Qadim", *Bulletin of the American Society of Papyrologists,* 23, 1986, pp. 1-60. See A. BÜLOW-JACOBSEN *et al.*, "The Identification of Myos Hormos: New papyrological evidence", *BIFAO,* 94, 1994, pp. 27-42.

7. BAGNALL, *op. cit.*, cat. 45.5.

curator praesidii which may have numbered 50 to 100 men.[8] Internal documents suggest the garrison was in place from the beginning of the 1st through the first quarter of the 2nd century.[9] This agrees with numismatic evidence of occupational activity; the three seasons of excavations produced only one worn Ptolemaic issue and one coin of the third century. The vast majority of the coins were bronze (*aes*), with a few billon tetradrachms. The identifiable coins are attributable to the reigns of Claudius, Nero and the Flavian emperors (41-96 A.D.) and a later coin of Hadrian (117-138 A.D.); this suggests an activity in the first and early second centuries. One should caution that of the coins identifiable as Roman only 1/5 could be attributed more precisely, due to wear and salt damage.[10]

The excavations produced an impressive list of languages used in or around this settlement: Latin, Greek, Demotic Egyptian, Tamil, Nabataean, and South Arabian. The occurrence of Tamil is perhaps the most interesting for the India trade. Two inscriptions on pottery have been shown to record personal names in old Tamil.[11] Not only do these graffiti correspond to Tamil on pottery at Arikamedu, but one of the names is actually found in the Arikamedu corpus.[12] The sherds were found in the structures across the road from the Roman "villa"; these buildings seems to encroach over the original street (see below), suggesting a second century date; such a date appears to agree with the palaeography.

This area also showed evidence of iron working, a traditional Indian activity; more important are the numerous ceramic types which appear to be in Indian style, if not actual manufacture. The nearby Roman "villa" had a cellar door made of cedar; and in the northwest, other architectural elements made of

---

8. *Idem*, 5.

9. *Idem*, 4.

10. S.E. SIDEBOTHAM, "Ancient coins from Quseir al-Qadim (an unpublished report)"; see his comments in *Roman economic policy,* p. 55.

11. D. WHITCOMB and J. JOHNSON, *Quseir al-Qadim 1978, Preliminary report,* Cairo, American Research Center in Egypt, 1979, Pl. 27j (hereafter, *Quseir 1978*), and *idem., Quseir al-Qadim 1980, Preliminary report*, Malibu, Undena publications, 1982, pp. 263-64, Pl. 61o (hereafter, *Quseir 1980).* The original discussion of the Tamil was contributed by I. Mahadevan.

12. R.E.M. WHEELER, "Arikamedu: An Indo-Roman trading-station on the east coast of India", *Ancient India,* 2, 1946, pp. 109-114. This was noted by R. SALOMON, "Epigraphic remains of Indian traders in Egypt", *JAOS*, 111, 1991, pp. 731-36; Salomon also discusses an ostracon written in Prakrit said to be from Quseir in the Cairo Museum.

teak. Analysis of other small wood artifacts of the Roman period indicated that virtually all came from outside of Egypt, and most from species native to Iran and India.[13] Connections with Arikamedu have been explored before; one might repeat here that the *terra sigillatas*, amphorae, and coinage (with the exception of gold) found at Arikamedu are precisely duplicated in the assemblages recovered at Quseir.

B. The Settlement

The overall character of the site is an orthogonally planned complex, arranged against the steep, western edge of the raised coral beach (see *fig. 1* and 2). There was no wall around the settlement. The principal buildings are two large complexes of mounded earth, labelled Central Building A and Central Building B. To the northwest and southwest are extensive ranges of low structures and midden debris. To the southeast is the flat expanse of the *sabkha* or mud flats sloping toward the beach and small bay.

1. Central Building A

Portions of this building were excavated in all three seasons, revealing a series of rooms with vaulted ceilings on the southwestern side.[14] A corresponding series of rooms may be postulated under the mounding to the northeast, as well as closing rooms and walls to the north and south. Some indication of the unity of this structure is provided in a staircase located in the northwest corner of the building.[15] Other than one amphora and a few vessels fallen from upper floors, most materials had been cleaned from these rooms before abandonment. Attached to the west of this building was a row of rooms, each measuring 9 x 4 m., called the White Building (due to the light yellow bricks used).[16] The floors were carefully tiled with bricks and one room had a

---

13. J. JOHNSON, *Quseir 1980,* 337. F.T. HIEBERT, "Commercial organization of the Egyptian port of Quseir al-Qadim: Evidence from the analysis of the wooden objects", *Archéologie islamique,* 2, 1991, pp. 127-59.

14. The fallen brick vaulting rested on piles of debris, suggesting a period of abandonment before its collapse. Walls were standing 2.5-3.0 m. high, but the solid mass of caliche or rock salt near the surface made it feasible to excavate only alternate squares. Much of this information is included here, since the 1982 season has not yet been published.

15. This staircase turned around a pillar and was made a limestone treads; controlled access was from an anteroom with locking doorway.

16. Most of the bricks used at Quseir are a red-brown (all are unfired). The superior quality of these yellow clay bricks led to extensive robbing out and reuse during the

series of holes against the wall, presumably for standing amphorae. A burial wrapped in Roman textiles was placed in the collapse of the vaulting, indicating destruction during the Roman period.

Central Building A may be provisionally identified as an *horreum*. Following Rickman's analysis, warehouses of the Roman period tended to be courtyard in plan. The *Horreum* of Epagathiana in Ostia (*fig. 3a*), dated to the mid-2nd century A.D., provides a startling parallel to the elements excavated and suggested by surface contours at Quseir.[17] This *horreum* measures 28 x 36 m., with an attached row of shops (8 m. deep) opening on to the street. Storerooms are ranged around a courtyard with two corner staircases leading to the second floor. This building is a distinctive type at Ostia and opinions vary as to its character; it seems to have been a private storehouse for expensive goods, one in which individual merchants might rent a storeroom, rather like an oriental khan.[18] The plan is not unlike the granary C65 excavated at Karanis in the Fayyum (*fig. 3b*).[19] While the courtyard, stairs and arrangement of rooms are similar, the size is about 1/4 the area and dominated by two floors of grain bins. The details of construction techniques at Karanis have many parallels in Central Building A and others at Quseir. The Ostian "khan" is no doubt the more immediate functional model.

2. Central Building B

This high mound forms the most prominent feature on the site, lying above the beach and east of the remainder of the site. Several small soundings revealed a complex of mud brick walls and fallen debris cemented into a hard mass of caliche. Little of the architectural character of this building was revealed; the artifactual assemblage was consistent with the remainder of the site. A relative depression in the center suggests a courtyard arrangement.

A working hypothesis is that, in the absence of a city wall, this was the locus for administration and protection of the town, the *castellum* defending the town. Small forts of the early Roman empire are relatively rare in the East and,

---

Islamic period, a millennium after abandonment.

17. G. RICKMAN, *Roman Granaries and Stone Buildings,* Cambridge, 1971, pp. 30-38, fig. 3. See G. BECATTI, "Horrea Epagathiana et Epaphroditian", *Notizie degli Scavi di Antichità,* 18, 1940.

18. RICKMAN, *op. cit.,* 37-38. He notes the emphasis on locking mechanisms for each door. Further parallels may be sought in Syria and the Levant from this period and later times.

19. E.M. HUSSELMAN, *Karanis: Topography and Architecture,* Ann Arbor, 1979, map 12, plans 19-21.

based on better known models from European provinces, probably conformed to the "playing-card" shape, rectangular with rounded corners and internal towers (if any).[20] The size of these forts ranges from 1.5 ha. to a more regular 3.5 ha. Fortunately there is just such a fort in the Eastern Desert of Egypt, that of Mons Claudianus in the Wādi Umm Hussein (see *fig. 3c*).[21] The earlier phase of this fort is dated to the mid-2nd century and has a rectangular plan without towers (its area is *c*. 3.85 ha.). The dimensions of this *castellum* are 75 x 52 m., a configuration which fits comfortably in the mounding at Quseir.[22] Constructions at Mons Claudianus are arranged against the exterior walls with the center left relatively open. The discovery of a small temple in this fort suggests the possibility that Central Building B may have also contained an otherwise unattested religious focus for Quseir al-Qadim. One might also note that the fort at Mons Claudianus forms an irregular rectangle; a failure to achieve four right angles may also be observed in Central Building A.

3. A Northeast structure

The original survey of the site revealed a rectangular structure north of Central Building B. In contrast to that complex, however, the limited structural debris in the northeast suggests only a simple enclosure. This suggests a function as a stable, or "animal-lines". Parallels may be drawn from Mons Claudianus (also in *fig. 3c*) and a number of stations on the Abu Sha'ar road, most of which have stables in a similar position relative to the principal building.[23]

4. The Northwest and Southwest areas

At this point, one might inquire about the strong resemblances between the remains at Quseir and Mons Claudianus. Indeed, both places had similar functions, they were specialized settlements for an economic purpose — the one for extracting architectural stone and the other for facilitating the India trade.

---

20. D. KENNEDY and D. RILEY, *Rome's Desert Frontier from the Air*, Austin, University of Texas, 1990, pp. 138ff.

21. T. KRAUS *et al.*, "Mons Claudianus — Mons Porphyrites: Bericht über die zweites Forschungsreise 1964", *MDAIK*, 22, 1967, pp. 116-29, Abb. 5.

22. Another *castellum* in the eastern desert is Abu Zawal (= Fatira?) with very similar dimensions and architecture; see REDDÉ and GOLVIN, *op. cit.*, p. 40.

23. Such animal lines are ubiquitous and discussed in D. MEREDITH, "The Roman remains in the eastern desert of Egypt", *JEA*, 38, 1952, p. 96. This same reference makes a back-handed admission that the road to Myos Hormos described by Strabo (17.1.45) fits the Quseir road better than that to Abu Sha'ar (*idem*, n. 1). See REDDÉ and GOLVIN, *op. cit.*, p. 56.

Neither settlement was a Roman city in its classical sense.[24] These were not loci for entertainment or comfortable living, much less intellectual pursuits. The potential for urban embellishments might have been felt by the inhabitants of Quseir, but the key factors of administrative, religious, and commercial functions were rudimentary, or more accurately, geared toward the primary purpose of international trade.

Thus, beyond the individual structures described above, the remainder of the site exhibited an homogenous archaeological character, plentiful indications of thin mud brick walls and piles of refuse, concentrations of sherds and organic remains. A number of soundings into these structures were made; one of the most substantial was labelled, not without some irony, the Roman "villa". This structure seems typical of the architecture of the entire western part of the site; that is, this was the residential sector of the settlement. This residence fronted a street and, with surface remains planned, gave some indications of the axial organization of this area (*fig. 2*). One may posit the beginnings of city plan, that the site may have received attentions from some *agrimensores*. These land surveyors were normally responsible for centuriation of country areas in founding new colonies; this work also involved laying out of new towns. The basic unit of measure was the *actus* (120 Roman feet on each side, or 35.5 m.); four *actus* made an *heredium.*[25] In practice, the layout of cities was in *insulae* of widely varying size.

Given the size of the Quseir ruins, it seems unlikely that standard imperial *insulae* were contemplated, even if a potential for expansion and prosperity was imagined. Nevertheless, an analysis of these remains in terms of *heredia* may reflect the initial layout or foundation of the port. A base line or *limites* west of the shops attached to the *horreum* was taken as the line of the *cardo,* the principal north-south street. The northwest corner of this structure produces a "best-fit" for a series of *heredia* along the western part of the site.[26] The

---

24. Thus Sidebotham characterizes the Red Sea ports as "surprisingly squalid places"; see his "Ports of the Red Sea and the Arabia-India trade", in *Rome and India: The Ancient sea trade,* V. BEGLEY and R.D. DE PUMA, eds., Madison, University of Wisconsin, 1991, pp. 12-38. He also recognizes the underlying Hippodamian plan at Quseir al-Qadim, *ibid.*, p. 27.

25. One hundred *heredia* made a *centuri*; O.A.W. DILKE, *Greek and Roman maps,* London, 1985, pp. 88*sqq*. The Roman foot (*podes*) was 0.296 m. and the *actus* measured 71 x 71 m. Some indication of early imperial *insulae* may be seen at Carthage, measuring 1 x 4 *actus.* This information is taken from F. CASTAGNOLI, *Orthogonal Town Planning in Antiquity*, Cambridge, MA, 1971, pp. 112-115.

26. In the same spirit of aggrandizement which led to the "villa", each of these units

northern *heredium,* Reg. I, was only incompletely developed and seriously encroached over the *cardo.* The *limites* between this and Reg. II follows a major drainage line (possibly worn down from travel) and may be extended as a line north of the stables. This line may have been a "wall" of the original rectangle; this suggestion is strengthened by surface remains of a square structure at the crossing of the *cardo* and this line, possibly marking an original gate or tetrapylon. This street might have been the *decumanus* connected to the principal route inland (see below). Reg. II contains the "villa" fronting the *cardo.* The less regular structures across the street seem to be encroachments on the original street, a pattern which may have predominated over the idealized plan presented here. Two further *heredia* may be plotted to the south, Reg. III and IV; numerous lines among the surface remains seem to indicate planning according to this orientation. There is some indication that additional *actus,* possibly an *heredium* labelled Reg. V, were planned toward the southwest. The ground becomes very dissected at this point, limiting the scope (or need) for planning.

5. The Harbour area

South of the above ruin fields is a relatively uniform *sabkha,* or mud flats. The northeast and southwest edges, where the sloping ruins began, were marked by parallel wall fragments. The slope behind the southwest wall was excavated as L8c, attention was focused on surface indications of intensive burning. The 1980 excavations revealed a circular structure set into a rectangular building with a number of small rooms or bins. These bins and much of the surrounding area were filled with ashes and numerous heat-cracked basalt grinding stones. This complex may now be identified as a bakery on the strength of a better preserved example found at Abu Sha'ar.[27] It may be noted that the bakery at Abu Sha'ar was associated with *horrea* identical to the "White Building" (see below).[28]

Between the parallel walls edging the *sabkha* was a sort of spine extending

---

will be labelled *regio* in this report.

27. This trench was the subject of many frustrations as various hypotheses were tested as the complex was dissected; its field designation was "confusion hill". There is no small satisfaction in seeing a better preserved parallel, nearly identical in numerous details (AS91-N); see S.E. SIDEBOTHAM, "Preliminary report on the 1990-1991 seasons", p. 153.

28. The *horrea* were AS91-R; both this structure and the bakery appear to belong to the earlier, 4th century occupation, *ibid.*, p. 154. A similar installation, another probable bakery with a corner location, is reported at al-Zarqa *in* N. Grimal, *BIFAO*, 94, 1994, p. 421 (see BÜLOW-JACOBSEN *et al.*, *op. cit.*).

into the *sabkha*; this mounding resembled nothing so much as a mole and contained several walls of similar orientations, seen in 1978 test trenches and surface indications. A number of walls joined this spine at right angles, suggesting shallow structures. The northwest limit of the *sabkha* was a heavily eroded slope with numerous lengths of a wall again at right angles to the spine and peripheral walls. The resulting configuration of these planned walls is a rectangle measuring 60 m. by 48 m., a structural element of the port labelled Reg. VI. This space is less than the *heredia* posited for the above regions. If this area was developed as a structural complex, its area corresponds precisely with that occupied by the internal structures of Abu Sha'ar, *i.e.* the functional elements of that *castellum* stripped of its fortifications (*fig. 3d*). Like that site, the spine may be interpreted as a central passage or street with *horrea* and other structures on either side.[29] The structures of Reg. VI have an orientation differing from the remainder of the town; this characteristic of quays and other harbour elements is well attested in other ports, Alexandria being an obvious parallel (*fig. 3e*).[30]

An extension of the western wall of this area also marks the limit of the "island", extensively excavated in 1978. This mound was hypothesized to have been the spoil of dredging operations, an ancient effort to keep the harbour clear.[31] This interpretation was apparently overlooked by Peacock, who also failed to notice the series of soundings placed into the *sabkha* in a preliminary effort to determine the existence of the harbour.[32] Presuming some shallow holding capacity in the *sabkha* area, the relatively narrow entry from the bay suggests a *cothon* type of harbour, such as at Carthage or Motya.[33] It is

29. Over half of Abu Sha'ar contained barracks, which structures would be located in the *castellum* postulated above.

30. There is some question as to whether this open, central area might have been the forum for this town. If one rejects the necessity of a central temple and other ceremonial structures, there may have been some overlap in functions.

31. D. WHITCOMB, *Quseir 1978,* p. 43. The excavators remain indebted to Prof. Fred Wendorf, who visited the site in 1978 and offered his experience with harbour facilities in the Fayyum.

32. D.P.S. PEACOCK, "The site of Myos Hormos: a view from space", *JRA*, 6, 1993, pp. 226-32. Whether satellite image or ground truth, a careful attention to antecedent observation and interpretation seems a useful procedure. The beginnings of such investigation of the *sabkha* are of course inadequate for a comprehensive reconstruction of the ancient landscape; see *Quseir 1978*, pp. 61-62.

33. B.S.J. ISSERLIN, "New light on the'cothon' at Motya", *Antiquity*, 45, 1971, pp. 178-86.

nevertheless difficult to imagine these quays and even this small bay servicing more than a dozen dhows, let alone 120 Roman merchantmen which Strabo reports sailed from here to India yearly. A careful reading of Strabo gives a somewhat different picture. He stresses the increased trade under Roman rule (of his friend Aelius Gallus) by saying that as many as 120 ships were *available* for the India trade after 25 B.C. (It can be surmised that these were the remnants of the Arabian campaign invasion fleet, over 200 vessels of burden and warships; 16.4.23.) This fleet was presumably distributed among several ports, especially the arsenal at Arsinoe.[34] The mention in connection with Myos Hormos reflects only this port's predominance in the India trade (Strabo 16.4.24, 17.1.45).

The presumed existence of a lagoon (see *fig. 4*) functioning as a shallow harbour may have had a minimal size of 700 x 200 m. (14 ha.).[35] This lagoon was gradually silted from the Wādi al-Anz (Wādi Abu Unis) on the north and the Wādi Quseir al-Qadim on the south. That the catchment area for these wadis is not as large as that of modern Quseir (the Wādi Ambagi system) may have offered a relative advantage to harbour facilities here. The Wādi Quseir al-Qadim was the only practical route to the Wādi Hammamat and the Nile valley;[36] this suggests that land transportation would have followed a track west and north of the lagoon and entered the town in line with the street between Reg. II and III, convenient to both the *horreum* and animal lines.

6. Town organization

This settlement was founded from outside the region rather than arising from a local population concentration. As such, the settlement is artificial and totally dependent on external relationships. The principal players were a diverse group of the Romans, Egyptians, Indians, and Arabs of the Red Sea region, as implied from the languages discovered. The analysis of the organization of the settlement suggests a separation of residential from official structures, the *castellum*, *horreum*, and harbour. The community had two foci, the *castellum*

---

34. On the character of this fleet, see S.E. SIDEBOTHAM, *Roman economic policy*, pp. 69-71.

35. Peacock suggests a lagoon about 5 times larger, stretching farther to the south, *op. cit.*, fig. 2.

36. This wādi also leads to Bir Nakheil (*praesidium* and mining settlement, QRS-16 and 18) and northwest to the Semna gold mines and Mons Claudianus; see M. PRICKETT, "Quseir regional survey", *Quseir 1978*, pp. 320-22 and fig. 47. The pass between the Wādi Quseir al-Qadim and Wādi Nakheil has a guard tower (QRS-26) with early Roman ceramics (PRICKETT, *op. cit.*, p. 314, fig. 44).

embracing administrative, protective, and possibly religious functions, and the harbour localizing economic functions.

The analysis of the original design of the town, that laid out by the *agrimensores,* is only one aspect of its physical organization. It seems unlikely that further excavations would find only this precise configuration. There are two reasons for this expectation. The first is that close adherence to this town plan would require constant governmental supervision, one resulting from incremental investment in urbanization typical of a classical town. Manifestly, this did not occur; the profits (and reinvestments) from commerce were taken elsewhere. In other words, the urban identity of this settlement did not take root, presumably because of the hostility of the environment. The second reason is that its population of very diverse origins, as noted above, brought a variety of settlement experience and expectations of urban environment. Little is known of the structural organization of Arabian and Indian settlements of size (whether or not "cities"); and the extent to which traditional Egyptian town organization might be applied outside the agriculturally based Nile valley remains to be studied. The point here is that the study of Roman period remains at Quseir has a strength in the interlocking lines of evidence from different regions; but this situation also implies a marginalized, temporary settlement which ultimately cannot be a typical phenomenon, except perhaps at another port.

Regional historic context

The long-standing debate on the location of Myos Hormos illustrates the peculiar nature of classical studies, one which either ignores or improperly evaluates archaeological data. Reddé and Golvin clearly illustrate the variety of port sequence attested in the various classical authors.[37] One little-noticed feature is the tendency of Philoteras to wander up and down the coast with little creditable evidence to pin this "city" to one spot. On the other hand, the port of Leukos Limen (Albus Portus) is accepted with great confidence by the majority of observers solely on the basis of a single mention in Ptolemy. The identification with Quseir has continued to be accepted (even by the excavators) in spite of the fact that this new name appears in Ptolemy's text *after* major occupation ceased on this site (witness the coins, epigraphy, and Arretine wares discovered at Quseir al-Qadim).

The long-standing identification of Abu Sha'ar with Myos Hormos invites

---

37. *Op. cit.*, p. 62.

comparison of these archaeological remains. The harbour area and architectural details in the bakery and *horreum,* as described above (*fig. 3d*), suggest that these ports share a commonalty in the architectural traditions from which they have drawn. The structure of Abu Sha'ar, stripped of its defensive shell, seems to coalesce the elements found at Quseir, ranged along either side of a main street. Excavated evidence indicates that Quseir al-Qadim was abandoned by the early third century and Abu Sha'ar may have begun later in that same century; in other words, there may be a sequential relationship between these two ports. The identifying features of Myos Hormos, as described in the Classical authors, are well known. Both sites have fortified ruins, nearby springs,[38] a harbour with winding entrance, and a dazzling red hill (more convincing as the Jebel Hamrawein at Quseir). The three wooded islands in tradition of Agatharchides is another matter; such islands do not exist at Quseir, but find ready identifications near Abu Sha'ar. The islands are, indeed, one of the main underpinnings of this localization of Myos Hormos.[39]

A careful reading of Strabo suggests an alternative explanation for the three wooded islands at Myos Hormos. In the presentation of the northeast coast of the Red Sea, the textual tradition from Agatharchides includes the Aelanite gulf (the gulf of Aqaba), Nabataea, a fertile plain and large island, and a gulf of 500 stadia with three islands full of olive trees.[40] The large island may be modern Tiran, known as Iotabe in late antiquity;[41] the three wooded islands may be the modern Shusha, Barqan, and Sinafir islands, opposite 'Aynuna. The Wādi 'Aynuna has an extensive archaeological site and port of the Nabataean and Roman periods (see *fig. 5*); these ruins have been proposed as those of the port of

38. The spring (the *Fons Tadnos* of Pliny) is found at Abu Sha'ar (MURRAY, *op. cit.*, p. 141, with earlier identifications) and at Bir Kareim (*Quseir 1980,* pp. 391-96).

39. The three islands, once covered with trees are said to be Shadwan, Tawila, Jubal?, MURRAY, *op. cit.*, p. 141. One of the islands is said to have had numbers of guinea-fowl (*Numida meleagris*); the excavations at Quseir al-Qadim have produced quantities of Roman bird bones, mainly *Gallus gallus* (chickens).

40. Strabo 16.4.18; Agatharchides 87a. The olive trees are specified as an Ethiopic type, one which may be identified as the mangrove or *shora*; see S.M. BURSTEIN, *Agatharchides of Cnidus on the Erythraean Sea,* London, Hakluyt Society (1989), p. 136, n. 4. For a concise discussion of the mangrove in Roman context, see J. DESANGES and M. REDDÉ, "La côte africaine du Bab el-Mandab dans l'antiquité", *Hommages à Jean Leclant,* vol. 3, pp. 183-85.

41. P. MAYERSON, "The Island of Iotabê: A Reprise", *BASOR*, 287, 1992, pp. 1-4. The continuing presence of a customs facility, presumably under Roman control, is suggestive of a similar early role.

Leuke Kome.[42] Further, it has been suggested that Leukos Limen might be a corruption by Ptolemy of the better attested Leuke Kome.[43] In addition to the three wooded islands, 'Aynuna claims a famous water source in its springs and an approach through a "tortuous channel".[44] Finally, one of the islands had the remains of a shrine of Isis, a deity associated with Aphrodite (see below). Thus the islands in the description of Myos Hormos may have been copied from that of Leuke Kome in this geographical tradition and have no bearing on the association of Quseir al-Qadim with Myos Hormos.[45]

Myos Hormos of the Ptolemies

The foundation of Myos Hormos by Ptolemy II Philadelphus (285-246 B.C.) has been widely assumed, yet there is no direct evidence. The attribution is implied from the tradition of Agatharchides, written over 150 years later and available only in quotations (Diodorus, Strabo, and Photius). As Burstein has pointed out, the name implies an unofficial, non-royal foundation; the other ports of Ptolemy II are all named for his female relatives.[46] The text of Agatharchides, as found in Photius, states that a later name for the port was Aphrodite's harbour.

The location of the Ptolemaic port of Myos Hormos cannot be at Quseir al-Qadim from its archaeological evidence, which is consistently early Roman.[47]

---

42. M.L. INGRAHAM *et al.*, "Saudi Arabia Comprehensive Survey Program: c. Preliminary report on a reconnaissance survey of the northwestern province", *Atlal,* 5, 1981, pp. 76-78. This identification has been accepted by CASSON, *Periplus*, pp. 143-44.

43. BÜLOW-JACOBSEN *et al.*, *op. cit.*, n. 7.

44. BURSTEIN, *op. cit.*, p. 152, n. 2. Only the brilliant red mountain and guinea-fowl remain unaccounted, see n. 35.

45. For a discussion of the location of Leuke Kome, see P-L. GATIER and J-F. SALLES, "Aux frontières méridionales du domaine nabatéen", *L'Arabie et ses mers bordières,* Lyon (1988), pp. 186-87. It is a disquieting thought that the way to Leuke Kome led on toward another Berenice, that of Aila (Aqaba); Josephus, *Jewish Antiq.* 8.6.4 .

46. BURSTEIN, *op. cit.*, p. 136, n. 1.

47. There remains the possibility that the *castellum* might bear evidence of Ptolemaic occupation. Nevertheless, the cumulative evidence of three seasons of excavations can hardly be considered limited in extent and chronologically unrepresentative, as

There remains the possibility of a Ptolemaic port at, or more precisely under, the modern town of Quseir. This idea hinges on four hieroglyphic inscriptions from a Ptolemaic temple discovered by Weigall in 1907. He notes that "[...] on one of them was the name Duau, followed by the hieroglyph representing a town written twice to indicate the existence of the two ports". Recent consensus among Egyptologists stands against this reading; a more plausible reading might be "deities of the underworld", rather than a proper name.[48] The stones do seem to indicate a temple to Hathor, which goddess was identified with Aphrodite. Although this was the principal Egyptian deity worshipped east of the Nile, a temple of Hathor strengthens the tradition of Aphrodite's harbour and may refer to the site of modern Quseir.

Prickett suggests that a series of square towers or route markers may lead toward the modern town and may be Ptolemaic in date.[49] Identification of Ptolemaic sites and, more specifically, Ptolemaic ceramics will hinge on the results of recent excavations at Coptos. This material has been used for identification of Hellenistic components of sites along routes in the eastern desert.[50] The architectural evidence from Coptos, also known as an *emporion* to Strabo, seems limited to the temples, churches, and *temenos* walls recovered by Petrie and Reinach.[51]

Peacock would suggest (*op. cit.*, p. 232).

48. A.E.P. WEIGALL, *Travels in Upper Egyptian deserts,* London, 1909, p. 61, Pl. X, 21-24. The reading is limited by the hand-copy of Weigall, which indicates some damage. Nevertheless, the name Douaou may be ruled out. The author is indebted to Profs. J.H. Johnson, E. Wente, and L. Bell for this reading. Further stones, apparently from a Ptolemaic temple, were found in 1978 in the modern town. This was reported by Prof. A.M.A.H. Sayed but remains unpublished.

49. *Quseir 1978,* 319. This point is discussed in REDDÉ and GOLVIN, *op. cit.*, p. 58.

50. H. T. WRIGHT and S. HERBERT, *Archaeological survey in the eastern desert of Egypt ... 1993* (unpublished manuscript), p. 11. This survey was primarily concerned with routes toward Berenice.

51. A.J. REINACH, "Deuxième rapport sur les fouilles de Koptos", *Bulletin de la Societé des fouilles archéologiques*, 1910.

The Isthmus

Strabo's conceptualization of the structure of the eastern desert may be of some relevance to the location and history of these ports and their trade (*fig. 5*). Strabo states that there was an isthmus from Coptos to Berenice, a way founded by Philadelphus (Ptolemy II).[52] He next offers that Berenice was not far from Myos Hormos and that Coptos was not far from Apollonopolis (Edfu), "so that there are two cities at either end defining the isthmus". He then describes the pre-eminence and improvements on the Coptos — Myos Hormos route in his day, early Roman period. Finally, he mentions the Smaragdus mines "on the isthmus" no doubt referring to the emerald mines near Berenice; this anticipates his description of Berenice. The routes describe, for Strabo, a difficult passage between the easy sailing of the Red Sea and the Nile; it is not accidental that he likens the camel-merchants to mariners navigating this narrow, hostile zone of desert.

While we may never know the inspiration for this analysis by Strabo, one may consider the most famous isthmus in the classical world, that of Corinth (*fig. 6*). The isthmus of Corinth separates the gulf of Corinth from the Saronic Gulf. As described by Strabo, the importance of the isthmus was in the exchange of merchandise. For this purpose, there were two ports, Cenchreae and Lechaeum, "the one leads straight to Asia, the other to Italy" (8.6.20). He further notes the harbour (*limen)* of Schoenus which is connected to Pagae in Megaris by the roadway called the Diolcus, the line of the canal (8.6.22). One may note that Cenchreae was a naval station (*naustathmon*), the same term used for Myos Hormos (8.6.4; 17.1.45). The isthmus was thus defined by the two roadways and two principal port cities, Cenchreae and Lechaeum standing for Myos Hormos and Coptos. This geographical configuration may have served as a model for the structure connecting Nilotic and Erythraean ports, joining the worlds of the Mediterranean and Indian Ocean.

Donald WHITCOMB
The Oriental Institute
University of Chicago

---

52. Strabo 17.1.45. The author is indebted to T. Dousa and B. Precourt for assistance with implications of the Greek terminology; they would no doubt wish to be absolved of association with interpretations written herein.

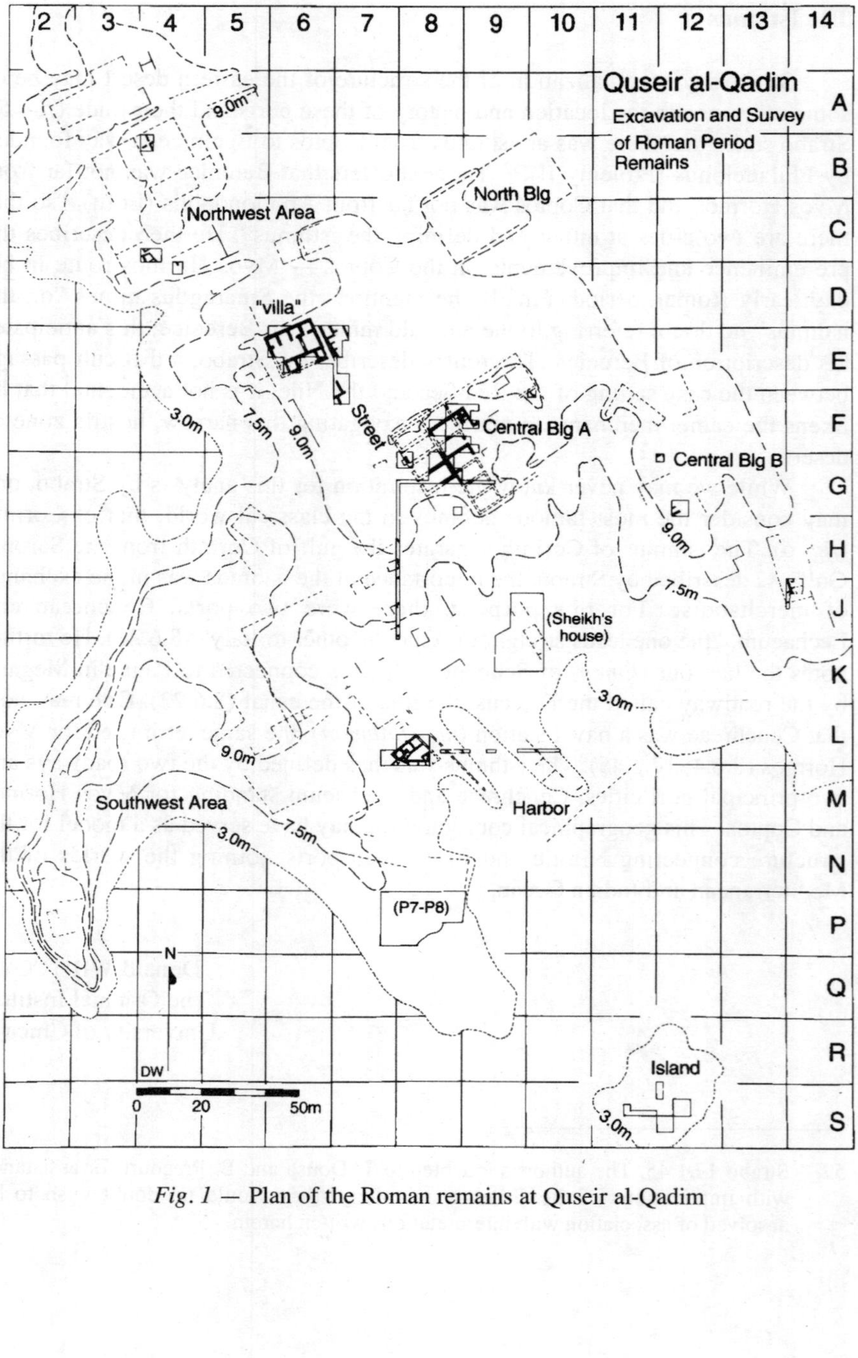

Fig. 1 — Plan of the Roman remains at Quseir al-Qadim

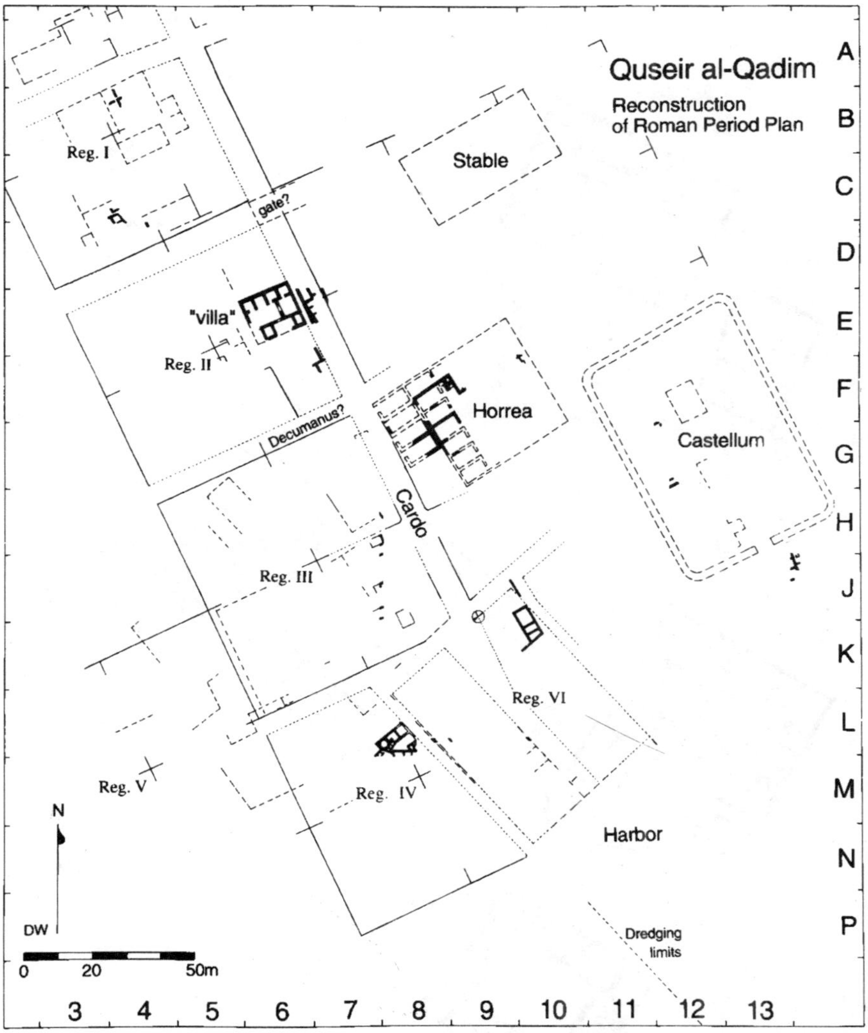

Fig. 2 — Reconstruction of the Roman town plan at Quseir al-Qadim

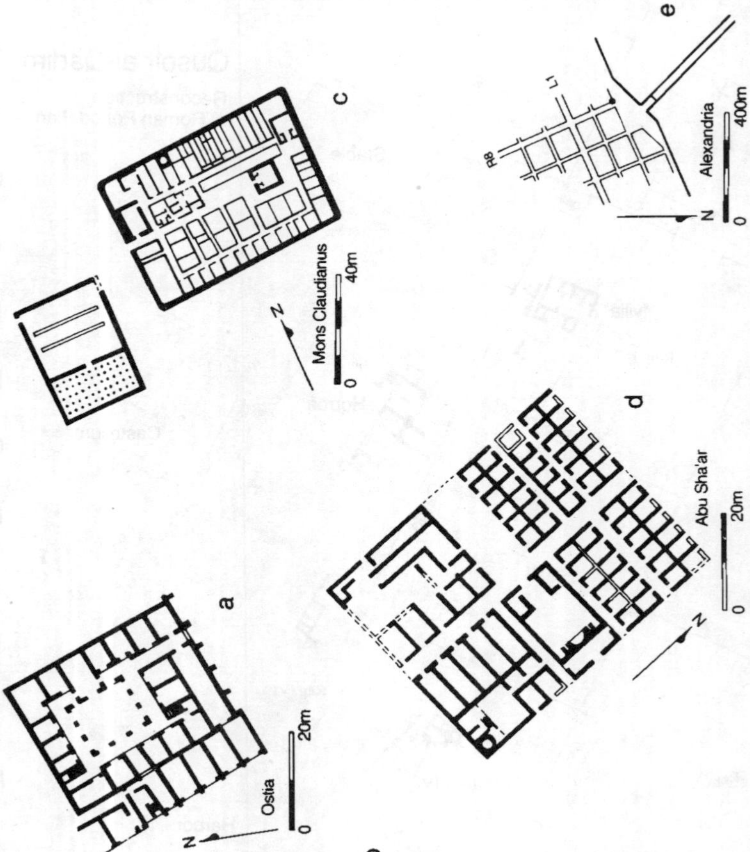

Fig. 3 – Plans of architectural comparisons

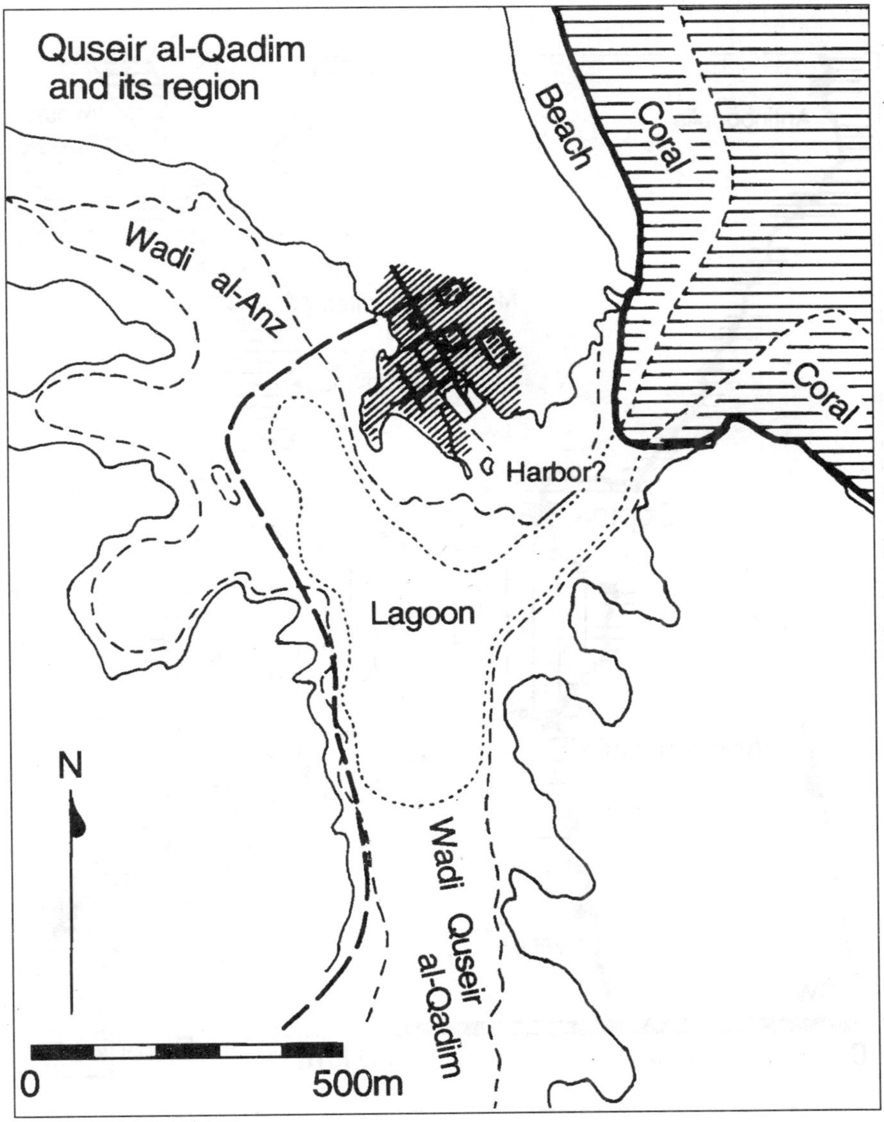

Fig. 4 — Map of the region around Quseir al-Qadim

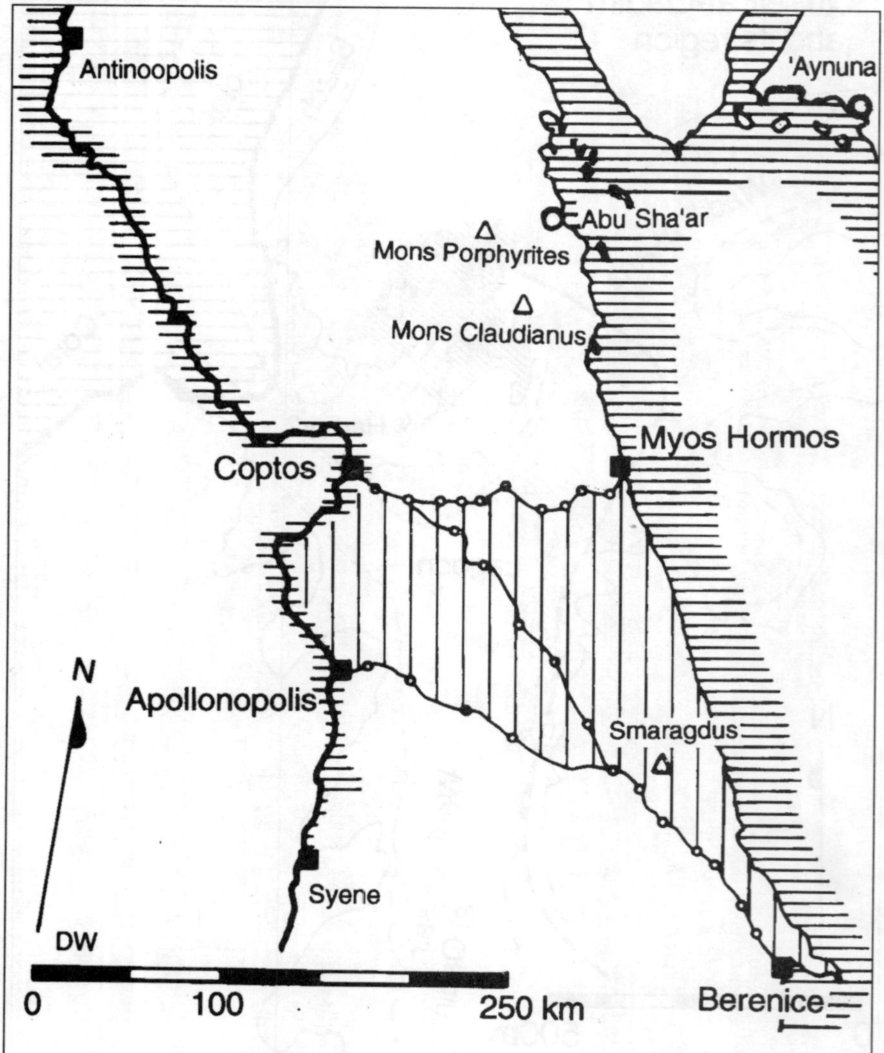

Fig. 5 — Map of the Isthmus described in Strabo and sites mentioned in the text

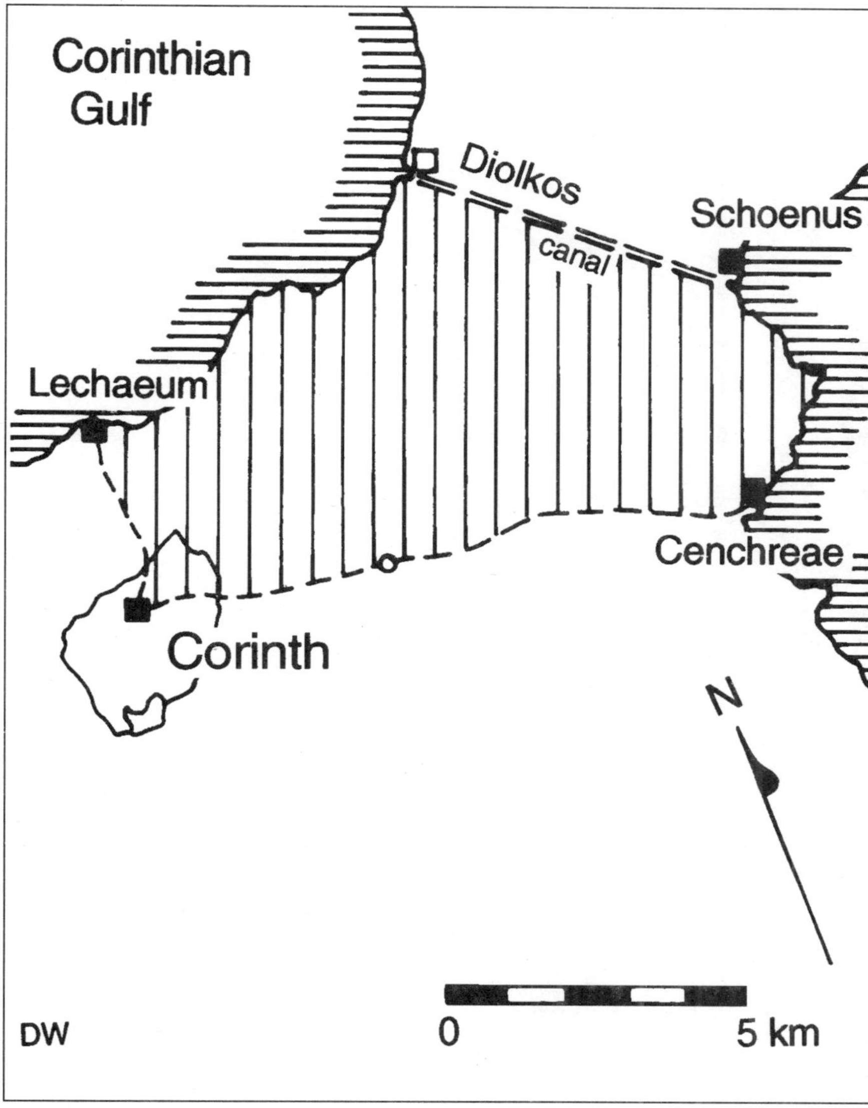

Fig. 6 — Map of the Isthmus of Corinth

AN OVERVIEW OF ARCHAEOLOGICAL WORK

in the Eastern Desert and Along the Red Sea Coast of Egypt by the University of Delaware - Leiden University, 1987 - 1995

This overview is broken down into three main categories: 1) excavations conducted by the University of Delaware during five seasons at and in the vicinity of Abu Sha'ar between 1987-1993, 2) on-going excavations carried out at Berenike by the University of Delaware and Leiden University in the winters of 1994 and 1995, and 3) extensive surveying in the Eastern Desert from 1987-1993 by the University of Delaware and in 1994 and 1995 in collaboration with Leiden University. Survey and excavation data complement each other and together they provide a broader picture of the history of the region and the interrelationships among its sites and with areas beyond the Eastern Desert than could be gleaned solely from excavation at a few sites.

ABU SHA'AR AND ENVIRONS

Our initial work at Abu Sha'ar sought to identify the site — through archaeological work — with the Ptolemaic-Roman port of Myos Hormos.[1] Previous visitors and most, though not all, scholars prior to 1987 (and some

---

1. Ancient sources mentioning Myos Hormos include Agatharchides 5.83a = S.M. BURSTEIN, *Agatharchides of Cnidus On the Erythraean Sea*, London, The Hakluyt Society, 1989, pp. 135-136; Diodorus Siculus 3.39.1-2; Strabo, *Geography* 16.4.5, 2.5.12, 16.4.25, 17.1.45; Pliny the Elder, *Natural History* 6.26.102-103, 6.33.168; *Periplus Maris Erythraei* 1, 19; Claudius Ptolemy, *Geography* 4.5.8; Petrie Ostraca nos. 195-304 [*in* J.G. TAIT, *Greek Ostraca in the Bodleian Library at Oxford and Various Other Collections*, London, Egypt Exploration Society, 1930, pp. 106-125].

since) have equated Abu Sha'ar with Myos Hormos.[2] Our fieldwork at the site [3]

---

2. Those identifying Abu Sha'ar with Myos Hormos include: J. BURTON, *Collectiones Aegyptiaca* Add. Mss. 25,624, London, British Library (unpublished); J. BURTON, *Collectiones Aegyptiaca* Add. Mss. 25,626, London, British Library (unpublished); J.G. WILKINSON, "Notes on a Part of the Eastern Desert of Upper Egypt", *JRGS* 2, 1832, 48, pp. 50-51; J.G. WILKINSON, *Topography of Thebes and General View of Egypt,* London, John Murray, 1835, pp. 411-412; J.R. WELLSTED, *Travels in Arabia* vol. 2, London, John Murray, 1838, pp. 124-125; R. LEPSIUS, *Letters from Egypt, Ethiopia, and the Peninsula of Sinai,* London, Henry G. Bohn, 1853, p. 289; O. SCHNEIDER, *Über den roten Porphyr der Alten*, Dresden, Gilbers'sche königl. Hof-Verlagsbuchhandlung, 1887, Taf. II; T. BARRON and W.F. HUME, *Topography and Geology of the Eastern Desert of Egypt Central Portion*, Cairo, Government Press, 1902, p. 86, 88; A.E.P. WEIGALL, *Travels in the Upper Egyptian Deserts,* Edinburgh-London, W. Blackwood and Sons, 1913, p. 109; J. BALL, *Egypt in the Classical Geographers,* Cairo, Government Press, 1942, 53n, 65, 68, 79, 82n, 83, 106, 183-185; G.W. MURRAY, "The Roman Roads and Stations in the Eastern Desert of Egypt", *JEA* 11, 1925, pp. 141-142, 146-147; G.W. MURRAY, "Trogodytica: The Red Sea Littoral in Ptolemaic Times", *GJ* 133, 1967, p. 32; G.W. MURRAY, *Dare Me to the Desert,* S. Brunswick-New York, A.S. Barnes & Co., 1968, p. 40, 116, 119 ; C.H.O. SCAIFE, "Two Inscriptions at Mons Porphyrites (Gebel Dokhan). Also a Description, with Plans, of the Stations Between Kainopolis & Myos Hormos Together with Some Other Ruins in the Neighborhood of Gebel Dokhan", *Bulletin of the Faculty of Arts University of Egypt* 3/2, 1935, pp. 81-86; C.H.O. SCAIFE, "Further Notes on Myos Hormos and Tadnos Fons", *Bulletin of the Faculty of Arts University of Egypt,* 1936, pp. 55-56; L.A. TREGENZA, *The Red Sea Mountains of Egypt,* London-New York-Toronto, Oxford University Press, 1955, pp. 89-108; D. MEREDITH, "The Roman Remains in the Eastern Desert of Egypt", *JEA* 38, 1952, pp. 94-98 ; D. MEREDITH, "Myos Hormos Road. Inscriptions and Ostraca", *CE* 31/62, 1956, pp. 356-362; D. MEREDITH, *Tabula Imperii Romani Sheet N.G. 36 Coptos,* Oxford, Society of Antiquaries of London, 1958, 12 and map sheet; E.A. FLOYER, "Notes on a Sketch-Map of Two Routes in the Eastern Desert of Egypt", *Proceedings of the Royal Geographical Society*, 1887, p. 667, 730 map; J. COUYAT, "La route de Myos Hormos et les carrières de porphyre rouge", *BIFAO* 7, 1910, pp. 22-24; F. BISSON DE LA ROQUE, "Voyage au Djebel Shaïb", *BSRGE* 11, 1922, p. 113; H. KEES, *PW* 16, *s.v.* "Myos Hormos", 1935, pp. 1081-1083; T. KRAUS, J. RÖDER and W. MÜLLER-WIENER, "Mons Claudianus-Mons Porphyrites Bericht über die zweite Forschungsreise 1964", *MDAIK* 22, 1967, pp. 203-205; J. DESANGES, *Recherches sur l'activité des méditerranéens aux confins de l'Afrique, VIe siècle avant J.-C. - IVe siècle après J.-C.,* Rome, 1978, pp. 270-271; M.J. KLEIN, *Untersuchungen zu den kaiserlichen Steinbrüchen an Mons Porphyrites und Mons Claudianus in der östlichen Wüste Ägyptens,* Bonn, Habelt, 1988, p. 18, 120, Abb. 1; L. CASSON, *The* Periplus Maris Erythraei. *Text with Introduction, Translation, and Commentary,* Princeton, Princeton University Press, 1989, pp. 94-97, 273. For the most recent treatment of this question and identification of Myos Hormos with Quseir al-Qadim see D.P.S. PEACOCK, "The site of Myos Hormos: a view from space", *JRA* 6, 1993, pp. 226-232 and A. BÜLOW-JACOBSEN *et al.,* "The Identification of Myos Hormos. New Papyrological Evidence", *BIFAO* 94, 1994, pp. 27-38.

(27°22.13' N/33°40.97' E) *c.* 20 km. north of Hurghada and approximately 355 km. south of Suez unearthed a late Roman fort erected (possibly rebuilt), according to a Latin inscription which originally sat over the west gate, in A.D. 309-311.[4] The fort accommodated a mounted *ala.*[5] Sometime before the end of the fourth century the military abandoned the fort. There followed a period of unknown duration when the installation seems to have been uninhabited except, possibly, by the occasional passerby. By the late fourth-early fifth century Christian hermits or monks reoccupied the fort.[6] The *principia* was converted into a church and the main entrance to the site was no longer the larger west gate as it had been during the military occupation, but, rather, the smaller north gate, then adorned with dozens of Christian graffiti, written in Greek, in the form of personal names and crosses together with two more formal ecclesiastical inscriptions.[7] The interior of the fort seems to have housed fewer people in this

---

3. For excavation reports on work at Abu Sha'ar see S.E. SIDEBOTHAM, J.A. RILEY, H.A. HAMROUSH and H. BARAKAT, "Fieldwork on the Red Sea coast: The 1987 Season", *JARCE* 26, 1989, pp. 127-166; S.E. SIDEBOTHAM, "University of Delaware Archaeological Project at 'Abu Sha'ar, The 1990 Season", *NARCE* 153, spring 1991, pp. 1-6; S.E. SIDEBOTHAM, "A Roman Fort on the Red Sea Coast", *Minerva* 3/2, March/April 1992, pp. 5-8; S.E. SIDEBOTHAM, "The 1991 Season of Archaeological Fieldwork at 'Abu Sha'ar (Red Sea Coast), Egypt Conducted by the University of Delaware", *Archaeological News* 17, 1-4, 1992, pp. 31-34; S.E. SIDEBOTHAM, "University of Delaware Archaeological Project at 'Abu Sha'ar: The 1992 Season", *NARCE* 161/162, spring/summer 1993, pp. 1-9; S.E. SIDEBOTHAM, "Preliminary Report on the 1990-1991 Seasons of Fieldwork at 'Abu Sha'ar (Red Sea Coast)", *JARCE* 31, 1994, pp. 133-158; S.E. SIDEBOTHAM, "University of Delaware Fieldwork in the Eastern Desert of Egypt, 1993", *DOP* 48 1994, pp. 263-275; S.E. SIDEBOTHAM, "The Fort at 'Abu Sha'ar", *in* K. BARD, ed., *The Archaeology of Ancient Egypt: An Encyclopedia*, forthcoming. See also R.S. BAGNALL and J.A. SHERIDAN, "Greek and Latin Documents from 'Abu Sha'ar, 1990-1991", *JARCE* 31, 1994, pp. 159-168; R.S. BAGNALL and J.A. SHERIDAN, "Greek and Latin Documents from 'Abu Sha'ar, 1992-1993", *BASP* 31, 1994, pp. 109-120; W.Z. WENDRICH and W. VAN NEER, "Preliminary notes on fishing gear and fish at the late Roman fort at 'Abu Sha'ar (Egyptian Red Sea Coast)", *in* W. VAN NEER, ed., *Fish Exploitation in the Past. Proceedings of the 7th Meeting of the ICAZ Fish Remains Working Group. Annales du Musée Royal de l'Afrique Centrale, Sciences Zoologiques* no. 274, Tervuren, Musée Royal de l'Afrique Centrale, 1994, pp. 183-189. The final report is in preparation.

4. For this inscription see BAGNALL and SHERIDAN, *JARCE* 31 (1994) (*supra* n. 3), pp. 159-163 ; see also R.S. BAGNALL, *Egypt in Late Antiquity,* Princeton, Princeton University Press, 1993, p. 145.

5. BAGNALL and SHERIDAN, *JARCE* 31 (1994) (*supra* n. 3), pp. 162-163. The unit was, in all likelihood, a dromedary and not a cavalry detachment, cf. SIDEBOTHAM, *DOP* 48, 1994 (*supra* n. 3), p. 272, n. 43.

6. SIDEBOTHAM, *DOP* 48, 1994 (*supra* n. 3), pp. 273-275.

7. See SIDEBOTHAM, *NARCE* 161/162, 1993 (*supra* n. 3), pp. 6-7.

later Christian phase than in the earlier military one; much trash was dumped into some rooms which were clearly unoccupied in that later period.[8]

The bath outside the north gate no longer seems to have served that purpose in the later Christian occupation though what function it had at that time (a baptistery?) remains unknown.[9]

Ceramic evidence for the Christian occupation is very difficult to date closely, but it seems to have lasted until the later sixth, less likely, into the early seventh century.[10] It appears by the period of the Muslim Arab invasions of Egypt in the 640s that the fort had already been abandoned for some unknown length of time. It was never reoccupied though the occasional traveller camped here from time to time.[11]

There are several possible explanations for the fort's location at this point on the Red Sea coast. The late third-early fourth centuries witnessed great military activity on the Roman frontiers as Diocletian (A.D. 284-305), his colleagues and immediate successors sought to reorganize defenses. Throughout the empire numerous fortifications were erected and military units reassigned and reorganized in this period.[12] Thus, Abu Sha'ar fits well into the context of

---

8. SIDEBOTHAM, *Archaeological News* (*supra* n. 3), p. 33 ; SIDEBOTHAM, *JARCE* 31, 1994 (*supra* n. 3), p. 156 ; SIDEBOTHAM, *DOP* 48, 1994 (*supra* n. 3), p. 273.

9. SIDEBOTHAM, *DOP* 48, 1994 (*supra* n. 3), pp. 270-272.

10. SIDEBOTHAM, *JARCE* 31, 1994 (*supra* n. 3), p. 156 ; SIDEBOTHAM, *DOP* 48, 1994 (*supra* n. 3), pp. 273-274.

11. SIDEBOTHAM *DOP* 48, 1994 (*supra* n. 3), p. 274.

12. For Tetrarchic-Constantinian military reforms in general see A.H.M. JONES, *The Later Roman Empire 284-602,* Norman, University of Oklahoma Press, 1964, pp. 52-60, 97-101, 607-609; D. VAN BERCHEM, *L'Armée de Dioclétien et la réforme constantinienne,* Institut français d'Archéologie de Beyrouth, Bibliothèque archéologique et historique, vol LVI, Paris, Imprimerie nationale-Libràirie Orientaliste Paul Geuthner, 1952, *passim,* for Egypt pp. 59-71, Map IV; D. VAN BERCHEM *in* S. APPLEBAUM, ed., *Roman Frontier Studies 1967. The Proceedings of the Seventh International Congress of Roman Frontier Studies held at Tel Aviv,* Tel Aviv, Students' Organization of Tel Aviv University, 1971, pp. 123-127; A.K. BOWMAN, "The Military Occupation of Upper Egypt in the Reign of Diocletian", *BASP* 15, 1-2, 1978, pp. 25-38; B. ISAAC, *Limits of Empire. The Roman Army in the East,* Oxford, Clarendon Press, 1990, pp. 162-171; S.E. SIDEBOTHAM, "A *Limes* in the Eastern Desert of Egypt: Myth or Reality?", *in* V.A. MAXFIELD and M.J. DOBSON, eds, *Roman Frontier Studies 1989. Proceedings of the XVth International Congress of Roman Frontier Studies*, Exeter, University of Exeter Press, 1991, pp. 494-497; S.E. SIDEBOTHAM, "Römische Straßen in der ägyptischen Wüste", *Antike Welt* 22/3, p. 1991, pp. 177-189; for Egypt and elsewhere in the East see J.-M. CARRIÉ, "Les *Castra Dionysiados* et l'évolution de l'architecture militaire romaine tardive", *MEFRA* 86/2, p. 1974, p. 837; U.A. WARETH and P. ZIGNANI, "Nag Al-Hagar. A Fortress with a Palace of the Late Roman Empire Second Preliminary Report", *BIFAO* 92, 1992, pp. 185-210; SIDEBOTHAM, *JARCE* 31, 1994 (*supra* n. 3), p. 158, n. 59-68.

these times. In part its purpose was, undoubtedly, to monitor movements of peoples in the adjacent desert, along the coast and on the sea lanes. The (re)dedicatory inscription over the west gate mentions *mercator(um)* suggesting that the fort served some economic function probably related to the revival of the Red Sea-Indian Ocean trade.[13] A graffito found at the west gate reinforces this interpretation.[14]

Abandonment by the military and later reoccupation by Christians also fits a pattern found elsewhere in the Roman east at that date.[15] Remote in the desert complete with defensive structures and a nearby water supply it is hardly surprising that early monastic (cenobitic)-oriented Christians would occupy the installation. It was in an ideal location to facilitate Christian pilgrim movements between Upper Egypt, the monasteries in the Eastern Desert (*e.g.* St. Antony's and St. Paul's), onward sea travel to Sinai for St. Catherine's Monastery or to Aila and thence to the Jerusalem area. The installation at Abu Sha'ar was itself a pilgrimage center. Human adult male bones wrapped in cloth found in front of the altar inside the church[16] indicate that Abu Sha'ar was a shrine to some unknown martyr or saint, a common practice in Coptic Christian Egypt at that date.[17]

An artesian well *c.* 1 km. west of Abu Sha'ar provided water to the main fort via an underground conduit made of terracotta pipes. This was in use in the military period and seems to have continued to function, based upon ceramic evidence, during the Christian occupation.[18]

About 5.5-6 km. west of Abu Sha'ar, at the foot of Gebel Abu Sha'ar is a small fortified water station (*hydreuma*) (27°22.14' N/33°37.98' E) connected by a rubble and mortar water pipeline *c.* 500 metres long to wells at Bir Abu Sha'ar el-Qibli. Occupants of the *hydreuma* used the water for irrigation of agricultural

13. SHERIDAN and BAGNALL, *JARCE* 31, 1994 (*supra* n. 3), pp. 162-163.

14. BAGNALL and SHERIDAN, *BASP* (*supra* n. 3), p. 112.

15. For Judaea see Y. HIRSCHFELD, *The Judean Monasteries in the Byzantine Period*, New Haven, Yale University Press, 1992, pp. 47-54.

16. SIDEBOTHAM, *JARCE* 31, 1994 (*supra* n. 3), p. 138, 158.

17. J. KAMIL, *Coptic Church History and Guide,* revised ed., Cairo, The American University in Cairo Press, 1990, p. 78; cf. P. MAYERSON, "An Inscription in the Monastery of St. Catherine and the Martyr Tradition in Sinai", *DOP* 30, 1976, pp. 375-379; A. PIETERSMA and S.T. COMSTOCK, "Coptic Martyrdoms in the Chester Beatty Library", *BASP* 24, 3-4, 1987, pp. 143-163.

18. The well is 27°21.92' N/33°40. 42' E ; see SIDEBOTHAM, *DOP* 48, 1994 (*supra* n. 3), pp. 267-268.

land, no doubt to supply food for themselves and for the main military garrison and, later, the Christian inhabitants, of Abu Sha'ar.[19]

Some animals and, possibly, humans may have drunk the water, but it is, now, too brackish for human consumption; farmers today still use water from these wells to irrigate their crops.

Indeed, the placement of the late Roman fort at Abu Sha'ar may well have been dictated, in part, by knowledge of the existence of these wells and the small *hydreuma* nearby long before the fourth century. The *hydreuma* near Bir Abu Sha'ar el-Qibli was a station on the second century Via Hadriana remains of which we found nearby.[20] Ostraca from the site confirm occupation by the early second century.[21] We do not know whether the Via Hadriana was continuously used from the time of its construction in the first half of the second century A.D. until late antiquity. Poor preservation of the *hydreuma* at Bir Abu Sha'ar el-Qibli and relative dearth of artifacts did not allow us to determine if occupation of this small installation was continuous from the second century into the period of Christian occupation of the main fort at Abu Sha'ar or whether there were periods of abandonment which, like the main fort at Abu Sha'ar, punctuated its history.[22]

---

19. Postulated by SIDEBOTHAM, *JARCE* 31, 1994 (*supra* n. 3), p. 157; see also SIDEBOTHAM, *DOP* 31, 1994 (*supra* n. 3), 267 and n. 14; cf. R. MACMULLEN, *Soldier and Civilian in the Later Roman Empire,* Cambridge, MA, Harvard University Press, 1963, pp. 1-22. For parallels among early Christian monastic settlements in the desert and modern Bedouin practices see WILKINSON 1832 (*supra* n. 2), p. 31 and O.F.A. MEINARDUS, *Monks and Monasteries of the Egyptian Deserts,* revised ed., Cairo, The American University in Cairo Press, 1989, p. 19 for gardens in St. Anthony's monastery ; for gardens in St. Paul's monastery see WILKINSON, pp. 34-35 and MEINARDUS, p. 40. For Ma'aza Bedouin desert gardens see J.J. HOBBS, *Bedouin Life in the Egyptian Wilderness,* Austin, University of Texas Press, 1989, pp. 45-46. Sidebotham saw one of these desert plots in the Wādi al-Ghuzza when taken there by Zaid Faraj Suleiman on August 2, 1991; G.W. MURRAY, "Water from the Desert: Some Ancient Egyptian Achievements", *GJ* 121, 1955, pp. 171-181; for Sinai A. KINGLAKE, *Eothen,* Oxford-New York, Oxford University Press (reprint 1982), pp. 232-233 and A. PEREVOLOTSKY, "Orchard Agriculture in the High Mountain Region of Southern Sinai", *Human Ecology* 9/3, 1981, pp. 331-357.

20. Traces of the Via Hadriana near the small *hydreuma* are at 27°22.36' N/33°37.71' E; see SIDEBOTHAM, *DOP* 48, 1994 (*supra* n. 3), pp. 266-267.

21. SIDEBOTHAM, *DOP* 48, 1994 (*supra* n. 3), pp. 265, 266-267; BAGNALL and SHERIDAN, *BASP* 31, 1994 (*supra* n. 3), pp. 116-119.

22. These periods of potential abandonment might have occurred sometime between the early second and fourth centuries (before the occupation of the main fort at Abu Sha'ar), and, thereafter, may have coincided with the military abandonment of the main fort in the late fourth-early fifth century and, again, after the Christian abandonment of the main fort at Abu Sha'ar in the late sixth/early seventh century.

BERENIKE AND ENVIRONS

A joint University of Delaware-Leiden University expedition at Berenike has completed two seasons of survey and excavation (1994 and 1995).[23] A number of ancient authors and ostraca mention the port — (23°54.62' N/35°28.42' E) *c.* 800 km. south of Suez and *c.* 260 km. east of Aswan — as a prominent one in the lucrative Red Sea-Indian Ocean trade.[24] The emporium was a principal western terminus in the world's first extensive commercial maritime network connecting East Asia, South Asia, Arabia, coastal sub-Saharan Africa, the Red Sea and the Mediterranean. The site covers *c.* 2 km^2 with the densest area of occupation encompassing *c.* 7 hectares. An extensive road network radiated to/from Berenike enhancing its importance both as a commercial as well as an administrative center.[25]

Although we recovered some bronze coins of Ptolemy II Philadelphus during excavations in 1995, we have yet to confirm, archaeologically, Pliny the Elder's (*Natural History* 6.33.168) foundation date of the third century B.C. (*c.* 275 B.C.) for the port. Results from the 1994 and 1995 seasons suggest that Berenike was occupied, if not used as a port, into the sixth century A.D. The slight amount of evidence recovered so far points to continuous habitation

---

23. S.E. Sidebotham and W.Z. Wendrich are co-directors of this project.

24. Ancient sources on Berenike include: Strabo, *Geography* 2.5.12, 16.4.4 ff., 17.1.13, 17.1.45; Pliny the Elder, *Natural History* 6.24:84-85, 6.26.101, 12.30.54, 12.32.63-65, 12.41.84, 12.42.85 ff., *Periplus Maris Erythraei* 1, 2, 18, 19, 21; *Petrie Ostraca* nos. 195-304 (= TAIT [*supra* n. 1], pp. 106-125). Diodorus Siculus 3.39.3 and Agatharchides 5.84b (= BURSTEIN [*supra* n. 1], pp. 137-138) both refer to Cape Ras Benas just north of Berenike and the practice of dragging ships across that peninsula. For a similar *diolkos* at Corinth see D. ENGELS, *Roman Corinth,* Chicago, University of Chicago Press, 1990, pp. 58-59.

25. For road networks leading from Berenike northwest towards Apollinopolis Magna (Edfu) and Coptos (Qift): see Pliny the Elder, *Natural History* 6.26.102-103; Claudius Ptolemy, *Geography* 4.5.8; *Tabula Imperii Romani*, segment VIII; *Itinerarium Antoniniana* 171.5-173.4; *Ravenna Cosmography* 2.7; S.E. SIDEBOTHAM *in* S.E. SIDEBOTHAM and W.Z. WENDRICH *et al.*, eds, *Berenike 1994. Preliminary Report of the 1994 Excavations at Berenike (Egyptian Red Sea Coast) and the Survey of the Eastern Desert,* Leiden, CNWS, 1995, pp. 85-101; S.E. SIDEBOTHAM and R.E. ZITTERKOPF, "Routes Through the Eastern Desert of Egypt" *Expedition* 37/2, 1995, pp. 39-52. For the road (Via Hadriana) leading north along the Red Sea coast and eventually to Antinoë: see SIDEBOTHAM, *DOP* 48 (1994) (*supra* n. 3), pp. 266-267 and n. 11-13 for bibliography; for roads leading to the southwest towards the forts in Wadi Kalalat, Shenshef, Hitan Rayan: see SIDEBOTHAM *in* SIDEBOTHAM and WENDRICH (1995), pp. 87-98 and S.E. SIDEBOTHAM and R.E. ZITTERKOPF, "The Survey", *in* S.E. SIDEBOTHAM and W.Z. WENDRICH, eds, *Berenike 1995. Preliminary Report of the 1995 Excavations at Berenike (Egyptian Red Sea Coast) and the Survey of the Eastern Desert,* Leiden, CNWS, 1996. For the importance of Berenike as an administrative center see SIDEBOTHAM *in* MAXFIELD and DOBSON (*supra* n. 12), pp. 494-497.

between the putative third century B.C. foundation and the apparent sixth century A.D. abandonment. The size of the emporium in different periods most certainly also varied reflecting the waxing and waning of the maritime commerce which passed through it.

The port, in addition to being a conduit for commodities imported and exported between the Mediterranean and the Red Sea-Indian Ocean basins, was also a manufacturing center. Metals (iron and copper) glass and beads, were produced here though whether for local or export consumption cannot be determined at this point. The discovery of a Tamil-Brahmi graffito of the first century A.D., an Indian textile, a possible Indian sherd and sorghum, rice and peppercorns found in the excavations in 1994 and 1995 provide evidence of commerce between Berenike and India spanning the early to late Roman periods. The recovery of a garbled "South-Arabian/Axumite" ostracon of *c.* A.D. 400 and the presence of coconut shells and shell bangles in fifth-sixth century contexts also indicates continued contact between Berenike and other areas of the Red Sea-Indian Ocean littoral in late antiquity.

Excavations at Berenike in 1994 and 1995 suggested that the Blemmyes may have resided in the city in the fifth-sixth centuries A.D., a time when they are known to have occupied portions of the desert between Berenike and the Nile.[26]

There is questionable literary evidence that Berenike was the seat of a Christian bishop in the fourth-fifth century though given the rapid Christianization of Egypt and Nubia at that time such a possibility cannot be ruled out.[27] The discovery of a fourth century Christian cross graffito scratched on the bottom of a terracotta lamp found on the surface of the site in 1995 suggests a Christian presence at the port at that time.

---

26. See Olympiodorus, *History* fragment 35.2 *in* R.C. BLOCKLEY, *The Fragmentary Classicizing Historians of the Later Roman Empire* II, Liverpool, Francis Cairns, 1983, pp. 198-199; Priscus, fragments 27.1-2 *in* BLOCKLEY, *ibid.*, pp. 322-325; Procopius, *History of the Wars* 1.19.28-36; Ammianus Marcellinus 14.4.3, 22.15.24; cf. discussion *in* SIDEBOTHAM and WENDRICH 1995 (*supra* n. 25), pp. 8-10, 41-43, 105-106 and SIDEBOTHAM and WENDRICH 1996 (*supra* n. 25). See also R.T. UPDEGRAFF, "The Blemmyes I: The Rise of the Blemmyes and the Roman Withdrawal from Nubia Under Diocletian", *ANRW* 2.10.1, 1988, p. 71 and n. 167. Cf. SIDEBOTHAM and WENDRICH 1996 (*supra* n. 25).

27. On the questionable literary evidence for a bishop at Berenike see G. GABRA, "Bemerkungen zu den Aussagen des arabischen Synaxars der Kopten über Nabis, den Bischof von 'Aidab", *in* M. KRAUSE, ed., *Nubische Studien Tatungsakten der 5. Internationalen Konferenz der International Society for Nubian Studies Heidelberg, 22.-25. September 1982*, Mainz, Philipp von Zabern, 1986, pp. 231-236. For the rapid Christianization of Egypt in the fourth century see R.S. BAGNALL, *Egypt in Late Antiquity* (*supra* n. 4), pp. 278-289; cf. F. ALTHEIM and R. STIEHL, *Christentum am Roten Meer,* vol. 2, Berlin-New York, Walter de Gruyter, 1973, pp. 303-332 for Nubia and the Blemmyes.

SURVEY OF THE EASTERN DESERT

The survey work we have undertaken has had some important results. We have visited many scores of ancient (mainly Ptolemaic, Roman and Byzantine) sites, recorded their locations as precisely as modern Global Positioning System (GPS) technology allows, drawn (and continue to draw) very accurate plans of dozens of sites with remains surviving above ground (forts, *hydreumata,* watering points, and settlements) and dated all sites mainly through surface artifact (essentially ceramic) analysis.[28] These sites and roads linked various Nile emporia to their counterparts on the Red Sea coast and/or to various mines, quarries and *hydreumata* in the Eastern Desert. Our goal is to have as complete a picture as possible of activity in the entire region between the Nile and the Red Sea coast from the Wadis Sha'ayb-'Araba (the paved road between Al-Kraymant on the Nile and Za'afarana on the Red Sea) in the north to the Sudanese border in the Ptolemaic-Roman-Byzantine period.

We have revisited the majority of the sites recorded by travellers since the early nineteenth century and have, in addition, found several dozen new sites previously unrecorded by any « western » visitors. We have also plotted hundreds of route marking cairns, signal towers and road segments. We have determined, for example, that the course of the route from Berenike to Edfu in the segment close to Edfu is, in fact, different from the one which traditionally appears in earlier publications.[29] There was substantial Ptolemaic activity in the Eastern Desert especially in gold mining regions and along roads between Berenike and Apollinopolis Magna (Edfu) and between Marsa Nakari (Nechesia?) and Apollinopolis Magna.[30] Undoubtedly, there was more activity

---

28. Dr. R.E. Zitterkopf, Dr. Hans Barnard and Mr. Brian Cannon were architects for these surveys. For results of the University of Delaware Eastern Desert surveys see R.E. ZITTERKOPF and S.E. SIDEBOTHAM, "Stations and Towers on the Quseir-Nile Road", *JEA* 75, 1989, pp. 155-189; S.E. SIDEBOTHAM, R.E. ZITTERKOPF and J.A. RILEY, "Survey of the 'Abu Sha'ar-Nile Road", *AJA* 95/4, 1991, pp. 571-622; SIDEBOTHAM *in* SIDEBOTHAM and WENDRICH 1995 (*supra* n. 25), pp. 85-101; SIDEBOTHAM and ZITTERKOPF *in Expedition* (*supra* n. 25), pp. 39-52; SIDEBOTHAM and ZITTERKOPF *in* SIDEBOTHAM and WENDRICH 1996 (*supra* n. 25).

29. Eg. G.W. MURRAY, "The Roman Roads and Stations in the Eastern Desert of Egypt", *JEA* 11, 1925, map on plate XI and D. MEREDITH, *Tabula Imperii Romani Sheet N.G. 36 Coptos* (*supra* n. 2), map sheet; they have the route passing from Abu Midrik to el-Kanaïs south of Abu Rahal. In fact, the route passes through Abu Rahal and Abu Rahal West before reaching el-Kanaïs.

30. For gold mines see R. KLEMM and D.D. KLEMM, "Chronologischer Abriß der antiken Goldgewinnung in der Ostwüste Ägyptens", *MDAIK* 50, 1994, pp. 206-211; for the Berenike-Edfu road see SIDEBOTHAM and ZITTERKOPF, *Expedition* (*supra* n. 25), pp. 45-48; for the putative Marsa Nakari-Edfu road see S.E. SIDEBOTHAM, "The

in the region in the Ptolemaic period, but evidence of those endeavours has probably been erased somewhat, overlain by later Roman and Byzantine construction.

There was a substantial increase in activity in the Eastern Desert in the early Roman period. Most sites we have studied during this extensive survey provide ceramic evidence of first-second century A.D. activity/occupation. There are indications of activity at some sites into the third century, but an upsurge in the fourth and subsequent centuries. Some sites seem to have been built and occupied only in this later period (fourth century on).

Clearly, the late Roman/Byzantine period was one of continued extensive mining and quarrying in and travel and trade with and through both the desert and the Red Sea coast (*e.g.* at Berenike, Marsa Nakari, Abu Sha'ar and Clysma-Qolzoum-Cleopatris-Suez).[31]

The desert sites were, by necessity, dependent upon the Red Sea coast and Nile valley for supplies and manpower. The degree of that dependency, on supplies at least, may not have been as great, in many cases, as previously believed. The situation at Abu Sha'ar described above is a case in point. I suspect that if any one of these other desert sites were examined extensively in a concerted campaign of excavation and regional survey that many will be shown to have produced a sizeable amount of their own food requirements.

CONCLUSION

We have made progress in the study of Hellenistic, Roman and Byzantine era sites and road networks in the Eastern Desert and along the Red Sea coast, but much remains to be done. Given the rapid growth of tourism and encroachment of Egypt's rapidly burgeoning population into the desert areas our research takes on new urgency as the ancient sites come under increasing assault by man. We must accelerate our survey and excavation programme to record as much as possible before many of these sites cease to exist.

Steven E. SIDEBOTHAM

Roman Frontier in the Eastern Desert of Egypt", *Proceedings of the XVI International Congress of Roman Frontier Studies 1995*, forthcoming.

31. For late Roman-Byzantine activity in the Eastern Desert see SIDEBOTHAM (*supra* n. 30), forthcoming.

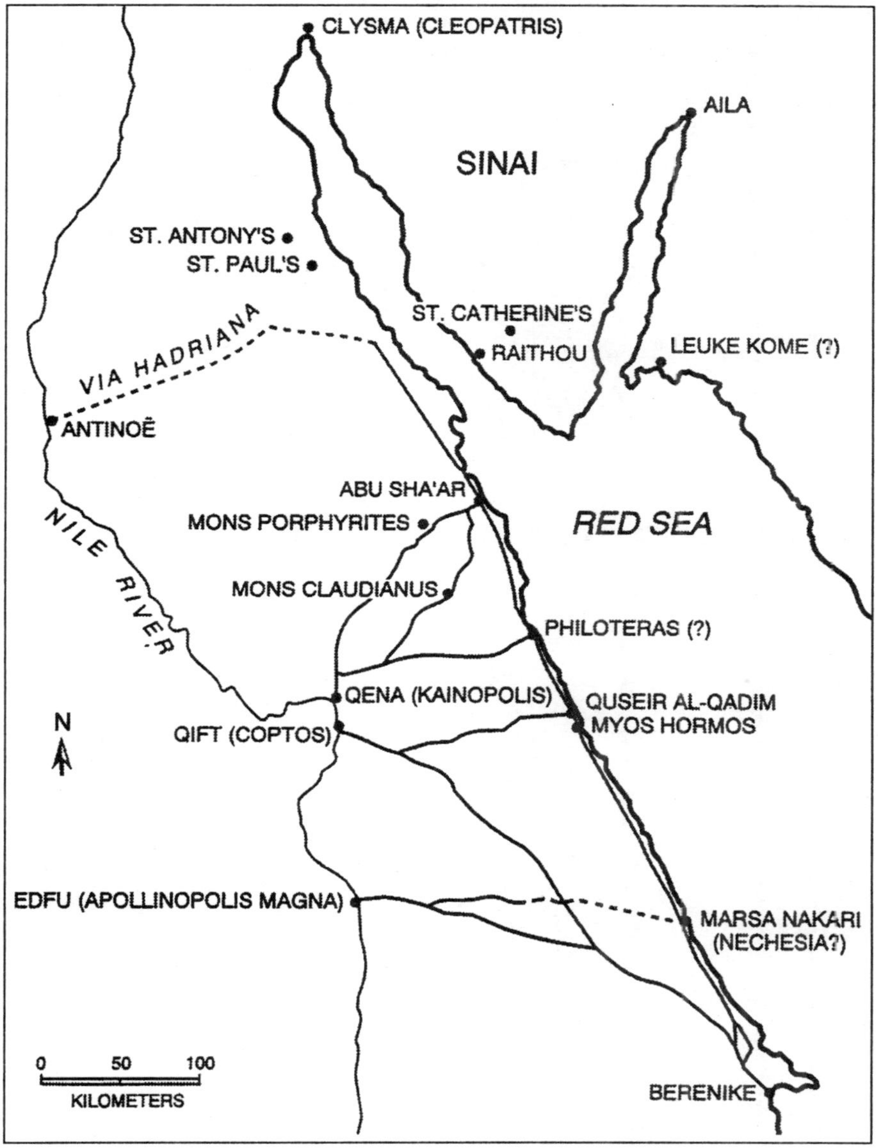

Fig. 1 — The Red Sea Coast in Ptolemaic-Roman-Byzantine Times

FROM THE MEDITERRANEAN TO THE INDIAN OCEAN EGYPT AND LONG DISTANCE TRADE IN THE ROMAN PERIOD: THE EVIDENCE OF THE CERAMICS

The present article is the result of field research conducted in Egypt and the Eastern Desert on long distance trade in Roman times.

It is an attempt to take stock of the knowledge about the origin of pottery found in the Eastern Desert of Egypt (*fig. 1*). All caravans going from the Nile to the Red Sea ports had to pass through the Eastern Desert. This became one of the major trade routes linking the Mediterranean system to the Red Sea and the straits zone bounded on the west by North-East Africa and on the east by "Blessed Arabia".

One of the results of the annexation of Egypt to the Roman Empire in 30 B.C., and its coming under the direct control of Augustus in 27 B.C. was the development of trade with the Far-East. The Nile, the Eastern Desert and the Red Sea became the main routes for approaching the Indian Ocean and it was possible to give up the hazardous routes through the Syrian hinterland and the northern part of the Arabian Peninsula.

The Ptolemies had already tried to develop the Red Sea ports,[1] thus avoiding the lands controlled by the belligerent Seleucids, in their efforts to trade with the Far-East. Archaeological evidence relating to the Hellenistic period is still quite meagre. In all the settlements in the Eastern Desert, with the exception of the quarries of Wādi Hammamat which have been explored for a long time and where recent excavations have revealed levels ranging from the end of the

---

1. P.M. FRAZER, *Ptolemaic Alexandria*, I, Oxford, 1972, pp 173-184, presents a detailed picture of the trade between Egypt and the countries of the South and the East; H. CUVIGNY, "Alexandrie, ville nouvelle", *ROMM* 46, 1987-4, pp. 25-27; S.E. SIDEBOTHAM, "Ports of the Red Sea and the Arabia-India Trade", *Rome and India. The Ancient Sea Trade*, Oxford University Press, 1992, pp. 12-38.

A Gateway from the Eastern Mediterranean to India. The Red Sea in Antiquity
P. BALLET, pp. 117-147

Late Dynastic Period to the end of the Early Roman Empire,[2] only a few pieces of Hellenistic pottery were found at Samut situated on the road from Edfu (Apollonopolis Magna) to Berenike.[3]

From Egypt, the survey was extended to the zone of the straits and the shores of the Indian Ocean (*fig. 2*). Two modest settlements in the Horn of Africa, al-Heis and Damo, on the coast of former Somaliland, provided a small amount of glassware and pottery.[4] Though there was only a small quantity of pottery, it adds to our knowledge about goods that crossed through the region of the straits. The *emporion* of Qana (Bir'Ali) — situated on the southern coast of the Arabian Peninsula washed by the Indian Ocean and therefore closer to the borders of the Far-East and the Indian sub-continent — allows us to appreciate the extreme diversity of the different groups of pottery and their varied origins.

One of the main questions pertains to the diverse origins and the volume of the products involved in this trade. Pottery, which testifies to its existence, is but one aspect. It does not necessarily imply a linear movement covering the distance from the starting to the finishing point. Actually, the movement was far more complex and we have to take into account coastal and inland navigation, transit and redistribution points: in other words, the various intermediate stages which make it more difficult to define trade routes.

I. The Eastern Desert of Egypt and its Sea Ports (*fig. 1*)[5]

It is necessary to have a list of the Egyptian imports and products manufactured in the workshops in the Valley to understand trade during the Roman period. It enables us to appreciate the importance of international, national and regional trade flows.

We will give an idea of the major sites in the Eastern Egyptian Desert, most of which go back to the Early Roman Empire.

---

2. IFAO excavations conducted in 1987 and 1988 under the supervision of A. Gasse.

3. *Infra.*

4. J. DESANGES, M. STERN & P. BALLET, *Sur les routes antiques de l'Azanie et de l'Inde. Le fonds Révoil du Musée de l'Homme (Heïs et Samo en Somali)*, MAIB (N.S.) XIII, 1993.

5. For an appraisal of the question and a preliminary inventory of the settlements in the Eastern Desert, M. REDDÉ & J.-Cl. GOLVIN, "Du Nil à la Mer Rouge: documents anciens et nouveaux sur les routes du désert oriental d'Égypte", *Karthago* 21, 1987, pp. 5-64.

Excavations were recently carried out in three settlements. The **Mons Claudianus,** which is being printed[6] at present, describes one of the major Roman settlements where an extensive programme of excavation and investigation was undertaken. These granodiorite quarries provided durable building material to construction sites in the western world, especially Rome.[7] None of the pottery found here seems to have been produced locally and imports from the Mediterranean region are few.[8] Most of the fine pottery, as well as the common ware and amphorae came from the Nile Valley. Two groups were subjected to a detailed study.[9] Some pieces of the fine red-slipped ware found here have shapes that were popular in the Mediterranean region during the Roman Empire. Amphorae with bifed handles, probably from the Maryut region, are imitations of post-Koan and Italic amphorae (Dressel 2-4). There is in addition a group of brown bitroconical amphorae made of alluvial clay from the Valley (Thebes region or Middle Egypt). They constitute the biggest group in the assemblage and show some resemblance to the amphorae of Al-Zarqa which probably came from the same production centres.

On the road connecting Coptos (Quft) to Myos Hormos (Qosseir), "the isthmus of Coptos",[10] **Al-Zarqa** is one of the military posts (*praesidium*) that supervised caravans travelling on this road. We refer our readers to J.-P. Brun's recent article[11] which gives detailed information and enriches our knowledge about the pottery of the Eastern Desert. We find that imports were very limited amounting to just about 1% of the material found whereas Egyptian pottery abounds. There are brown amphorae, water-jugs and "fine" pottery probably exported by the workshops of Upper Egypt — the Thebes region, to be more

---

6. J. BINGEN, "Première campagne de fouille au Mons Claudianus. Rapport préliminaire", *BIFAO* 87, 1987, pp. 45-52; J. BINGEN *et alii*, "Quatrième campagne de fouilles au Mons Claudianus. Rapport préliminaire", *BIFAO* 90, 1990, pp. 65-81; J. BINGEN, A. BÜLOW-JACOBSEN, W.E.H. COCKLE, H. RUBINSTEIN & W. VAN RENGEN, *Mons Claudianus. Ostraca graeca et latina, I (O. Claud. 1 to 90), Doc. FIFAO* 29, 1992. We will mention below the preliminary articles dealing with the pottery discovered in Mons Claudianus studied by R. Tomber. The entire material on pottery will be published in one volume which is being prepared at present.

7. D.P.S. PEACOCK, "The Roman quarries of Mons Claudianus, Egypt. An interim report", in N. HERTZ & M. WAELKEN (eds), *Classical Marble, Geochemistry, Technology, Trade*, Dordrecht, 1988, pp. 97-102.

8. R. TOMBER, "Mons Claudianus", *BCE* 13, 1988, pp. 35-37; *id.*, "Mons Claudianus", *BCE* 14, 1990, pp. 26-27.

9. R. TOMBER, "Early Roman Pottery from Mons Claudianus", *CCE* 3, 1992, pp. 137-142.

10. Strabo, 17, 1, 45.

11. J.-P. BRUN, "Le faciès céramique d'Al-Zarqa. Observations préliminaires", *BIFAO* 94, 1994, pp. 7-26.

precise. Several categories of fine pottery from Aswan, typical of the Early Roman Empire, are seen among them.

The occupation of **Wādi Hammamat** goes far beyond this chronological framework. *Bekhen* and other kinds of stones were quarried here from the Old Kingdom onwards. During the excavations carried out by IFAO in 1987 and 1988 the base of rockfaces was uncovered and it was possible to go down to levels dating back to ancient times.[12] It was found that it was occupied at two different periods. One phase went back to the very end of the Late Dynastic Period or even to the very beginning of the Hellenistic period while the second could be dated to the Early Roman Empire. Pottery was conveyed from the Valley, the Thebes region being the main source followed by the workshops of the first cataract which provided a smaller amount. The few imports consisted mainly of *Eastern Sigillata* ware.

We will take a quick look at the material from **Quseir al-Qadim (Myos Hormos)**,[13] the seaport on the road connecting Coptos and the Nile to the Red Sea. Technical indications mentioned in the publication do not always give any indication about the source of the pottery except for some pieces where the morphology by itself is enough to recognise the production group. However, Egyptian pottery from the Valley seems to predominate whereas imports are larger than those found in sites in the heart of the desert.[14]

The road from **Coptos** to **Berenike** was explored in 1987 and 1988.[15] The principal sites uncovered were situated on the caravan route going south-east from Lakeita towards the port of Berenike. These sites were Bir Daghbag, Bir Abu Qreiya (Iovis), Bir Beizah, Wadi Gerf, Wadi Dweig and Wadi Gemal. A second road coming from Edfu (Apollonopolis Magna) and joining the Lakeita-Berenike road at Wādi Dweig was also explored and the most noteworthy settlements discovered were those of al-Kanaïs and Samut.

Some pieces of pottery were collected during these exploratory visits. The results obtained after a preliminary study[16] reveal a great similarity to the

---

12. Its purpose was to find out if there were any inscriptions on the lower level of the working face obstructed from view by heaps of rock and rubble.

13. D.S. WHITCOMB & J.H. JOHNSON, *Quseir al-Qadim 1978. Preliminary Report*, ARCE, Princeton, 1980; *ead., Quseir al-Qadim 1980. Preliminary Report*, ARCE Reports 7, 1982.

14. We will discuss their origin in the following paragraphs.

15. The team included J.-Cl. Golvin, S. Hegazy, M. Reddé, M. el-Saghir and R. Vergnieux.

16. The documentation deposited in the Franco-Egyptian Centre in Karnak was examined in 1989.

potteries found in sites along the northern route going from Coptos to Quseir (Myos Hormos) and those on the southern route going to Berenike on the Red Sea coast.

I.1. About the Origin of Pottery in the Eastern Desert. The Workshops (*fig. 3*)[17]

The Workshops of Aswan

The workshops of Aswan were among the largest exporters of pottery in the Eastern Desert.[18] Based on the use of kaolinitic clay, associated with the granite complex of the first cataract, the light coloured products of Aswan made of fine clay are attested as far back as the Hellenistic period.[19] Nevertheless, it was during the Early Roman period that the manufacture of pottery from kaolinitic clay developed considerably. A recently discovered workshop on the western bank of Aswan[20] was one of the production centres during the Early Roman period. Aswan pottery was then distributed all over the country and particularly in the Eastern Desert.

Fine pottery (*fig. 4-6*) such as jugs accompanied by kettles and, more rarely, cooking pots are regularly found in the Eastern Desert from Wādi Hammamat (*fig. 4*) to Quseir al-Qadim, passing through al-Zarqa[21] and on the road from Coptos to Berenike (Bir Abu Qreiya, Bir Beizah Wādi Gerf) (*fig. 5*).

---

17. A paper analysing Egyptian workshops and products during the Hellenistic and Roman periods can be found in P. BALLET, "Céramiques hellénistiques et romaines d'Égypte", *Céramiques hellénistiques et romaines*, III, edited by P. Lévêque & J.-P. Morel (being printed).

18. Apart from the articles dealing with the detection of workshops and the spread of pottery made in Aswan mentioned below, there is a recent monograph on the pottery of Elephantine from the Early Roman period to the early years of the Arab conquest by R.D. GEMPELER, *Elephantine X. Die Keramik römischer bis früharabischer Zeit, Archäologische Veroffentlichungen* 43, 1992.

19. M. RODZIEWICZ, "Field Notes from Elephantine on the Early Aswan Pink Clay Pottery", *CCE* 3, 1992, pp. 103-107. Pottery belonging to the pharaonic period is made of alluvial clay.

20. P. BALLET, F. MAHMOUD, M. VICHY, M. PICON, "Artisanat de la céramique dans l'Égypte romaine tardive et byzantine. Prospections d'ateliers de potiers de Minia à Assouan", *CCE* 2, 1991, p. 142; P. BALLET & M. VICHY, "Artisanat de la céramique dans l'Égypte hellénistique et romaine. Ateliers du Delta, d'Assouan et de Kharga", *CCE* 3, 1992, pp. 113-116.

21. BRUN, *op. cit.*; group A, p. 14, fig. 7; group P, p. 20, fig. 11, may be added.

But their source has not been always recognised and it is necessary to identify some of the fine wares and jugs found in Quseir al-Qadim[22] as products of the first cataract. Potteries of category P from al-Zarqa[23] can also be classified as originating from Aswan. Of course, the colours varying from light brown to beige are noticeably different from the usual shades of syenitic clay which makes it more difficult to identify them. However, colour variations verging on beige are often characteristic of the Aswan group and probably a result of overfiring. Similarly, a bowl with a head painted on the inner bottom[24] matches perfectly with the well-known series of "bowls with a dancer" (*fig. 6*)[25] and originates from Aswan without a shadow of a doubt. There is no doubt that these potteries were manufactured for export.

The origin of bowls with barbotine decoration continues to be uncertain. In Egypt, they are of two types. The first type found in Al-Zarqa is made of very fine, compact and slightly micaceous alluvial clay ranging in colour from brown to red, but the workshop is not known.[26] The second type made of kaolinitic clay and ranging in colour from pink to beige definitely comes from the workshops of Aswan and is recognised as such in Mons Claudianus.[27]

We must mention in particular the amphorae of Aswan, especially those of the "type from the workshop of the Aga Khan" with a hollow ring-shaped base

---

22. There is no doubt that the "bowl with the dancer" was definitely from Aswan as pointed out by WHITCOMB & JOHNSON, *Quseir al-Qadim 1978*, pl. 26, e, as also the jugs and kettles only the top part of which often exist, *ibid*, pl. 23, e, pl. 30, f, pl. 31, c. These recipients bearing marks of fire are found in other parts of Egypt (Douch/Kysis, Umm al-Brigat/Tebtynis) and they were also products for export.

23. J.-P. BRUN, "Le faciès céramique d'Al-Zarqa. Observations préliminaires", *BIFAO* 94, 1994, p. 20, fig. 11.

24. *Ibid*, p. 20, fig. 11, p. 1.

25. The article by H. JACQUET-GORDON, "A Group of Egyptian Figure Painted Bowls of the Roman Period", *Mélanges Gamal Eddin Mokhtar, Bd'E* XCVII/1, 1985, pp. 409-417, does not recognise the use of kaolinitic clay or that these bowls originate from Aswan. The hypotheses on p. 417 claiming that they are the products of a workshop in Fayum or in Middle Egypt must be rejected. One of the pieces comes from Quseir, WHITCOMB & JOHNSON, *Quseir al-Qadim 1978*, p. 84, e, E 7a-9, pl. 26, e. Another specimen found in Schedia (Kôm Giza), Alexandria's domestic customs post, can be added to the series of "bowls with dancer" (OAE excavations; unpublished).

26. BRUN, *op. cit.*, group M, p. 20, fig. 11. Should this type be linked with the bowls wirh barbotine decoration of Mons Claudianus which, according to me, are from Aswan?

27. R. TOMBER, "Mons Claudianus", *BCE* XIV (1990), pp. 26-27. We hesitate to identify the exact origin of the barbotine wares of Quseir which could quite easily have come from Aswan, WHITCOMB and JOHNSON, *Quseir al-Qadim 1978*, pl. 22, a; pl. 23, f; pl. 24, c; pl. 32, a.

(*fig. 7*).[28] Dating back to the Early Roman Empire, they are found in small quantities in the Eastern Desert. Though absent from the finds of al-Zarqa, the amphorae of Aswan dating from the Early Roman Empire are found sporadically in Wādi Hammamat. Also found along the southern road from Coptos to Berenike, in Bir Abu Qreiya and also in Bir Beizah, they are very small in number. They should be considered as an occasional export to the Eastern Desert as distinguished from a regular commercial flow.[29]

The Workshops of Upper Egypt – from Thebes to Coptos

This region is known for its pottery made from calcareous clay. Right from the Middle Kingdom, if not earlier,[30] the workshops of Thebes used calcareous clay[31] which acquired a light colour after firing. The geological conditions were favourable, layers of clay being placed between stratified levels of the calcareous plateau and also due to the banks of clay deposited by torrential streams at the mouth of wādis in the Valley. In addition, there is another type of pottery made from silty clay whose colour ranges from red to brown after firing. But the inventory of the different zones of production in the Thebes region is far from complete.

Between Tôd and Coptos, there is a concentration of ribbed jars made of calcareous clay,[32] produced between the Persian period and the beginning of the Hellenistic period[33] This homogenous group suggests the existence, if not of a large centre, then at least of several smaller workshops producing a type of

28. P. BALLET - M. VICHY, "Artisanat de la céramique dans l'Égypte hellénistique et romaine. Ateliers du Delta, d'Assouan et de Kharga", *CCE* 3, 1992, pp. 114-116.

29. It is likely that as far back as the Early Roman Empire, the Aswan amphorae were sold by numbers in the Nubian region which served as a market and outlet for a large part of the goods transiting through the first cataract, BALLET - VICHY, *op. cit.*, pp. 115-116. This is also the case with Aswan amphorae during the Late Roman Empire.

30. We are reminded right away of tubular shapes and jars with fluted handles from the later neolithic period generally associated with the successive cultures of Upper Egypt, especially those of Nagada.

31. Cf. J. JACQUET, "Fouilles de Karnak Nord. Neuvième et dixième campagnes (1975-1977)", *BIFAO* 78/1, 1978, p. 47, pl. XIII (jar of calcareous clay) while awaiting the publication of material on the pottery of North Karnak.

32. Some fine specimens of these jars can be seen among others in K. MYSLIWIEC, *Keramik und Kleinfunde aus der Grabung im Tempel Sethos'I in Gurna, Archäologische Veröffentlichungen* 57, 1987, Nos. 397-402.

33. According to the stratigraphy of recent excavations in Tôd, G. PIERRAT, M. ETIENNE, D. LECONTE & C. BARBOTIN, "Fouilles du Musée du Louvre à Tôd. 1988-1991", *Cahiers de Karnak* X, 1995, p. 463, fig. 54a.

pottery peculiar to this area. However, it has not been possible to identify a single workshop to this day.[34]

In the Arabian Desert, under the later local dynasties, ribbed jars used for storing things other than wine[35] represent the largest collection of storage vessels. In Wādi Hammamat, they are found everywhere from levels going back to the 5th century B.C. to the beginning of the Hellenistic period. The fact that they are quite commonly found in the desert areas to the east of the Nile that were dependent on the Thebes and Coptos regions for food supplies and other goods of daily use is a further proof of the location of pottery workshops in the area between Coptos and Tôd.

This announces the situation during the Roman period when sites in the Eastern Desert were logistically dependent on the Nile Valley which supplied food and other daily necessities to settlements of quarrymen and military outposts.

In spite of the decline of pottery made from calcareous clay during the Roman period in the region extending from Thebes to Coptos, the production of a very specialised type of water-jugs (*fig. 8*) continued during the Early Roman Empire.[36] These water-carrying vessels, characterised by a flat rim and sometimes a narrowing of the inner neck (used as a strainer), are found in the later resettlements, both funerary and residential, in the western necropoleis of Thebes. They constitute one of the main groups of Theban pottery spread all over the Eastern Desert. They are found in the "isthmus of Coptos", from the Nile to the Red Sea, in Wadi Hammamat (*fig. 8*), in al-Zarqa[37] and also in Quseir al-Qadim.[38] As for the southern road leading to Berenike, only Bir Abu Qreiya has a few specimens.

---

34. However, in Medamud to the north of Karnak, a few sporadic traces on the surface indicate the existence of potters using local calcareous clays. The products consisting of smooth-surfaced jars of a type different from the one mentioned here and common pottery could be dated to the pre-Ptolemaic period, or even the beginning of the Ptolemaic period, BALLET, MAHMOUD, VICHY & PICON, *op. cit.*, p. 139.

35. They could be water jars.

36. M. GABOLDE & C. GRATALOUP, *Les Réserves de Pharaons. L'Égypte dans les collections du musée des Beaux-Arts de Lyon*, 1988, p. 87, No. 5; P. BALLET in L. GABOLDE, H.I. AMER, P. BALLET & M. CHAUVEAU, "Le 'Tombeau suspendu' de la 'Vallée de l'Aigle'", *BIFAO* 94, 1994, p. 223, No. 84.

37. BRUN, *op. cit.*, p. 16, fig. 8, B 50.

38. WHITCOMB & JOHNSON, *Quseir al-Qadim 1978*, p. 98 e, pl. 33 e.

A part of the brown bitroconical (AE 3) amphorae made of alluvial clay recorded in settlements in the Eastern Desert[39] can probably also be assigned to the Theban region. The Theban type represented by an amphora from Karnak, published in 1969,[40] may be completed by the fine specimens found in later settlements of the temple of Sethi I at Gurna (*fig. 9*).[41] It is also found frequently in the wādis of West Thebes.[42]

These brown bitroconical amphorae are found on the road between Coptos and Quseir in al-Zarqa,[43] Wādi Hammamat (*fig. 10*) and even in Quseir (*fig. 11*).[44] They are made of brown alluvial clay and their morphology is similar to the Theban specimens. They have a long cylindrical neck with small handles fixed to the upper portion, a shoulder slightly marked and the lower part of the vessel tapers to a pointed foot.

This type also predominates on the road from Coptos to Berenike and is found in Bir Daghbag, Bir Abu Qreiya and Bir Beizah (*fig. 12*). However, we cannot rule out the possibility that these brown amphorae found in this part of the Eastern Desert were produced by the workshops of Apollonopolis Magna (Edfu).[45]

---

39. The name is given to amphorae having a similar structure produced in the workshops of Lake Maryut, see lastly J.-Y. EMPEREUR & M. PICON, "La reconnaissance des productions des ateliers céramiques: l'exemple de la Maréotide", *CCE* 3, 1992, p. 148, fig. 3. The term should not give any false ideas. Mareotis centres do not have a monopoly over bitroconical amphorae because they were also produced in Fayum and also in Middle and Upper Egypt.

40. P. ANUS & R. SA'AD, "Fouille aux abords de l'enceinte occidentale à Karnak", *Kêmi* XIX, 1969, p. 235, photo 4, a and e.

41. MYSLIWIEC, *op. cit.*, Nos. 947-955.

42. P. BALLET in L. GABOLDE, H.I. AMER, P. BALLET & M. CHAUVEAU, "Le 'Tombeau suspendu' de la 'Vallée de l'Aigle' ", *BIFAO* 94, 1994, p. 225, Nos. 87-88.

43. BRUN *op. cit.*, p. 23, fig. 12.

44. WHITCOMB & JOHNSON, *Quseir al-Qadim 1978*, p. 74 z, pl. 21, p. 76 d, e, g, pl. 22, p. 78 o, p, q, pl. 23, p. 88 k, pl. 28.

45. Workshops have been identified on the brick wall surrounding the temple and the settlement on the western side, BALLET, MAHMOUD, VICHY & PICON, *op. cit.*, p. 140. The amphorae of Edfu can be subdivided into two groups, one made of brown alluvial clay containing a large proportion of vegetal temper and the second made of fine brown alluvial clay with a reddish pink slip. Since these features have not been seen in the specimens found on the road from Coptos to Berenike, there is still some doubt about whether these amphorae were made in Apollonopolis Magna.

The Mareotic Workshops[46]

There could be two groups of Mareotic amphorae spread over the Eastern Desert: Dressel 2-4 (AE 4) (*fig. 13*) and a part of the bitroconical amphorae (AE 3) (*fig. 14*). To our knowledge, there are no other Egyptian workshops producing the first type of amphorae whereas workshops producing bitroconical amphorae are found all over the country. Outside the Maryut, workshops producing amphorae similar in shape to the bitroconical amphorae from West Alexandrian chora have been identified in Fayum,[47] in Middle Egypt[48] and in the Theban region.[49] The clays are different from those used for making the Mareotic amphorae except in the case of some specimens found in Mons Claudianus.[50] Bearing in mind the abundance of bitroconical amphorae in the Theban region and even in Middle Egypt, it could be said that they were among the exporters of this type of amphora.

On the contrary, there is no doubt about the large-scale presence of Dressel 2-4 amphorae of Mareotis[51] in the Eastern Desert. This is one of the most significant findings of the pottery excavations in Mons Claudianus.[52] They represent *c.* 1% of the material found in al-Zarqa[53] and also figure among the Egyptian amphorae found on the Coptos-Berenike road (Bir Abu Qreiya/Lovis and probably Wadi Gerf).

---

46. Among the most recent publications on the amphora workshops of Lake Mareotis, J.-Y. EMPEREUR, "Un atelier de Dressel 2-4 en Égypte au IIIe siècle de notre ère", *suppl. BCH* XIII, 1986, pp. 599-608; J.-Y. EMPEREUR & M. PICON, "Les régions de production d'amphores impériales en Méditerranée orientale", *CEFR* 114, 1988, pp. 227-228, pp. 234-235; J.-Y. EMPEREUR & M. PICON, "La reconnaissance des productions des ateliers céramiques : l'exemple de la Maréotide", *CCE* 3, 1992, p. 149, fig. 4.

47. Unpublished material from excavations in Tebtynis/Umm al-Brigat; the first volume on ceramics is under preparation (P. Ballet & A. Poludnikiewicz).

48. BALLET, MAHMOUD, VICHY & PICON, *CCE* 2, 1991, p. 138, fig. 15.

49. *Supra*, p. 125.

50. TOMBER, *CCE* 3, 1992, p. 141, fig. 2, 4, remarks on the similarity between the Dressel 2-4 and the bitroconical amphorae of Mons Claudianus; she suggests with due caution that they may have the same source without forgetting to point out that it would be necessary to carefully examine the bitroconical amphorae of Middle Egypt.

51. *Supra*, n. 46.

52. TOMBER, *CCE* 3, pp. 140-141.

53. BRUN, *op. cit.*, p. 20.

The Workshops of Middle Egypt (?)

We have been talking about the bitroconical amphorae of the Eastern Desert which may have come from different sources and there is a possibility that Middle Egypt may have been one of the exporters of these amphorae.[54]

There is also some uncertainty about a group of fine pottery with a red slip found in Mons Claudianus.[55] While we do not find any trace of this type in Wādi Hammamat, one sherd found on the Coptos-Berenike road could be linked to it. The texture of the clay and the glossy red slip also characteristic of the *K Group*[56] belonging to a later date suggest that Middle Egypt could be one of the areas that produced this type of pottery. However, we cannot rule out the possibility that it was produced in workshops situated further south. Fine wares of alluvial clay with a red slip have been found in the Theban region but their peculiar features have not been carefully defined.[57]

I.2. Pottery Imported from Outside Egypt found in the East Egyptian Desert

Imports, mainly from the Mediterranean region, are quite rare. That is the immediate conclusion that can be drawn on looking at the tables indicating the percentage of local and imported wares.

In al-Zarqa, some fine wares and a small number of amphorae reveal that the import of non-Egyptian pottery was quite rare. In fact, imports constitute only 0.005% of the fragments[58] found among which there are two of *Eastern*

---

54. Cf. *supra*. Later specimens were made on the west bank at Hermopolis Magna (Ashmunein), D. BAILEY in *Ashmunein (1982), British Museum Expedition to Middle Egypt, BM Occasional Paper No. 37* (1982), pl. 35 a (4th or 5th century) and on the west bank in Zawyet el-Maietin, BALLET, VICHY & PICON, *CCE* 2, 1991, p. 138, fig. 15.

55. TOMBER, *CCE* 3, 1992, pp. 141-142.

56. The real K(armin) group figures among the main types of fine wares. During the Late Roman period, its production area was situated in Middle Egypt, M. RODZIEWICZ, *La céramique fine romaine tardive d'Alexandrie, Alexandrie* I, 1976, pp. 50-51; J.W. HAYES, *Late Roman Pottery. A Catalogue of Roman Fine Ware,* BSR, London, 1972, p. 399 (*Egyptian B*) and BALLET, MAHMOUD, VICHY & PICON, *op. cit.*, pp. 136-138. There are many Egyptian fabrics which are similar to the K group in the region between the Delta and Thebaid. They cannot however be confused with the red-slipped ware of Middle Egypt made from a fin micaceous clay with a brown break and a thick glossy slip sometimes covered with fine cracks.

57. As far as we know, macroscopic studies of clays of the Theban region are not sufficiently advanced.

58. BRUN, *op. cit.*, pp. 10, 12-13, fig. 6.

Sigillata, three wine amphorae (one Gauloise 4, one Cnidian, one amphora from Asia Minor)[59] and three oil amphorae (African Ostia LIX and Tripolitan 1).

Although there is a wide variety of imports from Baetica, Gaul, Italy, Tripolitania and Crete at Mons Claudianus,[60] the number of specimens of each category is quite small and amounts to less than 5% of the total finds. Among the imported fine ware, only a few specimens of *Eastern Sigillata* A are mentioned.

We are presenting here three specimens of *Eastern Sigillata* A (*fig. 15-17*) found in Wādi Hammamat.[61] On the basis of their chemical composition,[62] it has been suggested that they may be from Cyprus, if not Pamphylia. There is no imported amphora discovered in the Roman contexts during the excavations conducted by the Institut français d'archéologie orientale.

As regards the settlements situated on the Coptos-Berenike route, the number of imported wares discovered is very small. The most numerous are the Mau XXVII-XXVIII amphorae probably from Cyprus.[63] [However, some non-Egyptian imported storage vessels could not be identified]. It is surprising to find this type of amphora in sites all along the Coptos-Berenike route. It is believed to originate from Cyprus and is not seen in other parts of the Eastern Desert but is found frequently on the Mediterranean coast, *e.g.* Alexandria,[64] Marina el-Alamein[65] and also Pelusium.[66]

---

59. Of the Robinson F65-66 type which is generally classified with the *Late Roman Amphora 3 group* made of a very micaceous clay.

60. R. TOMBER, "Mons Claudianus", *BCE* XIII, 1988, pp. 35-37; *id.*, "Mons Claudianus", *BCE* XIV, 1990, pp. 26-27.

61. Material studied in 1987 and 1988 during the epigraphical and archaeological studies conducted by IFAO at Wādi Hammamat under the supervision of A. Gasse. The search for inscriptions hidden under masses of fallen stones necessitated the excavation and uncovering of the lower portion of the rock faces. We will only deal with material from the Roman period.

62. X-ray fluorescence analyses conducted by the Laboratoire de Céramologie in Lyon reveal that figures 15 and 16 come from the same workshop. The third specimen, whose chemical composition is noticeably different, could be linked with wares from the eastern Mediterranean.

63. They have also been found in Bir Abu Qreiya, Wadi Gerf and Wadi Dweig.

64. Excavations conducted on land by the Centre d'Études Alexandrines.

65. W.A. DASZEWSKI, G. MAJCHEREK, Z. SZTETYLLO & I. ZYCH, "Excavations at Marina el-Alamein 1987-1988", *MDAIK* 46, 1990, p. 46, type 4. The specimens found on the Coptos-Berenike route have a coarser texture than those found in Marina el-Alamein.

66. P. BALLET, "Péluse. Le théâtre romain", in *An Introduction to the Pottery of the Northern Sinaï. Preliminary Results of the Rescue Campaigns (1990-1994), CCE* 5, edited by J. Bourriau & D. Valbelle, 1997, Nos. 15-16.

Imported fine wares are limited to a small group consisting of a dozen specimens of Italian *sigillata* (*fig. 18-19*) and *Eastern Sigillata* A found only in Wadi Gemal.

The results obtained during the last ten years in the research of Egyptian wares and imports call for a thorough re-examination of the pottery of Quseir (Myos Hormos). Imports are evidently more numerous here than in the interior of Egypt.

Among these, the Italian *sigillata* wares occupy an important place[67] together with *Eastern Sigillata*.[68] Among the amphorae, the Dressel 2-4, whose exact origin cannot be determined,[69] are in a majority; one notices also some coming probably from Rhodes[70] and an amphora of the type Agora M 54 from southern Turkey.[71] As for amphorae from the southern Mediterranean coast, there is also a substantial part of Tripolitanian wares (*fig. 20*)[72] while there are also some specimens of African I & II wares[73] from Tunisia.

It is undoubtedly necessary to make a distinction between the sites occupied by quarrymen (Mons Claudianus)[74] and the caravanserais and military check-posts or *praesidia* in the Eastern Desert to interpret the nature of imported wares. In the first case, it may be supposed that the pottery found in these places satisfied the daily needs of their residents consisting of quarrymen, managers and handymen. In the second case, pottery from convoys heading for the Red Sea, which ended up in these inns for a variety of reasons, was essentially meant for export.

The case of Wādi Hammamat during the Early Roman Empire and Wādi Fawakhir during the Late Roman Empire is more complicated. Located on the Coptos-Quseir route, they are permanent settlements of quarrymen and also halting-places for caravans heading towards the Red Sea ports

---

67. WHITCOMB & JOHNSON, *Quseir al-Qadim 1978*, pl. 20, a-h; pl. 21, f-g; WHITCOMB & JOHNSON, *Quseir al-Qadim 1980*, pl. 29, j-k, aa, dd, ee; pl. 30, e, k-l, p-s, w.

68. Group A is better represented than group B, WHITCOMB & JOHNSON, *Quseir al-Qadim 1978*, pl. 20, k; pl. 21, b-c; WHITCOMB & JOHNSON, *Quseir al-Qadim 1980*, pl. 29, a-b, d-i, m-o, q-u, w, y, bb, cc; pl. 30, c, f, j, m-n, t-v.

69. It is difficult to distinguish between the amphorae with bifid handles from Italy, from the Aegean and from Egypt.

70. WHITCOMB & JOHNSON, *Quseir al-Qadim 1978*, pl. 24, h-l; however, there is some doubt about it.

71. *Ibid.*, pl. 27, f.

72. *Ibid.*, pl. 24, I, pl. 27, h, pl. 30, d; WHITCOMB & JOHNSON, *Quseir al-Qadim 1980*, pl. 15, e.

73. WHITCOMB & JOHNSON, *Quseir al-Qadim 1978*, pl. 23, m.

74. We must add to these the excavations being conducted in Mons Porphyrites.

Until recently, archaeologists were agreed that Egypt and the Eastern Desert which were at the heart of a communications network bringing together the West and the Far-East had a large amount of material that made it possible to study the export trade of Western, Aegean and Near-Eastern pottery towards India. Results provided by research during the last ten years in the eastern part of Egypt have modified these assumptions to a certain extent. The *praesidia* and quarrymen's settlements cannot be compared to Quseir (Myos Hormos), the main port on the Red Sea, or to major Mediterranean ports like Alexandria and Pelusium if we consider the inventory and the volume of imports. The interior of the Eastern Desert provides a small number of amphorae and fine wares both from the Western and Eastern Mediterranean. In spite of the apparent diversity of imported amphorae originating from Gaul, Cnidia and Tripolitania, it must be borne in mind that there are only a few specimens of each type. There may be two reasons for this. Firstly, the amphorae from the West, from Greece and the Levantine coast constituted only a tiny part of cargo shipped to the East and the Far-East. Secondly, amphorae transiting through Egypt were probably meant for more distant lands. We should be able to find substantial traces of these wares in lands beyond Egypt and its dependencies such as the *emporia* on the Red Sea, the Erythraean Sea and even those in the Indian sub-continent.

II. Towards India (*fig. 2*)

The study conducted on the Revoil Fund, which is kept in the Musée de l'Homme, gave a rough idea of the spread of eastern and western wares through sea routes and made it possible to reconstruct some of the trade links with the Indian Ocean. Two Somalian halting places in the Horn of Africa, viz. al-Heis and Damo, provide limited but significant documentation.[75] The pottery collected from these two settlements is mostly of western origin. It consists of fragments of Dressel 2-4 amphorae from Campania (*fig. 21*),[76] Western *Sigillata* of Arretine ware type (*fig. 22*). We can add to them two specimens of *Eastern Sigillata* A type.[77] If the pottery fragments cannot be classified with any

75. In collaboration with J. DESANGES & M. STERN, *Sur les routes antiques de l'Azanie et de l'Inde: le fonds Revoil du musée de l'Homme*, Mémoires de l'Académie des Inscriptions et Belles-Lettres, n.s. XIII, 1993.

76. The presence of blackish inclusions of a volcanic type, the general appearance of the texture and colour of the amphorae supported by chemical analyses (Laboratoire de Céramologie de Lyon) are quite peculiar to Campanian wares, *ibid.* p. 65.

77. The origin of the respective fine wares has also been confirmed by chemical analysis. The *ESA* of al-Heis have a composition very similar to the *Eastern Sigillata* found in Wādi Hammamat.

certainty as belonging to Egyptian ware,[78] the pieces of mosaic glass which constitute a major part of the finds could have been made by glass-makers, if not of Alexandria, then at least of Egyptian origin.[79] Evidence regarding their date provided by glassware and fine pottery points out to the first half or even the middle of the 1st century A.D.

Despite the absence of Egyptian pottery, the geographical position of these two sites, which were anchorages rather than real *emporia*, and the presence of Egyptian glassware indicates that these goods had to necessarily pass through Egypt.

The ancient port of Qana (Bir 'Ali) on the South Yemen coast occupied a position of vantage on the trade route between Rome and India and is mentioned as one of the *emporia* in the *Periplus of the Erythraean Sea.* It served as a warehouse for incense from the kingdom of Eleazos and also as its principal redistributor.[80] The large variety of pottery imported both from the West and the East is an archaeological proof of prime importance also confirming its role as a redistributor and a port of call in the vast trade network bringing together the West and the Far-East.

Although we are unable to reconstruct with any accuracy the different ways in which these wares were shipped to Qana, we will present a picture based on the results of systematic excavations undertaken in Bir 'Ali since 1985 by the Russian Institute of Oriental Studies.[81] Three main phases of occupation have been identified. They are mentioned in a chronological order from I to III extending from the Early to the Late Roman period.[82]

---

78. The fragment with a glazed zigzag pattern, No.7, *ibid.*, p. 67, could be from southern Mesopotamia or the Persian Gulf area according to J.-F. Salles. (Oral communication).

79. M. STERN, in DESANGES, STERN & BALLET, *op. cit.*, pp. 29-30. According to Stern, *op. cit.*, p. 30, the port of embarkation was probably Berenike and not Quseir (Myos Hormos).

80. L. CASSON, *The* Periplus Maris Erythrei. *Text with Introduction, Translation and Commentary*, Princeton University Press, 1989, § 27, p. 67.

81. Academy of Sciences, Moscow. A general presentation of the site and archaeological and epigraphical documents can be found in A. SEDOV, "New Archaeological and Epigraphical Material from Qana (South Arabia)", *AAE* 3/2, June 1992, pp. 110-137.

82. We will deal only with the later periods in order to reconstruct an overall view of the goods that passed through Qana during the occupation of this site.

We will confine ourselves to underlining the presence of some imported pottery groups of known origin while awaiting the final publication of results[83] and without broaching the subject of local or regional workshops.[84]

In the earlier occupied levels (phase I), specimens of the *Eastern Sigillata* A are probably the earliest pieces of pottery found in Qana going back perhaps to the last years of the Hellenistic period if not the very beginning of the Roman Empire. There are two main shapes. Firstly, a shallow dish with slightly rounded walls rising almost vertically towards the mouth (Form 4 in *Atlante* classification) and secondly a convex bowl (form 22A in *Atlante*) (*fig. 23*). The reference types are generally dated from the end of the 2nd century B.C. to the beginning of the 1st century A.D. Made of a very thick light coloured clay with a mildly adhesive glaze whose lustre is not very resistant, these wares originating from the Eastern Mediterranean have all the features of *Eastern Sigillata* wares, more precisely of the *Eastern Sigillata* A group. The two types found here are among the wares most commonly found all over the East and also Egypt. They abound in Alexandria,[85] in Pelusium they are quite conspicuous[86] but they are found occasionally in Fayum[87] and in the Eastern Desert.[88] The Qana specimens are an important landmark in the spread of *Eastern Sigillata* A towards the Far-East where it seems they have not been recognised.[89]

---

83. During the two missions granted by the Maison de l'Orient méditerranéen to study the pottery of Bir 'Ali (UMR 5649, F.-Courby), I was able to examine the entire material and determine the origin of some pottery groups.

84. They will be dealt with at length in the final volume on the Qana excavations to be brought out by the publications division of the Maison de l'Orient méditerranéen. Apart from a local pottery with coarse walls containing a vegetable temper meant for storage purposes, it is necessary to draw attention to the presence of jars and bowls with a wavy pattern. The hard clay and medium fine texture is red or dark grey. In the latter case, the colour is evidently the result of overfiring. Similar wares have been found in the Oman peninsula according to M. Mouton (Oral communication). An associated research project will enable us to study later the trade relations between the hinterland of the Arabian-Persian Gulf and coastal settlements in Southern Arabia thereby confirming the existence of a regional trade network.

85. From the foundation layer of the Majestic wall dating back to the end of the 1st century B.C.

86. P. BALLET, "Péluse. Le théâtre romain", in *An Introduction to the Pottery of the Northern Sinaï. Preliminary Results of the Rescue Campaigns (1990-1994)*, *Cahiers de la Céramique Égyptienne* 5, IFAO, Caire (1997), Nos. 3-8.

87. In Tebtynis (Umm al-Brigat) during the joint excavations conducted by the Institut Français d'Archéologie Orientale and the Institute of Papyrology of Milan University.

88. *Supra*, p. 128.

89. K. WARNER SLANE, "Observations on Mediterranean Amphoras and Tablewares Found in India", *op. cit.*, p. 208. On the contrary, pieces of *Eastern Sigillata* B have been identified in Arikamedu, *ibid.*, pp. 207-208.

It is quite certain that during the Early Roman period (phase I), the West was represented by *Sigillata* wares which can be qualified without much accuracy as Italian wares (*fig. 24*). Their pinkish colour, the fineness of the clay and the quality of the glaze which is both adhesive and lustrous, make them akin to the wares produced in the peninsula. The specimens found in Qana having the same features as the Arretine *sigillata* ware found in Al-Heis and Damo can be linked with the North Italian group.[90] It appears possible to date them to the 1st century A.D. and more precisely to the first half of that century.

They probably accompanied the Campanian amphorae of the Dressel 2-4 type recognised by the brick red colour of their cracks, the lighter surface and the coarse clay having numerous blackish inclusions. It was quite obviously the pyroxenic clay peculiar to Campania. These Campanian amphorae can be easily distinguished from the other amphorae with bifed handles found in Qana. The latter are made of a fairly fine and dense light coloured clay which makes them akin, if not to the Koan group, then at least to the Aegean group.[91] They can be dated back to the end of the Hellenistic period in the same way as the *Eastern Sigillata* A of Qana.

Even though they cannot be precisely dated in the Early Roman period (1st to 3rd century A.D.), the Egyptian amphorae are represented by the type with bifed handles derived from the Campanian Dressel 2-4 or the Koan amphorae with bifed handles. We are aware of the existence of one Egyptian production centre in Mareotis.[92] The clay used for making the Egyptian amphorae of Qana is closer to alluvial clays than to the calcareous clays of Maryut. This means that there were other workshops producing Dressel 2-4 wares in Egypt that are yet to be identified or that it is necessary to re-examine the clay samples from the Maryut region. The batch of Egyptian Dressel 2-4 is completed by a few bitroconical amphorae (*fig. 25*) made of brown micaceous alluvial clay. In the absence of a chemical analysis, we cannot determine their exact origin as several Egyptian workshops produced this type of amphora[93] very similar to the containers of Upper Egypt spread all over the Eastern Desert[94] as we have seen earlier.

---

90. According to analyses conducted by the Laboratoire de céramologie in Lyon, DESANGES, STERN & BALLET, *Sur les routes antiques de l'Azanie et de l'Inde: le fonds Revoil du musée de l'Homme*, p. 65.

91. A more analytical account will be given in the final publication. It is also necessary to point out the presence of amphorae from Rhodes and Tripolitania.

92. *Supra*, p. 126.

93. *Supra*, pp. 124-125.

94. *Supra*, p. 125.

The presence of Egyptian containers[95] at Qana casts a new light on the spread of amphorae towards the Far-East. Till now, the amphorae with bifed handles from Arikamedu were classified into two groups according to their probable origin: a Koan or, at least, an Aegean group and an Italic (pseudo-Koan) group.[96] The data collected in Qana will undoubtedly enable us to re-examine and add to the list of "western" imports, especially amphorae, on the shores of the Indian peninsula.

Among the Egyptian imports found in the Qana *emporion* there are several specimens of Egyptian jugs, identical in every way to the wares of calcareous clay from the Theban region that were regularly sent to the Eastern Desert during the Early Roman Empire.[97] We may say that they served as individual containers since they were water jugs carried by sailors and transport agents.

Finally, the presence of fine wares from Aswan (*fig. 26*), though in a small number, is a sufficient proof of the widespread use of kaolinitic wares of the first cataract under the Roman Empire. The inventory of Aswan pottery exported outside Egypt must be drawn up systematically. Found on the coast of North Sinaï and in some places on the Levantine coast, these wares figure among those commonly seen in transit sites and ports on the eastern bounds of the Mediterranean.

Information regarding Qana's Egyptian pottery is far from trifling. It confirms the importance of the Nilotic waterways and of Egypt's Arabian Desert in long distance trade with far-flung areas of the Far-East.

During the Late Roman Empire (phases II and III), there continues to be a great diversity of pottery. But the origin of these different wares reflects a certain shift in the economic centres. In the West, North Africa took over from South Italy. Cylindrical amphorae[98] and *Late Roman A* fine wares were found in Qana while the major workshops in the Eastern Mediterranean also sent their products there. As a matter of fact, from the 5th century onwards, *Late Roman 1* type

95. These Egyptian Dressel 2-4 amphorae were shipped to Italy during the first century of the Roman Empire and were mixed with other local wares in the Yumurtalik workshop on the south-east coast of Turkey, J.-Y. EMPEREUR, "Un atelier de Dressel 2-4 en Égypte au IIIe siècle de notre ère", *Recherches sur les amphores grecques, Suppl. BCH* XIII, 1986, p. 606; J.-Y. EMPEREUR & M. PICON, "Les régions de production d'amphores impériales en Méditerranée orientale", *Amphores romaines et histoire économique. Dix ans de recherche, CEFR* 114, 1989, pp. 228-229.

96. E. LYDING WILL, "The Mediterranean Shipping Amphoras from Arikamedu", in V. BEGLEY & R.D. DE PUMA, eds., *Rome and India. The Ancient Sea Trade*, Oxford University Press, 1992, pp. 151-153; K. WARNER SLANE, "Observations on Mediterranean Amphoras and Tablewares Found in India", *op. cit.*, pp. 204-205.

97. *Infra, fig. 8.*

98. They were in all likelihood preceded during phase I and the earlier part of phase II by amphorae of the African I type. But they have not yet been definitely identified.

amphorae[99] were spread all over the Mediterranean region. Qana was no exception to this rule confirming once more the enormous production and distribution potential of the workshops of the Near East during the Late Roman Empire. It is not surprising that a second group of eastern amphorae, the *Late Roman 4* type, was found in large numbers during the excavations at Qana of levels dating back to the Late Roman Empire. They actually represent one of the main groups of amphorae spread all over the Mediterranean area and its borders.

A workshop producing the amphorae (*fig. 27*) with a slightly ridged body was recently discovered at Ayla, the ancient port of Aqaba.[100] They pose a delicate problem regarding their chronology. The activities of potters settled in the port of Aqaba, whose development seems to have been linked with the settling of Muslim conquerors in the Gulf, do not date back further than the mid 7th century. After this date the amphorae spread, if not in Egypt,[101] then at least in the direction of the Arabian Peninsula and in the Aksum region.[102] All the archaeological, epigraphical and numismatic data collected in Qana suggests that it was occupied not later than the end of the 6th century. This inconsistency could be corrected eventually by attributing the production of similar amphorae to a workshop both geographically and technologically close to the one in Ayla.

During this later period there appears a fairly substantial batch of hand-made pottery with an incised or engraved geometrical pattern made in North-East Africa (*fig. 28*). This pottery fits in well with the technical traditions of Upper Nubia and the Aksum region, but for the time being it is not possible to establish parallels with the published documentation. On the contrary, there are exact replicas among the Red Aksum Ware[103] of a moulded bowl with an

---

99. *Late Roman I* type amphorae were produced in several workshops in the Eastern Mediterranean, J.-Y. EMPEREUR & M. PICON, "Les régions de production d'amphores impériales en Méditerranée orientale", *op. cit.*, pp. 236-243.

100. D. WHITCOMB, "Evidence of the Umayyad Period from the Aqaba Excavations". *The Fourth International Conference on the History of Bilad al-Sham during the Ummayad Period*, ed. by M.A. Bakhit & R. Schick, Amman, 1989, fig. 5; *id., Ayla Art and Industry in the Islamic Port of Aqaba*, The University of Chicago, 1994, pp. 23-25.

101. This type of amphora does not seem to be found in Egypt. Perhaps, it has not been possible to identify it due to the lack of accurate knowledge about its morphology and its clay, unless it has been confused with the *Late Roman I* amphora.

102. F. ANFRAY, *Les anciens Éthiopiens. Siècles d'histoire*, Paris, 1990, p. 131; it is a "Mediterranean" amphora found in Matara, 70 km to the south-west of Adulis. S.C. MUNRO-HAY, *Excavations at Aksum. An Account of Research at the Ancient Ethiopian Capital Directed in 1972-4 by the late Dr. Neville Chittick*, London, 1989, pp. 314-315, fig. 16, pp. 468-470. The source of this group has been wrongly situated in Egypt.

103. MUNRO-HAY, *op. cit.*, fig. 16, pp. 75-76 and fig. 16, 92, 94.

inverted pattern (*fig. 29*) reproducing gadroon motifs. There is no doubt that these wares were imported from the Aksum kingdom.

And What About Indian Pottery?

We will end our account of the trade between Rome and India based on the wares found in different places by referring to the ceramics produced in India. Were they, as storage vessels or simply subsidiary merchandise, a part of the regular shipments leaving Indian shores? We will not dwell on the potteries of the Indian sub-continent as they merit a detailed study which we are not in a position to undertake here.[104] We will therefore make do with a brief account.

A group of potteries found at Quseir al-Qadim has been recognised as "Indian".[105] According to the meagre details available about the morphology and the type of clay used for the "Indian" potteries of Quseir, it is doubtful if they can be called so. The shapes do not appear to be any different from those of common Egyptian wares belonging to Roman times and the technical information available to us suggests that these so-called Indian vessels may have come from Egypt.

Given the present state of knowledge, it seems that no Indian pottery penetrated the Egyptian hinterland between the Red Sea and the Nile.[106]

As for Qana, I have not found any convincing confirmation of the presence of Indian pottery.[107] One complete piece, supposed to originate in the Far-East, is not representative of the products of the Indian sub-continent (*fig. 30*). The texture of its clay and its coating indicate that it has more in common with fine wares from the Eastern Mediterranean.

We cannot completely rule out the presence of Indian vessels on sites and in regions covered by this international trade. Any unidentified group of wares in a particular place cannot by default be deemed as a product of the workshops of the Far-East about which little is known. We will have to look for more

104. The author of the *Periplus* gives very little information about the merchandise coming from India. He mentions that chartered ships from India halted at Eudaimôn Arabia on the southern Arabian coast, to the east of modern Aden, without specifying what their cargo contained, CASSON, *Periplus*, p. 65, while the inventory of goods coming from India mentions iron and cotton among the other goods that passed through Adulis, *ibid.*, p. 54.

105. WHITCOMB & JOHNSON, *Quseir al-Qadim 1978*, pp. 67-70.

106. The most recent publications do not mention it.

107. Although the Qana excavators drew attention to the presence of Red Polished Ware, A. SEDOV, "Qana (Yemen) and the Indian Ocean: The Archaeological Evidence", (being printed), p. 17.

convincing evidence based on the shape and the type of clay used which is now being put together on the borders of the Mediterranean world.[108]

Pascale BALLET
Université de Haute-Bretagne

108. Research undertaken by A. Marangou-Lerat and S. Elaigne under the guidance of J.-Fr. Salles in Bangladesh and in India. One study already provides valuable information on the spread of Indian pottery in Southern Iran and in the eastern part of the Arabian Peninsula: M. KERVRAN, "Indian Ceramics in Southern Iran and Eastern India. Repertory, Classification and Chronology", in H.P. RAY & J.-F. SALLES, eds, *Tradition and Archaeology, Early Maritime Contacts in the Indian Ocean*, Manohar, New Delhi, 1996, pp. 37-58.

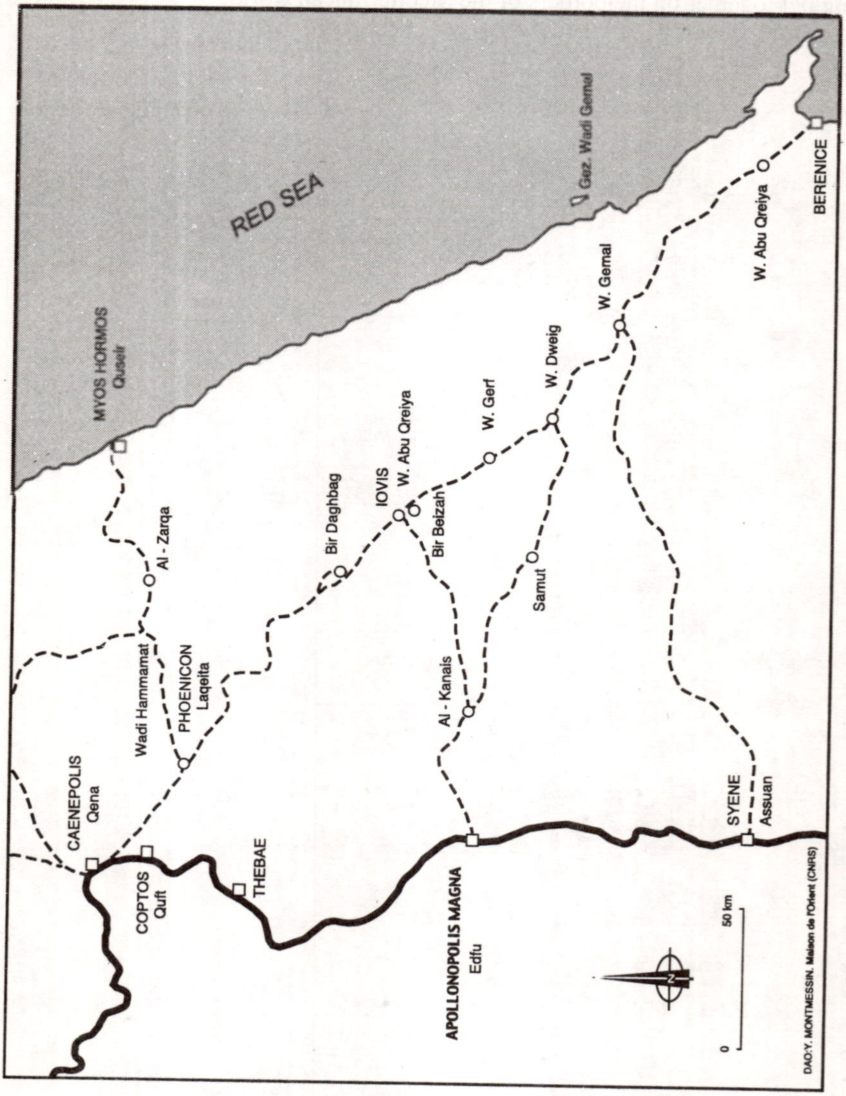

Fig. 1 – The Eastern Desert of Egypt. Principal routes between Coptos and the Red Sea

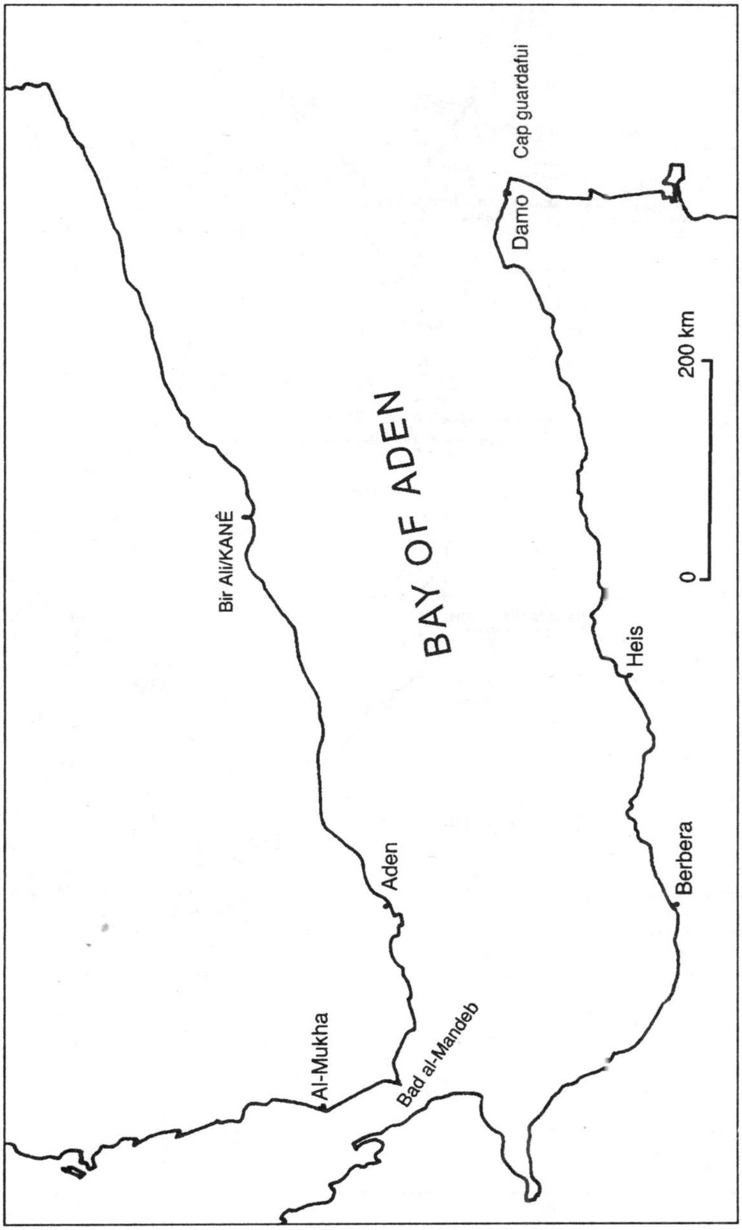

Fig. 2 – The straits zone leading from the Red Sea to the Indian Ocean

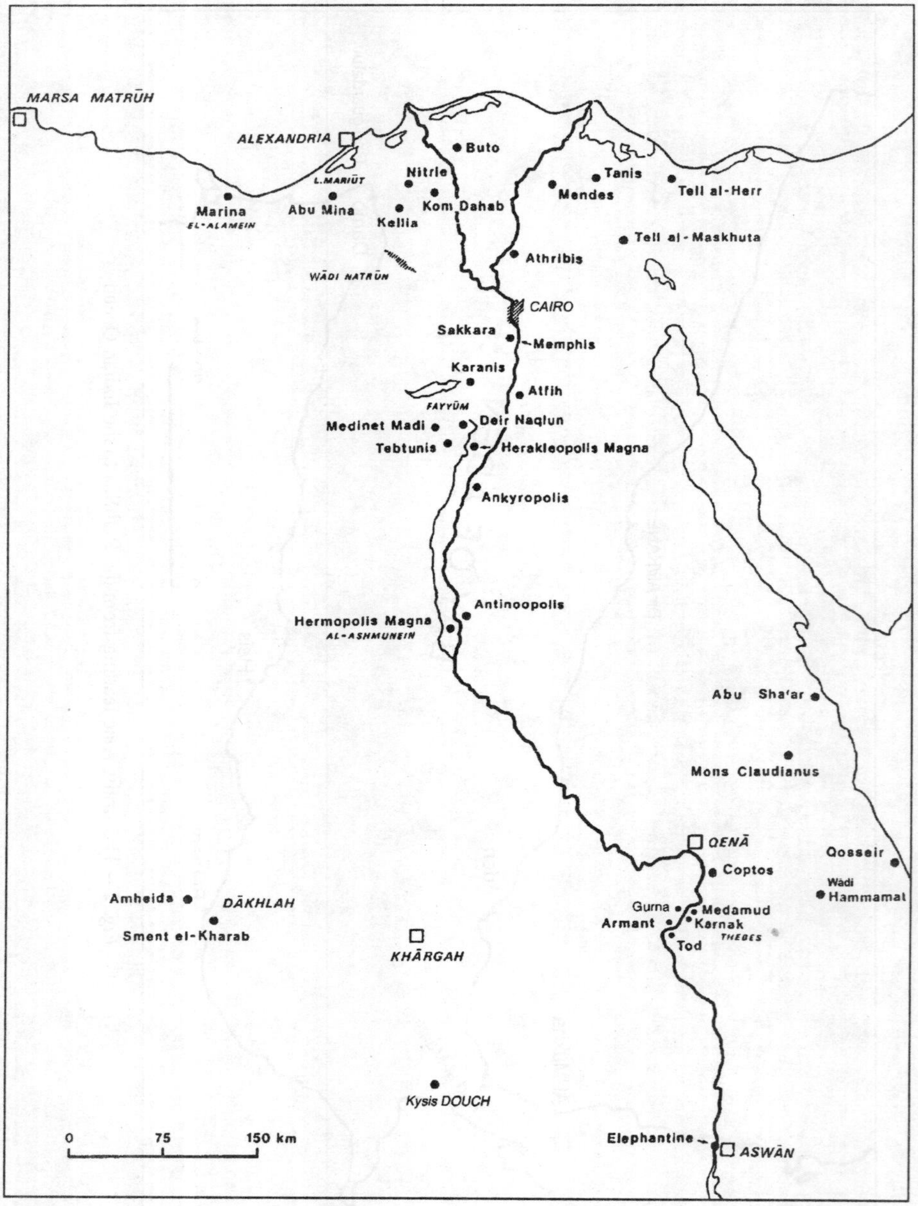

Fig. 3 – Egypt during the Roman period. Principal sites mentioned in the article

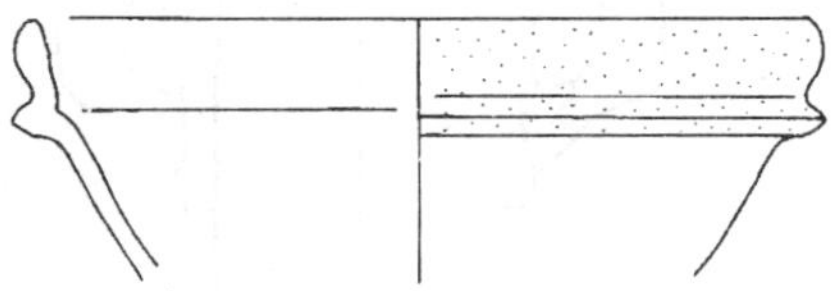

Fig. 4

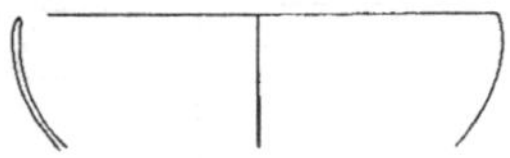

Fig. 5

Fig. 6

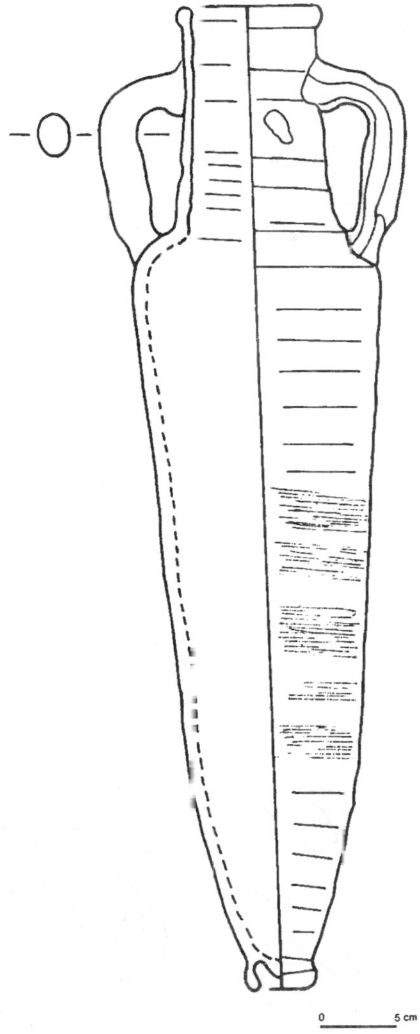

Fig. 7

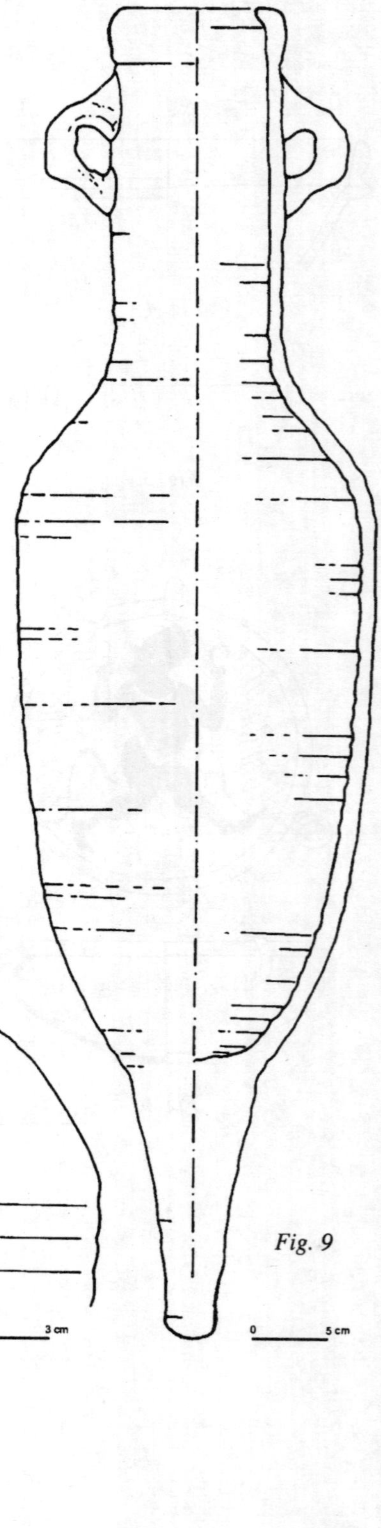

Fig. 9

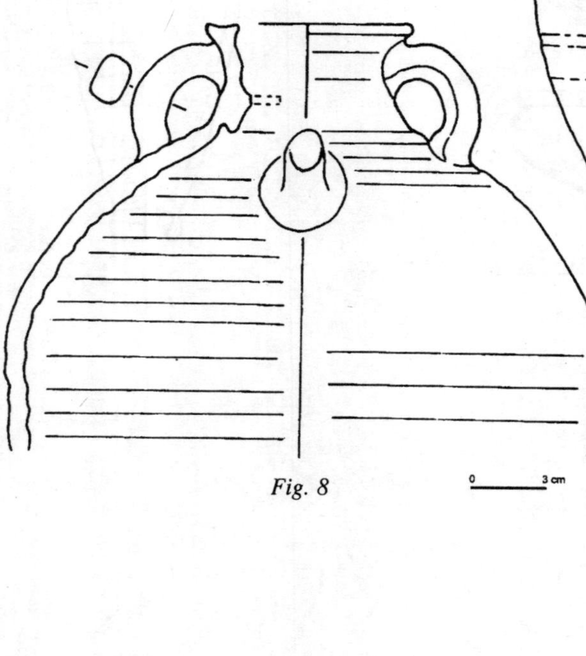

Fig. 8

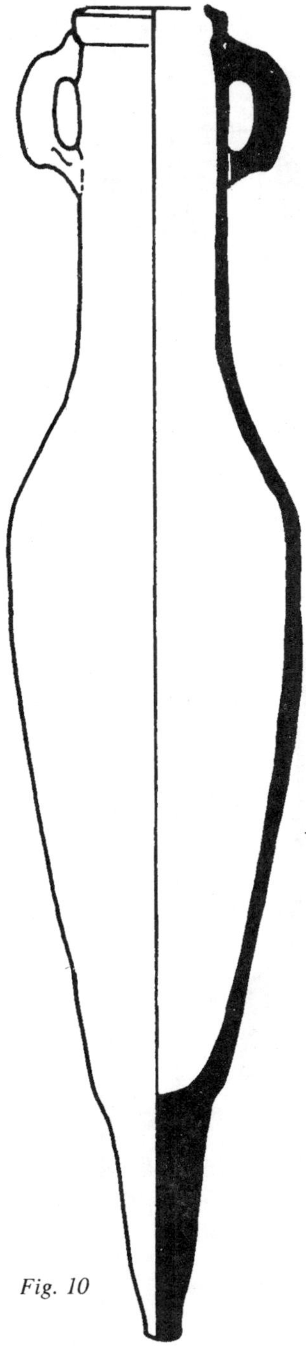

Fig. 10

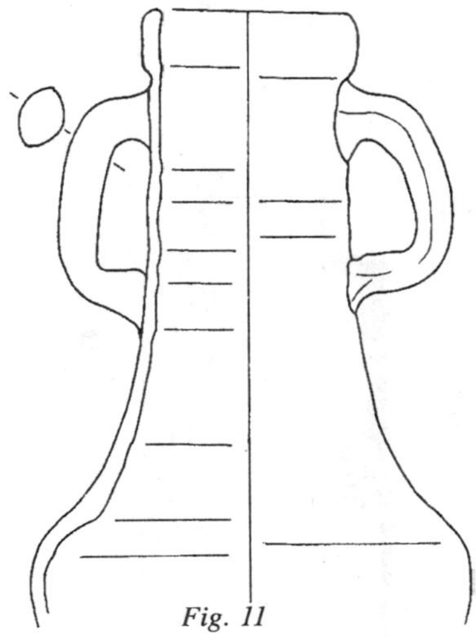

Fig. 11

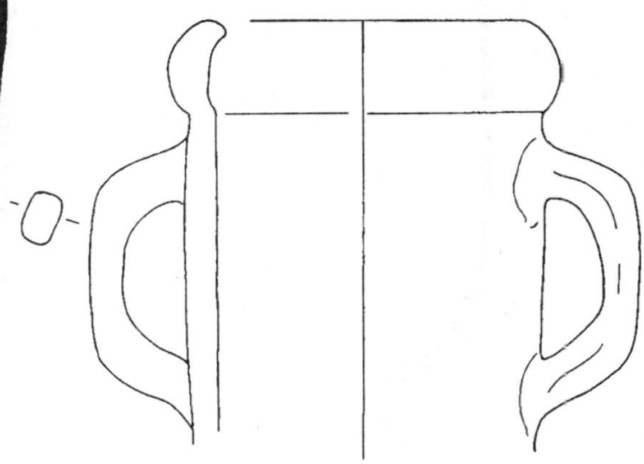

Fig. 12

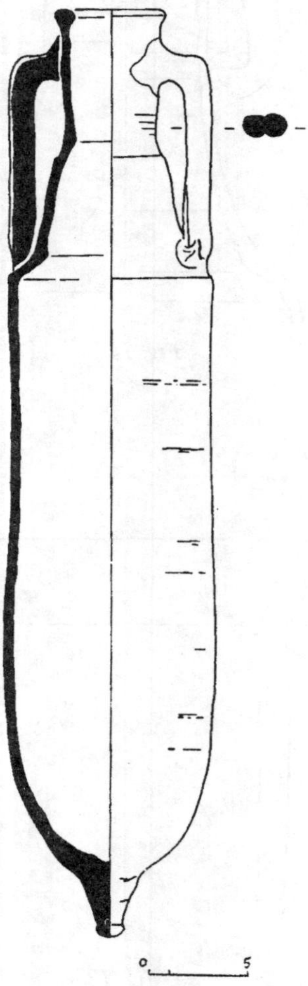

Fig. 13

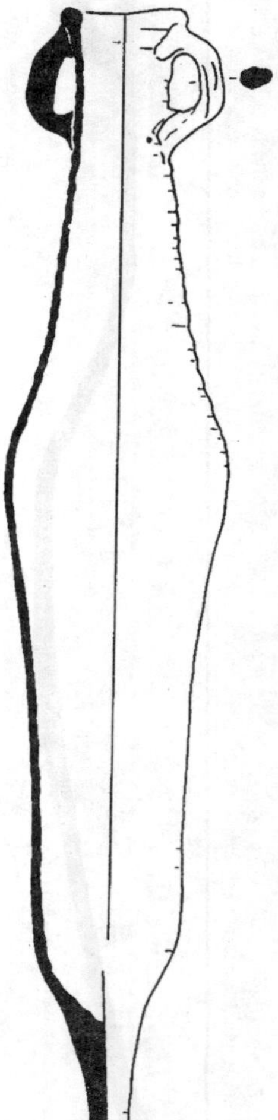

Fig. 14

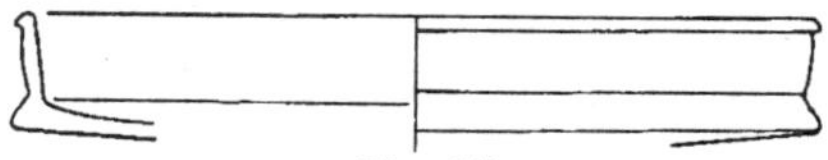

Fig. 15

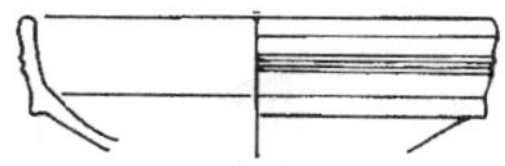

Fig. 16

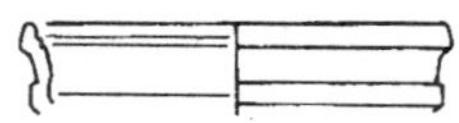

Fig. 17

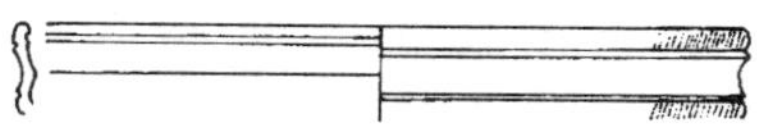

Fig. 18

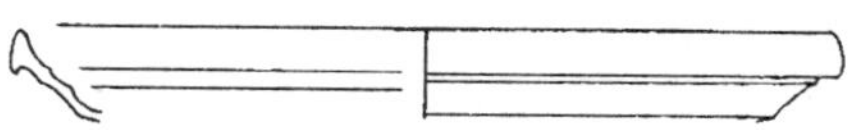

Fig. 19

0 3 cm

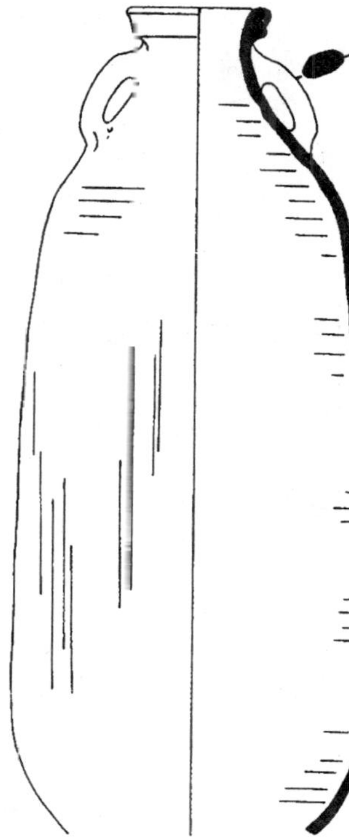

Fig. 20 0 10 cm

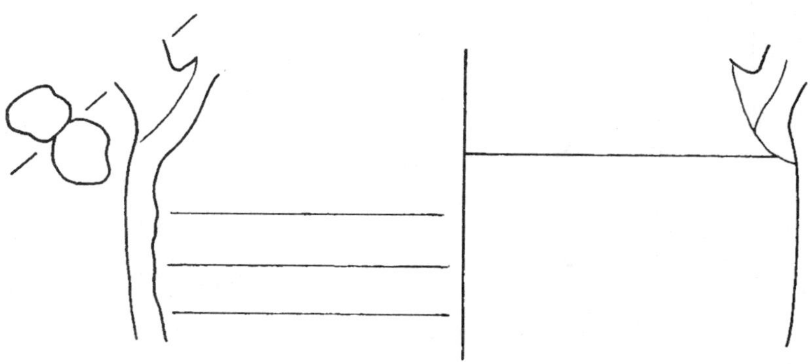

Fig. 21

0 3 cm

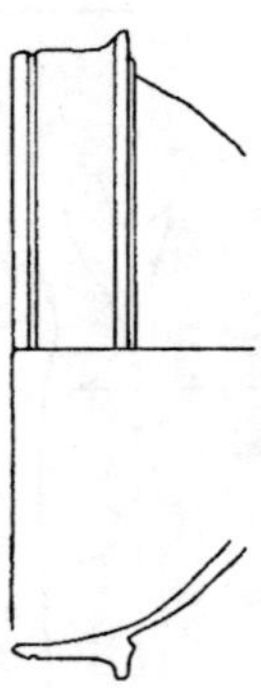

Fig. 22

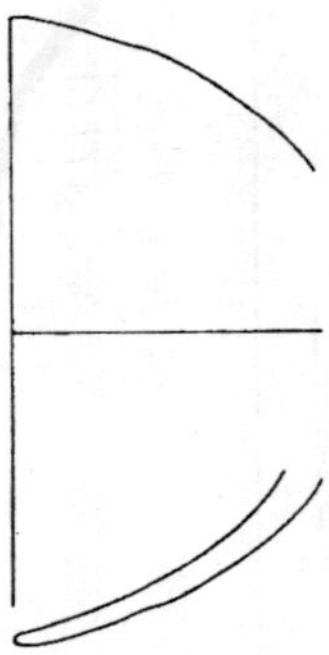

Fig. 23

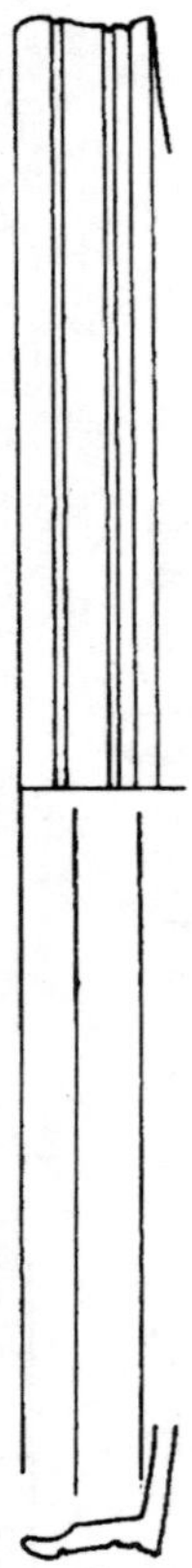

Fig. 24

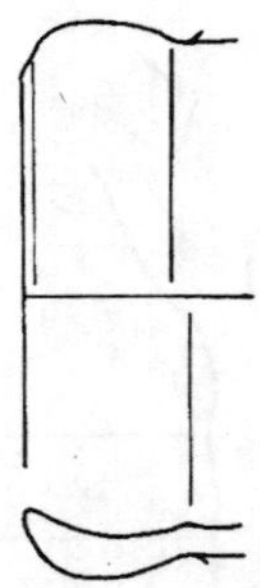

Fig. 25

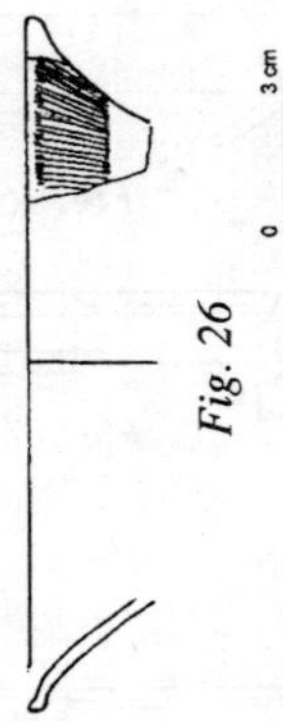

Fig. 26

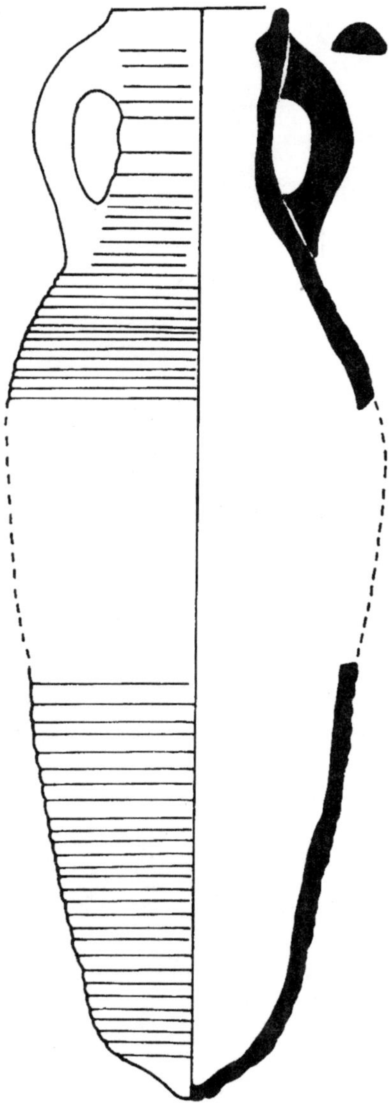

Fig. 27

0 5 cm

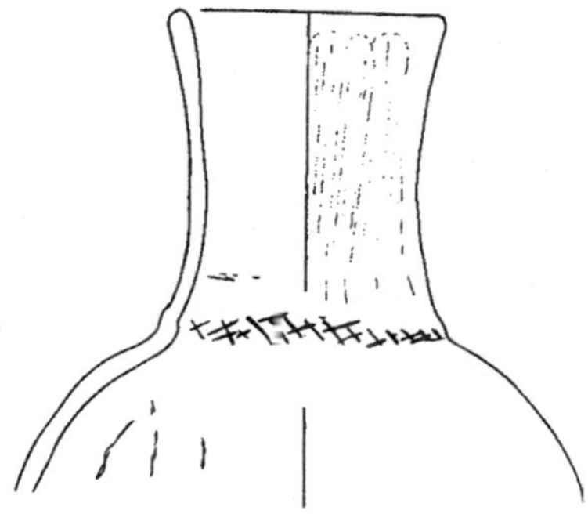

Fig. 28

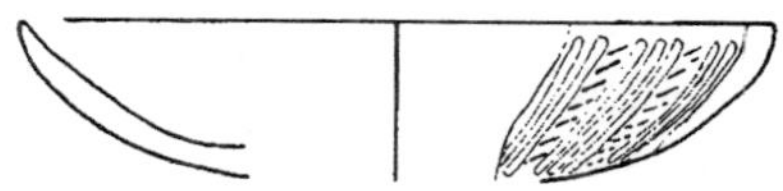

Fig. 29

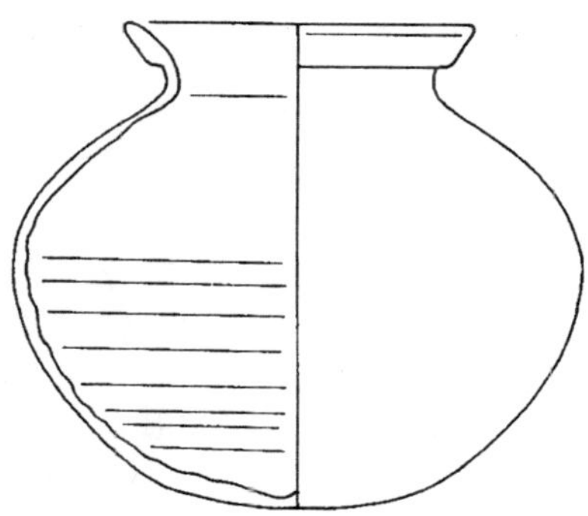

Fig. 30

0 3 cm

IVORY AND PTOLEMAIC EXPLORATION OF THE RED SEA THE MISSING FACTOR*

Like the voyages of Christopher Columbus, the campaigns of Alexander the Great marked the beginning of a great age of exploration that profoundly changed western conceptions of world geography. For the first time, Greek geographers had at their disposal sufficient knowledge to draw relatively accurate maps of the Old World from the Atlantic Ocean to India.[1] One area where the gain in Greek geographical knowledge was particularly remarkable was the Red Sea and its African hinterlands.

Despite its harsh climate and treacherous coasts, the Red Sea was one of the principal commercial arteries of the ancient world. During the second and early first millenniums BCE Egyptian and Phoenician ships plied its waters in search of the wealth of Northeast Africa and Southern Arabia. The Greeks were comparative latecomers to the Red Sea. Greek awareness of the Red Sea began in the sixth century BCE, when the Carian shipmaster Scylax of Caryanda published an account of the voyage he had made from India to Egypt in the service of the Persian king Darius I.[2] Scylax's work is no longer extant, but traces of its influence can be detected in most later classical accounts of the lands along his route. Almost two centuries later an expedition dispatched from Egypt on orders from Alexander the Great in 323 BCE to circumnavigate Arabia

* I would like to thank Professors R. Bagnall and W. Clarysse for their assistance with this paper.

1. Strabo 1. 2. 1 [C 14]; J.O. THOMSON, *History of Ancient Geography,* Cambridge England, 1948, pp. 123-125; O.A.W. DILKE, *Greek and Roman Maps*, London, 1985, pp. 31-35.

2. The fragments of Scylax's works are collected in *FGrH* 3C 709. For the influence of Scylax's works see K. KARTTUNEN, *India in Early Greek Literature, Studia Orientalia* 65, 1989, pp. 65-68.

A Gateway from the Eastern Mediterranean to India. The Red Sea in Antiquity
S.M. BURSTEIN, pp. 149-157

provided further information.[3] It was only in the third century BCE, however, that a permanent Greek presence in the Red Sea basin was established and that a flood of new information about the region was provided by the reports of explorers sent out by Ptolemy II and his successors, Ptolemy III and Ptolemy IV. As a result, Greek geographers were able to describe the coasts of the Red Sea and its hinterlands with a degree of precision and detail that would not be surpassed in the West until publication of the first Portuguese accounts of the area in the sixteenth century CE.[4]

Ptolemaic activity in the Red Sea was unusual in that it is almost the only known example in antiquity of a sustained programme of exploration undertaken on the initiative of a government. Unlike their Egyptian and Phoenician predecessors, however, Ptolemaic interest in the Red Sea was not primarily commercial but military: their desire to find a secure source of war elephants. Despite their mixed record in battle, Hellenistic monarchs had assigned a high priority to the acquisition of war elephants ever since the reign of Alexander. Cut off by geography and politics from what had hitherto been the only source of war elephants and elephant handlers, India, Ptolemy II and his successors turned to the interior and coastal regions of Northeast Africa south of Egypt in their search for a source of war elephants that would be safe from interference by their Seleucid rivals; and they succeeded.

At first, the Ptolemies attempted to reach the elephant hunting grounds in the central and Southern Sudan by means of the Nile valley.[5] Beginning in 270-269 BCE, however, with the foundation of Ptolemaïs of the Hunts — modern Aqiq — near the entrance of the Baraka River valley,[6] and continuing for almost three quarters of a century thereafter, Ptolemaic elephant hunting activity increasingly focused on the Red Sea and its hinterlands. The results were impressive. By the second half of the third century BCE, the Ptolemies were able to employ significant numbers of war elephants in their wars with their Seleucid rivals.[7] Equally impressive, however, was the magnitude and cost of the effort required to achieve these results. As Lionel Casson pointed out in his recent

---

3. Theophrastus, *History of Plants* 9. 4. 3-4; cf. P. HÖGEMANN, *Alexander der Grosse und Arabien, Zetemata* 82, 1985, pp. 80-87.

4. A. KAMMERER, *La Mer Rouge: l'Abyssinie et l'Arabie depuis l'Antiquité*, 3 vols., Cairo, 1929-1949, 2, pp. 363-464.

5. J. DESANGES, "Les chasseurs d'éléphants d'Abou-Simbel", *92e Congrès national des sociétés savantes, Strasbourg et Colmar (1967), Section d'archéologie*, Paris, 1970, pp. 31-50.

6. V. TSCHERIKOWER, *Die hellenistischen Städtegründungen von Alexander dem Grossen bis auf die Römerzeit, Philologus* Suppl. 19. 1, 1927, p. 14; Agatharchides of Cnidus, *On the Erythraean Sea*, edited and translated by Stanley M. BURSTEIN, London, 1989, p. 144, n. 2.

7. Ptolemy III: *OGIS* 54, lines 10-13. Ptolemy IV: Polybius 5. 79. 2.

comprehensive study of Ptolemaic elephant hunting:[8] "It involved the setting up, in remote and primitive areas, of bases fitted with elaborate facilities and the staffing of them with p had to be recruited and specially trained for their jobs. It involved as well launching a fleet of boats of new design to bring the captured beasts back to Egypt. Within Egypt itself it involved the establishment of staging areas and of permanent stables; there seem to have been staging areas around Koptos and in the Fayum, and the stables may have been in Memphis".

Scholarly interest in Ptolemaic elephant hunting has been high ever since the beginnings of modern Hellenistic historiography in the nineteenth century.[9] Three issues have been at the center of much of that scholarship: the political and military significance of Ptolemaic elephant hunting, the organization and infrastructure of the hunts, and the analysis and evaluation of the geographic and ethnographic information produced by them. Remarkably little attention has been devoted to analyzing the conduct of the hunts themselves or, equally important, to explaining the steady southward shift of the location of the principal elephant hunting grounds during the third century BCE that is one of its most striking features and was responsible for the remarkable expansion of Greek knowledge of the geography of the Red Sea basin with which this paper began. Thus, while the chief center for elephant hunting during the reign of Ptolemy II was Ptolemaïs of the Hunts on the central Sudanese coast of the Red Sea, during the reign of his successor Ptolemy III the focus of Ptolemaic elephant hunting moved South to the coast of modern Eritrea, and by the time organized elephant hunting ended during the reign of Ptolemy IV, Ptolemaic hunters had left the Red Sea entirely and pushed out along the Northern coast of Somalia in search of their prey.

In part, of course, scholarly neglect of this phenomenon has resulted from the fact that the explanation for it is, at first glance, obvious. As L. Casson observed, "the reason for the continuous advance southward [sc. of Ptolemaic elephant hunting] very likely was the gradual exhaustion of each hunting ground".[10] This answer, however, ignores a further and more significant question: how could the Ptolemies have exhausted the Red Sea hunting grounds in less than a century? Casson himself was aware of the problem, but could

8. L. CASSON, "Ptolemy II and the Hunting of African Elephants", *TAPhA* 123, 1993, p. 259.

9. Useful accounts are: E. BEVAN, *The House of Ptolemy: A History of Egypt under the Ptolemaic Dynasty*, London, 1927, pp. 175-177; P.M. FRASER, *Ptolemaic Alexandria*, 3 vols., Oxford, 1972, 1, pp. 177-179, 2, pp. 304-308, n. 359-372; H.H. SCULLARD, *The Elephant in the Greek and Roman World*, London, 1974, pp. 126-137; I. HOFMANN, *Wege und Möglichkeit eines indischen Einflusses auf die meroitische Kultur*, Vienna, 1975, pp. 46-111; BURSTEIN, *supra*, n. 6, pp. 4-12; and CASSON, *supra*, n. 8, pp. 247-260.

10. CASSON, *supra*, n. 8, p. 256.

suggest only that the Ptolemies opened new hunting grounds, "when all the herds within easy reach had been caught".[11] This, however, is unlikely.

The ancient sources, it is true, credit the third century Ptolemies with the possession of very large numbers of war elephants, but these numbers are open to serious question. The problems are twofold. First, there is wide variance in the numbers reported in the sources. Appian[12] and Porphyry[13] credit Ptolemy II with 300 and 400 elephants respectively, and the author of *3rd Maccabees* [14] claims that Ptolemy IV possessed 500 elephants. Second and equally important, in 217 BCE, when the survival of the Ptolemaic kingdom itself was at stake and the Ptolemaic government attempted to mobilize the strongest possible army, Ptolemy IV still was able to field a force of only 73 elephants at the Battle of Raphia.[15] Taken together these considerations strongly suggest that the Ptolemaic elephant corps was much smaller than that implied by the high figures found in the sources. Equally clearly, the capture of the relatively few animals each year that would be required to build and maintain a force of this magnitude could not by itself have led to the decimation of the Northeast African elephant herds implied by the southward movement of the focus of Ptolemaic elephant hunting. Another factor must have been involved, and there is one obvious candidate: ivory.

The failure by modern scholars to consider the acquisition of ivory as a possible goal of Ptolemaic policy in the Red Sea is surprising.[16] Throughout history the desire for ivory has been the single most important factor in the decimation of elephant populations in Africa and Asia;[17] and Northeast Africa was one of the principal sources of ivory in antiquity, particularly after the extermination of the elephant populations of western Asia in the first half of the first millennium BCE.[18] From very early times governments in the region strove to acquire large stocks of ivory. Already in the Old Kingdom Egyptian caravans

11. *Ibid.*
12. Appian, Preface 3.
13. Porphyry, *FGrH*, 2B 260 F 42.
14. *3rd Maccabees* 5. 2.
15. Polybius 5. 79. 2.
16. Only suggested to my knowledge by O. KRZYSZKOWSKA, *Ivory and Related Materials: An Illustrated Guide*, London, 1990, p. 18.
17. The literature on the ivory trade and its deleterious effects on elephant populations is enormous. A good general survey is D. WILSON and P. AYERST, *White Gold: The story of African Ivory*, New York, 1976.
18. SCULLARD, *supra*, n. 9, pp. 26-28; R. D. BARNETT, *Ancient Ivories in the Middle East and Adjacent Countries*, *Qedem* 14, 1982, pp. 5-7; KRZYSZKOWSKA, *supra*, n. 16, pp. 15-16.

travelled far up the Nile into upper Nubia to trade for ivory.[19] During the New Kingdom tomb paintings [20] and inscriptions [21] at Thebes record the arrival of ivory in Egypt as part of the tribute of Kush, the Egyptian term for the various states that occupied the Nile Valley in Nubia. In the second and early first millennia BCE, however, the focus of the ivory trade began to shift to the Red Sea. Elephant tusks are prominent among the goods brought back to Egypt by the fleet the Egyptian queen Hatshepsut sent to Punt,[22] roughly the coast and hinterland of the central Sudan, in the early 15th century BCE. Almost five hundred years later Phoenician and Israelite ships also sailed the Red Sea in search of ivory and other luxuries to bring back to Solomon,[23] while inscriptions [24] and reliefs [25] record the arrival in Persepolis of "gifts" of ivory from Kush, *i.e.* the central Sudan, during the period of Persian rule in Egypt. The evidence is clear, moreover, that, like their Egyptian and Near Eastern predecessors, the Ptolemies also succeeded in acquiring large stocks of African ivory.

Almost three quarters of a century ago W.W. Tarn [26] pointed out that a sharp drop in the prices of ivory mentioned in inscriptions at Delos during the reign of Ptolemy II suggests that the supply of ivory reaching the market increased significantly during his reign; and two hundred years later Ptolemy XII and Ptolemy XIII still possessed sufficiently large quantities of ivory to make two large gifts of ivory to the temple of Apollo at Didyma for the decoration of the temple doors.[27] But how did the Ptolemies obtain their ivory?

As already mentioned, the traditional ways of obtaining ivory were trade and diplomacy, and the Ptolemies employed both methods. Thus, Demotic

---

19. J. H. BREASTED, *Ancient Records of Egypt*, 5 vols., Chicago, 1906, 1, p. 54.

20. J. VERCOUTTER, "The Iconography of the Black in Ancient Egypt: From the Beginnings to the Twenty-fifth Dynasty", *The Image of the Black in Western Art* 1, New York, 1976, pp. 47-51.

21. BREASTED, *ARE* 2, p. 494, 502.

22. *Ibid*., p. 263, 272 ; cf. 2, p. 486 (Thutmose III). For the location of Punt see K.A. KITCHEN, "Plunt and How to Get There", *Orientalia*, Ser. 2, 40, 1971, pp. 184-207.

23. 1 *Kings* 10, 18, 22.

24. R. KENT, *Old Persian Grammar Texts Lexicon, American Oriental Series* 33, 2nd ed., New Haven, 1953, p. 144 DSf 40-45; cf. Herodotus 3. 97. 3, who says the Aithiopians brought the Persians twenty large elephant tusks every third year.

25. G. WALSER, *Die Völkerschaften auf den Reliefs von Persepolis*, Berlin, 1906, pp. 100-102, pl. 30, 81, 82.

26. W. W. TARN, "Ptolemy II", *JEA* 14, 1928, p. 258; cf. BARNETT, *supra*, n. 18, p. 65.

27. *I. Didyma* 218, II, lines 5-10, 314, lines 14-18; cf. H.W. PARKE, "The Temple of Apollo at Didyma: The Building and its Function", *JHS* 96, 1986, p. 131.

ostraka from Elephantine containing receipts for payment of ivory tax attest to the continued operation of the Nilotic ivory trade during the reign of Ptolemy II,[28] while the presence of 600 elephant tusks carried by "Aithiopian gift-bearers" in the great procession mounted by the same king in 275 BCE [29] clearly reflects the continuation of the sort of diplomatic "gift" exchange that had been traditional in the region for millennia. Unlike any of their predecessors, however, the Ptolemies also had access to a potential third source of large quantities of ivory: the same elephant hunting organization that they created to acquire their war elephants. The question is: did they use it?

It is certainly difficult to believe that Ptolemaic elephant hunters would have limited their activity to the capture of live elephants and ignored the opportunity provided by the hunts to acquire large amounts of ivory, especially since the sale of ivory would have helped offset the huge expenses incurred by the Ptolemaic government in organizing and conducting the hunts.[30] Evidence that the hunts also functioned as sources of ivory is, however, surprisingly sparse. The extant literary sources for Ptolemaic activity in the Red Sea basin, which are based primarily on the reports of Ptolemaic explorers,[31] are silent on the details of the hunts, concentrating instead on the establishment of the elephant hunting system itself and the dramatic story of the dangers involved in the transportation of the captured elephants to Egypt.[32] Fortunately, as so often happens in the history of Ptolemaic Egypt, critical evidence that is lacking in the literary sources is provided by a papyrus, namely, *P. Petrie* III, 114.[33]

P. Petrie III, 114 records payments made to a number of soldiers, who participated in elephant hunting expeditions up to and including the 25th year of Ptolemy III (223-222 BCE). Like the rest of the papyri discovered by Flinders

---

28. S.V. WÄNGSTEDT, "Demotische Steuerquittungen aus ptolemäischer Zeit", *Orientalia Suecana* 17, 1968, pp. 29-34.

29. Kallixeinos of Rhodes, *FGrH*, 3C 627 F 2. 32. For the date of the procession see V. FOERTMEYER, "The Dating of the Pomp of Ptolemy II Philadelphus", *Historia* 37, 1988, pp. 90-104. Ptolemy VI also claimed to have received ivory as tribute (cf. HOFMANN, *supra*, n. 9, pp. 70-71).

30. The very high cost of the elephant hunting project was pointed out by Cl. PRÉAUX, *L'économie royale des Lagides*, Brussels, 1939, pp. 34-39.

31. The main source for Ptolemaic elephant hunting is the *On the Erythraean Sea* of Agatharchides of Cnidus. For his use of the reports of Ptolemaic explorers see BURSTEIN, *supra*, n. 6, pp. 29-35.

32. *Ibid.*, F 85. Ptolemy II (E. NAVILLE, "La stèle de Pithom", *ZÄS* 40, 1902, p. 73, line 24) and Ptolemy III (*OGIS* 54, lines 10-13) both boasted of their success in bringing elephants back to Egypt alive.

33. The most recent edition of *P. Petrie* III, 114 is B. HEMMERDINGER, "Comptes de chasseurs d'éléphants (*P. Petrie* III, 114)", *APF* 20, 1970, pp. 25-28.

Petrie at Gurob in 1889,[34] *P. Petrie* III, 114 was recovered from cartonage used to wrap mummies. The text, therefore, is fragmentary, and much remains and will remain unclear about its original provenance, character and purpose. Fortunately, however, the text is clear on the one issue that concerns this paper: the payments listed in the papyrus were connected somehow with ἀναστamάτων,[35] that is, elephant tusks, that are specifically described as having been obtained "from the elephant hunts (ἀπὸ τῆς θήρας τῶν ἐλεφάντων)".[36]

Although firm data about the extent of Ptolemaic elephant hunting is lacking, it would be a mistake to underestimate its scale and potential impact on local elephant populations. The demand for ivory in antiquity was enormous. On the basis of references to ivory in Greek and Latin literature E.H. Warmington compiled the following incomplete list of the uses of ivory in the classical world: "statues, chairs, beds, scepters, hilts, scabbards, chariots, carriages, tablets, book-covers, table-legs, doors, flutes, lyres, combs, brooches, pins, scrapers, boxes, bird-cages, floors..."[37] Equally enormous were the costs of meeting this demand. Fully three hundred elephants were required to produce the six hundred tusks Ptolemy II paraded through the streets of Alexandria in 275 BCE. Still, these tusks may represent the cumulative result of several years of diplomatic gift exchange between Ptolemaic Egypt and its southern neighbours. More indicative of the situation is the fact that sixty eight tusks — the product of thirty-four elephants — weighing almost four thousand pounds were required to decorate a single set of doors in the temple of Apollo at Didyma in the first century BCE![38] With the demand for ivory being on this scale, it is easy to understand how overhunting by Ptolemaic hunting expeditions, which could

---

34. For the discovery of the Gurob papyri see W.M. FLINDERS PETRIE, *Ten Year's Digging in Egypt*, London, 1891, pp. 135-136.

35. For the meaning of ἀνάσταμα see HEMMERDINGER, *supra*, n. 33, p. 26, n. 2b.

36. *P. Petrie* III, 114, lines 5, 9, 16, 20. The papyrus is too fragmentary to confirm the theory of H. RAÏOS CHOULIARA ("La chasse et les animaux sauvages d'après les papyrus grecs", *Anagennesis* 1, 1981, pp. 78-79) that *P. Petrie* III, 114 records payments both for tusks obtained from animals killed in hunts and for tusks scavenged from elephants that died in captivity.

37. E.H. WARMINGTON, *The Commerce between the Roman Empire and India*, 2nd. ed., London, 1974, p. 163. There is, unfortunately, no comprehensive survey of ivory in the classical world. Useful preliminary studies are SCULLARD, *supra*, n. 9, pp. 260-261; BARNETT, *supra*, n. 18, pp. 56-72; and the papers collected in J. LESLEY FITTON (ed.), *Ivory in Greece and the Eastern Mediterranean from the Bronze Age to the Hellenistic Period*, 199.

38. See *supra*, n. 27. For other examples of ivory doors see A. OLIVER Jr., "Ivory Temple Doors", *Ivory in Greece*, pp. 227-231.

number over two hundred hunters,[39] could have helped produce the bleak situation attested in early Roman period sources such as Pliny the Elder and the *Periplus of the Erythraean Sea*,[40] which document the disappearance of elephants from the hinterlands of the Red Sea and locate the main sources of ivory either far to the West of the Red Sea in modern Sennar in the Southern Sudan or in India. Viewed in this perspective, Ptolemaic activity in the Red Sea and the expansion of geographical knowledge that resulted from it can be seen as constituting yet another chapter in the dismal story of the decimation of the elephant populations of the Old World during antiquity. Fortunately, however, that is not the whole story.

The shift of the focus of elephant hunting away from the Red Sea basin and its hinterlands toward the interior of Africa and India in the late Hellenistic and early Roman Periods had two important but unanticipated results. First, it allowed the elephant populations in some parts of the Red Sea hinterlands, at least, to recover so that by the end of antiquity the region was again a significant supplier of ivory.[41] Second, and equally important, was its impact on state formation in the area. For almost a millennium following the end of Egyptian rule in Nubia the native peoples of the region had controlled the ivory trade in Northeast Africa. The creation of the Ptolemaic elephant hunting system in the third century BCE had threatened to put an end to that monopoly. The end of organized elephant hunting in the Red Sea basin, however, eliminated this threat and effectively re-established local control of the ivory trade, thereby helping to make possible two of the key developments in the history of Northeast Africa in the early centuries of the Common Era: the economic resurgence of the

39. An expedition of 231 hunters is mentioned in a papyrus of the year 223 BCE (L. MITTEIS and U. WILCKEN, *Grundzüge und Chrestomathie der Papyrus Kunde*, 4 vols., Leipzig/Berlin, 1912, n°. 451).

40. Pliny, *N. H.* 8. 4. 7; *Periplus of the Erythraean Sea* 3-4. The scale of the Indian Ocean ivory trade is well illustrated by a recently published papyrus (cf. L. CASSON, "New Light on Maritime Loans: P. Vindob G 40822", *ZPE* 84, 1990, pp. 195-206) containing a contract for a miscellaneous consignment of India goods loaded at Muziris that includes 7,478 pounds of ivory representing more than one hundred individual elephants.

41. Sixth century CE sources refer to large numbers of elephants near Axum and to the export of ivory from Ethiopia to both the Mediterranean and the countries around the Indian Ocean (Nonnosos *apud* Photius, *Bibliotheca* 3, 2b; Cosmas Indicopleustes, *The Christian Topography*, London, 1897, 11, 339).

kingdom of Meroe in the central Sudan[42] and the emergence of the kingdom of Axum in the Ethiopian highlands.[43]

Stanley M. BURSTEIN
California State University, Los Angeles

42. An indication of this is the discovery of the remains of a large store of ivory in one of the storage rooms of a first century CE Meroitic palace at Wad-ban-Naga (J. VERCOUTTER, "Un palais des 'Candace', contemporain d'Auguste [Fouilles à Wad-ban-Naga 1958-1960]", *Syria* 39, 1962, p. 280; HOFMANN, *supra*, n. 9, p. 139). For Aithiopia (the upper Nile valley) as a source of ivory in the Roman period see Pausanias 5. 12. 3 and Philostratus, *Life of Apollonius of Tyana* 6. 2.

43. For the role of Axum and its principal port, Adulis, in the ivory trade in the first century CE see *Periplus of the Erythraean Sea* 4 and Pliny, *N. H.* 6. 34. 173.

ROMANS AND ARABS IN THE RED SEA*

Exploitation of the Red Sea for communication and commerce has taken place since the predynastic period of Egyptian history (prior to *c.* 3100 B.C.).[1] We know more about activities here from later Egyptian and classical (Greco-Roman) records and from archaeological evidence, especially at the northern end of the Red Sea than from any other contemporary sources.[2] Therefore, our views of Romans and Arabs in the Red Sea will, to a large extent, be coloured by this bias in the surviving or more easily accessible "classical" literary and

---

* I wish to thank Prof. D.F. Graf for reading a draft of this paper, commenting on it and providing useful bibliography which would otherwise have been missed.

1. Cf. J. ZARINS, "Ancient Egypt and the Red Sea Trade: The Case for Obsidian in the Predynastic and Archaic Periods", *in* B. WILLIAMS and A. LEONARD, eds., *Essays in Ancient Civilization Presented to Helene J. Kantor (Studies in Ancient Oriental Civilization,* vol. 47), Chicago, Oriental Institute, 1989, pp. 339-368; J.A. MONTGOMERY, *Arabia and the Bible,* Philadelphia, University of Pennsylvania Press, 1934, p. 176; G.W. VAN BEEK," The Land of Sheba", *in* J.B. PRITCHARD, ed., *Solomon & Sheba,* London, Phaidon, 1974, p. 47; M.G. RASCHKE, "New Studies in Roman Commerce with the East", *ANRW* 2.9.2, 1978, p. 911, n. 1055 on the pharaonic period; pp. 929-930, nn. 1130, 1132 on the Achaemenid Persian period in Egypt; C.A. NALLINO, "L'Égypte avait-elle des relations directes avec l'Arabie méridionale avant l'âge des Ptolémées?", *BIFAO* 30/2, 1930, pp. 465-475.

2. For trade in the Red Sea-Indian Ocean in the Roman-Byzantine period see Raschke (*supra* n. 1): pp. 604-1378; S.E. SIDEBOTHAM, *Roman Economic Policy in the Erythra Thalassa 30 B.C.-A.D. 217* (*Mnemosyne* supplement no. 91), Leiden, E.J. Brill, 1986, *passim;* D.G. LETSIOS, *Byzantium and the Red Sea Relations with Nubia, Ethiopia and South Arabia Until the Arab Conquest, Historical Monographs* 5, Athens, S.D. Basilopoulos, 1988, *passim*; L. CASSON, *The* Periplus Maris Erythraei *Text with Introduction, Translation, and Commentary* Princeton, Princeton University Press, 1989, *passim*; V. BEGLEY and R.D. DE PUMA, *Rome and India: The Ancient Sea Trade,* Madison, University of Wisconsin Press, 1991, *passim.*

A Gateway from the Eastern Mediterranean to India. The Red Sea in Antiquity
S.E. SIDEBOTHAM, pp. 159-171

archaeological evidence rather than in pre-Islamic "Arabic" sources though the latter do provide important evidence.

First, it is essential to define and differentiate "Roman" and "Arab". During the course of the first century B.C. and first and second centuries A.D. many Roman "subjects" in the eastern Roman empire (which encompassed all or parts of modern day Georgia, Armenia, Azerbaijan, Turkey, Syria, Iraq, Jordan, Lebanon, Israel, Egypt and northwestern Saudi Arabia) included Arabs.[3] Some were merely subjects, others were full-fledged Roman citizens; in A.D. 212 all or nearly all free subjects in the Roman Empire became citizens.[4] Also, not all Arabs lived in the Roman Empire; many lived beyond its borders. For the purposes of this paper, an Arab will be defined as a nomad or one of nomadic descent who spoke Arabic or one of its pre-Islamic dialects whether or not he/she was a Roman subject or citizen and whether or not he/she lived inside the Roman realm.[5] Among the Arabs different groups should be distinguished; in this paper the major ones are the Nabataeans, Palmyrenes, Minaeans, Sabaeans and Himyarites. All other non-Arab groups will be considered Roman (subjects/citizens no matter what their ethnic origins) or have some other ethnic nomenclature appended to them.

The Arabs began exploiting the Red Sea as a communication-commercial thoroughfare long before the Romans arrived in the area. Contact between the King Solomon of Israel and Sheba (Saba), an "Arab" kingdom located either in the southwestern corner of the Arabian peninsula or in Eretria-Ethiopia, in the tenth century B.C. is merely one of the more famous examples.[6] Direct Roman involvement in the Red Sea only began after the annexation of the Ptolemaic Kingdom of Egypt as a Roman province by the emperor Octavian/Augustus in 30 B.C.[7] This direct Roman contact with the Red Sea expanded with the eventual annexation of the Arab kingdom of the Nabataeans in A.D. 106 as the Roman Provincia Arabia.[8] Although the southern boundaries of Provincia

---

3. SIDEBOTHAM (*supra* n. 2), pp. 83-102.
4. A.N. SHERWIN-WHITE, *The Roman Citizenship,* 2nd ed., Oxford, Clarendon Press, 1973, pp. 279-287, 380-394.
5. Cf. I. EPH'AL, *The Ancient Arabs: Nomads on the Borders of the Fertile Crescent, 9th - 5th centuries B.C.*, Leiden, E.J. Brill, 1982, pp. 5-12.
6. I *Kings* 10:1-10,13 = II *Chron.* 9:1-9,12; *Isaiah* 60:6; cf. MONTGOMERY (*supra* n. 1), pp. 176-181; VAN BEEK (*supra* n. 1), pp. 47-48; P. CRONE, *Meccan Spice Trade and the Rise of Islam,* Princeton, Princeton University Press, 1987, p. 14 for the Sabaeans as a north Arabian tribe and Sheba as a north Arabian ruler.
7. Strabo, *Geography* 17.1.11-12; Dio Cassius 51.17.1; for a summary of Ptolemaic activity on the Red Sea see SIDEBOTHAM (*supra* n. 2), pp. 1-12.
8. Dio Cassius, *Epitome* 68.14.5; G.W. BOWERSOCK, *Roman Arabia,* Cambridge, Harvard University Press, 1983, pp. 76-89; SIDEBOTHAM (*supra* n. 2), pp. 148-154; B. ISAAC, *The Limits of Empire. The Roman Army in the East,* Oxford, Clarendon

Arabia cannot be established with precision, it seems that Roman military power and political influence extended outside and to the south of this province to include areas of present day Hejaz and along the Wādi Sirhan in northwestern Saudi Arabia. Roman commercial interests, of course, extended much farther afield.[9]

Even after Roman political and military power physically dominated the northern end of the Red Sea, however, the evidence is insufficient to indicate whether "Romans" or "Arabs", "Axumites/Ethiopians", "Indians" and others primarily controlled the commerce passing here. Our ignorance on this point stems from two deficiencies in our sources. First, the ancient classical sources eschew, except in the most general way, any reference to quantification of the evidence; precise numbers of entrepreneurs, their "nationalities" (an anachronistic, but convenient term), volume and cost of trade goods broken down by categories are few and of questionable value.[10] Second, throughout the classical period of interest in the Red Sea-Indian Ocean (*i.e.* from the campaigns of Alexander the Great at the end of the fourth century B.C. until the Muslim Arab conquests of the Near East in the seventh century A.D.) there was a tendency among classical Mediterranean authors to conflate one ethnic group with another. It was quite common, for example, for classical authors to interchange the identities of Indians, Ethiopians and South Arabs.[11] Rarely did the classical sources accurately name and differentiate various Arab/"Saracen" groups.[12]

Press, 1990, 119; F. MILLAR, *The Roman Near East 31 BC-AD 337,* Cambridge, MA-London, 1993, 92-97.

9. For the southern boundaries of Provincia Arabia see I. SHAHÎD, *Rome and the Arabs. A Prolegomenon to the Study of Byzantium and the Arabs,* Washington, D.C., Dumbarton Oaks Research Library and Collection, 1984, p. 20 and n. 5; D.F. GRAF, "Qura 'Arabiyya and Provincia Arabia", *in* P.-L. GATIER *et al.*, eds., *Géographie historique au Proche-Orient*, Paris, CNRS, 1988 pp. 171-211; cf. P.-L. GATIER and J.-F. SALLES, "Aux frontières méridionales du domaine nabatéen", *in L'Arabie et ses mers bordières*, Lyon, TMO no. 16, 1988, pp. 173-190. For the geographical extent of Roman commercial interests see nn. 1-2 *supra*.

10. SIDEBOTHAM (*supra* n. 2), 13-47, pp. 83-102.

11. For the Roman period until the early third century see SIDEBOTHAM (*supra* n. 2), pp. 40-41; for the fourth century on see SHAHÎD (*supra* n. 9), pp. 53-54 and P. MAYERSON, "A Confusion of Indias: Asian India and African India in the Byzantine Sources", *Journal of the American Oriental Society* 113/2, 1993, pp. 169-174.

12. SHAHÎD (*supra* n. 9), pp. 123-141; for the term Saracen in Near Eastern sources see M. O'CONNOR, "The Etymology of *Saracen* in Aramaic and Pre-Islamic Arabic Contexts", *in* P. FREEMAN and D. KENNEDY, eds., *The Defence of the Roman and Byzantine East Proceedings of a colloquium held at the University of Sheffield in April 1986, British Institute of Archaeology at Ankara* (monograph no. 8) (*BAR* is 297, ii), Oxford, British Archaeological Reports, 1986, pp. 603-623.

With the literary sources in such confusion it is impossible for us to ascertain which of the disparate ethnic groups dominated commercial or other activity in the Red Sea at any particular point in the period under consideration. We know all of these groups were involved in the trade, but will probably never know which, if any, group dominated. Certainly, at different periods one or more groups may have been more active in the region than at other times. Particular groups, certainly the Arabs, would have dominated the overland caravan portions of the Red Sea trade network on the Arabian side of the Red Sea while others — and this is less certain — notably Romans and Graeco-Roman-Egyptians would have dominated the maritime portions of the Red Sea trade-communication network at least at its northern end. At the southern end of the Red Sea many, though certainly not all, cargoes would have been trans-shipped from the vessels of northern Red Sea origin (Romans, Graeco-Roman-Egyptians and, perhaps, Nabataeans) to those of South Arabs, Indians, Axumites/Ethiopians and others for conveyance to more distant ports in the Persian Gulf and Indian Ocean littoral.[13]

Archaeological remains and epigraphic evidence indicate that certain groups of Arabs also participated in — there is no evidence that they dominated — the commercial caravan traffic between the Red Sea coast of Egypt and the Nile. In Egypt Nabataeans and Palmyrenes, but also South Arabs including Sabaeans, Himyarites and Minaeans actively participated in the caravan traffic for several centuries, the Nabataeans and Minaeans even before the advent of the Romans.[14] The Nabataeans undoubtedly dominated this caravan traffic between the Red Sea coast of Arabia Nabataea/Provincia Arabia and Petra and over to the Mediterranean coast, mainly in and around Gaza for this was their homeland.[15]

---

13. J.-P. REY-COQUAIS, "L'Arabie dans les routes de commerce entre le monde méditerranéen et les côtes indiennes", *in* T. FAHD, ed., *L'Arabie préislamique et son Environnement historique et culturel, Actes du Colloque de Strasbourg, 24-27 juin 1987, Université des Sciences Humaines de Strasbourg, Travaux du Centre de Recherche sur le Proche-Orient et la Grèce Antiques* 10, Leiden, E.J. Brill, 1989, pp. 225-239; CASSON (*supra* n. 2), 20-21, 31-35, pp. 169-170. For a contrary view see R. LEBARON BOWEN, Jr., "Ancient Trade Routes in South Arabia", *in* R. LEBARON BOWEN, Jr., and F.P. ALBRIGHT, eds., *Archaeological Discoveries in South Arabia,* Baltimore, The Johns Hopkins Press, 1958, p. 35.

14. G. WAGNER, "Une dédicace à Isis et à Héra de la part d'un négociant d'Aden", *BIFAO* 76, 1976, pp. 277-281 = A. BERNAND, *Les Portes du désert,* Paris, CNRS, 1984, pp. 193-195 no. 65; SIDEBOTHAM (*supra* n. 2), pp. 94-96, 98-99; see C. TOLL, "Two Nabataean Ostraca from Egypt", *BIFAO* 94, 1994, pp. 381-382 for the Quseir-Nile road.

15. Diodorus Siculus, *Bibliotheca Historica* 19.94.4-5; *Periplus Maris Erythraei* 19; Pliny the Elder, *Natural History* 12.32.63-64; M.I. ROSTOVTZEFF (trans. D. and T. Talbot Rice), *Caravan Cities,* New York, AMS Press, 1971, pp. 37-54; P.C. HAMMOND, *The Nabataeans. Their History, Culture and Archaeology, SIMA*

Although the date of their appearance is debated, the Nabataeans seem to have been first attested in Assyrian inscriptions of *c.* 650 B.C.[16] The earliest classical Mediterranean reference to them is in 312 B.C.[17] at which point they appear to have abandoned, at least partially, their nomadic ways for a more settled/mercantile life. From their capital at Petra they engaged in caravan trade with South Arabia and with Gerrha on the Persian Gulf.[18] They also appear to have engaged in piracy in the Red Sea sometime in the Hellenistic period (323-30 B.C.), but an expedition — the details of which are vague — launched against them by one of the Ptolemaic monarchs seems to have stopped or at least curtailed this practice.[19] The Nabataeans had an important emporium at Leuke Kome (identified with Kuraybah-'Aynunah in Saudi Arabia near the Straits of Tiran) [20] and probably another at Aila (Aqaba at the northern end of the Gulf of Aqaba). The latter was certainly important in the Roman period as terminus for a major highway and, most likely, as a port.[21] The *Periplus Maris Erythraei* (19)

---

xxxvii, Gothenburg, Paul Åstroms Förlag, 1973, pp. 65-74; BOWERSOCK (*supra* n. 8), pp. 1-11.

16. J.B. PRITCHARD, *Ancient Near Eastern Texts Relating to the Old Testament,* 3rd ed. with Supplement, Princeton, Princeton University Press, 1969, pp. 298-300; cf. D.F. GRAF, "The Origin of the Nabataeans", *Aram* 2: 1 & 2, 1990, pp. 45-75.

17. Diodorus Siculus, *Bibliotheca Historica* 19.94.1; BOWERSOCK (*supra* n. 8), p. 13.

18. For Gerrha see D.T. POTTS, *The Arabian Gulf in Antiquity.* Volume II. *From Alexander the Great to the Coming of Islam,* Oxford, Clarendon Press, 1990, pp. 16-17, 56-57, 85-97, 178-179.

19. Diodorus Siculus, *Bibliotheca Historica* 3.43.4-5; Strabo 16.4.18; W. DITTENBERGER, ed., *OGIS*, Leipzig, S. Hirzel, 1903-1905, no. 132 of 130 B.C. shows how the Ptolemies protected their merchants; W.W. TARN, "Ptolemy II and Arabia", *JEA* 15, 1929, pp. 15-16 argues for Ptolemy II launching the expedition against the Nabataeans. D. LORTON, "The Supposed Expedition of Ptolemy II to Persia", *JEA* 57, 1971, pp. 160-164 believes that Ptolemy II's expedition recorded on the Pithom Stele was directed into Syria-Palestine in 276 B.C. and not into northwestern Arabia. For a late Hellenistic date for Nabataean piracy and a Ptolemaic response to it see Graf (*supra* n. 16). Perhaps the appearance in the late second century B.C. in Ptolemaic sources of an official termed στρατηγὸς καὶ ἐπιστράτηγος τῆς Ἐρυθρᾶς καὶ Ἰνδικῆς θαλάσσης indicates, in part, an attempt by the Ptolemies to curtail Nabataean piracy in the region. On the possible commercial duties of this official see SIDEBOTHAM (*supra* n. 2), pp. 8-9, 11. For Nabataean trade see J. TEIXIDOR, *Un Port romain du Désert. Palmyre et son Commerce d'Auguste à Caracalla, Semitica* 34, Paris, Librairie d'Amérique et d'Orient Adrien-Maisonneuve Jean Maisonneuve Successeur, pp. 42-45.

20. *Periplus Maris Erythraei* 19; SIDEBOTHAM (*supra* n. 2), pp. 106-108, 120-130 = S.E. SIDEBOTHAM, "Aelius Gallus and Arabia", *Latomus* 45/3, 1986, pp. 590-602.

21. Strabo, *Geography* 16.2.30; 16.4.4; cf. Procopius, *History of the Wars* 1.19.3, 1.19.19-20, 1.19.24; Y. GHAWANMEH, "The Port of 'Aqaba and its Role in the Indian Ocean Trade in Ancient and Medieval Times", *Annual of the Department of Antiquities of Jordan* 30, 1986, pp. 311-318; D.S. WHITCOMB, *Aqaba Port of*

records the arrival of small Arab ships to Leuke Kome and we may presume, though the sources are silent, to Aila as well in this period. The Nabataeans continued their caravaning activities even after Roman annexation in A.D. 106 not only in Arabia, but also, as noted above, in Egypt.

The Palmyrene Arabs, whose capital was at Palmyra in Syria, also had a caravan/trade-driven economy.[22] They, too, were active in, though they never could have dominated, the Red Sea trade especially, as epigraphic evidence suggests, at emporia on the Nile in Egypt.[23] They seem to have been more involved in the organizational aspects of this commerce than in the actual conveyance of commodities at least in Egypt. The presence of Palmyrene political and military power in the northern Red Sea was quite short: 269-270/271 A.D. when Queen Zenobia's forces conquered Egypt.[24] This brief

---

Palestine on the China Sea, Amman, Al Kutba Publishers, 1988, *passim*; H.I. MACADAM, "Fragments of a Latin Building Inscription from Aqaba, Jordan", *ZPE* 79, 1989, pp. 163-172 for an imperial Latin inscription of the fourth century and for two Trajanic milestones from A.D. 111/112; J.W. EADIE, "Strategies of Economic Development in the Roman East: The Red Sea Trade Revisited", *in* D.H. FRENCH and C.S. LIGHTFOOT, eds., *The Eastern Frontier of the Roman Empire, Proceedings of a colloquium held at Ankara in September 1988, British Institute of Archaeology* monograph no. 11, *BAR* is 553 (i), Oxford, British Archaeological Reports, 1989, 117; Z. RUBIN, "Byzantium and Southern Arabia. The Policy of Anastasius", *in* D.H. FRENCH and C.S. LIGHTFOOT, eds., *The Eastern Frontier of the Roman Empire,* p. 385, 388 ; ISAAC (*supra* n. 8), pp. 164-165 and n. 16. For recent excavations at Roman Aqaba see S.T. PARKER, "Preliminary Report on the 1994 Season of the Roman Aqaba Project", *BASOR,* 305, 1997, pp. 19-44.

22. Appian, *Civil Wars* 5.1.9; M.I. ROSTOVTZEFF, "Les Inscriptions caravanières de Palmyre", *Mélanges Gustave Glotz* 2, Paris, Les Presses Universitaires de France, 1932, pp. 793-811; ROSTOVTZEFF (*supra* n. 15), pp. 91-119 for Palmyra and Dura, pp. 120-152 for ruins of Palmyra; J. STARCKY and M. GAWLIKOWSKI, *Palmyre,* Paris, Librairie d'Amérique et d'Orient, 1985, pp. 73-88; Ern. WILL, "Marchands et chefs de caravanes à Palmyre", *Syria* 34, 1957, pp. 262-277; I.A. RICHMOND, "Palmyra Under the Aegis of Rome", *JRS* 53, 1963, pp. 43-54; I. BROWNING, *Palmyra,* Ridge Park, NJ, Noyes Press, 1979, pp. 12-18; 25-27; R. DREXHAGE, "Der Handel Palmyras in römischer Zeit", *Münstersche Beiträge zur Antiken Handelsgeschichte* I,1, 1982, pp. 17-34; M. GAWLIKOWSKI, "Palmyre et l'Euphrate", *Syria* 60, 1983, pp. 53-68; J.F. MATTHEWS, "The Tax Law of Palmyra: Evidence for Economic History in a City of the Eastern Roman Empire", *JRS* 74, 1984, pp. 157-180; R. DREXHAGE, *Untersuchungen zum römischen Osthandel,* Bonn, Habelt, 1988, *passim*; ISAAC (*supra* n. 8), pp. 141, 144-146; TEIXIDOR (*supra* n. 19), *passim;* see now R. STONEMAN, *Palmyra and its Empire Zenobia's Revolt Against Rome,* Ann Arbor, University of Michigan Press, 1992, pp. 31-49, 59-63.

23. *OGIS* (*supra* n. 19), no. 639; J. BINGEN, "Une dédicace de marchands palmyréniens à Coptos", *CE* 59, 1984, pp. 355-358 = BERNAND (*supra* n. 14), pp. 262-263 no. 103; SIDEBOTHAM (*supra* n. 2), pp. 94-96.

24. *(Scriptores) Historia Augusta Probus* 9.5 ; D.F. GRAF, "Zenobia and the Arabs", *in* D.H. FRENCH and C.S. LIGHTFOOT, eds., *The Eastern Frontier of the Roman Empire,* pp. 144, 145, 146-147; D. GRAF, "Rome and the Saracens: Reassessing the

occupation hardly allowed the Palmyrenes time to establish any hegemony over the commerce in this region. Their main interest lay in the routes between India, the northern end of the Persian Gulf leading north along the Tigris-Euphrates and traversing thence westward, via Palmyra, to the Mediterranean coast. Their wealth derived from direct participation in the trade, from acting as middlemen in the commerce and in taxing merchants passing through their territory.[25] This desert trading empire eventually disappeared in 273/274 A.D. after conquest by Rome.[26]

Several other Arab groups bear scrutiny. The Kingdom of Ma'in in present day northern Yemen was active in the overland caravan trade in the Arabian peninsula by about 400 B.C. It established trade links northward into the peninsula in the Hejaz and also founded a number of colonies along the Red Sea coastal route to Palestine the most famous of which was Dedan.[27] Their presence in Egypt and on the Aegean island of Delos in Hellenistic times attests to wide-ranging commercial interests.[28] Later, in the course of the first century B.C., Ma'in was absorbed by its southern neighbour the Kingdom of Saba; colonies in the north eventually lost their Minaean identity.[29]

The Sabaeans produced frankincense and myrrh much demanded in the Mediterranean world and controlled trade through their territory deriving income from tolls levied on passing caravan traffic.[30] From their capital at Marib (Marsiaba) they held sway over large portions of the southwestern Arabian

---

Nomadic Menace", *in* T. FAHD, ed., *L'Arabie préislamique et son Environnement historique et culturel* (*supra* n. 13), 391 ; ISAAC (*supra* n. 8), pp. 222-223 and nn., 227 for bibliography; STONEMAN (*supra* n. 22), pp. 158-159, 160-161.

25. BROWNING (*supra* n. 22), pp. 12-18; TEIXIDOR (*supra* n. 19), pp. 20-23, 31-42; for caravan revenues 49-54, for the municipal tariff 57-90; DREXHAGE, "Der Handel ... " (*supra* n. 22), *passim*; DREXHAGE, *Untersuchungen...* (*supra* n. 22), *passim*; STONEMAN (*supra* n. 22), pp. 31-49, 59-63.

26. (*Scriptores*) *Historia Augusta, Aurelian* 31.1-6; Zosimus, *Historia Nova* I.60-61; STONEMAN (*supra* n. 22), 155-179.

27. For the second century B.C. see S.M. BURSTEIN, ed., trans., *Agatharchides of Cnidus on the Erythraean Sea*, second series no. 172, London, Hakluyt Society, 1989, p. 149 (5.89a-89b); for the first century B.C. see Strabo, *Geography* 16.4.18; SIDEBOTHAM (*supra* n. 2), p. 99.

28. SIDEBOTHAM (*supra* n. 2), pp. 98-100.

29. MONTGOMERY (*supra* n. 1), pp. 60-61, 133-138, 182-184; S. MOSCATI, *Ancient Semitic Civilizations*, New York, G.P. Putnam's Sons, 1957, pp. 183-194; in general cf. C. ROBIN, "L'Arabie du Sud et la date du *Périple de la mer Érythrée* (nouvelles données)", *Journal Asiatique* 279, 1-2, 1991, pp. 1-30.

30. BURSTEIN (*supra* n. 27), p. 167 (5.103a-104a); Diodorus Siculus, *Bibliotheca Historica* 3.46.1-3.47.9; Strabo, *Geography* 16.4.19; Pliny, *Natural History* 12.32.63-65; cf ROBIN (*supra* n. 29), pp. 1-30.

peninsula until the early centuries A.D.[31] The Sabaeans were also active in some of the overland caravan traffic between the Egyptian Red Sea ports and the Nile. Graffiti along these routes and from the Egyptian Red Sea port of Quseir al-Qadim attest to their presence there.[32]

Later, the Kingdom of Himyar with its capital at Zafar dominated this trade until the rise of Axum, an African Kingdom on the west coast of the Red Sea in the fourth century.[33] Thereafter, these two powers battled for control of the lucrative trade routes in the region. These power struggles culminated in a series of invasions of Himyarite territory by the Axumites in the course of the fourth and sixth centuries.[34] The motivation was partly commercial, but also political

---

31. MOSCATI (*supra* n. 29), pp. 183-194; VAN BEEK (*supra* n. 1), pp. 40-63.

32. SIDEBOTHAM (*supra* n. 2), 16-17; D.S. WHITCOMB and J.H. JOHNSON, *Quseir al-Qadim 1978 Preliminary Report,* Princeton, ARCE, 1979, *passim*; D.S. WHITCOMB and J.H. JOHNSON, *Quseir al-Qadim 1980 Preliminary Report, American Research Center in Egypt Reports* vol. 7, Malibu, CA, Undena Publications, 1982, *passim;* D.S. WHITCOMB and J.H. JOHNSON, "1982 Season of Excavation at Quseir al-Qadim", *Newsletter of the American Research Center in Egypt* 120, 1982, pp. 24-30; for the question of the identification of Leukos Limen and Myos Hormos with Quseir al-Qadim see J. DESANGES, *Recherches sur l'activité des méditerranéens aux confins de l'Afrique (VIe siècle avant J.C. - IVe siècle après J.C).*, Paris, Collection de l'École française de Rome, 38, 1978, pp. 269-270; G.W.B. HUNTINGFORD, *The Periplus of the Erythraean Sea,* London, Hakluyt Society, 1980, p. 86; M. REDDÉ and J.-C. GOLVIN, "Du Nil à la Mer Rouge: Documents anciens et nouveaux sur les Routes du Désert oriental d'Égypt", *Karthago* 21, 1986-87, pp. 63-64; D.P.S. PEACOCK, "The Site of Myos Hormos: A View from Space", *JRA* 6 (1993), pp. 226-232. An IFAO team excavating in winter 1994 at Zerkah station (the ancient Maximianon) on the road between Coptos and Quseir/Quseir al-Qadim found ostraca mentioning the port of Mycs Hormos: A. BÜLOW-JACOBSEN *et al.*," The Identification of Myos Hormos. New Papyrological Evidence", *BIFAO* 94, 1994, pp. 27-38. This writer believes that Ptolemaic Myos Hormos is beneath modern Quseir and that Quseir al-Qadim represents a Roman period port founded after the Ptolemaic period one *c.* 6-8 km farther south (under modern Quseir) had, for some reason, been abandoned. For Islamic activity at Quseir al-Qadim see above and D. WHITCOMB, "Quseir al-Qadim, Egypt: Text and Context in the Indian Ocean Spice Trade", *Al-'Usur al-Wusta* 7/2, October 1995, pp. 25-27.

33. On Axum see Y.M. KOBISHCHANOV (L.T. Kapitanoff, trans.), *Axum,* London - University Park, PA, Pennsylvania State University Press, 1979, pp. 171-189 and S. MUNRO-HAY, *Aksum. An African Civilisation of Late Antiquity,* Edinburgh, Edinburgh University Press, 1991, pp. 33-35, 166-179; on Roman/Byzantine relations with Axum and South Arabia see LETSIOS (*supra* n. 2), *passim.* Ethiopian tradition believes that Sheba was from Axum which later conquered the southwestern corner of Arabia as part of the kingdom of Sheba (Saba).

34. CRONE (*supra* n. 6), pp. 42-48; RUBIN (*supra* n. 21), pp. 390-392. For evidence of Axumite presence along the Berenike-Nile road in Egypt in the fourth century see E. LITTMANN and D. MEREDITH, "An Old Ethiopic Inscription from the Berenice Road", *Journal of the Royal Asiatic Society* 3rd series, 1954, pp. 119-123.

and religious; the Axumites were African Christians, the Himyarites were Arabs although one of their rulers in the sixth century, Dhu Nuwas, was Jewish and there was a sizeable Jewish community in the region.[35] Graffiti from along the roads and from Quseir al-Qadim indicate that the Himyarites, too, were involved in the overland caravan traffic between the Egyptian Red Sea ports and the Nile.[36]

It was not all competition. Rome and Axum had an extended period of friendly relations based partly on their common religion, Christianity, and on their interests in diverting trade from the Sassanian Persians (see *infra*).[37] Cooperation may have included attempts at controlling the depredations of nomadic tribes in northeastern Africa especially from the late third-fourth centuries A.D. until the seventh. The Nabatae and Blemmyes were particularly troublesome and their activities may have had a negative impact on Roman control over any transdesert caravan traffic passing between the Nile and the Red Sea coast in that period. The Blemmyes seem to have controlled aspects of this commerce in the Eastern Desert and Red Sea coastal areas of Egypt.[38] Blemmyes power undoubtedly extended south of the Roman sphere of influence and both Rome and Axum would have sought each other's help to deal with this situation.[39]

---

35. B. LEWIS, *The Jews of Islam*, Princeton, Princeton University Press, 1984, pp. 74-75; RUBIN (*supra* n. 21), p. 389, 390; F. de BLOIS, "The date of the 'Martyrs of Nagrān'", *Arabian Archaeology and Epigraphy* I, no. 2/3, Dec. 1990, pp. 110-128.

36. SIDEBOTHAM (*supra* n. 2), pp. 16-17, 56, 100; G. COLIN "À propos des graffites Sud-Arabiques du Ouādi Hammāmāt", *BIFAO* 88, 1988, pp. 33-36.

37. CRONE (*supra* n. 6), pp. 40-42; RUBIN (*supra* n. 21), pp. 383-386; A. WINK, *Al-Hind The Making of the Indo-Islamic World,* vol. 1. *Early Medieval India and the Expansion of Islam 7th-11th Centuries,* Delhi, OUP, 1990 p. 47.

38. Olympiodorus, *History* fragment 35.2 *in* R.C. BLOCKLEY, *The Fragmentary Classicizing Historians of the Later Roman Empire* II, Liverpool, Francis Cairns, 1983, pp. 198-199; Priscus, fragments 27.1-2 *in* BLOCKLEY, pp. 322-325; R.T. UPDEGRAFF, "The Blemmyes I: The Rise of the Blemmyes and the Roman Withdrawal from Nubia Under Diocletian", *ANRW* 2.10.1, 1988, p. 71 and n. 167. For possible Blemmyes presence at the Red Sea port of Berenike see S.E. SIDEBOTHAM and W.Z. WENDRICH, eds., *Berenike 1994. Preliminary Report of the 1994 Excavations at Berenike (Egyptian Red Sea Coast) and the Survey of the Eastern Desert,* Leiden, Centre for Non-Western Studies, 1995, pp. 8-10, 41-43, 105-106, and S.E. SIDEBOTHAM and W.Z. WENDRICH, eds., *Berenike 1995. Preliminary Report of the 1995 Excavations at Berenike (Egyptian Red Sea Coast) and the Survey of the Eastern Desert,* Leiden, Centre for Non-Western Studies), 1996.

39. Procopius, *History of the Wars* 1.19.29-33; RUBIN (*supra* n. 21), pp. 385-386; J. DESANGES, "Les relations de l'Empire romain avec l'Afrique nilotique et érythréenne, d'Auguste à Probus", *ANRW* 2.10.1, 1988, pp. 33-40; R.T. UPDEGRAFF,

In general, to discern which groups may have dominated activity in the Red Sea we must remember not only the time frame which we are considering, but also the geographical region of the Red Sea under discussion.

We know, for example, that the Kingdom of Axum and several of the South Arabian Kingdoms (*e.g.* Ma'in, Saba and later Himyar and the al-Kinda federation) *seem* to have dominated trade in the southern part of the Red Sea throughout the last centuries B.C. until the seventh century A.D. while the Romans *seem* to have dominated the northern part of the Red Sea trade at least until the end of the second century A.D.[40] From the late third/fourth century A.D. these southern Red Sea powers increasingly dominated commercial activities in the entire region at the expense of the Romans.[41] Ancient literary sources and sketchy archaeological evidence, however, suggest that Romans remained active in the Red Sea throughout the entire period of Roman presence in the area. Although the intensity of that activity declined during the third century, there was a renaissance in the fourth-sixth centuries.[42] After the Muslim Arab conquests of Egypt and the Near East in the seventh century A.D. Rome played no direct role in the Red Sea commerce.[43]

There were military and political attempts by Rome to influence events beyond her borders in the Arabian peninsula. Some were successful; others were not. The famous invasion of South Arabia by the Roman governor of Egypt Aelius Gallus with a 10,000 man army in 26-25 B.C. was the earliest endeavour by Rome to influence decisively events in the Arabian peninsula. Although the expedition was a military failure, foundering at the gates of Marib (Marsiaba), it seems to have reaped for Rome tremendous political, diplomatic and, concomitantly, commercial advantages. Other Roman/Byzantine expeditions in alliance with the Axumites, are believed to have taken place in the fourth century and known to have taken place during the reign of Justin I (A.D. 518-527).[44]

ANRW 2.10.1, 1988, pp. 44-97 and L. TÖRÖK, "Additional Remarks", *ANRW* 2.10.1, 1988, pp. 97-106.

40. For Axum, KOBISHCHANOV (*supra* n. 33), pp. 171-189 and MUNRO-HAY (*supra* n. 33), pp. 33-35, 166-179; for Saba, BURSTEIN (*supra* n. 27), pp. 166-167 (5.103a-104a-104b) and VAN BEEK (*supra* n. 1), p. 40, 63; for Minaeans, BURSTEIN (*supra* n. 27), p. 149 (5.89a-89b).

41. KOBISHCHANOV (*supra* n. 33), pp. 171-189; MUNRO-HAY (*supra* n. 33), pp. 33-35, 166-179.

42. SHAHÎD (*supra* n. 9), p. 40; SIDEBOTHAM and WENDRICH (*supra* n. 38), *passim*. S.E. SIDEBOTHAM and W.Z. WENDRICH, eds., *Berenike 1995*, 1996.

43. Cf. A.J. BUTLER (P.M. Fraser, ed.), *The Arab Conquest of Egypt and the Last Thirty Years of the Roman Dominion*, 2nd ed., Oxford, Clarendon Press, 1978, pp. 194-495.

44. For Gallus see SIDEBOTHAM (*supra* n. 2), pp. 120-130 = SIDEBOTHAM (*supra* n. 20), pp. 590-602; for the later expeditions see SHAHÎD (*supra* n. 9), p. 15, pp. 41-43;

Later in the second century A.D. after the Roman annexation of Arabia Nabataea four inscriptions — one bilingual Greek-Nabataean, two Greek and one Nabataean — from Ruwwafa (Saudi Arabia) dating from the joint reigns of the Roman emperors Marcus Aurelius and Lucius Verus (A.D. 161-169) record a treaty among warring Thamudic Arab tribes or, perhaps, between the Thamudic and Safaitic tribes.[45] These important inscriptions suggest that Roman authorities negotiated peace between warring factions of Arab tribes. Arabs from a number of tribes regularly served in the Roman and later Byzantine armies as *foederati* (auxiliary allied troops).[46]

Another inscription from Namara dated to A.D. 328 indicates Roman relations, through a chieftain named Imru' al-Qays, with the Lakhmid tribe which acted as *foederati* to the Roman forces.[47] Since, however, Arab tribes traditionally conducted periodic raids against one another and against settled peripheral areas of the Roman Empire, such a peace would not have been long-lasting. Rome wanted stability, no doubt, to keep trouble away from her borders and to perpetuate the proper atmosphere for continued conduct of the lucrative overland caravan trade passing between the empire on the one hand and South Arabia and the Persian Gulf on the other.[48] Whatever peace may have been achieved was short lived: tribal unrest disrupted regions of Provincia Arabia perhaps in the Severan period (A.D. 193-235) and certainly more severely after

---

CRONE (*supra* n. 6), pp. 47-48; LETSIOS (*supra* n. 2), pp. 239-274; for additional bibliography on Roman-Axumite relations see *supra* n. 33.

45. D.F. GRAF, "The Saracens and the Defense of the Arabian Frontier", *BASOR* 229, 1978, pp. 9-12; M. SARTRE, *Trois études sur l'Arabie romaine et byzantine, Collection Latomus* 178, Brussels, 1982, pp. 27-29; BOWERSOCK (*supra* n. 8), pp. 96-98; I. SHAHÎD, *Byzantium and the Arabs in the Fourth Century,* Washington, D.C., Dumbarton Oaks Research Library and Collection, 1984), p. 30, 128, 138; SHAHÎD (*supra* n. 9), pp. 330-345, 394; GRAF (*supra* n. 9), pp. 171-211.

46. GRAF (*supra* n. 45), pp. 4ff; for Arabs as *foederati* in the later Roman period see SHAHÎD (*supra* n. 9), pp. 18-24 and *s.v.* "foederati", "Arab' in index 613-614; I. SHAHÎD, *Byzantium and the Arabs in the Fifth Century* Washington, D.C., Dumbarton Oaks Research Library and Collection, 1989, pp. 10-12, 464-465 for Arab units and *foederati* in Egypt and *s.v.* "*foederati,* Arab" in index 585-586; D.G. LETSIOS, "The Case of Amorkesos and the Question of the Roman Foederati in Arabia in the Vth Century", *in* T. FAHD, ed., *L'Arabie préislamique et son environnement historique et culturel* (*supra* n. 13), pp. 525-533.

47. MILLAR (*supra* n. 8), pp. 434-435. The Lakhmids also supported the Sassanians when it suited them: SHAHÎD (*supra* n. 9), pp. 31-53; LETSIOS (*supra* n. 2), pp. 185-186, 338-339.

48. In general for the earlier period D.T. POTTS, *The Arabian Gulf in Antiquity,* Volume I. *From Prehistory to the Fall of the Achaemenid Empire,* Oxford, Clarendon Press (1990), *passim;* in general for the later period in the Gulf see POTTS (*supra* n. 18), *passim.*

the fourth century.[49] The examples of the Ruwwafa and Namara inscriptions illustrating Roman attempts to control unrest amongst the Arab tribes on and beyond her political borders are not isolated cases, and the results of the efforts recorded on these inscriptions were probably ephemeral. Rome failed to impose any long term solutions to troubles created by Arab tribes on the edges of its eastern frontier.

There is another factor to consider when discussing Romans and Arabs in the Red Sea and their roles in the commercial activity there. The political situation in the Red Sea basin did not remain static throughout the period of Roman activity there. Between 30 B.C. and the seventh century A.D. Rome politically dominated the northern portion of the Red Sea. Such cannot be said for the southern end, however, where political power ebbed and flowed to and from various states both on the Arabian and on the African sides of the Red Sea. The absorption of the Minaeans by the Sabaeans, the Roman expedition of 26-25 B.C. and conflicts among the Axumites themselves and among the Axumites, Byzantines and Himyarites noted above[50] are but a few of the events which left the southern end of the Red Sea less politically stable than the northern portion.

One other factor must be considered when analyzing Romans and Arabs in the Red Sea and that is the political, commercial and military power first of Parthia from the third century B.C. until the third century A.D.[51] and then of Sassania from the third until the seventh century A.D.[52] Parthia and then Sassania were the greatest organized states Rome ever faced and the Romans perceived them as constant and serious threats to their power in the Near East from the first century B.C. until the seventh century A.D.[53] In fact, one major reason Rome sought to exploit the Red Sea as a commercial-communication link between the Mediterranean basin and the Indian subcontinent was to avoid the more expensive, Parthian-Sassanian controlled overland trade routes to the East.

---

49. S.T. PARKER, *Romans and Saracens : A History of the Arabian Frontier,* Winona Lake, Indiana, American Schools of Oriental Research, 1986, pp. 129-131; ISAAC (*supra* n. 8), pp. 68-77 believes that the nomadic tribes were not a source of trouble before the fourth century. See also D. KENNEDY and D. RILEY, *Rome's Desert Frontier from the Air,* Austin, University of Texas Press, 1990, pp. 36-39.

50. See *supra* n. 44.

51. N.C. DEBEVOISE, *A Political History of Parthia,* Chicago, University of Chicago Press, 1938, *passim;* M.A.R. COLLEDGE, *The Parthians*, New York-Washington, Praeger, 1967, 36-56.

52. BUTLER (*supra* n. 43), pp. 54-92; cf. Z. RUBIN, "Diplomacy and War in the Relations between Byzantium and the Sassanids in the Fifth Century AD", *in* P. FREEMAN and D. KENNEDY, eds., *The Defence of the Roman and Byzantine East, Proceedings of a colloquium held at the University of Sheffield in April 1986, British Institute of Archaeology at Ankara* monograph no. 8 (*BAR* is 297, ii), Oxford, BAR, 1986, pp. 677-695.

53. See *supra* nn. 51-52.

Circumvention of Parthia and Sassania were uppermost concerns in the Roman decision to exploit and Red Sea-Indian Ocean option at least in its trade with India. To this end Rome cooperated with two major powers at the southern end of the Red Sea in the fourth-sixth centuries: the Arab Kingdom of Himyar and the African Kingdom of Axum. These latter powers were also anxious to cooperate with Rome to divert the eastern trade away from Parthian-Sassanian controlled overland routes to the Red Sea and Indian Ocean.[54]

It is interesting to note that our knowledge of "Indian" views on this "western" competition between Rome and Parthia-Sassania is marginal to non-existent; in many cases the Tamil and other Indian literary terms for "westerners" — Yavanas — do not precisely discriminate between "Romans" and others dwelling in lands west of India.[55]

Chinese sources, however, seem to indicate that the Persian intermediaries tried to discourage direct contacts between China and Rome[56] and, we may assume by analogy, probably between India and the Mediterranean, too, in order to preserve their middleman status.

This brief overview of Romans and Arabs in the Red Sea shows the complexities of attempting to simplify and label different groups of peoples and has demonstrated the difficulties of studying their activities in the region. Only continued, extensive archaeological work will shed additional light on the history of Roman and Arab activity in the Red Sea.

Steven E. SIDEBOTHAM

---

54. DEBEVOISE (*supra* n. 51), pp. 203-212; SHAHÎD (*supra* n. 45),p. 15.

55. There is a large and growing bibliography on the Yavana question. Cf. O. STEIN, "Yavanas in Early Indian Inscriptions", *Indian Culture* I, 1935, pp. 343-357; P. MEILE, "Les Yavanas dans l'Inde Tamoule", *Journal Asiatique* 232, 1940, pp. 85-123; K. ZVELEBIL, "The Yavanas in Old Tamil Literature", *in* F. TAUER *et al.*, eds., *Charisteria Orientalia praecipue ad Persiam pertinentia*, Prague, Nakladatelství Ceskoslovenské Akademie Ved, 1956, pp. 401-109; R. SORACI, *L'Unità dei Greci e il Nome Yauna,* Catania, Tipogr. "Le Celere" (1958), *passim;* P.T. SRINIVAS IYENGAR, *History of the Tamils from the earliest times to 500 A.D.* reprint ed., New Delhi, Asian Educational Services, 1982, pp. 297-298, 305, 315, 390, 541-542; F. DE ROMANIS, "Roma e i Nótia dell'India ricerche sui rapporti tra Roma e l'India dravidica dal 30 A.C. all'età flavia", *Helikon* 22-27, 1982-1987, pp. 169-179.

56. Cf. D.F. GRAF, "The Roman East from the Chinese Perspective", forthcoming.

ARCHAEOLOGY IN THE RED SEA

In 1969, a group of Israeli archaeologists spent a summer excavating the remains of an immense ship that had burned and sunk at anchor in the port of Sharm el Sheikh, now the military harbour there. They found more than 1,000 thin, earthenware water vessels, some pipes, and pieces of broken porcelain on a well preserved ship of the early 18th century (RABAN 1971). Other sites in the Sinai also received attention; they include a mercury-carrier of the late medieval period and several scatter wrecks that include anchors (RABAN 1973 and 1990). With the increasing popularity of sport diving in the Red Sea, other shipwreck sites were discovered, but most have been seriously looted.

Since 1994, the Institute of Nautical Archaeology-Egypt (INA-Egypt)[1] in cooperation with the Supreme Council of Antiquities for Egypt (SCA), has documented archaeological sites in the Red Sea and the Mediterranean through shipwreck surveys and the excavation of an Ottoman-period vessel. In the Red

---

1. Acknowledgements. Egypt's Supreme Council of Antiquities provided crucial support for the excavation through the participation of archaeological inspectors Abdel el Rigal, Sameh Ramses, Mohammed Mustafa and Mohammed el Sayed. We are also grateful to the Egyptian Navy for the liaison duties carried out by Lt. Tarek Abu el Elaa, to the American Research Center in Egypt and its Cairo director Mark Easton for logistical support, and to archaeologists Douglas Haldane, Emad Khalil, Elizabeth Greene, Alan Flanigan, Peter Hitchcock, Layne Hedrick, Marsten Morgan and Chris Stephens and to our illustrators Netia Piercy, Kendra Burnett, and Lara Piercy.

Funding and support for the 1995 season were generously supplied by Billings Ruddock, The Amoco Foundation, CityBank, The John and Donnie Brock Foundation, CIB, Kodak, Pfizer - Egypt, DHL, Bilkent University, the Institute of Nautical Archaeology, Harry and Joan Kahn, Richard and Mary Rosenberg, Sea-U-Underwater, Robert and Fran Vincent, Richard and Bari Benia, Hermes Diving Center, and Scuba-Doo Diving Center.

A Gateway from the Eastern Mediterranean to India. The Red Sea in Antiquity
C. HALDANE, pp. 173-188

Sea, few remains dating before the 14th century AD have been identified, although one site seems to be of the Roman period. Along the Mediterranean coast west of Alexandria, 17 sites dating from the 4th century BC through the 7th century AD have been located, but most are poorly preserved or isolated finds. Each year, we plan to continue the exploration of Egypt's coast through surveys while continuing an excavation programme designed to study wrecks from important periods of Egyptian history. All finds from INA-Egypt work are currently stored and undergoing conservation in the Alexandria Conservation Laboratory for Submerged Antiquities, located in the Maritime Museum. The lab itself is another joint project of the SCA and INA-Egypt.

The 1994 Red Sea Shipwreck Survey

For five weeks in 1994, a small international team investigated reported wreck sites and anchorages in an area between Quseir and Hurgada as well as in the Sinai (HALDANE 1994). Seventeen of the sites we visited produced archaeological material, and we learned of several additional wrecks from local sports divers. None of the artifacts we recorded was retained due to restrictions placed on us by the SCA. The most significant of these sites date to the Ottoman period.

In the modern harbour of Quseir, surface survey of the sandy bottom provided a collection of late 17th and early 18th century clay pipes, cups, and jars. Much of the harbour is less than 5 m deep, and recovering 300-year-old objects from the surface of the seabed there was surprising to us, as we had expected sand deposition to have hidden both recent and historical traces. Historical material was mixed with modern sheep bones; local residents told us that a ferry carrying sheep had sunk at the harbor a few years earlier.

At Quseir al Qadim, 12 km north of the modern city, we recorded an 18th-century iron anchor on the south side of the harbour. A later visit to this site included a dive on a deep, poorly preserved Roman period wreck. Excavators of the Roman/Mamluk settlement associated with the harbour have convincingly suggested that the sea formerly reached nearly a kilometre further inland (WHITCOMB and JOHNSON 1982), so the infilled area may be a better place to search for wrecks.

Despite the possibility of finding pharaonic remains at Mersa Gawasis, the site of several Middle Kingdom shrines excavated by Dr. Abdel Monem al Sayed (1978), we found only a transport jar fragment of indeterminate date and two iron anchors in the anchorage. As at Quseir al Qadim and other inlets along this coast, sand is created and deposited at a rapid rate through erosion and the life cycles of reef inhabitants. Remote sensing is likely to be more productive than visual survey.

Near Hurgada, sports divers showed us a medieval keg amphora concreted to the seabed, but it seems to be an isolated artifact. Also in the area are two large porcelain wrecks of late 17th/early 18th century date and several historical wrecks under intense pressure from sports divers. Porcelain from a site in Hurgada wreck is comparable to objects from the Sadana Island shipwreck further south (see below) and the Sharm el Sheikh ship excavated by A. Raban (1971); clay vessels resemble objects from those two sites as well as harbour deposits at Sharm el Sheikh and on a wreck site near Tiran Island that we visited. The survey concluded with visits to previously documented sites (RABAN 1973, 1990), a much disturbed wreck probably of the 18th century, and examination of medieval sherd scatters in the many small anchorages of the Sharm el Sheikh area.

The Sadana Island Shipwreck

Several Egyptian sport divers who wanted to protect an unusual resource told us about the Sadana Island shipwreck. One group dived more than 500 times on the wreck in 1991, examining the wreck and, later, moving some artifacts to less visible locations. Before them, an unknown group apparently had illegally worked at the site, leaving concrete blocks and white plastic labels behind; we have no information about their identity, but find it shocking that individuals clearly practicing archaeology would do so without permission from the Supreme Council of Antiquities for Egypt.

In 1994, one of the Egyptian sport divers we spoke with described the site's general location, and we spent three days determining the extent and nature of the shipwreck. The construction of the ship shared some features with the Sharm el Sheikh wreck, but was clearly an undocumented tradition. Qing Dynasty Chinese porcelain of the Kangxi period had made the site attractive to looters as well, and pressure on the site was increasing. The Sadana Island Shipwreck could provide a large and diverse collection of well dated artifacts of the late 17th/early 18th centuries, a time often neglected by archaeologists, and supply information about a poorly documented period in the northern Red Sea. With these points in mind, INA-Egypt began excavating the Sadana Island Shipwreck in 1995 with the cooperation of the SCA.

The Site

The Sadana Island shipwreck covers an area approximately 50 x 25 m along the sandy, sloping base of a coral reef. The site lies between 28 and 40 metres, and a group of anchors east of the wreck may be associated with it. Three stacked grapnel anchors mark the bow, and the port frames are visible along the length of the site, including some covered by coral within the reef. The starboard side of the ship broke away at or near the keel: only a few planks near the assumed centerline are visible. A 7 x 6 m area filled with more than 1,000 earthenware water vessels delimits the stern; a sandy slope west of this area is sterile.

To a visitor's eyes, the ship is surprisingly empty. About 30 large storage or transport jars clustered dominate the center of the site, and a copper and porcelain objects can be distinguished in the lower regions. Large timbers running the length of the hull and other hull components protrude from the sand, but much of the original cargo seems to have been lost. Historical documents tell us that organic goods, especially textiles, coffee, and sugar, made up much of the Red Sea trade during the Ottoman period; if the Sadana ship carried the products, natural processes of decay may be responsible for the "emptiness" of the site. Excavation techniques designed to recover organic materials already have given us clues to the ship's original cargo.

After setting our datum points for mapping the site, we began to move all large objects from the central part of the site. At the same time, some teams of archaeologists planned and removed all visible porcelain and copper objects to make the site less attractive to looters. Still others used a water dredge to excavate two test trenches for investigating the hull's structure. Over the nine-week season, more than 1,000 dives on the site allowed the controlled excavation of a large number of porcelain, copper, earthenware, and organic objects. All artifacts are stored and conserved in the Alexandria Conservation Laboratory for Submerged Antiquities, a joint SCA/INA-Egypt project located in Alexandria's Maritime Museum.

Summary of finds

Porcelain objects make up the largest single class of artifacts excavated in 1995, followed by other ceramics. The 320 porcelain objects represent a special class of export wares created by kiln centers in China for the Middle Eastern market. Religious injunctions against the representation of human figures meant that most porcelain sold in the Middle East featured floral designs, and agents for cargoes destined for the Red Sea were strongly warned against buying any other type. The Topkapi Saray Museum in Istanbul offers the closest comparative collection for the Sadana porcelain; many pieces are virtually identical (KRAHL and AYERS, 1986). Monochrome glazed, enamelled, celadon, white, and blue-and-white decorated wares allow us to look at the variety of Chinese porcelain known and used in the Ottoman world.

The Sadana collection includes several types of the popular blue-and-white porcelain traded to Europe and elsewhere in large numbers. At least 140 large blue-and-white dishes decorated with a peony scroll motif on the interior and two bare branches on the exterior were excavated in 1995 (*fig. 1*). The dishes measure either 34.4 cm or 37.8 cm in diameter like those represented in the Topkapi collection and are dated to the late 17th or early 18th century (KRAHL and AYERS, 1986: 1026, no. 2208). Two other saucer-shaped dish designs also at Sadana are dated to the early 18th century (KRAHL and AYERS, 1986: 1072, no. 2405 and 1073, no. 2408).

Nearly 70 cups of nine different designs include celadon (*fig. 2a*) and monochrome brown glazed examples (*fig. 2b*), one brown glazed type having a quatrefoil medallion filled by an underglaze blue plum-family blossom (*fig. 2c*).

The brown cups are usually dated to the mid/late 17th century. In *fig. 2d*, only the underglaze blue decoration remains of a pattern once bright with enamelled colours such as red, yellow, green or gold. Enamel colours rarely are found on pieces that come from the sea, but, with patience and raking light, it is possible to trace their original location on the porcelains because they last long enough to protect the glazed surface from the effects of salt water. This kind of work must be done after the object has been desalinated and dried, so few of the Sadana pieces have had their "ghosting" defined.

One notable exception is bowl 2-65 (*fig. 3*), with day lilies and chrysanthemums preserved only as ghosts (solid lines) in a framework of underglaze blue leaves, flowering grasses, and panels. Topkapi Saray Museum bowl TKS 4062 is almost identical to the Sadana example (KRAHL and AYERS, 1986 : 1216, no. 3011), but is about 15% larger. It is dated to the early 18th century.

Intricate ghosting also has been identified on several other pieces. A bowl with vine-leaf-shaped medallions and another with spiralling blue panels from Sadana also find parallels in the Topkapi collection (KRAHL and AYERS, 1986: 1296, no. 3343; 1339, no. 3525). These, however, are dated to the second half of the 18th century and 1730-60 respectively.

Almost 50 smaller bowls of two styles also featured colours applied after firing. On one, a fence, decorative rocks, and floral elements are easily seen in blue (*fig. 4*); the other is decorated with flowers and floral sprays on the outside while inside, a central rosette of 10 alternating light and dark "petals" and, at the rim, a now-invisible diaper border enclosing blue-flowered panels complete the design. The catalogue of enamelled wares may also embrace some shallow dishes and plates, now only white, but some of which were originally painted with other colours. Thirty plates and dishes with bracket-lobed and ridged rims have six pendants that extend to the cavetto.

As noted in the descriptions of different types, the dating for Sadana Island porcelain spans a century according to traditional interpretations. It is unlikely that the porcelain itself was made over such a long period and traded only after 1750. Because porcelain wares within this period rarely bear reign marks that could provide a precise date, it is likely that the Sadana Island ship's cargo eventually will help resolve new and existing questions about Qing Dynasty chronology.

Less finely made but as varied are more than 100 earthenware water vessels excavated this year. At least 20 different designs and shapes are known from this group of objects. Hollow arms join the mouth and body of a shape that imitates a Ming dynasty lidded piece (*fig. 5a*); applied strips and dots of clay enhance an elaborate, double-handled jar (*fig. 5b*). Other shapes resemble waterpipe bowls; still others have filters at the junction of neck and body. All are made of a thin, gray/brown fabric designed to allow water to evaporate through it quickly to cool the remaining water.

In addition to large and small glazed and plain clay bowls, we also recovered a handled jar (1-1, *fig. 6*). Its interior is dark green and crazed; so far, it is unique. Also unusual is a yellow and brown glazed bowl with a central spiral and lotus-like blossoms on "arms" extending from the center (*fig. 7)*. Clay pipes, a red-slipped tobacco holder, incense burners, handled jars, and a small spouted pot also were excavated this year.

Other containers on the site were made of green and brown glass (case bottles) and of copper-based metal. Archaeologists recovered a coffee pot, two tripod grills lined with a ceramic insulator, a kettle, ewers, and cooking pots. Copper metal also was used in the manufacture of a large pulley wheel and a lidded box, possible an expanding lantern.

Chance finds of large and small container lids, rope, wood, charcoal, and coconut husks showed that organic materials were well preserved on site. Systematic examination of all jar contents and dark-coloured deposits produced pepper, coriander, coffee beans, aromatic resin and weed seeds from the ship's last voyage. These finds are especially important as we suspect that much of the ship's original cargo was organic. Separating organic remains from sediment is a tedious but simple procedure known as bucket flotation; gross morphological features and sections of recovered seeds are compared to modern ones for identification just as pottery designs can be compared to known examples. Archaeobotanical studies contribute tremendously to our understanding of shipping activity from all periods because they provide hard evidence for cargo, shipboard life, trade routes and even seasonality.

The hull

Studying methods of ship construction gives us the opportunity to look at the most complex machines built before Industrial Revolution (STEFFY 1994). If a Mediterranean and a European shipwright had looked at the Sadana Island ship, they would have been puzzled to see the combination of familiar and unfamiliar elements it incorporates. The ship is large (about 50 metres long), yet its frames are smaller than they would be familiar with from their own traditions.

Up to three keelsons and sister keelsons, timbers stretching the length of the ship above the keel, are not unusual in either Mediterranean or European shipbuilding, but the Sadana ship had at least 10 of these timbers spread across its bottom and fastened only every 50 cm to frames. Frames do not fit the planking well, and wooden shims fill gaps of up to 4 cm. Iron fastenings are sparse compared to more well documented traditions, and yet we have not, to date, found any evidence of edge fastening.

The ship's frames are spaced about 47-52 cm apart center-to-center, and measure about 22 cm sided and 26 cm molded. Several composite frames and either a half frame or futtock end also were noted. Shims filling gaps in the area between the frame and the planking were documented beneath several frames in one of the test trenches. Above the frames are timbers running along the length of the ship; iron concretions suggest that these timbers were fastened to each frame, at least in the midships area.

In 1995 we opened three test trenches to begin documenting this unusual ship, and found ourselves almost more puzzled than when we began. Each trench included features so different than those of other trenches that we would have suspected several ships had sunk in the same area had we not the evidence of solid runs of frames and long timbers throughout the site. Because of these differences, full discussion of the shipbuilding techniques, and their possible point of origin, will wait until after the 1996 season when much of the port side will be uncovered.

Conclusions

Difficulties in dating the porcelain on the Sadana Island shipwreck precisely mean that we cannot directly relate it to economic and social conditions in the Red Sea other than through broad statements about the late 17th and early 18th centuries. When the excavation is completed and we are able to study all the finds at once, we will be able to assign a more precise date for its sinking.

The presence of the Sadana Island, Sharm el Sheikh and Hurgada wrecks in the northern Red Sea suggests that there was a strong interest in moving Chinese porcelain and other goods by sea north of Jidda, a point traditionally seen as the terminus of the sea trade from the Indian Ocean during this time (McGowan, 1994 and Raby 1986). Egyptians under Ottoman suzerainty controlled what was effectively internal trade until the late 18th century when European shipping began operating between Suez and Jidda.

Much of the Red Sea trade reached Egypt by a complicated route. Ships obtained goods in China and Indonesia, and often trans-shipped their goods at other centers such as Surat in India. From there, Indian and other ships caught the spring monsoons and headed for Mocha and other Red Sea ports, carrying local products as well as Far Eastern luxuries such as porcelain. In the first part of the 17th century, Mocha and Jidda were the destinations of ships from Arabia, East Africa, Southeast Asia, and, especially, from both sides of the Indian peninsula in addition to Dutch and Portuguese controlled vessels (Brouwer, 1991 and 1992).

Indian ships were known to carry goods north to Suez for French and other merchants periodically during the 17th and 18th centuries. In 1670 the ra'is Ahmed owned two Indian ships at Suez, and in 1682, port chronicles mention a markab hindi, or Indian sailing ship, anchored in the harbour there (Raymond 1973: 110, n. 5). In 1762, a foreign visitor noted that of the 14 ships that operated between Suez and Jidda, most were built in Suez where the industry was flourishing, but by the later 18th century, a French traveller commented that most Arab ships in the Red Sea were built in India (Raymond 1973: 110). For much of the 17th and 18th centuries, strong commercial ties existed between

Egypt and India, and it would not be surprising to find that Indian shipbuilding techniques were adopted by local Egyptian builders.

Could the Sadana Island ship be Indian or of local Egyptian construction? We know only that the Sadana ship was not built according to traditional Mediterranean or European construction practices at the time. It does not resemble Dutch, Portuguese, or English ships active in the Indian Ocean, and it is unlike what we know of Indian Ocean sewn ships of the time. When the wood used in building the ship is identified, we may learn more about where the materials for shipbuilding came from, but in a wood-poor region like the Red Sea, even wood was transported long distances by ship, either from Alexandria or further ports to the east.

The continuing excavation of the Sadana Island shipwreck furnishes an opportunity to explore the nature of the ship, its cargo, and its crew and master. It also ensures that this part of Egypt's nautical heritage will be investigated and preserved.

Cheryl HALDANE
INA-Egypt
P.O. Box 432, El Ibrahimia, Alexandria

References Cited

BROUWER 1991

C.G. BROUWER, "Non-Western shipping movements in the Red Sea and Gulf of Aden during the 2nd and 3rd decades of the 17th century, according to the records of the Dutch East India company. Part 1", *Die Welt des Islams* 31, 1991, pp. 105-67.

BROUWER 1992

C.G. BROUWER, "Non-Western shipping movements in the Red Sea and Gulf of Aden during the 2nd and 3rd decades of the 17th century, according to the records of the Dutch East India company. Part 2", *Die Welt des Islams* 32, 1992, pp. 6-40.

HALDANE 1994

C. HALDANE, "INA-Egypt's Red Sea survey", *INA Quarterly* 21.3, 1994, pp. 4-9.

KRAHL and AYERS 1986

R. KRAHL and J. AYERS, *Chinese ceramics in the Topkapi Saray Museum Istanbul III, Qing Dynasty porcelain,* London, 1986.

MCGOWAN 1994

B. MCGOWAN, "The age of the ayans, 1699-1812", in H. INALCIK and D. QUATAERT (eds), *An economic and social history of the Ottoman Empire 1300-1914,* Cambridge, 1994, pp. 637-758.

RABAN 1971
A. RABAN, "The shipwreck off Sharm-el-Sheikh", *Archaeology* 24.2, 1971, pp. 146-55.

RABAN 1973
A. RABAN, "The mercury carrier from the Red Sea", *International Journal of Nautical Archaeology* 2, 1973, pp. 179-183.

RABAN 1990
A. RABAN, "Medieval anchors from the Red Sea", *International Journal of Nautical Archaeology* 19, 1990, pp. 299-306.

RABY 1986
J. RABY, "The porcelain trade routes", in R. KRAHL and J. AYERS (eds), *Chinese ceramics in the Topkapi Saray Museum Istanbul* I, 1986, pp. 55-63.

RAYMOND 1973
A. RAYMOND, *Artisans et commerçants au Caire au XVIIIe siècle*, I, Damascus, 1973.

STEFFY 1994
J.R. STEFFY, *Wooden shipbuilding and the interpretation of shipwrecks*, College Station, 1994.

WHITCOMB and JOHNSON 1982
D. WHITCOMB and J.H. JOHNSON, *Quseir al Qadim 1980. Preliminary report,* American Research Center in Egypt Reports 7, 1982.

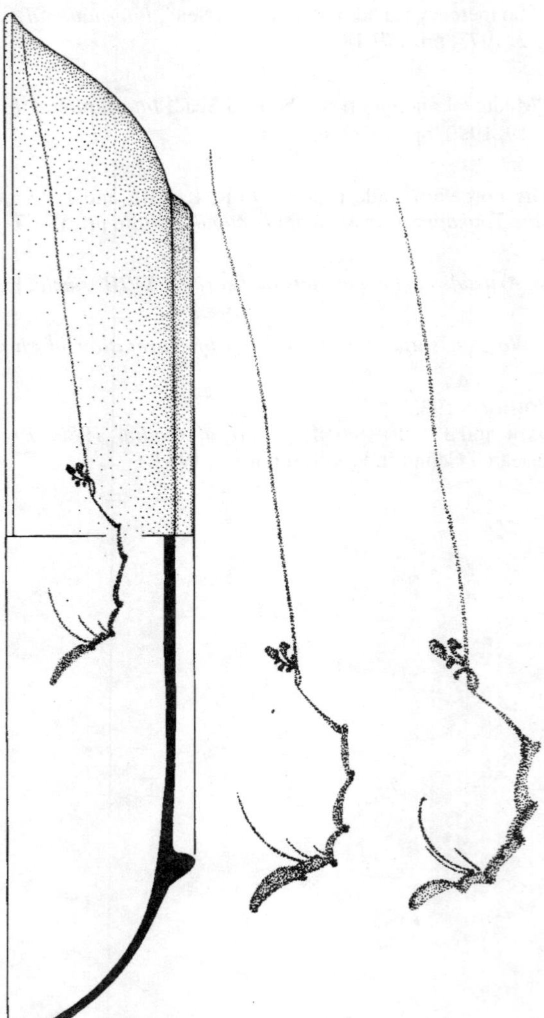

Fig. 1 — Exterior view of peony scroll dish R2-5, D 34.7 cm H 5.3 cm. (Drawing N. Piercy)

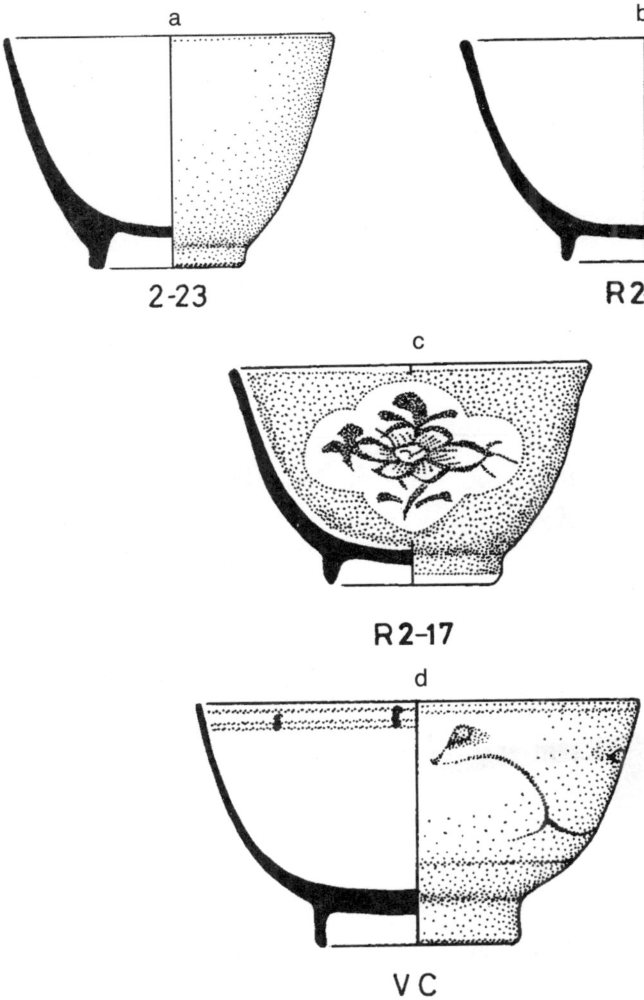

Fig. 2 — a) Celadon glazed cup, b) Monochrome brown glazed cup, c) Monochrome brown with underglaze blue blossom in quatrefoil medallion, d) Formerly enamelled cup with underglaze blue remaining (Drawings a, d by N. Piercy; b, c by L. Piercy)

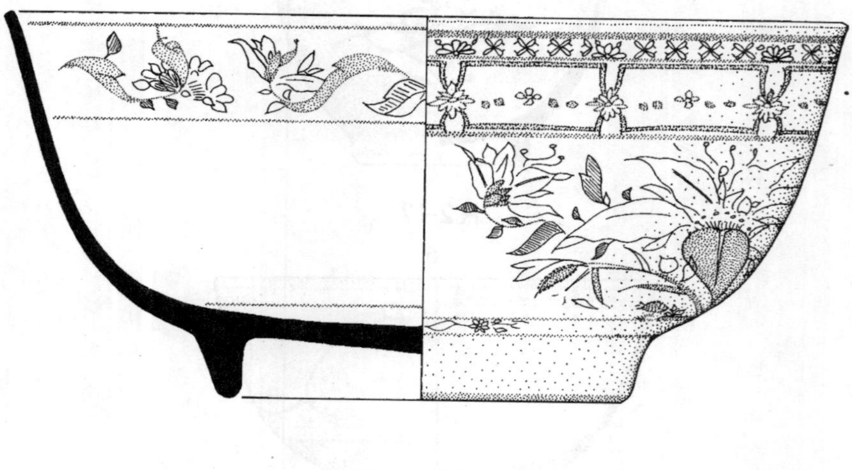

Fig. 3 – Enamel designs on this day lily and chrysanthemum bowl were preserved only by "ghosting", represented here by solid lines; the blue underglaze is indicated by stipling. D 26.7 cm H 12.7 cm (Drawing N. Piercy)

Fig. 4 — Blue underglaze provides the foundation for this design of rocks, a fence, and flowers. The flowers, once painted with bright colours, now exist only as nearly invisible differences in surface texture. (Solid lines indicate ghosting.) D 18.7 cm H 8 cm (Drawing N. Piercy)

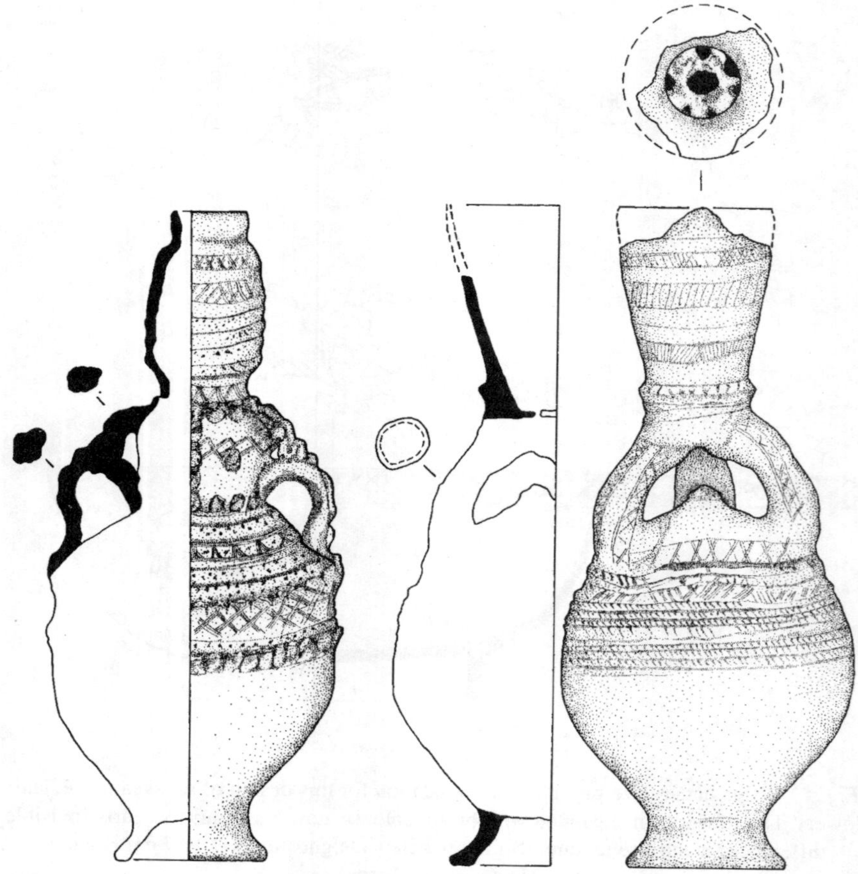

Fig. 5a -5 b – Two earthenware water vessels, light gray brown fabric with applied and incised designs. D 11.5 cm H 30 cm (Drawings K. Burnett)

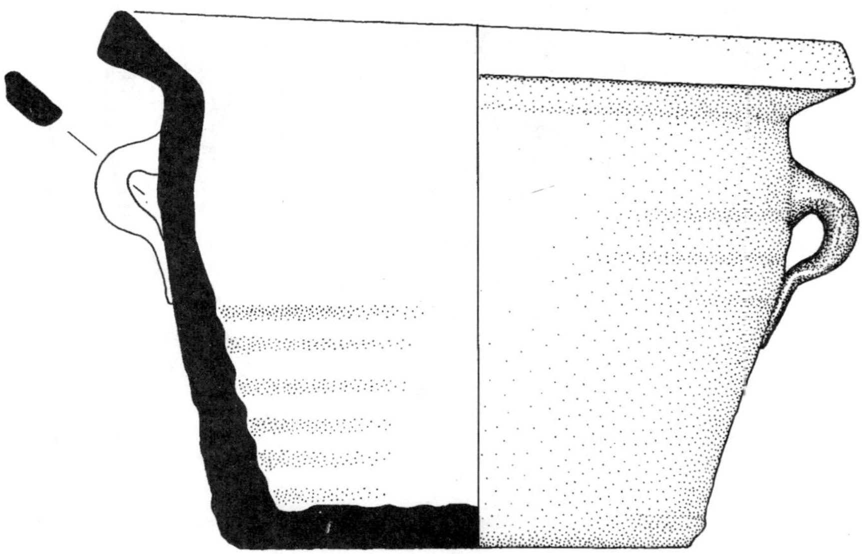

1-1

Fig. 6 — Buff fabric, wide-mouthed jar with dark green crackled glaze on interior. D 18.2 cm H 13.5 cm (Drawing N. Piercy)

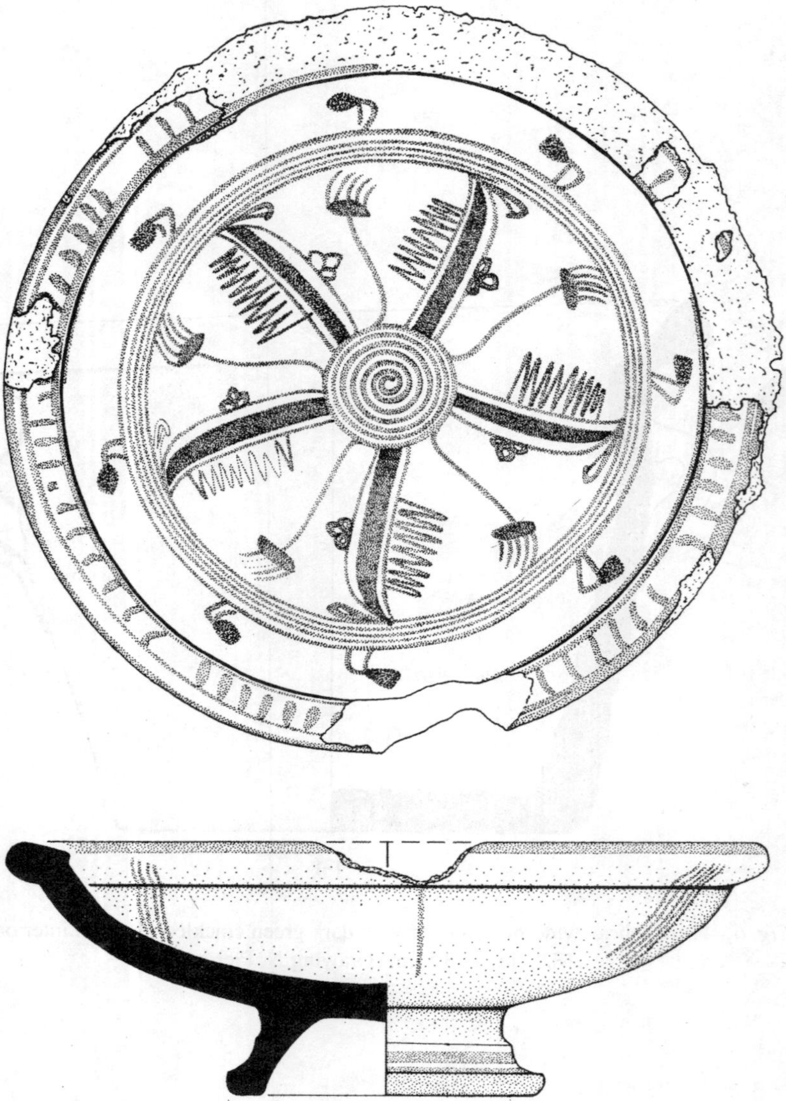

Fig. 7 – Yellow and brown glazed earthenware bowl, D 27.8 cm H 7.8 cm
(Drawing N. Piercy)

ANAXIKRATES' EXPEDITION TO WESTERN ARABIA

In book IX of his treatise on plants,[1] Theophrastus gives a detailed description (Chapter 4) of Arabian trees producing frankincense and myrrh, followed (Chapter 5) by more scanty and unreliable information about cinnamon and another closely related species called *kas(s)ia.*[2] As regards the former trees, Theophrastus declares that he has reproduced on-the-spot observations made by travellers who set sail from the Golf of Heroes or what is now called the Gulf of Suez (*HP* IX, 4,4). "These people said that as they sailed along the coast after leaving the Gulf of Heroes, they landed to look for water in the mountains and saw these trees and the collection of their produce."

---

1. Better known under its Latin name *Historia Plantarum* (*HP* in references). The most recent complete edition of this work is A.F. HORT's *Theophrastus. Enquiry into Plants*, The Loeb Classical Library, 2 vol., 1916 & 1926.

2. Both species of the genus *Cinnamomum* whose bark is consumed as cinnamon according to the most common interpretation (contested among others by F. de Romanis; for a detailed discussion see *The Enigmatic Cinnamon* in this volume). What the ancient apothecaries called "aromatic" or "clove-scented cassia" was really cinnamon, while what we call "cassia" today is a species belonging to the genus *Cassia* which is a Leguminosae and not a Lauraceae like *Cinnamomum*. It is distinct from cinnamon because of its laxative properties (as in the well-known French saying "Je vous passe la casse, passez-moi le séné" which may be translated literally as "I pass you the cassia and you will pass me the senna" but which really means "You scratch my back and I'll scratch yours"). The ambiguity of the term has led P. FAURE (*Parfums et aromates de l'Antiquité*, Paris, 1987, p. 291) to illustrate the entry on cinnamon with a picture of the *Cassia fistula* L. used for medicinal purposes. The name transfer is explained by the similarity between "sticks" of cinnamon (actually pieces of dried bark which roll themselves into tubes; see A. HERAUD, *Nouveau dictionnaire des plantes médicinales*, Paris, 1875, p. 299, fig. 164) and cassia "sticks" (which are actually long cylindrical pods [*ibid.* p. 93, fig. 47-48] which become tubular in shape once the pulp inside them dries up or is removed).

A Gateway from the Eastern Mediterranean to India. The Red Sea in Antiquity
S. AMIGUES, pp. 189-195

W.W. Tarn[3] compared this text with a passage from Arrian (*Indica*, 43, 7) which also mentions a shortage of water which, in this case, put an end to the attempt to circumnavigate Arabia from the west, undertaken on Alexander's orders after his return to Susa. "The sailors, who after leaving the Arabian Gulf near Egypt tried to go around Arabia to reach Susa and Persia, were able to continue as long as there was water on board, then they had to turn back".

The third document which must be taken into account is found in Strabo (XVI, 4,4 = C 768) who borrows the following information from Erastothenes: "The part of the Arabian Gulf along the side of Arabia, beginning at the Aelanites recess, measures fourteen thousand stadia according to the descriptions given by Alexander's companions and Anaxikrates."

When asked if these three accounts refer to the same expedition, Tarn replied in the affirmative without any hesitation. P. Högemann[4] has recently reopened the matter. He has closely studied each bit of evidence and come to a different conclusion. Theophrastus's text, *HP* IX, 4, can help us to select the most likely hypothesis and determine the exact date and circumstances.

We must first point out that Arrian (*An.* VII, 20, 7-9) says that eastern coast of Arabia was explored at the same time by three missions led by Archias, Androsthenes and Hieron of Soloi. The latter (§ 8) "had been ordered to go round the entire Arabian peninsula, right up to the Egyptian coast of the Arabian Gulf, somewhere near the town of Heroes; undoubtedly, he did not dare to go further although he sailed along a major part of the Arabian coast; but he turned round and came back to tell Alexander that the peninsula was exceptionally large". This misadventure is similar, if we may say so, to that of the sailors from the Gulf of Heroes (*Indica*, 43, 7). Why doesn't Arrian mention the name of their leader, which he had probably learnt from his sources? The simplest explanation would be that although there is a good reason to determine the role of each of the three expeditions that set out to explore Eastern Arabia, if only one tried to approach the peninsula from the west, the historian was not bound in any way to mention the leader's name. For us, this unique attempt, according to the information provided by Strabo, would be the expedition undertaken by Anaxikrates.

But just because in Strabo's account the length of the Western Arabian coast is measured from the "Aelanites recess" or the present Gulf of Aqaba, while the sailors mentioned by Theophrastus and Arrian came from Heroonpolis, P. Högemann unlike Tarn and Schmitthenner[5] refuses to accept that all the three authors refer to the same expedition led by Anaxikrates. He must have led at an

---

3. "Ptolemy II and Arabia", *JEA* 15, 1929, pp. 9-25; see p. 13.

4. *Alexander der Grosse und Arabien* (Zetemata, Monographien zür Klassischen Altertumwissenschaft, 82), Munich, 1985, pp. 80-87.

5. W. SCHMITTHENNER, art. *Anaxikrates* 8, in PAULY-WISSOWA, *RE*, Suppl. XIV, 1974, col. 44-47.

indeterminate date an expedition about which we would have known nothing except that it reached Bab el-Mandeb at the opposite end of the Arabian coast from the Gulf of Aqaba. Even if Anaxikrates had really set sail from Egypt, it would not make any difference to his calculation of the distance between the two ends of the Arabian coast. He just had to substitute concerning the "Aleanites recess" an approximation or a second-hand information for a measurement, if he had not covered the distance himself.

Theophrastus's account presents another possibility. The men who found, while they were looking for water, unguarded trees producing frankincense and myrrh (*HP* IX, 4, 5) "were able to collect, because they were undisturbed, a large amount of frankincense and myrrh which they loaded on *their boats* before setting sail". The plural τὰ πλοῖα (*ta ploia*) poses a problem because we know that Alexander gave to each of his explorers in the Persian Gulf[6] only one ship with thirty rowers to avoid the risk of losing a large part of his forces[7] in case of failure. Another reason was the problem of providing enough supplies to the crew. It is difficult to imagine that an entire fleet — the term employed by Högemann —[8] was engaged in such a risky operation without prior reconnaissance. The Red Sea expedition "probably coordinated with those led by Archias, Androsthenes and Hieron"[9] in the Persian Gulf must have been of the same kind. But we know that Alexander's inclination to simultaneously explore an area from two different directions, *e.g.* the successful meeting of his army and his fleet under Nearchus's command in Carmania, had encouraged him to undertake similar expeditions. It may therefore be assumed that a ship left Heroonpolis with the major part of the crew and that it was joined at the southern tip of the Sinai Peninsula by another ship which had set off earlier to "scientifically" reconnoitre the Aelanites Gulf. Of course, this is just a conjecture, but once Högemann's objection is refuted, it seems almost certain that a single expe-

6. Arrian, *An.* VII, 20, 7: "Archias (...) sent *on a ship with thirty rowers* to explore the route along the Arabian coast, reached the island of Tylos (...); Androsthenes, who left *on another ship with thirty rowers*, managed to sail along a part of the Arabian peninsula (...); Hieron of Soloi too received from Alexander *a ship with thirty rowers*".

7. This convincing explanation has been provided by J.-F. SALLES in "La circumnavigation de l'Arabie dans l'Antiquité classique", *L'Arabie et ses mers bordières. I. Itinéraires et voisinages* (under the guidance of J.-F. Salles), TMO No.16, Lyon, 1988, pp. 75-102 (see in particular pp. 86-88); taken up again (p. 83, n. 22) in "Découvertes du golfe Arabo-Persique aux époques grecque et romaine", *L'Océan et les mers lointaines dans l'Antiquité, REA* 94, 1992, pp. 79-97.

8. *O.c.*, p. 83: "Die Flotte musste spätestens im Frühsommer von Heroonpolis aufbrechen".

9. J.-F. SALLES, "La circumnavigation...", p. 91.

dition under Anaxikrates's command left Heroonpolis,[10] probably with two ships.

As for the dates, Högemann considers October 324 as the *terminus ante quem* in view of the navigation conditions in the Red Sea and the Gulf of Aden[11] which the sailors, who had set sail from Heroonpolis, had to cross in order to reach the land of myrrh and frankincense. It is to be regretted that Högemann does not refer to the evidence provided by Theophrastus in support of his views for it would have enabled him to determine more precisely the time and place of the anecdote related in *HP* IX, 4, 4-5. The myrrh-tree is presented in this anecdote (§3 & 7) as a shrub-like thorny bush akin to the terebinth with a thick short trunk covered with a smooth bark and "a leaf like that of the elm, except that it is curly and spinous at the tip like that of kermes-oak" which when "chewed tastes like that of the terebinth". This last detail rules out the *Commiphora myrrha* Engl. whose leaves are not aromatic.[12] One would think instead of the species that produces "the true Arabian myrrh",[13] *C. habessinica* (or *abyssinica*) Engl. Its appearance, at least in the thorny small-leaved form,[14] is closer to Theophrastus's description but its area in southern Arabia (stretching from Yemen to Oman) is too vast to allow us to determine without further information the exact spot where it was found by the Greek sailors.

After the botanical exploration conducted by him in 1977-78, Th. Monod has demarcated the χώρα λιβανωτοφόρος (*chôra libanotoforos*) more precisely, especially in the western part, the only one that concerns us. His studies have established the presence of the *Boswellia sacra* Flueck., the South Arabian frankincense tree, in various spots in Hadramaut extending right up to the region

---

10. Several experts on the ancient Middle-East cannot envisage any other possibility, *e.g.* J. DESANGES, *Recherches sur l'activité des Méditerranéens aux confins de l'Afrique*, Rome-Paris, 1978, p. 245; J.-F. SALLES, "La circumnavigation...", p. 91.

11. *O. c.*, p. 83: "The voyage along the southern coast of Arabia, from Aden to Oman, had to be completed before autumn. As a matter of fact, when the monsoon changed its direction in October and turned from the northeast to the west, it was no longer possible to sail eastward". For further details see P. SANLAVILLE, "Des mers au milieu du désert: mer Rouge et Golfe arabo-persique", *L'Arabie et ses mers bordières* (pp. 9-26), pp. 20-21.

12. A. ENGLER-K. PRANTL, *Die natürlichen Pflanzenfamilien*, t.19 a, Leipzig, 1931, pp. 429-443 for the genus *Commiphora* and its particularly complex systematics; for *C. myrrha* see p. 434, fig. 204, and p. 436, and also S. COLLENETTE, *An Illustrated Guide to the Flowers of Saudi Arabia*, Buckhurst Hill, 1985, p. 91 (note and colour photograph).

13. ENGLER-PRANTL, *o.c.*, p. 442.

14. Ilustrated by S. Stuart-Smith in A.G. MILLER-M. MORRIS, *Plants of Dhofar, the Southern Region of Oman. Traditional, Economic and Medicinal Uses*, Oman, 1988, p. 87; detailed note on p. 86 and pp. 306-307.

of Habban and Shabwa in the west.[15] At present there are a few scattered groves in the area, some of them with just a handful of trees. However, since the exploitation of a species over a long period of time leads, as a general rule, to its regression, it is quite likely that in 324 B.C. the frankincense-tree was commonly found in the coastal mountains starting from about a hundred kilometres to the west of Qana. Beyond this town, the coastal range between Mukalla and Sayhut now has the highest concentration of *Boswellia* trees in the entire Hadramaut area.[16] The botanical data therefore support Högemann's claim according to which the anecdote narrated by Theophrastus took place in the neighbourhood of Qana, the greatest frankincense market in ancient times.

The collection of myrrh and frankincense was in full swing at that time (*HP* IX, 4, 5): "There were two kinds of trees with incisions on their trunks and branches, but although it seemed as though the trunks had been hacked with an axe, the branches had smaller cuts; some of the gum drops fell on the ground but the rest remained sticking to the tree; in some places, palm-leaf mats were placed under the trees, in others there was nothing on the ground; the frankincense collected from the mats was pure and translucent, while the one on the ground was less so; what remained on the trees was scraped off with iron tools".[17] According to P. Faure, in August-September at the height of summer, droplets of white gum resin appear spontaneously under the bark of the frankincense-tree. Similarly, "after it has flowered, that is at the end of summer and before the autumn mists set in, double cuts are made on the bark of the myrrh-tree even today. The resin flows out like tears and falls on mats or coagulates on the trunk from where it is collected".[18] The most plausible date of the theft committed by the Greek sailors would hence be September 324. It must however be noted that in the case of frankincense, the information regarding the collection season varies a great deal according to the informants: "the scraping of the bark provides three harvests in a year" (Faure, p. 33); "sometimes, the collection takes place (mainly?) in winter, sometimes in any season, but the time between the tapping and the collection is longer in winter (25-30 days) than in summer (15 days); a Somali mentions ten tappings in a year (?)" (Monod, p. 149). The indications given by this writer (p. 150) about the supply of frankincense to the

---

15. Th. MONOD, "Les arbres à encens (*Boswellia sacra* Flückiger, 1867) dans le Hadramaout (Yémen du Sud)", *Bulletin du Muséum national d'Histoire naturelle*, series 4, 1 1979, section B, No. 3, pp. 131-169. See in particular pp. 134-136 (description of stations) and pp. 141-146: "L'aire de l'encensier sud-arabique".

16. See *ibid.* map on p. 136.

17. This description is considered to be "surprisingly apt" by A.G. MILLER - M. MORRIS (*o.c.*, p. 299) who affirm that the same collection technique is used to this day. On p. 81 of the same volume there is a picture of the traditional knife-cum-scraper. Similarly, Th. Monod gives an illustration, *o.c.*, p. 147, fig. 16-18, together with details (p. 149) about the tool and its use.

18. *O.c.* (cf. *supra*, n. 2), pp. 33-34.

market in Mukalla in 1977 reveal two peak seasons – March and November. We may, therefore, safely place the discovery of the Hadrami frankincense-tree by Anaxikrates's crew in September-October 324.

If, as it seems likely, the expedition reached Qana without any major mishap, why did it decide to give up the idea of proceeding further? One of the immediate reasons, as we have seen, was the unfavourable wind system. Besides, Arrian attributes the failure of attempts to explore Arabia to the shortage of water (*Indica*, 43, 7) and navigational dangers (*ibid.*, § 10) along deserted inhospitable coasts scorched by the sun (*ibid.*, § 3). But Nearchus came across the same obstacles in Gedrosia and managed to overcome them. It is also possible that the local population may have been hostile, wanting to protect its monopoly over frankincense[19] and determined to discourage all attempts by outsiders before they discovered the rich growth of frankincense-trees in Dhofar. There may even have been a ban on shipping which would have made the Indian Ocean a preserve of the "Indians (...), but particularly the Arabs who travelled its length and breadth in all directions".[20] Finally, the frame of mind of the various members of the expedition also played a key role. Unlike Nearchus who was guided, at least during a part of his voyage, by competent pilots[21] and who touched unknown lands at the head of a large fleet which permitted him to win the support of the local people by simple intimidation, Anaxikrates and his companions with just two or three ships must have found themselves alone and unarmed when faced by unprecedented problems. As for the rest, it is one thing to return — after facing the same risks — to known lands and finally to one's homeland, and it is something else to go further away from one's homeland day by day with the future shrouded in uncertainty. Alexander and his captains knew perfectly well how to bring back their troops to Persia but they were not able to force them to continue their march beyond the Indus. *A fortiori*, without Alexander, a few dozen men lost in depths of Arabia could not but be frightened and discouraged. Their raid on frankincense and myrrh, which visibly amused Theophrastus as a good trick played on the over-confident locals, reminds us of the more brutal plundering by the Ten Thousand at the end of *Anabasis*: tired of their adventure, all that the men want is to get some booty and go home.

Anaxikrates's career did not suffer because of the failure of his mission: Tzetzes[22] mentions him as one of the inspectors appointed by Seleucus Nicator

---

19. P. HÖGEMANN, *o.c.*, p. 87.

20. J.-F. SALLES, "Découvertes du golfe Arabo-Persique..." (cf. *supra*, n. 7), p. 79; also see p. 84, n. 27.

21. J.-F. SALLES, "La circumnavigation...", pp. 86-87, together with the hypothesis that "Nearchus had at his disposal, even before he left Karachi, accounts or ship's logs to guide his expedition; these data, inherited from the Achemenid period (...), made it possible to calculate reasonably well the risks involved in the adventure".

22. *Chil.* VII, vv. 177-180.

to supervise the foundation of city of Antioch. His expedition, though a failure, was not totally useless — at least from the scientific viewpoint. Androsthenes' report quoted by Theophrastus[23] informs us about the natural flora and crops of Tylos/Bahrein. Through a quotation from Athenaeus[24] we learn about the shells found in the Indian Ocean and pearl-fishing in the Persian Gulf. Thanks to Anaxikrates, Theophrastus has left us a "surprisingly apt"[25] description of South Arabian myrrh and frankincense.[26]

Suzanne AMIGUES
University of Montpellier

---

23. *HP* IV, 7, 7-8; *CP* II, 5, 5.
24. *Deipnosophists*, 93 a-b.
25. Cf. *supra*, n. 17.
26. I am very grateful to C. Robin for his remarks and for his kindness in providing me with the necessary documentation.

ON THE HIPPALOS SEA
FOLLOWING THE HIPPALOS WIND

In a short article,[1] which did not fail to draw the attention of specialists of the Red Sea and the Indian Ocean in Antiquity, the late S. Mazzarino has proposed a new interpretation, *hypalum* (acc.), of the name of the wind mentioned by Pliny the Elder in *Natural History* VI, 100. This new interpretation casts doubt on one piece of information in the *Periplus of the Erythraean Sea,*[2] according to which a pilot named Hippalos learned to navigate in the high seas in the Indian Ocean. It could certainly be assumed that the pilot was only an anthropomorphic figure inspired by the name of a wind.[3] But the lack of ambiguity of the adjective *hypalus* (from the Greek ὕφαλος "[came] from under the sea") debunks the *Periplus*'s claim that the 'libonotos' or southwestern wind on the route to India was named after the pilot. This would explain the silence maintained by Poseidonios regarding Hippalos in his famous account, preserved by Strabo,[4] of Eudoxus of Cyzicus' journeys across the Indian Ocean.[5] It is therefore advisable to closely examine S. Mazzarino's thesis.

The term *hippalus* occurs thrice in Pliny the Elder's *Natural History* if we refer to the editions of D. Detlefsen and C. Mayhoff in VI, 100; VI, 104 and VI, 172.

---

1. S. MAZZARINO, "Sul nome del vento *hipalus* ('ippalo') in Plinio", *Helikon*, XXII-XXVII, 1982-1987, pp. VII-XIII.
2. *Peripl. Mar. Erythr.*, 57 (henceforth referred to as *PME*).
3. This opinion is expressed by M. RODINSON in *Ann. EPHE*, IVe Section (1975-1976), pp. 208-209, rejected by L. CASSON, *The Periplus maris Erythraei*, Princeton, 1989, p. 224.
4. Str., II, 3, 4-5 (C 98-102).
5. J. DESANGES, *Recherches sur l'activité des Méditerranéens aux confins de l'Afrique (VIe s. av. J.-C.- IVe après J.-C.)*, Rome, 1978, pp. 151-165 (= Coll. EFR 38).

A Gateway from the Eastern Mediterranean to India. The Red Sea in Antiquity
J. DESANGES, pp. 197-202

Let us first consider VI, 100, which forms the basis of S. Mazzarino's thesis. The relevant passage runs as follows: *Postea ab Syagro* [codd. *siagro*] *Arabiae promunturio Patalen fauonio, quem hippalum ibi uocant, peti certissimum uidebatur,* which according to J. André's translation[6] means: "Later, it appeared that the safest route was to sail from Cape Syagros in Arabia to Patalen with the favonius which is called the hippalus in this region". Let us remember that in Pliny's wind rose[7] the favonius is shown as the wind coming from the equinoctial sundown or the west (and not the south-west as we would have expected[8] since it is the summer monsoon).

The following lessons can be drawn from the main manuscripts: hipalum *E*[s], hypilum *Fa*, ipilum *R*, pypylum *D*. The inconstancy in the use of **i/y*, which is not important, may be attributed to scribes (cf. *Syagro* written as *siagro* in the passage cited above) — provided, of course, that in this case the **y* is not the result of a misinterpretation of **ip* – but it is observed that the **p* is not doubled in any of the manuscripts. S. Mazzarino[9] has therefore suggested that the denomination of the wind used by Pliny should be restored in the form of *hypalos* and treated, as we have already said, as a transcription of the Greek adjective ὕφαλος. It is a wind coming from the sea, to be more precise "from under the sea" and the Italian scholar claims in support of his thesis Pliny's statement[10] that the south wind blows *ex imo mari, i.e.* "from the bottom of the sea". But Pliny curiously justifies this statement by emphasising that unlike the north wind, the south wind is *infernus* or a lower wind. As J. Beaujeu[11] says when commenting on this passage, "the south wind is *infernus* because of the ancient belief that the south is lower than the north on the earth's disk". Herodotus[12] says of the River Halys that as it flows, it rises towards the North Wind. Nothing similar can be claimed about a wind blowing from the west like

---

6. Pliny the Elder, *n.h.,* Book 2, part 2, text edited, translated and commented by J. André and J. Filliozat, Paris, Les Belles Lettres, 1980, p. 53.

7. Pliny, II, 119.

8. *PME*, 57, is right to link the summer monsoon with the libonotos.

9. S. MAZZARINO, *op. cit.*, p. X.

10. Pliny, II, 128.

11. Pliny the Elder, *n.h.,* Book II, text edited, translated and commented by J. Beaujeu, Paris, Les Belles Lettres, 1950, p. 209. The relevance of J. Beaujeu's commentary is fully apparent when one refers to the chapter (that he does not mention) devoted by Aulu-Gelle (II, 30) to the different effects of the movement of the south and north winds on the sea waves.

12. Hdt., I, 72.

the favonius, of which hypalos (?) may have been a local name. He cannot really be bothered about this speculation on north and south, "above" and "below".[13]

In the next instance — VI, 104 — Pliny tells us that it takes forty days to sail "with the hippalos wind" (*uento hippalo*) from *Ocelis* (on the Arabian coast of Bab el-Mandeb) to *Muziris* (Cranganore port on India's southwestern coast). Since in this case a manuscript (*a* of Vienna) gives a version with a geminated **p* (yppalo), S. Mazzarino[14] suggests that the form *hippalo* should be retained and points out that in Pliny's manuscripts, particularly when it is a question of Greek words belonging to the *hippos* family, a double **p* is never changed into a single **p* in all the manuscripts. (But is there a reciprocal proposition which obliges us to admit the existence of a double **p* when it is attested by only one manuscript?) He justifies the difference between the lessons adopted in VI, 100 and 104, because Pliny's sources were probably Hellenistic in the first passage and from the Roman period in the second when the name of the *hypalus* wind had already been corrupted to *hippalus*. It may be observed in passing that in our opinion Pliny follows from the beginning to the end of his historical review of the navigation for India Juba II's *Arabica*, so much so that "earlier writers" (*neminem priorum*) mentioned by the naturalist in VI, 105, are actually writers who preceded Juba. They are again unambiguously qualified as *priores* by Pliny in VI, 149. In any case, we shall consider the use of a double **p* in only one manuscript as a chance occurrence just as we refuse to deny its existence in one word for the simple reason that no manuscript shows any evidence of it. This *a silentio* principle seems unreasonable to us. Let us take for instance what we observe in Pliny IV, 70 *in fine*: the Hippuris (Amorgopoula) island, between Amorgos and Anaphe in the Aegean Sea, is mistakenly mentioned twice in succession by the manuscript tradition. To the form with a double **p* having several variants has been added another form with a single **p* having its own variants!

But let us leave aside for the time being the third probable instance of *hippalus* in Pliny (VI, 172) presented by the manuscripts as *hispalum* (acc.). It is in fact a delicate interpretation because the adjective is used this time to qualify a promontory. Let us go straight to the point: by reading Ptolemy's *Geographia*,[15] we learn of the existence of a Hippalus Sea (πέλαγος Ἵππαλον) that the best manuscript, the *Vatic. Graec.* 191 (X), mentions correctly whereas other manuscripts call it Ἵππαδον (*hippadon*). According to the Alexandrian geographer,[16] this sea stretches toward the east beyond the Avalite Gulf and joins the Indian Sea. According to the context, it seems to stretch right up to the area

13. On this point, cf. H. STÜRENBURG, *Relative Ortsbezeichung*, Leipzig & Berlin 1932, pp. 22-31.

14. S. MAZZARINO, *op. cit.*, pp. XI-XII.

15. Ptol., *Geogr.*, IV, 7, 12, Müller, p. 787.

16. *Ibid.*, IV, 7, 11.

of the Cape of Spices (Guardafui Cape). It is in any case a part of what we now call the Indian Ocean. Let us note in passing that according to Pliny,[17] the island of Dioscoridus (Socotra) is in the *Azanium mare* and according to Ptolemy,[18] it is in the Erythraean Sea. This suggests a certain inconsistency in designating parts of the same ocean by dividing it more or less arbitrarily. This disparity is further justified because *Azanium mare* refers to the land of *Azania* which, etymologically, is the land of dry heat, *aza* (ἄζα).

It must be added that in the *Itinerarium Alexandri Magni*[19] in Latin, published by C. Müller following F. Dübner's edition of Arrian, occurs the sentence "*Ipsa* [= India] *uero extrinsecus ubique oceano munitur, interfluo mari hippalo, cuius sinus Persas includit*, which means "But India itself is surrounded on all sides by the ocean before which flows the Hippalos Sea, a part of which embraces Persia".

It is quite clear that the Italian scholar's ingenious attempt to explain the origin of the adjective *hippalus* applied to a wind does not in any way help to explain the mention of a Hippalos Sea by Ptolemy and in the *Itinerarium Alexandri Magni* (middle of 4th century AD). How could this sea have been qualified by an adjective which means "under the sea"? On the contrary, one is forced to think that the name of a wind which carried ships from Arabia to India could only be closely linked with the name of a part of the Indian Ocean that these ships had to cross. The existence of a Hippalos Sea keeps us from challenging the existence of a Hippalos wind. Further, it is quite plausible — although it may not be certain — that not only the wind, as claimed by the author of the *Periplus of the Erythraean Sea,*[20] but also the Hippalos Sea was named after the man who was supposed to have been the first to use the wind to cross the sea away from the coastal waters.

Having established this, let us return to the third instance where *hippalus* occurs in Pliny (VI, 172). The naturalist mentions Ptolemais of the Hunts, which has not yet been precisely identified, but which may be situated in the region of Tokar and Aqiq, on the coast of modern Sudan, not far from the Erythraean border. Then he follows it up with: *Hinc Azanium mare, promunturium quod aliqui Hippalum* [cod. *hispalum*] *scripsere,* which means, "From there on it is the Sea of Azania, a promontory which some people have written as Hippalos". Geography forces us to consider this sentence as inappropriate, since it is understood that Pliny himself was probably responsible for this error. We are actually on the African coast of the Red Sea and Pliny soon mentions the town of the Adulites, in other words Adulis, also on the Red Sea in modern Eritrea. But

17. Pliny, VI, 153.
18. Ptol., VI, 7, 45, Nobbe, II, P. 109.
19. *Itin. Alex. M.*, 110, in F. DÜBNER, *Arriani Anabasis et Indica. Reliqua Arriani et scriptorum de rebus Alexandri M.*, Paris, Firmin Didot, 1846, p. 166.
20. *PME*, 57.

in another passage,[21] the naturalist reserves the adjective of *Azanius* for the ocean whose waters flow into the Persian and Arabian Gulfs and it would therefore be absurd to say that it is a part of the Arabian Gulf (our Red Sea). On the other hand, we have shown that he believes[22] that the *Azanium mare* washes the island of Dioscoridus (Socotra). If the controversial sentence were not a marginal note incorporated in an inappropriate context, one would expect right away that Pliny would suggest it to the reader two paragraphs later (VI, 174), before mentioning *sinus Aualitu* which in the form Aualites denotes the Gulf of Aden in Ptolemy's work[23] and could have been considered by the naturalist as a part of the *Azanium mare*.

Actually, it is likely that Pliny made a mistake because of his digression about the three Berenikes. As a matter of fact, after alluding in the right order to the first one (Berenike of the Trogôdytes: § 168), then the second and the third (respectively Berenike *Panchrysos* and Berenike *Epi Dires*: § 170), he comes back to his systematic description of the coast after the first Berenike, without mentioning it clearly to the reader. Then he mentions Ptolemais of the Hunts, comparing its position in relation to the solsticial midday sun with that of a Berenike, which he identifies only by a cross-reference to his second book. But then, immediately before backtracking, he was driven to mention the width of the straits marking the end of the Arabian Gulf, but in relation to Berenike *Epi Dires*. While trying to put the different pieces together, he ran a considerable risk of confusing not only his readers but also himself. The third time the adjective *hippalum* occurs and the reference to *Azanium mare* should, in Pliny's source, follow the short note related to Berenike *Epi Dires*, a trading post neglected by Juba.[24]

In truth, we are tempted to make a small correction by changing the order of the words. Let us suppose that *Azanium mare* and *promunturium* have been inverted. That would lead us to redo the Latin translation of the source used by the Roman naturalist: *Fauces Rubri maris $\overline{VII}$· D p. ab Arabia distant. Hinc promunturium, Azanium mare quod aliqui Hippalum scripsere* which means: "The straits of the Red Sea stretch over a distance of seven and a half miles from Arabia. Then, one comes to a promontory, the Azanian Sea that some have called Hippalus in their writings". Since Pliny describes the African coast, it would be quite natural to identify the unnamed promontory as Deire (ras Siyyan)[25] adjoining Berenike *Epi Dires*. But if we admit that the author was a little careless, which is not at all unlikely, we could consider another promon-

21. Pliny, VI, 108.

22. *Id.*, VI, 153.

23. Ptol. IV, 7, 3, pp. 760-763.

24. Pliny, VI, 170.

25. Cf. Str., XVI, 4, 4(C 769); Ptol., IV, 7, 2, p. 760.

tory, also unnamed. According to the naturalist,[26] for those coming from the Gulf of Aden this promontory comes before *Ocilia* (= *Ocelis*), i.e. ras Bab el-Mandeb or Manhali, because again according to Pliny,[27] "to go to India, the best way is to start from *Ocelis*" (*Indos autem petentibus utilissimum est ab Oceli egredi*). Even if one refuses to make this correction, which may appear too risky, it must be admitted that in addition to a Hippalus Sea and wind, there was also a promontory of the same name from where, according to all appearances, the intrepid and problematic pilot[28] was supposed to have set off toward India across the open sea. This promontory was therefore situated not in the Arabian Gulf, which we now call the Red Sea, but facing the open sea.[29]

Jehan DESANGES

26. Pliny, XII, 88.

27. *Id.* VI, 104.

28. On reading the paragraph from Pliny quoted *supra*, it would seem that the hippalus wind is the most reliable pilot: *inde* [= *ab Oceli*] *uento hippalo nauivant diebus XL ad primum emporium Indiae Muzirim*. As a matter of fact, a competent pilot is very necessary when crossing the straits and navigating along the Red Sea coast. When navigating, it is very important to know the seasons and this is what a shipwrecked Indian captain taught Eudoxus of Cyzicus.

29. If we were to look for this promontory at the eastern end of *Azanium mare*, as suggested in Pliny's text when it is accepted without any changes, it could be the Cape of Spices which is placed by Ptol., IV, 7, 3, pp. 760-766 between the Avalite Gulf and the Barbary Gulf. According to the *PME*, 57, many ships set off directly for India from this point.

HYPALOS: DISTANCES AND WINDS BETWEEN ARABIA AND INDIA IN THE HELLENISTIC KNOWLEDGE

Pliny, the *priores* and *nostri negotiatores*

In paragraph 96 of Book VI of his *Naturalis Historia*, while dealing with Carmania, Persia and Arabia, Pliny the Elder allows himself an *excursus*, mentioning the places touched by Alexander's fleet during his voyage from Patale to Susa, and then referring to that *nauigatio, quae his annis conperta seruatur hodie.*[1] Actually, after the voyage of Onescritus and Nearchus (96-100), the description of not one but three routes to India is given, which are said to have followed one another up to Pliny's time (100-106).

This history of *nauigationes in Indiam* is one of the very rare examples in ancient literature of a history of navigation, limited moreover to a specific geographical area. How did Pliny come to offer it? In a recent article, J. Desanges has claimed that Pliny borrowed it from *Arabica* by Iuba II. According to the French scholar, in fact, in the clause *quae* [...] *nomina apud neminem priorum reperiuntur* (VI 105) Pliny is not referring to all the authors older than himself (Iuba included) but only to those older than Iuba, who would be his source, just as in VI 149 the *priores* are undoubtedly the authors older than Iuba. Thus, we should assume that the king of Mauretania perceived such a history of navigation

1. Plin., *n.h.* VI 96: *sed priusquam generatim haec persequamur, indicari conuenit quae prodidit Onesicritus classe Alexandri circumuectus in mediterranea Persidis ex India, enarrata proxime a Iuba, deinde eam nauigationem, quae his annis comperta seruatur hodie.*

in the Indian Ocean, and the description of the route for Muziris should go back to the Augustan age.[2]

Desanges' theory is remarkably interesting and very attractive insofar as it would enable us to go back to a single source for the all *excursus* in paragraphs 96-106, which Pliny would have simply copied from Iuba. However, I have some difficulty in accepting this opinion, since a number of clues seems to prove that the genesis of those paragraphs of Pliny's text must have been much more tormented than Desanges admits. Above all, they prove that Iuba cannot be Pliny's source, not only for paragraphs 102-106, but not even for the end of paragraph 100; that is, not even as regards the first route for India, the Syagros-Patale, as I myself formerly believed.[3]

The assumption upon which Desanges builds his theory — the identification of the *priores* in VI 105 with the *priores* in VI 149 — proves to be fallacious upon careful consideration. At VI 149, the context makes it absolutely clear that *priores* means the authors previous to Iuba;[4] in fact, Pliny records Iuba's opinion in the first place, then he notes that this opinion differs from that of the *priores* and, finally, he refers to the stories of the merchants he mixed with. In this context *priores* cannot be taken as anything but *priores* to Iuba; that is, to the author whose opinion he has just quoted. It is a completely different matter in VI 105, where, as no other author is being quoted, the reader cannot help understanding *priores* as *priores* to Pliny himself, who is writing.

Furthermore, this impression is confirmed by the fact that the route for Muziris is the one which *his annis conperta, seruatur hodie* (96). Pliny sets it out in its entirety and in every detail, *nunc primum certa notitia patescente* (101), taking care to specify, indicating fresh information, *regnabat ibi, cum proderem haec, Caelobothras* (104).

Last but not least, the correspondence in the calendar between the 6th of Mechir in the Egyptians' revolving year and Ides of January in VI 106, as I have

---

2. J. DESANGES, "Sur la mer Hippale, au souffle du vent Hippale", *Topoi* 6, 1996, pp. 665-670. It is certain that Pliny knew (also?) Iuba's account of the voyage of Alexander's fleet, cfr. Plin., *n.h.* VI 96: [...] *enarrata proxime a Iuba.*

3. That Pliny depended on Iuba in the description of the two routes between Syagros and India (VI 100-101) has been judged probable by C. MÜLLER, *HGF*, III, p. 476 and F. JACOBY, *FGrHist* 275 F 28 Komm.; and certain by myself, cfr. F. DE ROMANIS, "Romanukharaṭṭha e Taprobane. Sui rapporti Roma-Ceylon nel I sec. d.C.", *Helikon* 28, 1988, p. 25, nt. 51 (english translation in F. DE ROMANIS/ A. TCHERNIA, *Crossings. Early Mediterranean Contacts with India*, New Delhi, 1997, p. 219, nt. 55).

4. Plin., *n.h.* VI 149: *ultra nauigationem inconpertam ab eo latere propter scopulos tradit Iuba praetermissa mentione oppidi Omanorum Batrasauaues et Omanae, quod priores celebre<m> portum Carmaniae fecere, item Homnae et Attanae, quae nunc oppida maxime celebrari a Persico mari nostri negotiatores dicunt.*

shown elsewhere, only took place in the years 49-52 A.D.[5] Unless it can be shown that in VI 106 Pliny is following sources different from those followed in VI 102-105, or unless Pliny, on his own initiative, can be supposed to have updated the calendar correspondence given by his source, we should admit that in this case too Pliny obtains his information from the *negotiatores* that he himself "interviewed" at first hand.[6] And we must suppose that those same *negotiatores* had taken part in commercial enterprises in southern India during the years 48/49-51-52 A.D.

Well then: similar to what happens with regard to the description of the coasts around Charax,[7] paragraphs VI 96-106 of the *Naturalis Historia* are based partly on information taken from the *priores* (Iuba, but other authors too, as we shall see) and partly on information obtained directly from the merchants. The information about southern Indian route (101-106) comes from the latter. Pliny must have considered this route among these *quas aut ignorauerant priores* — all the *priores*, Iuba included — *aut postea inuenerat uita.*[8]

1. DISTANCES

1. The distance between Syagros and Patale in Pliny

If Iuba is certainly Pliny's source for the voyage made by Alexander's fleet (VI 96-100), it can be shown, as I was saying, that the information relating the first Arabia-India route does not go back to Iuba. In a recent work, P. Arnaud has emphasised that in classical geographical literature there were two different systems of calculating maritime distances: the first one calculates the distance in spatial terms, *i.e.*, in number of stadia (sometimes translated in Roman miles); the second one, on the contrary, uses temporal terms, *i.e.*, the number of days

5. Plin., *n.h.* 106: *ex India renauigant mense Aegyptio Tybi incipiente, nostro Decembri, aut utique Mechiris Aegyptii intra diem sextum, quod fit intra idus Ianuarias nostras*, cfr. F. DE ROMANIS, "Romanukharaṭṭha e Taprobane", *cit.*, pp. 5-18 (english translation in DE ROMANIS/ TCHERNIA, *Crossings*, cit., pp. 161-172).

6. *Ibid.*

7. Plin., *n.h.* VI 139-140: *prius fuit a litore stadiis X – maritimum etiam Vipsan<i>a porticus habet –, Iuba uero prodente L p.; nunc abesse a litore CXX legati Arabum nostrique negotiatores, qui inde uenere, adfirmant*; ibid. 149: *ultra nauigationem inconpertam ab eo latere propter scopulos tradit Iuba praetermissa mentione oppidi Omanorum Batrasauaues et Omanae, quod priores celebre<m> portum Carmaniae fecere, item Homnae et Attanae, quae nunc oppida maxime celebrari a Persico mari nostri negotiatores dicunt.*

8. Plin., *n.h.* praef. 17.

necessary for navigation.[9] This opposition is found in the Plinian *excursus* on the *nauigationes in Indiam*: while in the description of the route to southern India the distances are always expressed by days spent in sailing — about thirty days from Berenice to Ocelis (or Cane), then forty from Ocelis (or Cane) to Muziris —,[10] in the description of the Syagros-Patale route, evidently drawn from another source of information, the distance is given as 1332 Roman miles.[11]

It goes without saying that the evaluation in Roman miles of the distance between Syagros and Patale in Pliny VI 100 is a translation of an evaluation in stadia of the Greek source from which Pliny draws either directly or indirectly; otherwise it would be difficult to explain the approximation to a Roman mile in the calculation of sea distances greater than a thousand Roman miles. It also goes without saying that it cannot be the translation of a distance in stadia according to the ratio usually found in Pliny, i.e., the one that makes 1 Roman mile equal to 8 stadia. If this were the case, in fact, the unlikely original distance would be 1332 x 8 = 10656 stadia, which is of foolishly ambitious precision. The hypothesis that 1332 stadia came from a ratio that makes 1 Roman mile equal to 7.5 stadia[12] seems much more likely; in this case, the original distance would be 1332 x 7.5 = 9990, that is to say, rounding it up a little,[13] 10 000 stadia.

2. Pliny and the "Babylonian" stadium

As we were saying, this is not the usual way in which Pliny translates into Roman miles the distances expressed in stadia. However, we can trace other distances in his work relating to geographical areas close to those of Syagros and Patale, in which the calculation in Roman miles appears to be the translation of one in stadia according to a ratio 1: 7.5.

---

9. P. ARNAUD, "De la durée à la distance: l'évaluation des distances maritimes dans le monde gréco-romain", *Histoire & Mesure* 8, 1993, pp. 225-226.

10. Plin., *n.h.* VI 104: *nauigare incipiunt aestate media ante Canis ortum aut ab exortu protinus ueniuntque tricesimo circiter die Ocelim Arabiae aut Canem turiferae regionis [...] Indos autem petentibus utilissimum est ab Oceli egredi; inde uento hippalo nauigant diebus XL ad primum emporium Indiae Muzirim.*

11. Plin., *n.h.* VI 100: [...] *postea ab Syagro Arabiae promunturio Patalen fauonio, quem hipalum ibi uocant, peti certissimum uidebatur, XIII (centena milia) XXXII (milia) p.* Reading *XIII (centena milia) XXXII (milia)* from **E**[s] is righlty preferred to *XIIII XXXV* from **DFRCha**. Also corrupt is *quadraginta duo milia* from **p**.

12. On the various equivalents Roman mile /stadium, cfr., e.g., F. LEHMANN-HAUPT, *R.E.* III A2, coll. 1931-1963.

13. One might suspect that the figure from **E**[s] (cfr. nt. 11) is slightly corrupt, since a reading *XIII (centena milia) XXXII<I> (milia) p.* would give a better approximation: 1333 x 7, 5 = 9997, 5 stadia. However, the existence of a similar case (cfr. *infra*, nt. 17) advises caution.

In the passage relating to the distances along the coasts of the Red Sea,[14] for example, while Artemidorus's calculations have been translated by Pliny (or by someone else for him) according to a ratio 1:8,[15] those of Agrippa — 1732 Roman miles for both shores of [illegible]ed Sea — on the contrary are based[16] on a ratio 1:7.5 stadia: 1 732 x 7.5 [illegible]990, that is to say, rounding it up,[17] 13 000 stadia.

The use of a ratio of 1:7.5 does, moreover, seem to occur in another fragment of Agrippa's work, also transmitted by Pliny. It concerns the dimensions of Media, Parthia and Persis on the one hand and of Mesopotamia on the other.[18] Here the distances passed on by Agrippa would give numbers rounded to tens, if converted into stadia at the ratio 1:8,[19] but give numbers rounded to hundreds — sometimes even thousands — if converted at the ratio 1:7.5. The *longitudo* of Media, Parthia and Persis would, in fact, be 1320 x 7.5 = 9 900; the *latitudo* would be of 840 x 7.5 = 6 300 stadia. The *longitudo* of Mesopotamia would be 800 x 7.5 = 6 000 stadia; the *latitudo* 360 x 7.5 = 2 700.

The adoption of such a ratio would appear much more likely when we consider how close the calculation of the Syagros-Patale distance is to the *longitudo* of Media, Parthia and Persis, measured from the Indus to the Tigris;[20] it is very difficult to consider this similarity as a coincidence. On the contrary, it seems to suggest some sort of relationship between the calculation of the distance between the Tigris and the Indus and that between Syagros and Patale, the Indian emporium at the mouth of the Indus.

---

14. Plin., *n.h.* VI 163: *nunc reliquam oram Arabiae contrariam persequemur. Timosthenes totum sinum quadridui nauigatione in longitudinem taxauit, bidui in latitudinem, angustias VII (milia) D p.; Eratosthenes ab ostio XII (centena milia) in quamque partem; Artemidorus Arabiae latere XVII (centena milia) L (milia). Trogodytico uero XI (centena milia) LXXXVII (milia) D p. Ptolemaida usque; Agrippa XVII (centena milia) XXXII (milia) sine differentia laterum.*

15. *Arabiae latus*: 1750 x 8 = 14 000 stadia; *Trogodyticum latus Ptolemaida usque*: 1187, 5 x 8 = 9500 stadia.

16. In stadia of 1/8 of a Roman mile the distance would be 13 856 stadia.

17. In this case too one might suspect a corruption from an original reading *XVII (centena milia) XXXII<I>* (milia), but cfr. *supra* nt. 13.

18. Plin., *n.h.* VI 137: *namque is [sc. M. Agrippa] Mediam et Parthiam et Persidem ab oriente Indo, ab occidente Tigri, a septentrione Tauro Caucasio, a meridie Rubro mari terminatas patere in longitudinem XIII (centena milia) XX (milia), in latitudinem DCCCXL prodidit, praeterea per se Mesopotamiam, ab oriente Tigri, ab occasu Euphrate, a septentrione Tauro, a meridie mari Persico inclusam, longitudine DCCC (milia) p., latitudine CCCLX (milia).*

19. *Longitudo* of Media, Parthia and Persis 1320 x 8 = 10560 stadia; *latitudo* of Media, Parthia and Persis 840 x 8 = 6720 stadia; *longitudo* of Mesopotamia 800 x 8 = 6400 stadia; *latitudo* of Mesopotamia 360 x 8 = 2880 stadia.

20. Respectively 1332 (or 1333?) Roman miles [= 10 000 stadia] e 1320 Roman miles [= 9900 stadia].

In conclusion: the calculation of the Syagros-Patale route in Roman miles as transmitted to Pliny VI 100 seems to be coherent with a system of measurement relating to certain Asian regions, which Pliny himself also found in Agrippa's work.[21]

3. The distance between Syagros and Socotra in Pliny

The island of Socotra, half-way between Arabia and Africa at the external edge of the Gulf of Aden, was at the crossroads of the sea routes between Southern Arabia, East Africa, the Persian Gulf and India for thousands of years. Perhaps it can be identified as the Happy Isles between Arabia and India, on which the fantastic Utopias of Euhemerus and Iambulus were set[22] and which, in Agatharchides's work, appear more clearly as the landfall of merchants sailing from the mouth of the Indus.[23] About two centuries later, it seemed evident to the author of the *Periplus Maris Erythraei* that the inhabitants of the island were of mixed race: the result of centuries of mingling with Indian, Arab and Greek

---

21. Probably derived from Agrippa and converted according to ratio 1:7.5 are also some maritime distances relating to the Black Sea: 2560 Roman miles (= 19 200 stadia) for the *circuitus Ponti* [IV 77: the reading *XXV (centena milia) LX (milia)* it is a certain emendation from Partsch of the impossible *XXIII (milia)* of the manuscripts; notice that in the Ian-Mayohoff edition of Pliny, due to a misprint, I imagine, there is *XL (milia)* instead of *LX (milia)*]; 560 Roman miles (= 4 200 stadia) for the coast *ab Histri ostio ad os Ponti* (IV 45; 78); 360 Roman miles (= 2700 stadia) from Phasis to Cimmerian Bosporus (VI 3): cfr. P. ARNAUD, "Les relations maritimes dans le Pont-Euxin d'après les données numériques des géographes anciens", *REA* 94, 1992, p. 71. As for the distance from the mouth of the Danube to Panticapaeum (IV 78) the manuscripts offer the reading *DCXXXV in* (*DCXXXV* F2), today generally emended in *DCXXXV* III (*milia*). Just because it seems to me that many of the Black Sea distances given by Agrippa are translations of original measurements in stadia according to a ratio 1 : 7.5 and also because the calculation of the *circuitus Ponti* makes it possible and suggests such a hypothesis, I would correct *DCXXXX (milia) inde*: 640 Roman miles of 7.5 stadia are 4 800 stadia. Vice versa, the distance from Calchedon to Phasis given by Agrippa (1 000 Roman miles: VI 3) comes from Eratosthenes (8 000 stadia: Strab. II 1, 39 = frg. III B 65 Berger) and is translated in Roman miles according to the usual ratio 1:8.

22. For Euhemerus Diod. V 41-46: the island of Panchaia has commercial relations with the Arabs (42, 2). From the eastern promontory of another island, at only 30 stadia from Panchaia, India is visible: φασὶ θεωρεῖσθαι τὴν Ἰνδικὴν ἀέριον διὰ τὸ μέγεθος τοῦ διαστήματος. For Diod. II 55-60, from the coasts of Αἰθιοπία, Iambulus reaches the happy isle in four months' sailing and then after more than four months he arrives at the shores of India.

23. Agatharch. 103 (*GGM* I, p. 191).

merchants.[24] Even today, the cult of Shikdara-mata, the goddess Socotra, is alive among the seamen of the Kutch and Gujarat coasts.[25]

As a comparison with Pomponius Mela's *Chorographia*[26] shows, Pliny seems to draw his information about the island Dioscuridu (Socotra) from a source different from the one — probably common to Pomponius Mela — that supplied him with the information about the island of Ogyris. While the measurements relating to this island are undoubtedly translated into Roman miles according to a ratio of 1 : 8,[27] the one relating to the distance from the promontory of Syagros to Dioscuridu have been converted into Roman miles according to a ratio of 1:7.5. In fact, in this case too [280 x 8 =] 2 240 is too exact a figure to be taken as the one translated by (the source of) Pliny, while [280 x 7.5 =] 2 100 stadia may well be the translation into linear distance of a voyage lasting for three temporal units, each of them equalling 700 Roman miles.

---

24. *PME* 30. In late antiquity, the island was thought to be colonised by Ptolemies, cfr. Cosm. Indic. III 169 B.

25. B. ARUNACHALAN, "Socotra in Indian Navigational Traditions", in S. CHANDRA, B. ARUNACHALAM, V. SURYANARAYAN, *The Indian Ocean and its Islands*, New Delhi, 1993, p. 118. Here important observations relating to XVIIth century Indian navigation maps, where the polar co-ordinates of South Arabian and Western Indian ports from Aden to Mangalore are given with reference to the island of Socotra. It is possible that in ancient times the island was a reference point for sailors in the Indian Ocean, sailing between Southern Arabia and India, as it is shown by a peculiar procedure followed by ships sailing towards the north-western coasts of India: after having sailed from Hisn el-Ghurab, in Southern Arabia, or from Cape Guardafui, these οὐ πλεῖον ἢ τρεῖς ἡμέρας ἀντέχουσι (*PME* 57). From the context of the passage (see L. CASSON, "The Sea Route to India: *Periplus Maris Erythraei* 57", *CQ* 34, pp. 473-479; A. TCHERNIA, "*Ad* Periplum Maris Erythraei 57", in M.-CL. AMOURETTI/ P. VILLARD, EYKRATA. *Mélanges offerts à Claude Vatin*, Aix-en-Provence (1994), pp. 131-136) we can infer that the relatively short ἀντέχειν of the ships sailing for the north-west coasts of India is absolutely equivalent to the τραχηλίζειν to which the ships making for Southern India are obliged during the whole voyage. In other words, the ships leaving from Hisn el-Ghurab or from Cape Guardafui and heading for the western coast of India, whether north or south, all took the same route during the very first part of the voyage. After a variable number of days – according to wheter they had left from Cane or from Cape Guardafui – but no more than three days in any case, they took different routes according to the various destinations.

26. Mela III 79: *aliquot sunt in medio insulae sitae, Ogyris quod in ea Erythrae regis monimentum est magis clara quam ceterae. alterum sinum undique Arabes cingunt;* Plin., *n.h.* VI 153: *insula in alto obiacet Ogyris, clara Erythra rege ibi sepulto; distat a continente CXXV (milia) p., circumitur CXII (milia) D. nec minus altera clara in Azanio mari Dioscuridu, distans a Syagro extumo promunturio CCLXXX (milia).*

27. The 125 Roman miles of the distance from the continent corresponds to 1 000 stadia; the 112.5 Roman miles of its perimeter equal 900 stadia.

We have already underlined the fact that the sea distance from Syagros to Patale appears in Pliny as the conversion of a distance given in stadia according to the exceptional ratio of 1:7.5. Now that very equivalence also seems to be suggested by the calculation of the distance between Syagros and the island of Dioscuridu. Thus it seems clear that Pliny drew his information as to the two distances from the same source.[28]

4. Pliny, Iuba, Artemidorus and the distances by sea in the Ἐρυθρὰ θάλασσα

The Greek geographical source from which Pliny (whether directly or indirectly) obtained the distances Syagros-Patale and Syagros-Dioscuridu cannot be identified as Iuba, because the distances by sea relating to Ἐρυθρὰ θάλασσα which Pliny takes from this author, when they are not kept in the original measurements in stadia,[29] are translated into Roman miles according to a ratio of 1:8.

Thus, in VI 175 (= *FGrHist* 275 F 5): *a Mossylico promunturio Atlanticum mare incipere uult Iuba praeter Mauretanias suas Gadis usque nauigandum coro, cuius tota sententia hoc in loco subtrahenda non est. a promunturio Indorum quod uocetur Lepte Acra, ab aliis Drepanum, proponit recto cursu praeter Exustam <ad> Malichu insulam XV (centena milia) p. esse, inde ad locum quem uocant Sceneos CCXXV (milia) p., inde ad insulas Adanu CL (milia): sic fieri ad apertum mare XVIII (centena milia) LXXV (milia) p.*[30]

Thus, in VI 203 (*FGrHist* 275 F 44): *Iuba de Fortunatis ita inquisiuit: sub meridiem quoque positas esse prope occasum, a Purpurariis DCXXV (milia) p., sic ut CCL (milia) supra occasum nauigetur, dein per CCCLXXV (milia) ortus petatur.*[31]

---

28. It would be rash to theorise that the Hellenistic route from Syagros to Patale envisaged, as perhaps occurred later for the routes from Cane or Cape Guardafui to India, an approach to the island of Socotra before crossing the ocean; rather, we should consider that the calculation of the maritime distance between Syagros and the island of Dioscuridu is to be associated with the development of commercial relationships between the Gulf of Aden and India, to which the "erythraean" islands also contributed (cfr. *supra* nt. 23).

29. As in Plin., *n.h.* XXXVII 108: *Iuba Topazum insulam in Rubro mari a continenti stadiis CCC abesse dicit.*

30. 1 500 x 8 = 12 000 stadia; 225 x 8 = 1 800 stadia; 150 x 8 = 1 200 stadia; 1 875 x 8 = 15 000 stadia.

31. 625 x 8 = 5 000 stadia; 250 x 8 = 2 000 stadia; 375 x 8 = 3 000 stadia. Ratio 1 : 8 is to be assumed also in VI 139 (50 Roman miles); VI 156 (4 000 Roman miles); XII 39 (10 Roman miles). The Babylon-Charax distance in VI 124 is almost certainly corrupt: the reading adopted by Mayhoff, CLXXV (milia) D, has not much chance to be the original; impossible XII (milia) D, the figure offered by **DF¹dTRa**.

Neither can Artemidorus be Pliny's source for the distances between Syagros and Patale and Syagros and Dioscuridu, since also the measurements of the Red Sea coasts supplied by the Ephesian geographer are translated by Pliny according to the most frequent ratio of 1 Roman mile = 8 stadia: *Artemidorus Arabiae latere XVII (centena milia) L (milia), Trogodytico uero XI (centena milia) LXXXVII (milia) D p. Ptol<e>maida usque.*[32]

2. WINDS

1. Etymology and history in the *Periplus Maris Erythraei*

Pliny's reconstruction of the history of navigation in India can be compared with the one put forward by the author of the *Periplus Maris Erythraei* on the evidence of two etymologies: that of the toponym 'Adan-Εὐδαίμων 'Αραβία,[33] and that of the name of the SW monsoon. According to the author of the *Periplus Maris Erythraei* the two names would seem to preserve the memory of an important period and of a great event in the history of trade in the Indian Ocean. Let us begin with an observation on the explanation of the name of the Arab port.

PME 26: Εὐδαίμων δὲ ἐπεκλήθη, πρότερον οὖσα πόλις, ὅτε, μήπω ἀπὸ τῆς Ἰνδικῆς εἰς τὴν Αἴγυπτον ἐρχομένων μηδὲ ἀπὸ Αἰγύπτου τολμώντων εἰς τοὺς ἔξω τόπους διαίρειν ἀλλ' ἄχρι ταύτης παραγινομένων, τοὺς παρὰ ἀμφοτέρων φόρτους ἀπεδέχετο, ὥσπερ 'Αλεξάνδρεια καὶ τῶν ἔξωθεν καὶ τῶν ἀπὸ τῆς Αἰγύπτου φερομένων ἀποδέχεται. νῦν δὲ οὐ πρὸ πολλοὺς τῶν ἡμετέρων χρόνων Καῖσαρ αὐτὴν κατεστρέψατο.

According to the author of the *Periplus Maris Erythraei*, then, the name Εὐδαίμων goes back to a fairly distant period before the work was written, even to the time when direct relations between Egypt and India[34] had not yet been established. At that time, Εὐδαίμων 'Αραβία would have been a *polis* acting as a trading *relais*. A splendid merchant, our author is not equally brilliant as a historian; not in these circumstances, anyway. This history of the place-name 'Adan, according to which an Arab *polis* (called 'Αραβία?) would have received, in a very distant past, a Greek nickname (Εὐδαίμων), is absolutely implausible. Especially when we take into account the fact that the Arab toponym 'Adan was

---

32. Plin., *n.h.* VI 163-164. 1 750 x 8 = 14 000 stadia; 1187, 5 x 8 = 9 500 stadia.
33. 'Αδάνη in Philostor. h. e. III 4; cfr. the adjectives 'Αδανηνός and 'Αδανείτης, the latter being attested in an inscription from Coptos of 70 d.C. (*IPortes* 65).
34. Also earlier, one would say, than the discovery of Hippalos, cfr. *PME* 57: τοῦτον δὲ ὅλον τὸν εἰρημένον περίπλουν ἀπο Κανῆς καὶ τῆς Εὐδαίμονος 'Αραβίας οἱ μὲν ‹πρότεροι› (Müller) μικροτέροις πλοίοις περικολπίζοντες ἔπλεον κτλ.

already indirectly attested, in a Greek inscription, in 70 A.D. If the author of the *Periplus Maris Erythraei* were right, ‘Adan would have to be considered a corruption of Εὐδαίμων Ἀραβία. Actually, as Müller realized, it is rather the case that Εὐδαίμων is a Greek adaptation of ‘Adan.[35] In short, the etymology given in the *Periplus Maris Erythraei* is one of the naive Greek etymologies of non-Greek place-names such as we often meet with in the geographical literature.[36] But if this is true, that is, if the name has an Arab origin and not a Greek one, then we may wonder how much the author's statements are worth in relation to ‘Adan's commercial role in a period so distant from his own. What other evidence did he have to say that earlier ‘Adan had been a city and had been at the center of the traffic between Egypt and India? Pliny (his source) does not assign any important role to ‘Adan in his history of the *nauigationes in Indiam*, therefore the suspicion that the description of ‘Adan as an Alexandria of the Indian Ocean is only a projection of the false etymology ‘Adan < Εὐδαίμων seems well-founded.[37]

2. Hippalos, the Etesian winds, and the λιβόνοτος of the Indian Ocean in the *PME*

The passage in which the author of the *Periplus Maris Erythraei* offers his explanation of the name *Hippalos* for the SW monsoon poses some interpretative and textual problems upon which it will be opportune to linger.

In the editions of Müller and Frisk, the text is established as follows: τοῦτον δὲ ὅλον τὸν εἰρημένον περίπλουν ἀπὸ Κανῆς καὶ τῆς Εὐδαίμονος Ἀραβίας οἱ μὲν ‹πρότεροι› (Müller) μικροτέροις πλοίοις περικολπίζοντες ἔπλεον, πρῶτος δὲ Ἵππαλος κυβερνήτης, κατανοήσας τὴν θέσιν τῶν ἐμπορίων καὶ τὸ σχῆμα τῆς θαλάσσης, τὸν διὰ πελάγους ἐξεῦρε πλοῦν, ἀφ᾽ οὗ καὶ τοπικῶς ἐκ τοῦ ὠκεανοῦ φυσώντων, [τῶν] (**L**, edd.) κατὰ καιρὸν τῶν παρ᾽ ἡμῖν, ἐτησίων ἐν τῷ Ἰνδικῷ πελάγει λιβόνοτος φαίνεται ‹ἵππαλος› (Müller) προσονομάζεσθαι (Salmasius: προσονομάζεται δὲ **P**) [ἀπὸ τῆς προσηγορίας τοῦ πρώτως ἐξευρηκότος (Gelenius: ἐξευρηκέναι **P**) τὸν διάπλουν].

35. *GGM*, I, p. 279: “Graeci mercatores in fortunatissimum Felicis Arabiae emporium nomen Εὐδαίμων Ἀραβία lusu quodam transtulisse videntur; ansam rei praebuerit *Aden* nomen Arabicum, quod sensim abiit in Εὐδαίμων”.

36. It may be enough to cite the parallel case of the oppidum Aduliton: Aegyptiorum hoc serui profugi a dominis condidere (Plin., *n.h.* VI 173).

37. On a different level is what appears in the text as a conquest of ‘Adan by a Καῖσαρ, an occurrence that the author places in times not much earlier than his own and that therefore he could have known not too vaguely: see the discussion in L. CASSON, *The* Periplus Maris Erythraei. *Text with Introduction, Translation and Commentary*, Princeton, 1989, p. 160; N. GROOM, “The Periplus, Pliny and Arabia”, *Arabian Archaeology and Epigraphy*, 6, 1995, pp. 183-184.

Accepting the corrections of his predecessors for all the rest, Casson has suggested: 1) deleting ἀφ' οὗ; 2) not taking προσονομάζεται δὲ – ἐξευρηκότος τὸν διάπλουν as a marginal gloss seeped into the text; and 3) rejecting the old salmasian correction προσονομάζεσθαι.

Both these readings leave us dissatisfied, however, since the relationship between the absolute genitive φυσώντων - ἐτησίων and the φαίνεται κτλ. is not clear. Indeed, what is the meaning in Müller's translation of "[...] quum pro locorum ratione, etesiae, eodem quo apud nos flant tempore, ex Oceano spirent in pelago Indico, libonotus ventus nominatus esse videtur Hippalus etc"?[38] There can be no casual or temporal relationship between the blowing of the Etesian winds and the name of Hippalos for the λιβόνοτος. Nor can one take φυσώντων – ἐτησίων as a partitive genitive, meaning that of all the various different Etesian winds blowing locally from the Ocean, only the λιβόνοτος was called Hippalos. If the ἐτησίων of *PME* 57 means the southern Etesian winds, these could not be identified as a whole except as the very same SW monsoon;[39] *i.e.*, with that wind that is called λιβόνοτος in *PME* 57. But since the Etesian winds in the *Periplus Maris Erythraei* clearly appear as winds altogether, or at least partly, different from the ἐν τῷ Ἰνδικῷ πελάγει λιβόνοτος, we should suggest a reading that does not force us to see the mentioned Etesians as Indian Ocean winds, i.e., which does not refer ἐκ τοῦ ὠκεανοῦ φυσώντων to ἐτησίων.

I would connect ἐτησίων with τῶν παρ' ἡμῖν[40] and refer to λιβόνοτος the ἐκ τοῦ ὠκεανοῦ φυσώντων τῶν: for example, as F. Angiò has suggested to me, I would read ἐκ τοῦ ὠκεανοῦ φυσῶν τ'ὤν τε κατὰ καιρὸν κτλ. Moreover, I believe it necessary to restore an ‹ὁ› before ἐν τῷ Ἰνδικῷ πελάγει, for which the attributive position with respect to λιβόνοτος seems to me evident. Thus I would not follow Casson in deleting ἀφ' οὗ, because it then becomes impossible to understand what logical connection could link the proposition concerning the discovery of Hippalos to the following proposition;[41] just as I would not accept in the text προσονομάζεται δὲ – ἐξευρηκότος (Gelenius: ἐξευρηκέναι **P**)

38. *GGM*, I, p. 298.

39. As in the historians of Alexanders and the Hellenistic geographical literature, the Etesian winds in the Indian Ocean are exclusively the SW monsoon, cfr. *infra* ntt. 56, 66.

40. For a similar formula, cfr. *PME* 29: τῶν παρ' ἡμῖν ἐν Αἰγύπτῳ δένδρων.

41. Casson is forced to put omission marks in his translation: "The ship captain Hippalos, by plotting the location of the ports of trade and the configuration of the sea, was the first to discover the route over open water (...). In this locale the winds we call "etesian" blow seasonally from the direction of the ocean, and so a southwesterly makes its appearance in the Indian Sea, but it is called after the name of the one who first discovered the way across" (CASSON, *The* Periplus Maris Erythraei, *cit.*, p. 87). The connection between the two clauses is very clear if we do not delete the reading ἀφ' οὗ and for the rest we emend the text like most of the editors: Hippalos's discoveries appear to be the origin of the name of the SW monsoon.

τὸν διάπλουν.[42] As for the rest, I think the integration of ‹πρότεροι› or similar justified; on the contrary, that of ‹ἵππαλος› is superfluous. If we preserve ἀφ' οὗ and we take it as a masculine referred to Ἵππαλος,[43] there is no more need to suppose a lacuna in the text.

To sum up, for the final part of the passage, the following reading could be proposed:

πρῶτος δὲ Ἵππαλος κυβερνήτης, κατανοήσας τὴν θέσιν τῶν ἐμπορίων καὶ τὸ σχῆμα τῆς θαλάσσης, τὸν διὰ πελάγους ἐξεῦρε πλοῦν. ἀφ' οὗ καὶ τοπικῶς, ἐκ τοῦ ὠκεανοῦ φυσῶν τ'ὤν τε[a] κατὰ καιρὸν τῶν παρ' ἡμῖν ἐτησίων, ‹ὁ› ἐν τῷ Ἰνδικῷ πελάγει λιβόνοτος φαίνεται ‹**›[b] [προσονομάζεται δὲ ἀπὸ τῆς προσηγορίας τοῦ πρώτως ἐξευρηκότος (Gelenius: ἐξευρηκέναι P) τὸν διάπλουν].

[a] φυσώντων τῶν P ([τῶν] L) [b] ‹προσονομάζεσθαι› uel ‹προσονομαζόμενος› uel sim.

and the following translation:

"After having considered the position of the emporia and the breadth of the sea, the pilot Hippalos was the first to discover how to sail in the open sea. It is evident (or: it seems) that the λιβόνοτος of the Indian Sea, (a wind) which blows from the Ocean in the (same) season of our Etesian, was called locally[44] after him".

Once again, the author of the *Periplus Maris Erythraei* links an important development in the history of seafaring in the Indian Ocean to a name, that of the SW monsoon. Hippalos is a name widespread in Ptolemaic-Roman Egypt:[45] is the etymology correct, this time?

3. Hypalus, hippalus, hispalus, hippallus, hipallus

As we noticed above, Pliny's history of *nauigationes in Indiam* is a patchwork from different sources. S. Mazzarino[46] has attributed to this very

42. With Müller and Frisk, I prefer to consider this a gloss penetrated into the text, taking the place of an original προσονομάζεσθαι or προσονομαζόμενος or another similar verb.

43. Similar nexus in *PME* 16 (ἀφ' ἧς) and 42 (μεθ' ἧς).

44. τοπικῶς is to be connected to the verb to be restored at <***>. The local nature of the name of the SW monsoon is also underlined by Plin., *n.h.* VI 100: [...] *fauonio quem ibi hypalum uocant.*

45. F PREISIGKE, *Namenbuch*, Heidelberg, 1922, col. 151; D. FORABOSCHI, *Onomasticon alterum papyrologicum*, Milano (1971), p. 149.

46. S. MAZZARINO, "Sul nome del vento *hipalus* ('ippalo') in Plinio", *Helikon* 22/27, 1982/1987, p. VII-XIV (english translation in F. DE ROMANIS/ A. TCHERNIA, *Crossings*, cit., pp. 72-79).

diversity the different spelling of the same name of the SW monsoon in two different passages of the *Naturalis Historia*, at least according to some manuscripts: in VI 100, the form *hypalus*, to be maintained, would be the one adopted by the late Hellenistic geographical source followed by Pliny; that is, the one whose stadion was calculated as 2/15 of a Roman mile, as we now know. In VI 104, the form *hippalus* — to be compared with the Ἵππαλος in *PME* 57 — depends on information obtained at first hand from merchants operating in 48/49-51/52 A.D.

I have set out below the readings of the main Pliny manuscripts relating to the denomination of the SW monsoon in VI 100 and VI 104. I have also added the readings relating to the denomination of a *promunturium* in VI 172,[47] where Detlefsen, Mayhoff, Desanges and many others believe the reading *Hippalum* should be restored.

	100	104	172
Par. Lat. 6795 (**E**^{S})	**hipalum**	**hipallo**	**hispalum**
Vat. Lat. 3861 (**D**)	**hypylum**[48]	**hippalo**	**hispalū**
Leidensis Voss. 7 (**F**)	**hypilum**	**hippalo**	**hispalū**
Ricc. 844 (**R**)	**ipilū**	**hippalo**	**hispalū**
Pierpont Morgan Lib.871	**hypylum**	**hippalo**	**hispalū**
Vindob. 234 (**a**)	**hypilū**	**yppalo**	**yspalū**
Pollinganus Lat. 11301 (**p**)	**ipalū**	**ypalo**	**hyspalū**
Par. Lat.6796A (**e**)	**hipalū**	**hipallo**	**hispalū**
Par. Lat. 6797	**hypilum**	**hyppolo**	**hispalum**
Toletanus Madrid Bibl. Nac. 10042	**hypilū**	**hyppolo**	**hispalū**

Without taking into account the hardly significant fluctuations between *-i-* / *-y-* and the omission of the initial aspirate, equally irrelevant, the three denominations — the first two, we repeat, referring to the SW monsoon, the third to a promontory at the beginning of the Azanian Sea — are given differently in the

47. J. DESANGES, *art. cit.*, pp. 668-670, proposes correcting the clause to *hinc promunturium, Azanium mare quod aliqui Hippalum scripsere* and suggests its re-siting after paragraph 174. The scholar, however, recognises that his suggestion might seem "trop risquée" and actually so it seems to me, too. Here we shall continue to speak about the *promunturium Hispalum.*

48. Not *pypylum*, as appears from Detlefsen, Mayhoff, André.

manuscript tradition: at VI 100 the simple *-p-* is unanimously attested, even when, as in **DFR** for example, the *-a-* in the second syllable is corrupt, by assimilation with the vowel of the first syllable, in *-i-/-y*. In VI 172, the manuscript tradition, also unanimous in this case, gives the reading *-sp-*. In VI 104, on the contrary, the double *-pp-* appears most often; in some cases, among them the authoritative Parisinus latinus 6795 (**E**[s]), the *-p-* is simple but the *-ll-* is double; in some others, both *-pp-* and *-ll-* are double.

Considering the problem only from the codicological point of view, we may observe that the spellings *-p-* and *-sp-*, unanimously attested by the manuscript tradition in VI 100 and VI 172 respectively, are precisely those which modern editors reject, in favour of a reading *-pp-*, attested, but not unanimously, in VI 104. The reasons for this choice, at first sight paradoxical, are to be found in the tradition relating to the Ἵππαλος κυβερνήτης: if the wind really takes its name from the anthroponym Ἵππαλος, a spelling such as *hypalus* is certainly to be rejected. And, on the other hand, since πέλαγος Ἵππαλος (or Ἵππαλον or Ἱππάλου) in Ptolemy is the name of the sea immediately to the west of the Indian Sea,[49] it would not seem unlikely that the name of the pilot is repeated exactly in that of the promontory, as well as in the names of the wind and the sea.

However, that in VI 172, the manuscripts's reading *Hispalum* should be preserved or, anyway, not corrected as *Hippalum* strikes me as evident from the context:[50] the formula *promunturium, quod aliqui Hispalum scripsere* betrays Pliny's surprise, perhaps even suspicion, at an unexpected spelling of the toponym.[51] If Pliny had read *Hippalum* in his own sources, just as he knew *Hippalus* to be the name of the SW monsoon, he would not have written *quod aliqui scripsere*. Of course, one can wonder whether the exemplars Pliny consulted did not already have a corrupt reading (*Hispalum* for an original *Hippalum* or *Hypalum*), but as far as Pliny's text is concerned, it must be observed that by correcting the attested *Hispalum* to *Hippalum*, a textual banalization is introduced, which is also inconsistent with the context; thus it is better to reject it.

Going on to the name of the SW monsoon in VI 104, although the form with single *-p-* and double *-ll-* finds a correspondence in the *Hippallo* of the Ambrosiam manuscript of the *Itinerarium Alexandri Magni,*[52] the spelling

49. Ptol., *geogr.* IV 7, 12.

50. Provided that other and more drastic corrections do not need to be made, cfr. *supra*, nt. 47.

51. Compare Plin., *n.h.* III 92: *Aethusa, quam alii Aegusam scripserunt*; VI 162: *nam et ipsum sinum nostri Laeaniticum scripsere, alii Aelaniticum, Artemidorus Alaeniticum, Iuba Leaniticum*; XXI 177: *trychno, quam quidam strychnon scripsere.*

52. *Itin. Alex. Magni* 110 Hausmann: *Ipsa uero extrinsecus ubique oceano munitur, interfluo mari Hippallo* (*Hippalio* Peiper: *Hippalico* Letronne), *cuius sinus*

hippalo, transmitted among others by **DFR** and supported by the "Ιππαλος of *PME* 57, must be definitively preferred to *hippallo* and *hipallo*. Like the author of the *Periplus Maris Erythraei*, the mid-first century A.D. merchants (Pliny's sources for VI 104) must have recognised the anthroponym "Ιππαλος in the name of the SW monsoon.

Is this a good enough reason to restore *hi<p>palum* to VI 100? In other words, does the explanation for the name of the SW monsoon, as the name of the inventor of sailing on the high seas between Arabia and India, really go back to the period of Pliny's (late Hellenistic) source, whose distances are translated according to the "Babylonian" ratio?

S. Mazzarino has suggested a different interpretation for the origin of the name of the SW monsoon: he has theorised that the name *hypalus* derives from ὕφαλος (sc. ἄνεμος or similar), "under-sea" (sc. wind), a qualification opposite to the name ἀπόγαιος, "from land" (sc. wind), given to the NE monsoon.[53] The changeover from *hypalus* to *hippalus* would have occurred precisely because of the spreading of the etymology, to be considered erroneous, which the author of the *Periplus Maris Erythraei* knew and gave credit to in the middle of the I century A.D.[54]

4. *Inferus ex imo mari spirat*: the southern Etesians in the Indian Ocean

For the classical authors, the SW monsoon has the evident characteristics of a sea wind. This is true not only for the relatively late author of the *Periplus Maris Erythraei*,[55] but also for the historians of Alexander, who had already noticed how India was characterised by the alternation of the land and sea monsoons: the wind ἐκ τοῦ ὠκεανοῦ ("from the ocean"), or ἀπὸ τῆς μεγάλης θαλάσσης κατὰ νότον μάλιστα ("from the great Sea, roughly from the South"), or again, ἐκ τοῦ πελάγεος ("from the sea"),[56] the SW monsoon, is sharply

---

Persas includit. In Müller's edition (in F. DÜBNER, *Arriani Anabasis et Indica. Reliqua Arriani et scriptorum de rebus Alexandri M.*, Paris, 1846, p. 166) the reading is given as *Hipallo*.

53. Strab. XV 1, 17-18 (= *FGrHist* 139 F 35; 133 F 18): τὴν δὲ θάλατταν ἄπλουν εἶναι τῶν ἀνέμων ἀντιπνεόντων, ἀπογαίας δὲ μηδεμιᾶς πνοῆς ἐκδεξαμένης. τοῦτο μὲν οὖν καὶ ὁ Νέαρχος λέγει *ibid.* 20 (= *FGrHist* 134 F 8): ταῖς δὲ τῶν ποταμῶν πληρώσεσι καὶ τῷ τοὺς ἀπογαίους μὴ πνεῖν ὁμολογεῖ καὶ τὸ λεχθὲν ὑπὸ τοῦ Ὀνησικρίτου.

54. Cfr. *supra* nt. 46.

55. *PME* 57: ἐκ τοῦ ὠκεανοῦ φυσῶν. Whatever are the readings accepted (cfr. *supra*) the clause is to be referred to the SW monsoon.

56. Arr., An. VI 21, 1-2 (= *FGrHist* 133 F 33): ἦν δὲ ἐν μὲν τῷ τότε ἄπορος ἡ ὥρα ἐς τὸν πλοῦν· οἱ γὰρ ἐτησίαι ἄνεμοι κατεῖχον, οἳ δὴ τῇ ὥρᾳ ἐκείνῃ οὐ καθάπερ παρ' ἡμῖν ἀπ' ἄρκτου, ἀλλ' ἀπὸ τῆς μεγάλης θαλάσσης κατὰ νότον μάλιστα ἄνεμον ἵστανται. ἀπὸ δὲ τοῦ χειμῶνος τῆς ἀρχῆς τὸ ἀπὸ Πλειάδων δύσεως ἔστε ἐπὶ τροπάς, ἃς ἐν χειμῶνι ὁ ἥλιος ἐπιστρέφει, πλόϊμα εἶναι ταύτῃ ἐξηγγέλλετο.

contrasted with the ἀπόγαιος ("the land wind"), the NE monsoon. But in what way can a wind be not simply and generally "from the sea", but actually ὕφαλος, "from under the sea"?

According to an ancient geophysical theory, briefly repeated by Pliny,[57] and at much greater length by Gellius,[58] winds from the South (particularly the *auster*, to which Gellius adds the *africus*, a SW wind) blow from the depths of the sea.[59] In fact, starting from the South Pole (*ad partem axis infimam depressi*) they would penetrate beneath the sea[60] in the northern hemisphere.

The theory that places at the South Pole the origin of the southern winds of the northern hemisphere is criticised in a passage of Aristotle's *Meteorologica*.

τότε γὰρ κατὰ γῆν μᾶλλον οἷα δὴ πολλῷ ὕδατι ἐξ οὐρανοῦ βεβρεγμένην αὔρας ἵστασθαι μαλθακὰς καὶ ἐς τὸν παράπλουν ταῖς τε κώπαις καὶ τοῖς ἱστίοις ξυμμέτρους; *id.*, *Ind.* 21, 1 (= *FGrHist* 133 F 1): ὡς δὲ τὰ ἐτήσια πνεύματα ἐκοιμήθη, ἃ δὴ τοῦ θέρεος τὴν ὥρην πᾶσαν κατέχει ἐκ τοῦ πελάγεος ἐπιπνέοντα ἐπὶ τὴν γῆν καὶ ταύτῃ ἄπορον τὸν πλοῦν ποιέοντα, τότε δὴ ὡρμῶντο κτλ.

57. Plin., *n.h.* II 128: *austro maiores fluctus eduntur quam aquilone, quoniam ille inferus ex imo mari spirat, hic summo ideoque post austros noxii praecipue terrae motus.*

58. Aul. Gell. II 30: *quid obseruatum sit in undarum motibus, quae in mari alio atque alio modo fiunt austris flantibus aquilonibusque. hoc saepenumero in undarum motu, quas aquilones uenti quique ex eadem caeli regione aer fluit, faciunt in mari austri atque africi. nam fluctus, qui flante aquilone maximi et creberrimi excitantur, simul ac uentus posuit, sternuntur et conflaccescunt et mox fluctus esse desinunt. at non idem fit flante austro uel africo; quibus iam nihil spirantibus undae tamen factae diutius tument, et a uento quidem iamdudum tranquilla sunt, sed mare est etiam atque etiam undabundum. eius rei causa esse haec coniectatur, quod uenti a septentrionibus ex altiore caeli parte in mare incidentes deorsum in aquarum profunda quasi praecipites deferuntur undasque faciunt non prorsus inpulsas, sed imitus commotas, quae tantisper erutae uoluuntur, dum illius infusi desuper spiritus uis manet. austri uero et africi ad meridianum orbis circulum et ad partem axis infimam depressi inferiores et humiles per suprema aequoris euntes protrudunt magis fluctus quam eruunt, et idcirco non desuper laesae, sed propulsae in aduersum aquae etiam desistente flatu retinent aliquantisper de pristino pulsu impetum. id autem ipsum, quod dicimus, ex illis quoque Homericis uersibus, si quis non incuriose legat, adminiculari potest. nam de austri flatibus ita scripsit*: ἔνθα νότος μέγα κῦμα ποτὶ σκαιὸν ῥίον ὠθεῖ, *contra autem de borea, quem 'aquilonem' nos appellamus, alio dicit modo*: καὶ βορέης αἰθρηγενέτης μέγα κῦμα κυλίνδων. *ab aquilonibus enim, qui alti supernique sunt, fluctus excitatos quasi per prona uolui dicit, ab austris autem, his qui humiliores sunt, maiore ui quadam propelli sursum atque subici. id enim significat uerbum* ὠθεῖ, *sicut alio in loco*: λᾶαν ἄνω ὤθεσκε ποτὶ λόφον. *id quoque a peritissimis rerum philosophis obseruatum est austris spirantibus mare fieri glaucum et caeruleum, aquilonibus obscurius atriusque. cuius rei causam, cum Aristotelis libros problematorum praecerperemus, notaui.*

59. Thus (*ex imo mari*) Pliny with reference to the *auster*. Gellius, writes *per suprema aequoris euntes*: are both translations from an original ὕφαλος/ὕπαλος?

60. And in the earth, hence the violent earthquakes.

Aristotle recognises that there is in the southern hemisphere a system of winds similar to that in the northern hemisphere and therefore he admits that there is an Etesian wind blowing from the South Pole. But he denies that this southern Etesian wind can be identified with the wind blowing from the South in the northern hemisphere. Indeed, for Aristotle, the "polar", Etesian winds remain within their own hemisphere without, moreover, covering its whole extent. Boreas, for example, although blowing strongly in the northern regions, does not reach the South Seas beyond the Λιβύη (Africa), where the εὗροι and ζέφυροι alternate.[61] The wind blowing from S in the northern hemisphere is formed in the torrid zone of the northern hemisphere and therefore it is not an Etesian wind.[62]

Aristotelian criticism clarifies the interpretation of the SW monsoon given by the historians of Alexander: contrary to the philosopher, they believed that the SW monsoon was an Etesian wind coming from the South (κατὰ νότον μάλιστα); that is, they believed that it was the wind which formed at the South Pole and arrived in the northern hemisphere blowing from the sea. It should be noted that later Hellenistic geography, while conceding some of Aristotle's objections,[63] basically follows the theory put forward by the historians of Alexander. The rainy seasons that were found to be similar in India, in Arabia[64] and in Upper Aethiopia[65] called for a single explanation, supplied precisely by the South Etesian winds, originating from the South Pole.[66]

---

61. Arist., *meteor.* 362 b-363 a: ἐπεὶ δ' ὁμοίως ἔχειν ἀνάγκη τόπον τινὰ πρὸς τὸν ἕτερον πόλον ὥσπερ ὃν ἡμεῖς οἰκοῦμεν πρὸς τὸν ὑπὲρ ἡμῶν, δῆλον ὡς ἀνάλογον ἕξει τά τ' ἄλλα καὶ τῶν πνευμάτων ἡ στάσις· ὥστε καθάπερ ἐνταῦθα βορέας ἐστίν, κἀκείνοις ἀπὸ τῆς ἐκεῖ ἄρκτου τις ἄνεμος οὕτως ὤν, ὃν οὐδὲν δυνατὸν διέχειν δεῦρο, ἐπεὶ οὐδ' ὁ βορέας οὗτος εἰς τὴν ἐνταῦθα οἰκουμένην πᾶσάν ἐστιν· ἔστιν γὰρ ὥσπερ ἀπόγειον τὸ πνεῦμα τὸ βόρειον [ἕως ὁ βορέας οὗτος εἰς τὴν ἐνταῦθα οἰκουμένην πνεῖ]. ἀλλὰ διὰ τὸ τὴν οἴκησιν κεῖσθαι ταύτην πρὸς ἄρκτον, πλεῖστοι βορέαι πνέουσιν. ὅμως δὲ καὶ ἐνταῦθα ἐλλείπει καὶ οὐ δύναται πόρρω διήκειν, ἐπεὶ περὶ τὴν ἔξω Λιβύης θάλατταν τὴν νοτίαν, ὥσπερ ἐνταῦθα οἱ βορέαι καὶ οἱ νότοι πνέουσιν, οὕτως ἐκεῖ εὗροι καὶ ζέφυροι διαδεχόμενοι συνεχεῖς ἀεὶ πνέουσιν.

62. *Ibid.* 363 a: ὥστ' ἀνάγκη τὸν ἀπὸ τοῦ κατακεκαυμένου τόπου πνέοντα ἄνεμον εἶναι νότον. ἐκεῖνος δ' ὁ τόπος διὰ τὴν τοῦ ἡλίου γειτνίασιν οὐκ ἔχει ὕδατα καὶ νομάς, αἳ διὰ τὴν πῆξιν ποιήσουσιν ἐτησίας.

63. Strab. I 3, 22 (= Eratosth. Frag. I B, 21 Berger): κατὰ γοῦν τὴν Αἰθιοπίαν μὴ πνεῖν νότον, ἀλλὰ κατωτέρω.

64. Strab. XVI 4, 2 (= Eratosth. *Frag.* III B, 48 Berger): [...] τὰ δ' ἔσχατα πρὸς νότον καὶ ἀνταίροντα τῇ Αἰθιοπίᾳ βρέχεταί τε θερινοῖς ὄμβροις καὶ δισπορεῖται παραπλησίως τῇ Ἰνδικῇ κτλ.

65. Strab. XVII 1, 5: οἱ μὲν οὖν ἀρχαῖοι στοχασμῷ τὸ πλέον, οἱ δ' ὕστερον αὐτόπται γενηθέντες ᾔσθοντο ὑπὸ ὄμβρων θερινῶν πληρούμενον τὸν Νεῖλον, τῆς Αἰθιοπίας τῆς ἄνω κλυζομένης, καὶ μάλιστα ἐν τοῖς ἐσχάτοις ὄρεσι, παυσαμένων δὲ τῶν ὄμβρων παυομένην κατ' ὀλίγον τὴν πλημμυρίδα· τοῦτο δ' ὑπῆρξε μάλιστα δῆλον τοῖς πλέουσι τὸν Ἀράβιον κόλπον μέχρι τῆς κινναμωμοφόρου καὶ τοῖς ἐκπεμπομένοις ἐπὶ τὴν τῶν ἐλεφάντων θήραν, καὶ εἴ

Finally, the fact that Hellenistic geographers describe the SW monsoon as Etesian winds coming from the South Pole, makes it possible, indeed suggests, that for them also the SW monsoon had a submarine route, as the *auster* and the *africus* had, according to Pliny and Gellius.

5. Hypalos: an Ionism?

But if the SW monsoon, on the basis of Hellenistic geographical theories, can be considered a submarine wind, the peculiarity of the form *hypalos* rather than *hyphalos* still has to be explained. Mazzarino thought that the exchange of mute for aspirate was due to the "barbarian" pronunciation of the Greek word by the merchants from Syagros or, less probably, from Patale. The use of the word in the mercantile "erythraean" environments is certain[67] and it is quite possible that in the popular pronunciation an original -φ- changed to -π-[68]. Nonetheless I would add the possibility that ὕπαλος is not a popular rendering, but the genuine and correct form of the Greek name for the SW monsoon. The term could be an Ionism (ὕπαλος for ὕφαλος) derived, as a technical term, from the Ionic science,[69] from which also the theory of Southern winds blowing from the depths of the sea might derive.[70]

τινες ἄλλαι χρεῖαι παρώξυνον ἐκεῖσε ἄνδρας προχειρίζεσθαι τοὺς τῆς Αἰγύπτου βασιλέας τοὺς Πτολεμαϊκούς.

66. Artemid. apud Strab. XVI 4, 17: ἔστι δ' αὐτοῖς χειμὼν μὲν ἡνίκα οἱ ἐτησίαι πνέουσι (κατομβροῦνται γάρ), θέρος δ' ὁ λοιπὸς χρόνος; Sen., *n.q.* V 18, 2: [...] *etesiae non patiuntur apud nos nubes consistere, idem totam Indiam et Aethiopiam continuis per id tempus aquis irrigant*; Plin., n.h. V 55: [...] *aut imbres Aethiopiae aestiuos, isdem etesiis nubila illo ferentibus e reliquo orbe.*

67. Cfr. *supra* nt. 44.

68. Cfr., e.g., *Pamen(oth)* in the inscription of C. Numidius Eros at the Paneion di Wādi Menīḥ, on which, recently, F. DE ROMANIS, *Cassia, cinnamomo, ossidiana. Uomini e merci tra oceano Indiano e Mediterraneo*, Roma, 1996, p. 211. There is no chance, however, that the passage ὕφαλος > ὕπαλος is due to a South Arabic prounúnciation of ὕφαλος, since South Arabic has no *p*, but only *b* or *f*. Normally, to a South Arabic *f* corresponds a Latin *f*: *carfiathum* < *ḫrf*, cfr. A.F.L. BEESTON, *A Descriptive Grammar of Epigraphic South Arabian*, London, 1962, p. 16.

69. The Ionic form was also used for another wind in Hellenistic Egypt, ἀπηλιώτης (for ἀφηλιώτης): E. MAYSER, *Grammatik der Griechischen Papyri aus der Ptolemäerzeit*, I 1, Berlin, 1970², p. 15.

70. This hypothesis would explain why the winds are reduced to two, the North and the South Wind, in Thrasyalces from Thasus, one of the ἀρχαῖοι φυσικοί. In his opinion, the most important winds (κυριώτατοι) are only Boreas and Notos: Strab. I 2, 21, cfr. H. BERGER, *Geschichte des wissenschaftlichen Erdkunde der Griechen*, Leipzig, 1903, p. 127.

6. From Hyp(h)alos to Hippalos

Between the two etymologies for the name of the SW monsoon, the one that derives it from Ἵππαλος and the one that derives it from ὕπαλος, the latter seems to me much more likely than the former. More likely because it is founded on a spelling (simple *-p-*) unanimously attested by the manuscript tradition, which is not methodical to correct if a coherent explanation can be found for it. More likely because Posidonius's silence weighs strongly against the derivation of the name of the SW monsoon from a pilot Hippalos; in fact, Posidonius does not mention Hippalos, but only Eudoxus of Cyzicus. More likely because elsewhere too the author of the *Periplus Maris Erythraei* is not unfamiliar with accepting or proposing historical reconstructions based only on naive etymologies.

Considering this evidence, it is not worth objecting that the later[71] hydronym πέλαγος Ἵππαλος (or Ἵππαλον or Ἱππάλου)[72] would mean "Submarine Sea".[73] Passed on to the I century A.D. merchants, ὕπαλος was assimilated with the anthroponym Ἵππαλος and then ended up evoking the pilot who first found the way to cross the ocean between Arabia and India. Later, only later, was the name of the wind and, by then, also that of the pilot, extended to the sea itself.

Nor can one object that for the source of Pliny the SW monsoon is a *fauonius*, a wind from the West, and it would not be correct to apply for it theories regarding southern winds. The definition ὕπαλος of the SW monsoon, in fact, is coherent with its direction from the South (κατὰ νότον μάλιστα). On the contrary, whoever called *fauonius* the SW monsoon rather considered it a wind from the West and denied that it was an Etesian wind. The fact that Pliny's source recalled that the wind was locally called ὕπαλος, does not mean he shared the theories underlying that denomination.

7. *Fauonius*: Posidonius and the SW monsoon

We have emphasised how the translation according to the "Baylonian" ratio of the distances between Syagros-Patale and Syagros-Dioscuridu leads us to reject the possibility that Iuba or Artemidorus are Pliny's sources for the relevant passages. In all probability, not even Agatharchides could have been Pliny's source, since he did not write about the island of Dioscuridu, but about the

---

71. If a πέλαγος Ἵππαλος (or Ἵππαλον or Ἱππάλου) was already known in the period of the author of *Periplus Maris Erythraei*, he would not have failed to recall that besides the wind, also the sea would be called after the pilot's name.

72. Ptol., *geogr.* IV 7, 12.

73. DESANGES, *art. cit.*, p. 666: "Comment cette mer eût-elle pu être qualifiée par un adjectif signifiant lui-même 'sous la mer'?".

"Happy Islands".[74] Pliny's source of VI 100 is also characterised by his definition of the SW monsoon as *fauonius,* a definition on which the local name of *hypalos* is juxtaposed. Thus, on the one hand this author could have information about the "erythraean" seafaring and about its technical terms; on the other hand, he gave a totally different interpretation of the SW monsoon from the one supplied by the historian of Alexander. We have seen that for them the SW monsoon was an Etesian wind and it blowed from the South. On the contrary, those who identified it as the *fauonius,*[75] implicitly denied its Etesian character, agreeing with Aristotle, for whom the southern seas, beyond the Λιβύη (Africa), are not reached by the Etesian wind, but are alternatively dominated by εὖροι and ζέφυροι συνεχεῖς ("constant east and west winds").

The same definition as *fauonius* occurs, defining the SW monsoon, in Pliny's Latin version of a passage from Posidonius,[76] while from another fragment of Posidonius, this time derived from Strabo,[77] it seems that the winds which make it possible to reach India from the West are the ζέφυροι συνεχεῖς ("constant west winds"). The same formula as the one adopted by Aristotle. Thus it is possible that the Latin *fauonius* — in Plin., *n.h.* VI 57, as ibid. 100 — is a translation, perhaps too precise, of ζέφυροι (συνεχεῖς), or even of the singular ζέφυρος, to be understood, like in the "Homeric" compass with only four winds, as the West wind.

Posidonius, author of the περὶ ὠκεανοῦ, was interested in the history of sailing on the Indian Ocean, as the story of Eudoxus's voyages proves: is he Pliny's source for the the Syagros-Patale route (and for Syagros-Dioscuridu distance)? Three clues would seem to strengthen this hypothesis: 1) interpretation of the SW monsoon as *fauonius* (ζέφυροι/ ζέφυρος) suggests a reorientation of

74. Cfr. *supra* nt. 23.

75. It has been rightly emphasised (DESANGES, *art. cit.*, p. 666) that the definition of *fauonius* given to the summer monsoon is, strictly speaking, incorrect, as it is a SW wind not a W one. It is more correctly called λιβόνοτος in *PME* 57.

76. Plin., *n.h.* VI 57 (= *FGrHist* 87 F 100 = F 212 E.-K. = 69a Th.): *Posidonius ab aestivo solis ortu ad hibernum exortum metatus est eam, aduersam Galliam statuens, quam <ab> occidente aestiuo ad occidentem hibernum metabatur, totam a fauonio; itaque aduersum eius uenti adflatu<m> iuuar<e> Indiam salubremque fieri haut dubia ratione docuit.* In Theiler's commentary, appropriate observations as to the Posidonian paternity; in Kidd's, emphasis on the importance of reorientation of the position of India in a NS direction, also in this case contrary to Eratosthenes' lesson. On this point cfr. A. TCHERNIA, "Moussons et Monnaies: les voies du commerce entre le monde gréco-romain et l'Inde", *Annales HSS* 5, 1995, p. 997.

77. Strab. II 3, 4 (= *FGrHist* 87 F 28 =F 49 E.-K. = F 13 Th.): πλεῖν ἐπὶ τὴν Ἰνδικὴν μετέωρον ζεφύροις συνεχέσι. The fact that Eudoxus actually had to sail in the Atlantic Ocean and not in the Indian Ocean does not matter here at all.

India in a North-South direction, which we know was Posidonius's;[78] 2) the definition of the SW monsoon as ζέφυρος evidently links it again to the anemography of the southern seas beyond the Λιβύη (Africa) in Aristotle, an author whose influence on Posidonius is well known;[79] 3) two different calculations of the earth's meridian are attributed to Posidonius, resulting in shorter lengths than the canonical "Eratosthenian" measurement of 252 000 stadia:[80] the circumstance that Pliny (or his Latin source) translates the distances from stadia into Roman miles using the "Babylonian" ratio could be explained by the necessity to balance the "Eratosthenian" measurements with that supplied by Posidonius.[81]

In any case, the calculation of the distance between Syagros and Patale offers a further proof of the solid basis for the commercial relations between Egypt, Southern Arabia and India in the late Hellenistic age.[82]

Federico DE ROMANIS

78. Cfr. *supra* nt. 76.

79. Cfr., p. ex., M. LAFFRANQUE, *Poseidonios d'Apamée*, Paris, 1964, p. 171-175.

80. Strab. II 2, 2 (= *FGrHist* 87 F 28 = F 49 E.-K. = F 13 Th.); Cleom. 94 (= *FGrHist* 87 F 97 = F 202 E.K. = F 287 Th.).

81. In this case, an exception to the more usual attitude seems possible. Generally speaking, in fact, "les géographes anciens, pour leur part, ne se sont guère souciés d'une possible différence des stades entre leurs diverses sources" (Y. JANVIER, "Les problèmes de métrologie dans l'étude de la cartographie antique", *Latomus* 53, 1993, p. 13, a paper containing useful methodological observations). Alternatively, it has to be admitted that, without being aware or without worrying about it, Pliny derived the data on the Syagros-Patale and Syagros-Dioscuridu island distances from a Latin source that constantly translated distances from stadia to Roman miles according to a "Babylonian" ratio, but this cannot be said for Agrippa.

82. ARNAUD, *art. cit.*, pp. 225-226: " [...] la référence à ces moyennes nous renseigne sur l'existence de véritables lignes de navigation assez frequentées pour que l'on connût précisément la durée normal de la relation et que l'on pût en inférer une distance". As to navigation in the Indian Ocean in the Hellenistic age, cfr. J.-F. SALLES, "Hellenistic Seafaring in the Indian Ocean. A Perspective from Arabia", in H.P. RAY/ J.-F. SALLES, *Tradition and Archaeology. Early Maritime Contacts in the Indian Ocean. Proceedings of the International Seminar "Techno-Archaeological Perspectives of Seafaring in the Indian Ocean 4th sent. B.C. -15th cent. A.D." New Delhi, February 28 - March 4, 1994*, New Delhi, 1996, pp. 293-309.

WHO USED TO READ THE *PERIPLUS MARIS ERYTHRAEI*?

Since Hjalmar Frisk's study in 1927[1] and Lionel Casson's commented edition published in 1989,[2] it is easier to judge and assess the language of *The Periplus Maris Erythraei* despite the persistence of difficulties due to the manuscript tradition, the lack of precision in determining the date of its writing and our insufficient knowledge about the Greek language during Roman times.

Let us remember that the text of the *Periplus* was transmitted through a minimal manuscript tradition. There is but one "primary" manuscript viz. *Palatinus gr. (Heidelberg.)* 398, belonging to the late 9th century (folios 40v-54v).[3] Its apograph, *Londonensis add.* 1939 1 (in the British Museum), folios 9r-12r, going back to the 14th century,[4] does not have much value except on account of the original which itself was corrected after the copy of this apograph.[5] As for

1. *Le* Périple de la mer Érythrée, *suivi d'une étude sur la tradition et la langue*, Göteborg, 1927. On pp. V-VI, Frisk gives a list of the earlier editions starting from Gelenius's first edition (Basle, 1533) to Müller's edition in the first volume of *Geographi Graeci minores*, Paris, 1853. H. Frisk has made a careful study of the manuscript tradition, especially of the language of the *Periplus*. His work is irreplaceable even though the documents now available allow us to add something.

2. *The* Periplus Maris Erythraei, Princeton, 1989. Regarding the value of this work, see among others J. ROUGE's *Archaeonautica* 10, 1990, pp. 265-269.

3. Cf. A. DILLER, *The Tradition of the Minor Greek Geographers*, Lancaster (USA) – Oxford, 1952, pp. IX and 3-14, indicates that the manuscript dates from the 9th century. L. CASSON, *The* Periplus Maris Erythraei, Princeton, 1989, p. 5, dates it, without any comments, to the early 10th century.

4. According to DILLER, *op. cit.*, p. 10; CASSON, *op. cit.*, p. 5, says "14th-15th century". DILLER's article which appeared in 1937 ("The Vatopedi Manuscript of Ptolemy and Strabo", *American Journal of Philology*, 58, 1937, 174-184 = *Studies in Greek Manuscript Tradition*, Amsterdam, 1983, 7-17), has been reused by the author, *op. cit.*, pp. 10-14.

5. Cf. FRISK, *op. cit.*, pp. 32-33.

A Gateway from the Eastern Mediterranean to India. The Red Sea in Antiquity
M. CASEVITZ, pp. 225-229

the date of its writing, it would be prudent to assign it to the second half of the 1st century A.D.[6] However, the papyrus edition and the publication of new works on the language of the papyri have slightly enriched our knowledge and enabled us to judge the language of the *Periplus* a little better.

As it stands at present, the text is in a piteous condition, partly due to the nature of its contents. As Frisk points out, "not having any literary merit, the *Periplus* has certainly never been the object of criticism by ancient philologists". The text provided by the *Palatinus* is full of mistakes due to the slipshod tradition. It would, however, be wrong to confuse the above mistakes with the clumsy use of a language which could be described as didactic (Frisk provides some useful advice in this regard, *op. cit.,* p. 35).

The author of *Periplus*, even if he were "a very uncultivated writer", to repeat another expression used by Frisk (*op. cit.,* p. 37), has written in the everyday language of his time. It is only after studying this language, such as we know it, we can answer the following question: for whom did the author write the *Periplus*?

From the very first page, the editor is obliged to make corrections, which are in no way negligible. Some are based on the assumption that the original copyists left behind a faulty version for the copyist of *Palatinus,* or because of slips made by the latter. Thus, in 1, 4-5,[7] it should be understood that δὲ (*de*) was inserted by mistake after κόλποι (*kolpoi*) by mixing up a whole line. We must therefore accept Müller's transposition. Later, a similar confusion (from μερῶν / *merōn* to μερόη / *meroē*) should explain the gap in 2, 11 which has undoubtedly been carefully copied by the scribe by leaving a blank after μερῶν (*merōn*) and by recopying the mistake in the original (σῆς μικρὸν /*sēs mikron*) which again is due to the earlier confusion with a later line. For all that, there is no guarantee that Schwanbeck's addition adopted by Müller and later editors (μητρόπολις λεγομένη Μερόη / *mētropolis legomenē Meroē*) is correct (as for us, we believe that the participle is not required and we would rather put it as ἡ μητρόπολις Μερόη, *hē mētropolis Meroē*).

What appears more important to us is the problem raised by the text of 3, 13 where editors have variously tried to change the text which, all said and done, seems to be beyond repair: τὸ πέρας τῆς ἀνακομιδῆς (*to peras tēs anakomidēs*). But would it not be possible to believe that these words have been displaced from one line to another and that they relate perhaps to the inland city mentioned earlier whose name is found in the gap indicated above? Thus the author mentions that this city is to be found "at the end of the search (for goods)". In 3,

---

6. For factors that can narrow down the date, see last of all Ch. ROBIN, *JA* CCLXXIX,1/2, 1991, pp.1-30.

7. References are given according to the paragraphs and lines in the Frisk edition.

14, the absence of the article[8] before Πτολεμαίων (*Ptolemaiōn*)[9] is surprising if the plural is to be retained and the singular is not to be used (cf. Ἀδριανοῦ θῆραι / *Adrianou Thērai*, Cassius Dio, 69, 10, 2,[10] Ælius Aristides, *Sacred Tales* (1), XLVII, 51-52 Keil).[11]

The text also has rare words or forms. One example should suffice although the text is full of them. In 6, 23 ἄγναφα (ἱμάτια) /*agnapha* (*himatia*) corresponds to[12] ἄγναπτος (*agnaptos*) and denotes rough garments (cf. *DELG sv* κνάπτω /*knaptō,* with reference to L. Robert, *Mélanges Orlandos*).

It was necessary to give a few examples of the difficulties entailed by the poor condition of the text that has come down to us to remind readers that it is not the author alone who is to be blamed for the coarse language of the *Periplus*. The manuscript tradition has certainly aggravated, albeit unintentionally, the incoherence mainly in the syntax.[13] What is certain though is that the author, even though he remains unknown and does not intrude on the text, addresses a well-defined readership, as almost all commentators agree, thanks to the contents of his writing. The *Periplus* was meant for merchants travelling by sea. Consequently, it gives the names of various ports and import-export centres, inland cities from where merchandise may be obtained, officials in different lands, the nature of the natives and, of course, the goods to be imported and exported.

But seafaring merchants are not the only identifiable readers. The author does not fail to point out to navigators the easy or difficult approaches to coasts, sea and river ports, the proper sailing seasons and the distance between various stopping places. The author thus enabled the community of sailors and travelling merchants to plan fruitful and timely voyages.

---

8. Frisk, *op. cit.*, does not mention this example pp. 67-72 (study on the use of articles).

9. The manuscript contains Πτολεμων (Ptolemōn), Bernhardy's correction must be accepted.

10. Ptolemais of the Hunts is a creation of Ptolemy Philadelphus, cf. *der Kleine Pauly, s.v.* "Ptolemais 7", and *RE, s.v.* [H. Treidler 1959].

11. One may also wonder if the original text did not contain ἐπὶ Πτολεμαίου τοῦ Πτολεμαίου (*epi Ptolemaiou tou Ptolemaiou*) (cf. the reconstructed text in Pausanias, I, 1, 1).

12. Cf. *Revised Supplement* of *LSJ*, Oxford, 1996, *s.v.* (The reference to a 3rd century papyrus already figures in the old *Supplement*).

13. Apart from the monotony and the platitudinous nature of the text in its original form, most of the time the sentences are connected by δέ or καί, sometimes by μὲν οὖν, ὁμοίως δὲ καὶ, and rarely by γάρ.

Is it possible that the author was also interested in a third category of travellers comprising tourists and curious persons of all kinds who certainly existed in Roman times? There are in fact notes of an ethnographic nature which bring to mind this category of readers. It is mentioned now and then that the inhabitants of the country with whom there is an import-export trade are "quite peaceful" (εἰρηνικώτεροι / *eirēnikōteroi* 8, 26) or that they are "quite rough" (σκληρότεροι / *sklēroteroi* 9, 5) but in the latter case the epithet ἔμποροι / *emporoi* is used. The nature of the inhabitants is indicated only to warn the merchants who have to trade with them. Similarly, when it is mentioned that the inhabitants are governed by a τύραννος (*tyrannos*) or a βασιλεῦς (*basileus*) or that they are "disorganised" (ἀτακτότεροι /*ataktoteroi*, 7, 21), it is only to facilitate the task of the Greek traders who must be aware of the trading conditions and the nature of the people they have to deal with. In the same way, the possible "friendliness" (φιλανθρωπία / *philanthrōpia*, 17, 17) of Barbarians, which can be won by paying them, is not intended to maintain good relations between them and travellers on a courtesy visit but it is necessary to win over the natives in order to trade with them. The exchange of gifts was an essential part of trading. In the reference to Zôskalès (who ruled over the lands mentioned in 4 and 5), we observe that the style of writing with a light touch of rhetoric betrays a literary concern, which is all the more commendable since it is the only example of its kind: ἀκριβὴς μὲν τοῦ βίου καὶ τοῦ πλείονος ἐξεχόμενος, γενναῖος δὲ περὶ τὰ λοιπὰ καὶ γραμμάτων Ἑλληνικῶν ἔμπειρος. The meaning of the expression ἀκριβής τοῦ βίου (*akribēs tou biou*) is not clear (although L. CASSON's commentary[14] does not say anything about it). Frisk (*op. cit.*, p. 55) says that the use of the genitive case with ἀκριβής (*akribēs*) is a trick "that I know, the only one of its kind". This leads him to propose (unlike Fabricius who translated "sparsam im Leben") for βίος (*bios*) not the word life but fortune or goods and to translate it as "jealous of his fortune" adding "which, besides, goes better with the following τοῦ πλείονος ἐξεχόμενος (*tou pleionos exekhomenos*)". It does not seem necessary to us to subscribe to this interpretation; ἀκριβής, like γενναίος which he is opposed to, should refer to a state of mind, a precision which when carried to the extreme becomes a defect. The parcimony of his kind of life (*τὸ ἀκριβὲς τοῦ βίου, *to akribes tou biou*), makes him in fact a stern, mean and miserly person[15] "bent on getting rich" (he is suffering from πλεονεξία / *pleonexia*), but "generous nonetheless and an expert in Greek literature". This ruler is not judged by a moralist but by a man who identifies himself with Greek merchants who have to keep in mind these flaws and qualities.

14. *The Periplus Maris Erythraei*, text with introduction, translation and commentary, Princeton, 1989. We include elsewhere in this volume critical remarks on this edition.

15. G.W.B. HUNTINGFORD, *The Periplus of the Erythraean Sea*, London, 1980, p. 21 and note on p. 60, translates it correctly "mean <in his way> of life" (the addition is unnecessary!). See CHANTRAINE, *DELG*, *s.v.* ἀκριβής (*acribēs*).

We cannot therefore include tourists among the intended readers of the *Periplus*. The text entertains us like a modern travel guide because of the picturesqueness of the exotic merchandise. But this is only a by-product, not author's main concern. At the most, we may point out a peculiarity mentioned in Chapter 41 (8-11) Σῴζεται δὲ ἔτι καὶ νῦν τῆς Ἀλεξάνδρου στρατιᾶς σημεία περὶ τοὺς τόπους, ἱερά τε ἀρχαῖα καὶ θεμέλιοι παρεμβολῶν καὶ φρέατα μέγιστα: "Traces of Alexander's expedition, old sanctuaries, foundations of camps and large wells are still preserved in these places". The only concession he makes for cultural interests is because his book was meant for Alexandrian travellers.

Michel CASEVITZ
University of Paris X Nanterre

TRAVELS TO THE EDGES OF THE WORLD
The Arab Trade through the *Seven Travels of Sindbad*

> "In a similar class to the work of Buzurg are the voyages of Sindbad, which appear in *Alf laila wa laila*. Whether extracts from genuine voyages have found their way into these stories is a matter of doubt, but the stories are certainly partly based upon *aja'ib* passages relating to south-east Asia which might be dated anywhere from the eighth to the tenth centuries
>
> TIBBETTS 1979, p. 10.

> "The voyages of Sindbad ... all being in the main tales taken from sailors, have no clear idea of the South-East as a whole, and give only hints here and there which can occasionally be fitted together to show some topographical relationship."
>
> TIBBETTS 1979, p. 76

Although Sindbad's seven wonderful voyages described in the *Thousand and One Nights*[1] have often been considered an event of great import in world literature, we feel that the historical and geographical study of this famous book has been somewhat neglected. There is no doubt that the places described appear to be situated at the very edge of the known world and if you confine yourself to the book, it seems quite difficult to determine their precise location. But if you forget for a moment the literary, religious and philosophical value of the message the book seeks to convey and compare it with other historical and geographical works in Arabic belonging to the same period, or commenting on it, you find that these seven voyages provide interesting information about Southeast Asia.

---

1. The Mardrus Edition, 1988, pp. 692-743.

A Gateway from the Eastern Mediterranean to India. The Red Sea in Antiquity
C. ALLIBERT, pp. 231-242

Besides, even though the period is supposed to be mythical, it corresponds perfectly with the reign of Harun al-Rashid when Islam was at the height of its glory (786-809).

Sindbad's seven travels always began from the capital, Baghdad, and he set sail from the port of Basra. And every time Sindbad was forced to travel by sea, even though the difficulties experienced during his earlier adventures had made him vow that he would never again go through a similar ordeal.

We do not wish to dwell on the literary merits of this great work although its cosmogonical elements (water-sea/navigation, air/flight of the Roc and of men, earth/chasms, tombs and galleries) have not been sufficiently highlighted. It is surprising that the philosopher Gaston Bachelard, known for his interest in the elements and the role they have played in mankind's daydreams, has not made use of this work to illustrate his philosophical vision of poetry.

It is also interesting to note that every voyage is presented as a rebirth, the hero having escaped from a shipwreck during the previous journey. What we have here is a game of survival because the shipwreck should normally have killed Sindbad. But his instinct for death (shipwreck) compels him to sail the seas again and again. His travels in wondrous lands are the sole object of our study although we would have a lot to say about the relation between the voyage as an object of death and rebirth, the strange coincidence that the visitor and the sailor are both called Sindbad, religion and its relationship with the real and the appearances and what is right and what is wrong, known only to God.

Let us study these seven voyages point by point — not by interpreting them as an act of initiation — but simply by comparing them to the ancient texts of Arab geographers.

The first voyage, during which the men land on the back of a whale mistaking it for an island and light a fire, has two elements that are worth thinking about. Firstly, the nature of King Mihrajan who receives Sindbad in a place where there are Indian visitors and secondly, the nearness of a land called Cabil whose distinctive feature is that it is the home of people who play drums and kettledrums in the night. The fact that there are Indian visitors means that the land is not India. Besides, if we refer to Kazwini (1203-1283),[2] we read:

> "Ibn al-Fakih said: On this island (the island of Bartayil, situated near the islands of Djawaga) (...) live people whose faces are like shields covered with leather, whose hair is like (the hair on) the tails of beasts of burden.[3] You can find rhinoceroses there; there are mountains where during the night you can hear the sound of drums and kettledrums, terrifying screams and a dreadful din. The sailors believe that the Antichrist lives there and that he will come from there (one day). Cloves are sold on this island which is why the merchants go there (...). The native dress consists of leaves in which they wrap

2. FERRAND 1914, Vol. 2, p. 304.

3. To our knowledge, the only explanation provided by critics is that the people so described wore masks. The second part of the sentence, however, could be a description of the thick straight hair of the Austronesians.

themselves up; the tree in question is called *lu.f*[4] They eat its fruit and wrap themselves up in its leaves (...). The natives of this island also eat fish, cloves, coconuts and bananas".

Apart from the fact that the name of the island is not exactly the same in the two accounts, the similarities are such that one cannot help feeling that they refer to one and the same place. Besides, the goods that Sindbad bought on the island — aloe-wood, camphor, incense and sandalwood — and also the king's name — Mihrajan — seem to suggest Indonesia. Tibbetts (1979, p.177) makes the same observation adding that the story of King Mihrajan's mare reminds us of the horse motif in Malaysian and Indonesian lore:[5]

> "The horses of Ibn Khurdadhbih are mentioned also in greater detail in the Sindbad story, where they are connected with the country of the Maharaja, but not specifically with the island of Bartayil (Kasil in Sindbad's story) (...). The Chinese triple-headed goddess Kwan-yin, the equivalent of India's Avalokitesvara, occasionally took the form of a horse (with marine accomplishments) and is reported to have been born in the southern seas and her father is said to have been a king with an empire extending between India, Siam, Fo-shih and Tienchen" (p. 179).

Therefore, it would not be unreasonable, as Tibbetts suggests (p. 179), to consider this island as "an unidentified Indonesian island", especially because of the reference to the rhinoceros.

The second voyage must be linked with the fifth insofar as it deals with the same subject: the Roc bird and its descent. In the first case, the bird's egg appears like an immense dome in the middle of the sea over which the bird is flying. Once the bird lands on its egg, Sindbad ties himself to one of its legs and finds himself carried to a valley strewn with diamonds. To escape the dangers awaiting him, he ties a quarter of meat around his body and the Roc, attracted by the meat, flies away with him. That is how he manages to get away from the valley carrying with him a rich hoard of diamonds. Once more, although the place is not given a specific name, there is no doubt that it is intended to be in Southeast Asia because of the presence of the rhinoceros (*karkadann*) and the camphor tree. What is more, Sindbad exchanges his diamonds (from Ceylon?) for gold and silver, metals which point to Sumatra and its neighbouring islands, as hinted by the author of the *Periplus of the Erythraean Sea* who calls it Krysè.

The Roc's egg[6] is brought up again in the fifth voyage when his companions break it and incur the bird couple's wrath. The rest of the voyage does not provide much information of interest to us and the location of the episode of the Old Man of the Sea and the city of monkeys is not clearly indicated. Certainly, the exchange of coconuts obtained with the help of the monkeys

---

4. See the complementary note at the end of the article.

5. It is worth undertaking a detailed comparative study of this motif.

6. We will not develop the theme of the Roc and its egg (see ALLIBERT 1992).

for pepper and cinnamon suggests a region that may be anywhere between the Indian sub-continent and Southeast Asia. Let us however note that some suggestions have been made on these two points. The (hairy) Old Man of the Sea has been interpreted as an orangutang. Moreover, Thomson draws a parallel between the technique used by the men in the fifth voyage to obtain inaccessible coconuts (by throwing stones at the monkeys to provoke them to throw back coconuts) and the techniques reported by ancient writers that Indians used to obtain pepper. According to Thomson, the Indians take advantage of the instinct that incites monkeys to imitate human actions and they use them to gather pepper found on trees in inaccessible places and drop it on the ground. They are so appreciative of the help provided by the monkeys that they protect them from the lions who prey on them.[7]

Thomson comments on this comparison, pointing out that Richard Hole believed that the story could be true and he compared it to the gathering of tea in China with the help of monkeys. He adds in a note that from Chinese drawings showing the gathering of tea, it appears that the monkey are doing a job for which they have been trained. This would tend to prove that the Chinese tame these animals to pick tea which grows on the top of high rocks and is therefore difficult to reach.[8]

This problem certainly needs to be studied, but this is not the right place because we are more interested in locating the places where the events described in Sindbad's fifth voyage occurred. That is why it is important to note that coconuts (not mentioned before the ship reached the sea of Harkand) were exchanged for pepper and cinnamon (associated by Arab writers with Java and Ceylon). Once again we are in a part of the sea[9] situated between Ceylon and Southeast Asia.[10]

It is also important to underline in passing the major role played by these trees and their land of origin in order to understand the nature of trade and the history of the Indian Ocean. Underwater archaeology is providing us more and more information about the antiquity of this trade although we may not know

---

7. THOMSON 1955, p. 42.

8. THOMSON 1955, p. 43. We would like to remind you that other Arab authors have mentioned the use of monkeys for domestic work, especially the author of *Merveilles de l'Inde* (SAUVAGET 1954, p. 238, paragraph 42 and the following paragraphs). Thus there is a reference to a monkey who "swept the house, opened the door to those coming in and closed it after them, lit the fire under the cooking pot and blew upon it until it burned properly, and fanned its master".

9. Let us recall the names of these seas: Fars (Persian Gulf), Larwi (Gujarat Sea), Harkand (Bay of Bengal), Salahit (Straits of Malacca), Andaman and Canhay (China Sea). Seven seas are listed in *Merveilles de l'Inde* but not all of them find mention in the works of Arab writers.

10. Let us also remember the role played by these two trees – pepper and cinnamon mentioned by Pliny in the 1st century A.D.

who was engaged in it. The wreck of a Roman ship that sank some 2200 years ago was recently discovered near the island of Elba. It was carrying a cargo of two hundred hermetically sealed wooden casks containing perfumes smelling of cinnamon, turmeric and cloves protected by sealed silver boxes. This discovery proves without doubt that this trade goes back to these early times.

Let us remember that the only source of cloves was the Moluccas and that cinnamon came from Southeast Asia and much later from Ceylon. Finally, as a matter of information, let us recall Miller's much discussed but disquieting hypothesis[11] regarding the origin of the word cinnamon. According to him, the word derived from the Malais *kayu manis* meaning "scented wood' corresponding to the Madagascan *hazo manitra* was known to the Hebrews who passed it on to the Greeks.

The third voyage was to the island of monkeys where a giant devoured spit-roasted humans who had been fed drugged food. The sailor, Tim Severin, whose adventures on the sea need no telling and who successfully completed Sindbad's voyage from Basrah to Canton, says that to the north of Sumatra food is laced with hashish. He concludes that this must be behind the Arab belief that the victims of cannibals were stuffed with drugs.[12]

Apart from the fact that the passage refers to the island of Salahata, it is also evocative of a famous passage from Homer — the story of the giant who was finally blinded by Sindbad with red-hot skewers cannot but remind us of the story of the Cyclop. If we need proof that the Arab tradition borrowed from the Greeks apart from other sources, it is to be found in this story.[13] As for Sahalata, there is no doubt that it is the Strait of Malacca (see WOLTERS 1965, pp. 178-179 and also TIBBETTS 1979, pp. 28-32 and 145) which, as we know, all sailors had to cross to reach China.

The sixth voyage lays much stress on the sea monsters:

> "And there before us on the foaming water, we saw coming towards the ship a monster as big and as tall as a mountain, then a second even bigger and a third following it as big as the first two put together. The last one suddenly sprang out of the sea whose waters separated in a yawning chasm; it opened its mouth which was larger than the chasm and swallowed three quarters of our ship with all that it contained".[14]

---

11. It was reassessed by J. de VERE ALLEN 1984 and B. DOMENICHINI-RAMIARAMANA 1990 but was rejected by CRONE 1987.

12. SEVERIN 1984, p. 220.

13. We refer to the article by BENCHEIKH (E.U. corpus 12). He believes that the stories of Sindbad were derived from an Indian source, but at the same time he points out that the Hellenic influence is also discernible in the Thousand and One Nights.

14. MARDRUS, p. 736.

This description reminds us of the description of a cyclone in *Merveilles de l'Inde*:

"I was told that there were enormous fearsome serpents in the sea called 'dragons'. When in the middle of the rainy season a cloud passes over the water's surface, the dragon comes out of the water and enters the cloud to escape the water's heat. In fact, during the rainy season, the sea-water is as hot as a cauldron. The dragon cannot leave the cloud because of the cold and the cloud pushed by the wind to the water's surface rises above the water: the dragon remains suspended there, it curls up and moves from one end of the horizon to the other. When the water in the cloud is exhausted, the cloud become less dense until it is reduced to a fine mist which separates and is ripped to shreds by the wind. And the dragon, having nothing to support it, falls into the sea or on land".[15]

We have there an excellent description of a meteorological phenomenon that is presented in almost the same manner in Sindbad's voyage and in *Merveilles de l'Inde*. However, this kind of meteor was already known as seen in *Voyage du marchand arabe Sulayman en Inde et en Chine*, a book written in the middle of the 9th century:

"Sometimes, one sees in this sea (Harkand) a white cloud covering the ships with its shadow; the cloud has a kind of tongue, long and thin, which becomes longer when it comes into contact with the sea; then the sea starts seething and this meteor turns into a whirlwind … When the whirlwind reaches the ship, it absorbs it. Then the cloud climbs higher and it rains".[16]

Once more, we find that what Todorov calls the "wonderful hyperbole of the *Thousand and One Nights*"[17] provides us with a much older view of this natural phenomenon called the tornado. The nature of this phenomenon was known to sailors long before the Arabs started navigating the seas as seen in the above passage from the voyage of the Arab merchant Sulayman.[18]

We must now refer to the dual purpose of Sindbad's seventh voyage. In fact, a more fantastic solution is the introduction of men who can fly. It seems quite difficult to analyse the message that this theme is meant to convey because, all said and done, it runs through all of Sindbad's adventures. On one occasion, he escapes from the valley of diamonds with the help of the Roc. But this time, he ties himself to a man belonging to a people who can fly once a year. We may however attempt a different interpretation. As Manguin tells us, the ability to fly was considered to be a characteristic peculiar to merchants in Southeast Asian texts:

15. SAUVAGET 1954, p. 215.
16. FERRAND 1922, p. 36.
17. TODOROV 1970, p. 82.
18. We refer to our earlier articles (1991 & 1992) where we explain this almost systematic duplication of the information provided by Arab writers.

"This ambivalence of merchants is possibly what prompted the author of a ninth century Javanese inscription to classify them among migratory birds: they were unattached, liable to transfer their trade activities to a rival harbour-city, hence dangerous. Again, a similar notion could have been conveyed by the 1079 C.E. Sriwijayan inscription at Canton which describes merchants as 'flying'".[19]

We observe that Sindbad's voyages correspond to *Merveilles de l'Inde.* Tibbetts tells us that they constituted the geographical basis of the great work. We could say that it is the romanticised version of the earlier work. We have pinpointed the real similarities: the Roc was added to the Ceylon episode involving the collection of diamonds while in *Merveilles* vultures were considered to be enough. But the Roc is also present in *Merveilles* and it is probably a reference to Madagascar and to the association Aepyornis/bamboo.[20]

We may wonder why Sindbad always travels eastwards and never to the south although Berbera is mentioned in *Merveilles* and archaeological research in the Indian Ocean has proved that Arabs did travel there. Perhaps, the passage to India, Southeast Asia and China was considered the archetype of a wonderful adventure. As a matter of fact, we find that the Zandjs and their country were added to the story by Abu Sayd Hasan about half a century later.

We cannot but take note of the auhor's thorough knowledge about the voyage from the Persian Gulf to Canton which lasted four months. The real intentions of traders like Sindbad the Sailor are quite evident:

"the desire to travel and enjoy the sight of lands and islands and look at unknown things with curiosity, without losing sight of buying and selling in different countries".

These trading activities were possible because the itinerary had been established earlier by the Persians. Proper commercial procedures were followed: you could either book a berth aboard a ship or you could buy a ship and sail it in your own name or for somebody else.

There is frequent mention of navigation problems in the area around the Strait of Malacca on the route to Canton. But the strait cannot be avoided and we are told that it was necessary to pay a tax:

"On arrival in Srivijaya, the king of Srivijaya demanded that he pay 20,000 dinars so that he could continue on his way without being stopped in the passage".[21]

This passage was closely guarded and according to the Chinese writer Tchao Jou Koua (1225):[22]

---

19. MANGUIN 1991, p. 51.

20. See ALLIBERT 1992.

21. *Merveilles*, p. 259.

22. FERRAND 1913, p. 13.

"This land lies in the ocean and rules over the straits through which foreign land and sea traffic must pass in both the directions".

On this subject, it is interesting to go further into Tchao Jou Koua's writings:

"In the past, they used an iron chain as a barrier to protect themselves from pirates of other countries. This chain could be raised or lowered with the help of an ingenious device. When a ship came, it was lowered. After some years of peace … it was removed and it lies coiled on the shore".

Let us now compare this document with a passage from *Merveilles de l'Inde:*[23]

"He told me that he had heard during his youth that M … one of the pilots who went to China and the land of gold, was said to have passed in the neighbourhood of the island of Javaga and spent one day between two horns which appear in the sea believing them to be two reefs; when he had passed them, they disappeared in the sea. He supposed then that they were the two pincers of a crab".

And again:

"Ismail … the ship's owner … told me that during one of his voyages to the land of gold, while he was close to the shore near Lampouri, he cast the big anchor into the sea because his ship had been damaged and he was forced to stop. But the ship did not stop … he then told the diver to go down the anchor cable and see what was the matter. The diver … looked. And there was the anchor between the pincers of a crab who dragged the ship along as it played with it".

We have no intention of interpreting all the wondrous elements in these texts. However, we may point out that it is quite possible that the story about the pincers of the giant crab was a fanciful representation of the chain stretching between the two shores of the strait under the control of the people of Sumatra.

By way of conclusion, it may be stated that the literary work narrating the seven voyages of Sindbad provides a better analysis of commercial information than *Merveilles de l'Inde*. Even if the latter represents the real geographical base for Sindbad's voyage, we find that some episodes in the seven voyages are not derived (cf. the saddle, the mares) from *Merveilles* but can be found in the accounts of Arab geographers of the same century.

We are told stories highlighting the importance of the reign of Harun al-Rashidi. These voyagers travel towards *lands of men*. In Sindbad's voyages, unlike contemporary texts and other passages from the *Thousand and One Nights*, the term *wakwak* is never used: perhaps because we are already in a period when the passage is well known. It is therefore necessary to interpret

23. SAUVAGET 1954, p. 193.

other stories in this work which refer to it as older geographical and historical terms.

To tell the truth, it is not as if Sindbad is telling his own story. What he really does is to put together the adventures of the sailors of his time and their direct or indirect knowledge — which after all is not as meagre as claimed by Tibbetts — of Southeast Asia and the remote areas of the world's seas.

Claude ALLIBERT
CEROI, INALCO

Complementary Note: Is the *luf* the banana tree?

The identification of this plant poses a real problem although Arab authors do not appear to have any doubts. As a matter of fact, the first time we come across it is in the *Agrégé des Merveilles* (towards the year 1000): "On the islands of the Green Sea … an island inhabited by a people who are the remnants of the *Nesnas*; these people possess a tree called the *luffa* whose fruits feed them and leaves clothe them…" (FERRAND 1913, p. 147).

Ferrand takes note of it (1913, I, p. 111) and gives this name to the tree mentioned at the end of the preceding paragraph by Kazwini (p. 146): "which grows in the land of people who sell cloves … it is said that these cloves … the inhabitants of the island eat them; they do not fall sick and they do not age. It is also said that they wear the leaves of a tree that grows in their country and which is unknown to other men".

If we confine ourselves to Arab texts, we are obliged to note Ibn al-Baytur's statement (FERRAND 1913, p. 237) according to which Adzan al-jil (elephant's ear) could either be the kulkas or the large variety of the *luf,* in which case the *luf* would be the *arum colocassia*, is not satisfactory. Even though the taro plant has large leaves, it does not have fruits but edible tubers. Further, it is supposed to be a tree, so it must have a trunk. Further, although the word *lufa* is not mentioned by Ibn Rosteh (FERRAND, p. 78), we would like to quote him: "We will look for *leaves of the banana tree* which are wide. They are large enough *to be wrapped around one or two men*". We start wondering if the *luf* would not be the banana tree whose fruit is edible, whose stem resembles a trunk and whose leaves are large. This seems to be confirmed by Muqaddasi's remark quoted by Miquel (1980, vol. 3, p. 417): "The colocassia … because of its leaves reminds us of the banana tree and moreover … it is known that if you cut a colocassia tubercule into two and put it back into the soil after inserting a date seed in it, a banana tree comes up".

The fact that Ibn-al Fakih (refer to the text corresponding to footnote 2) mentions the *luf* and later bananas without connecting the tree to the fruit is not considered a proof of their different natures. We have, as a matter of fact, shown in other circumstances (ALLIBERT 1991 & 1992) that Arab writers have compiled information without knowing how to bring it up to date. This happened particularly in the case of the *wakwak* tree whose fruit were the heads of young girls and the *nargil* coconut palm.

It is obvious that the initial resemblance between the leaves of the two trees, mainly due to their large size, must have confused the first Arab observers and this confusion persisted. That is why the word *luf* used to denote the plant or plants in question was no more than a general term referring to several plants. As Miquel puts it, it was "a term denoting, at will, the mandragor, a small melon from Egypt or Syria and the nectarine" (1980, p. 440) and referring to the roots as well as the fruits.

It is important to find the origin of the term *luf*. It seems difficult to link it with the Persian *lufa* which refers to the *centaurea* plant (DESMAISONS, p. 287). We may recall that Theophrastus mentions the banana in India (see Ch. Joret's study on the botanical research conducted by Alexander's expedition, 1903). Pliny is said to have given the common name *pala* to the banana trees on the Malabar coast.

Bibliography

ALLIBERT 1991

C. ALLIBERT, "Wakwak: végétal, minéral our humain? Reconsidération du problème", Paris, INALCO, *Études Océan Indien*, 12, 1991, pp. 171-189.

ALLIBERT 1992a

C. ALLIBERT, "Le monde austronésien et la civilisation du bambou: une plume qui pèse lourd: l'oiseau Rokh des auteurs arabes", *Taloha* 11, 1992, Antananarivo, pp. 167-181.

ALLIBERT 1992b

C. ALLIBERT, "L'île des femmes chez les auteurs arabes", *Hommages à J. Dez*, Paris, INALCO, *Études Océan Indien*, 15, 1992, pp. 261-267.

ALLIBERT 1993

C. ALLIBERT, "Accouplements rituels ou fantasmes zoophiles?", Paris, INALCO, *Érudes Océan Indien*, 16, 1993, pp. 171-179.

ALLIBERT 1995

C. ALLIBERT, "Les mouvements austronésiens vers l'Océan Indien occidental. La tradition arabico-malgache revisitée", *L'étranger intime. Mélanges offerts à Paul Ottino*, Université de la Réunion, 1995, pp. 61-76.

ALLIBERT in press

C. ALLIBERT, "The archaeology of knowledge about Austronesian influences in the Western Indian Ocean", paper presented at the World Archaeological Congress 3, New Delhi, December 4-11, 1994.

BENCHEIKH

J.E. BENCHEIKH, "Alf layla wa layla" in Corpus 12 of *l'Encyclopédie Universalis*, pp. 269-270.

CASSON 1989

L. CASSON, *The Periplus Maris Erythraei: Text with Introduction, Translation and Commentary* (by), Princeton University Press.

CRONE 1987

P. CRONE, *Meccan Trade and the Rise of Islam*, Oxford, B. Blackwell.

DESMAISONS 1908-1914

J.J.P. DESMAISONS, *Dictionnaire Persan-Français*, Rome, Imprimerie polyglotte vaticane.

DOMENICHINI-RAMIARAMANA 1990

B. DOMENICHINI-RAMIARAMANA, "Madagascar", *Histoire Générale de l'Afrique du VIIe au XIe siècle*, UNESCO/NEA, 1990, pp. 727-748.

FERRAND 1922

G. FERRAND, *Voyage du marchand arabe Sulayman en Inde et en Chine, rédigé en 851 suivi de remarques par Abû Zayd Hasan (vers 916)*, Paris.

JORET 1904

CH. JORET, "Les recherches botaniques de l'expédition d'Alexandre", Review of *Botanische Forschungen des Alexanderzuges*, Leipzig, 1903, par Dr. Hugo Bretzl, in *Journal des Savants*, Paris, 1904, pp. 498-504, 611-620.

MANGUIN 1991

P.-Y. MANGUIN, "The Merchant and the King: Political Myths of Southeast Asian Coastal Polities", *Indonesia*, 52, 1991, pp. 41-54.

MARDRUS

J.-C. Mardrus (contes traduits par) *Les Mille et une Nuits*, 1988, Paris, R. Laffont, Bouquins, 2 vol.

MIQUEL 1980

A. MIQUEL, *La géographie humaine du monde musulman jusqu'au milieu du 11e siècle*, Paris-The Hague, Mouton, 1980, 2 vol.

SAUVAGET 1954

J. SAUVAGET, *Les Merveilles de l'Inde*, Mémorial J. Sauvaget, Damascus, Institut Français.

SEVERIN 1984

T. SEVERIN, *Le voyage de Sindbad, sur les traces de Sindbad le Marin. Une extraordinaire odyssée d'Oman à Canton*, Paris, Albin Michel.

TIBBETTS 1979

G.R. TIBBETTS, *A Study of the Arab Texts Containing Material on South-East Asia*, Leiden-London, Royal Asiatic Society, 1979.

Theophrastus

Theophrastus, *Recherches sur les plantes*, Paris, Les Belles Lettres (1988-89), 2 vol. Text compiled and translated by S. Amigues.

THOMSON 1955

M.H. THOMSON, *Textes grecs inédits relatifs aux plantes*, Paris, Les Belles Lettres, 1955.

TODOROV 1970

T. TODOROV, *Introduction à la littérature fantastique*, Paris, Points Seuil, 1970.

VERE ALLEN 1984

J. VERE ALLEN, "Deux mystères dans l'histoire de l'océan Indien occidental", *Recherche, Pédagogie et Culture*, July-August-September 1984, pp. 10-16.

WOLTERS 1965

O.W. WOLTERS, *Early Indonesian Commerce. A Study of the Origins of Srivijaya*, Ithaca, New York, Cornell University Press, 1965.

C. MEYER, *Glass from Quseir al-Qadim and the Indian Ocean Trade, Studies in Ancient Oriental Civilization 3*, Chicago, The Oriental Institute of the University of Chicago, 1992.

A large number of studies are being carried out at present on the relations between the Eastern Mediterranean and the Far-East. Carol Meyer's book on glass discovered in the Red Sea port of Quseir al Qadim, which was a market for one of the trade-routes across the Arabian Desert starting from the Nile, makes an interesting contribution to the research in this field by providing new data to specialists in glass. This study of the glass trade during the first two centuries of the Christian era and during the period extending from the late 12th century to the early 14th century A.D. when the areas excavated by the American team were inhabited, supplements E. M. Stern's work relating to Antiquity[1] and is a novelty for the Islamic period. Besides, the dearth of publications on glass discovered in Egypt in the course of scientific excavations enhances the value of a book on this subject. As a matter of fact, the only recent monographs and articles that can be added to the old publications of the Cairo Museum[2] and those on Medamoud glass finds[3] relating to the Roman Empire is D. Harden's basic work on Karanis glass[4] and for the Islamic period his article on the Aidhab finds,[5] articles by G. Scanlon and R.H. Pinder-Wilson on glass finds at Fustat[6] and articles on the excavations conducted by the Japanese team also at Fustat and at al-Tur.[7]

---

* The titles of recently published articles and monographs will be included in this article.

1. See E.M. STERN, "Early Roman Exports of Glass in India", in V. BEGLEY and R. DE PUMA (eds), *Rome and India: The Sea Trade*, 1991, pp. 113-124; *eadem*, "Early Exports Beyond the Empire", in *Roman Glass: Two Centuries of Invention*, 1991, pp. 141-154; *eadem*, "The Glass from Heis", in *Sur les routes antiques de l'Azanie et de l'Inde (Le fonds Révoil du Musée de l'Homme), Heïs et Damo en Somalie*,, 1993, pp. 21-61.

2. M.C.C. EDGAR, *Catalogue général du Musée du Caire: Graeco-Egyptian Glass*, 1905.

3. R. COTTEVILLE-GIRAUDET, *Rapport sur les fouilles de Médamoud* (1930): *1ère partie. La verrerie alexandrine de Médamoud (Haute Égypte), BIFAO* 8/2, 1931, pp. 1-33.

4. D. HARDEN, *Roman Glass from Karanis* (1936).

5. *Idem*, "The Glass found at Soba", in P.L. SHINNIE, *Excavations at Soba*, 1955, pp. 60-76.

6. R.H. PINDER-WILSON & G.T. SCANLON, "Glass Finds from Fustat 1964-1971", *JGS* 29, 1987, pp. 60-71.

7. Y. SHINDO, "Glass", in K. SAKURAI & M. KAWATOKO (eds), *Al-Fustat 1978-1985*, 1992, Ch. IV and *eadem*, "Islamic Marvered Glass from al-Tur, South Sinai", *Annales du 12e Congrès l'Association Internationale pour l'Histoire du Verre, Vienne 1991*, pp. 297-305.

The book is chronologically divided into two parts, both having a similar plan — presentation of material and trade conditions during the Roman Empire (Ch. 2 & 3) and the Mameluke period (Ch. 4 & 5). They are preceded by a general introduction dealing mainly with the excavations at the site[8] (Ch. 1) together with a rich bibliography[9] and followed by a conclusion (Ch. 6), 21 plates and a very useful index.

The author clearly explains in the introduction that the purpose of this book is to present the glass finds from Quseir to facilitate more accurate studies on glassware found on the Egyptian soil. She also aims to provide a set of precisely dated parallels from the Middle-East and India, present a synthesis of the trading conditions between Alexandria and India and review the actual trade by trying to assess its importance, the existence of technology transfers and the difference between the trade networks under the Roman Empire and during the Mameluke period. So questions concerning manufacturing techniques and the function of various objects have been left out intentionally. The author has also avoided a quantitative breakdown of the various categories of glassware found at the site for want of a systematic collection of glass fragments during the excavation.[10]

In Chapter 2, the glassware from the Roman Empire is presented according to production techniques: monochromatic moulded glass from the late Hellenistic period, moulded glass from imperial Rome and blown glass. Fragments bearing decorative patterns belonging to objects whose shape cannot be reconstructed have been relegated to the end of the chapter together with elements of jewellery. A clearer chronological presentation would have been preferable. As a matter of fact, all the objects have been roughly dated as belonging to the first two centuries of the Christian era. However, it should have been possible to give more precise dates for some categories of objects. At least two fragments of mosaic glass (Nos. 309 & 310) and some fragments of moulded monochromatic bowls similar to those found in Delos[11] could be attributed to the later Hellenistic

---

8. The identification of Quseir el Qadim as Leukos Limen is discussed, see M. REDDÉ & J.-Cl. GOLVIN, "Quelques recherches récentes sur l'archéologie militaire en Égypte", *CRAI* 1986, pp. 172-196 and *Idem*, "Du Nil à la Mer Rouge: Documents anciens et nouveaux sur les routes du désert oriental d'Égypte", *Karthago* 21, 1987, pp. 5-64, which suggest that Quseir al Qadim is the same as the port of Myos Hormos and also see D.S. PEACOCK, "The Site of Myos Hormos: A View from Space", *JRA* 6, 1993, pp. 226-232, which re-examines the ancient descriptions of the Myos Hormos port in the light of satellite pictures of the Quseir site.

9. Correct p. XIX GAULMIER 1936, *Bulletin d'Études orientales* 6 and p. XXVI Whitehouse n.d. in WHITEHOUSE 1989, the article concerned was published in *JRA* 2, 1989, pp. 93-100.

10. See p. 15 note 1.

11. Considering its shape, fragment No. 298 could not have been cast upon a core towards the end of the Hellenistic period. It appears to be a piece of marbled glass

period (first half of the 1st century B.C.). A major part of the ribbed bowls as well as two fragments of linear-cut bowls should have been attributed to the second half of the 1st century B.C. in view of their shape, the relative irregularity of their pattern and the preponderance of fragments varying between yellow and brown. The virtual absence of such objects in Egypt pointed out by the author is due more to the dearth of publications than to their actual lack. We may mention the new fragments from Coptos preserved in the Fine Arts Museum in Lyon and also those recently discovered in Peluse, Tebtynis and Alexandria. The fragments of opaque glass with an incrusted pattern (No. 299), reticelli glass (Nos. 300 & 301), brightly coloured opaque glass (Nos. 302-305) and mosaic glass with floral patterns, which are different from those belonging to the Hellenistic period, can be assigned to the end of the 1st century B.C. and the beginning of the 1st century A.D.

The beautiful tableware cast out of colourless glass has been minutely studied by D. Grose[12] and assigned to the end of the 1st century A.D. The large number of fragments discovered at Quseir (114) confirms the hypothesis that these objects were produced in Egypt advanced earlier by D. Harden on the basis of the fragments found in Karanis. In addition to the three shapes presented by D. Grose, there are new shapes also seen in Tebtynis. The quality of glass used shows that the faceted goblets found in Quseir as well as in Karanis and Tebtynis belong to the same group. They have been studied in great detail by A. Oliver[13] and they constitute one of the dinner sets found in the cache in Begram.[14] The glass fragments with engravings of mythological scenes discovered in Begram enable us to push back, at least in the East, the earliest date of manufacture of these objects, one fragment of which was found in Quseir, to the end of the 1st century A.D. or the beginning of the 2nd century A.D.[15] It may be said that this piece depicts not a 'hero' but Serapis wearing the *calathos* on his head.

---

of the Mameluke period. For similar pieces see glass from Fustat, Y. SHINDO 1991, *op. cit.*, p. 300, fig. 3, No. 24-25.

12. D.F. GROSE, "Early Imperial Roman Cast Vessel: The Translucent Coloured and Colourless Fine Wares", in *Roman Glass: Two Centuries of Invention*, 1991, pp. 1-18.

13. A. OLIVER, "Early Roman Faceted Glass", *JGS* 26 (1984), pp. 35-38.

14. We may add to H. Hackin's *princeps* publication, B. HAMELIN's specialised studies in *Cahiers de Byrsa* 2, 1952, pp. 11-25; 3, 1953, pp. 121-128; 4, 1954, pp. 153-174 and the recent article by D. DELACOUR, "Redécouvrir les verres de Begram", *Arts Asiatiques* 48, 1993, pp. 53-71 giving detailed information about the finds in Begram.

15. On this point see G. DE TOMMASO, "Alessandria centro d'irradiazione del vetro inciso", in *Le vie del Vetro, Egitto e Sudan*, 1988, pp. 80-85 where this glass is assigned to the first half of the 2nd century as opposed to D. HARDEN *et al.*, *Glass of the Caesars*, 1987, p. 182 where these objects are assigned to the end of the 2nd century or the beginning of the 3rd century. The presence of a bowl of engraved and

It will be noticed that among the blown glass pieces there is a predominance of small and medium sized perfume vials. Some of these are beautifully made (No. 168-171) while others, strangely enough, are thick (No. 203-211). Contrary to what the author says, the latter are quite common in Egypt, more than fifty having been found in the recent excavations in Tebtynis and about twenty in the excavations in Coptos. On the basis of findings in Tebtynis and Karanis, they can be assigned to the late 1st century or the early 2nd century. The classification of blown glassware is a tedious job especially in the absence of complete pieces. But the author's method of separating the upper portion of the objects from their lower portion does not appear to be relevant. It is difficult to ascribe an exact date to the remaining glassware, except for the bowls with an elaborate engraved pattern (No.330-340) manufactured from the latter half of the 2nd century onwards. The 'glass corpus' presented in this book does not reveal if this glassware was meant for export or if it was meant for use by the residents of Quseir. The author deals with this question in the earlier part of the book.[16]

In the following chapter on trade, we must take note of the map showing the spread of glassware (pp. 60-61).[17] However, it is to be regretted that the author has neglected the problem of the circulation of goods in the Persian Gulf.[18] She gives only a rough idea by indicating the ports mentioned in *The Periplus of the Erythraean Sea* and detailing the various categories of glassware found.

It seems quite logical to agree with the author that the major portion of glassware discovered in Quseir was manufactured in Egypt, probably in more workshops than those mentioned by the author. In the following pages of the chapter, there is a second-hand summary of the conditions of trade between Alexandria and India regarding traders, means of transport, land[19] and sea routes. We must take note of the author's original interest in the material conditions of trade, e.g. types of packing, composition of caravans and duration of journey, types of boats used, their tonnage and crews. Perhaps, it was not necessary to repeat in detail all the ports mentioned in *The Periplus of the Erythraean Sea,* especially after the publication of the edition commented by Casson and works of M. Stern. The pages dealing with India could have been enriched with infor-

---

inscribed glass in the destruction layer in a part of Tebtynis going back to the first half of the 2nd century confirms the earlier date.

16. On pp. 73-74 in the conclusion of the chapter on trade under the Roman Empire.

17. The recent finds of glassware by the Russian team working in Qana in Yemen (oral announcement by A.V. Sedov) may be added.

18. On this point see J.-F. SALLES, "*The Periplus of the Erythraean Sea* and the Arabian-Persian Gulf", *Topoi* 3, 1993, pp. 493-523 bringing together archaeological data provided by sites in the Gulf and concluding that "in one way, the Arab-Persian Gulf was fed with western products by India".

19. Articles by M. REDDÉ & J.-CL. GOLVIN (see note 8) should have been mentioned in this context.

mation from R.N. Singh's recent book[20] which speaks of existence of local craftsmen specialised in making elements of glass jewellery.[21]

The second part of the book dealing with glassware from the Mameluke period will certainly stand out because it is one of the first publications about glassware found during scientific excavations while awaiting the promised studies of material, mostly belonging to an earlier period, found at Fustat,[22] Siraf,[23] the shipwreck of Serce Limani[24] and Aqaba.[25] Mameluke glassware is not as abundant as that belonging to the Roman period and it represents about a third of the glass pieces that have been exhumed and preserved. In most cases, it consists only of vessels of daily use with little decoration except for some small perfume containers of engraved glass (no. 466-473) or decorated with a feather motif (No. 548-553).[26] It will be noticed that there are a large number of closed vases, bottles or jars with different shaped mouths and also bracelets (more than forty pieces) either in the form of plain glass rings or with polychromatic patterns.[27]

Chapter 5 dealing with trade during the Mameluke period gives summaries, some rapid and others extensive, based on the works of S.D. Goitein and others on traders' organisations between the 11th and 14th centuries A.D. (Geniza archives in Cairo and sources relating to Karimi merchants), glassware production centres, the journey from Cairo to the Red Sea and merchant ships.[28]

---

20. R.N. SINGH, *Ancient Indian Glass :Archaeology and Technology*, 1989, particularly pp. 34-40 and pp. 123-140. Mention may also be made of the recent articles by S. GUPTA, "List of Explored and Excavated Early Historic Sites in India Yielding Material Evidence of Indo-Roman Trade", *Yavanika*, 3, 1993, pp. 75-91 and R.M. CIMINO, "Roman Glassware from India", in *Ancient Rome and India: Commercial and Cultural Contacts Between the Roman World and India*, 1994, pp. 161-163.

21. See for example P. FRANCIS, *Bead Emporium: A Guide to the Beads from Arikamedu in the Pondicherry Museum*, 1987.

22. See note 6 about American excavations. The publication about the finds of glassware in the excavations by IFAO is being prepared by D. Foy.

23. Being prepared by D. Whitehouse.

24. In the bibliography given by the author, we should add FR.H. VAN DOORNINCK, "The Serce Limani Shipwreck: An 11th Century Cargo of Fatimid Glassware Culled from Byzantine Glassmakers", in *1st International Anatolian Glass Symposium 1988*, 1990, pp. 58-63.

25. Being prepared by C. Meyer.

26. For a more recent study of this glassware see note 7.

27. Since then, there has been an article by M. SPAER, "The Islamic Glass Bracelets of Palestine: Preliminary Findings", *JGS* 34, 1992, pp. 44-62.

28. The article by L. VARADARAJAN, "Indian Boat Building Traditions: The Ethnological Evidence", *Topoi* 3, 1993, pp. 547-568 (with an extensive bibliography) will

The second part of the chapter is more original and brings together information about trade along the African coast,[29] in India and in the Far East[30] but gives a map limited only to the African coast and the West Indian coast. This map shows the settlements known through texts or archaeological finds but does not give details of glassware that has been discovered or is mentioned in the sources.

Carol Meyer's book is a good introduction to trade in the Red Sea and the Indian Ocean under the Roman Empire and during the Mameluke period through glassware, which is often neglected. The most original part of the book is certainly the one dealing with the Mameluke period both because of the material and explanations presented by the author.

Marie-Dominique NENNA
CNRS, Institut F. Courby UMR 5649
Maison de l'Orient

contribute new data to this part which is rather long and based on examples from the Mediterranean.

29. Completed by V.V. NAUMKIN & A.V. SEDOV, "Monuments of Socotra", *Topoi* 3, 1993, pp. 569-623, especially p. 596, fig. 15 and for the trade in beads, SH.J. SAITOWITZ, "The Archaeometry of Glass Beads and Trade between Southern Africa, Egypt and India AD 900-1250", in *Archaeology as an Indicator of Trade and Contact, World Archaeological Congress 3, New Delhi 1994*, pp. 1-20.

30. Regarding glass trade in the Far-east, it is necessary to add the basic articles by A. JIAYAO, "Early Chinese Glassware", *The Oriental Ceramic Society Translations* 12, 1987; *Idem*, "Dated Islamic Glass in China", *Bulletin of the Asia Institute* 5, 1991, pp. 123-137; and by E. JOHNSTON LAING, "A Report on Western Asian Glassware in the Far East", *Bulletin of the Asia Institute* 5, 1991, pp. 109-121.

A. BRESSON and P. ROUILLARD eds, *L'Emporion*, published by Centre Pierre Paris (URA 991), Diffusion De Boccard, Paris, 1993.

This book edited so brilliantly[1] and with such alacrity by A. Bresson and P. Rouillard brings together the papers presented at seminars held in Bordeaux under the auspices of the Centre Pierre Paris and in Paris from 1989 to 1991. The book's title discloses its subject while A. Bresson's introduction and P. Lévêque's concluding remarks ("La richesse foisonnante de l'*emporion*", pp. 227-231) determine its scope. There is no question of defining the term *emporion* (except for a personal interpretation, cf. M. Gras, p.104, or an attempt to summarise without giving a 'simplistic definition', A. Bresson, pp. 222-226; P. Lévêque, p. 230). All that has been done is to outline the concept diachronically and over the widest geographical area (from the Cassiterides or Sicily Islands to Tapobranè/Ceylon) which, as stated by P. Lévêque, may raise doubts about some comparative studies including those attempted in this review. But the sum total of reflections that the book offers is extremely rewarding as it underlines the uncertainties and sometimes the contradictions associated with the Greek term.

The very first uncertainty, which is a logical consequence of the non-definition of the term, emerges with the lack of a translation for the word as seen in the book's title. A. Bresson (pp. 163-164) insists that one should be cautious about using the Anglo-Saxon equivalent 'port of trade', closely linked with the Polanyan theories about ancient economy, which can be easily refuted in the case of the Greek term *emporion*. But none of the papers presented in French has proposed a translation of the term, most authors being quite content to mention the 'uses' which they do not always agree with (e.g. P. Counillon, p. 8, n.3). Conversely, "the common use of the word *emporion* in ancient literature to designate a big or small 'trading post' justifies the similar use of this word in contemporary scientific literature" (A. Bresson, p. 216). The Greek *emporion* thus remains *emporion* in French.[2] So, doesn't the term mean different things to different people? As a matter of fact, this is not far from the historical reality revealed in this book.

---

1. The only fault that I could find is the difficulty in locating the table of contents and what struck me most was the attractive dust jacket by J.-C. Golvin depicting Alexandria in the 2nd century A.D. which reminds of aerial photographs of modern cities in the Persian Gulf.

2. The term 'échelles' appears many times in the book, but nowhere is it claimed to be a translation of *emporion*. It undoubtedly refers to the existence of numerous *emporia* in Antiquity, but how can the same French word be used to designate what were once Alexandria, Delos or Ostia and Adanè or Zonè (list of *emporia* mentioned in the *GGM*, P. Counillon, pp. 54-55)? As for these lists, many authors point out the advantage of using the data bank of the *Thesaurus Linguae Graecae*.

Another contradiction in the term *emporion* emerges quite clearly in what I find is a well-documented and definitive paper on the problems of Al-Mina and Tell Sukas by J.Y. Perreault entitled "Les *emporia* grecs du Levant: mythe ou réalité? (Greek *emporia* in the Levant: Myth or Reality?), (pp. 59-87). In his philological analysis in the beginning of the book entitled "Emplois classiques et histoire du mot", (Conventional Uses and History of the Word), (pp. 9-22), M. Casevitz shows interest in the word *emporos* because *emporion* is the place where the *emporoi* or merchant-travellers are in control (p. 15). He refers to one of its uses by Herodotus (IV.154) "an *emporos* is a Greek or a Barbarian who leaves his country to settle down in a place to conduct business" (p. 13). Similarly, A. Bresson introduces in the concept of *emporion* the idea of "a small expatriate community engaged in trade" (p. 224). J. Y. Perreault, on his part, shows how the Greeks gradually started visiting the eastern ports on the Levantine coast from the latter part of the 8th century B.C. (earlier, the few goods imported from Euboea and Cycladia passed through the hands of Phoenician middlemen). They started settling down in these areas in the late 7th century B.C. and progressively assimilated themselves with the local population. Thus, Greek graffiti on the tombs in Tell Sukas or Bassit and especially the presence of an 'Athenian' house in Bassit (p. 80, n. 94) prove without any doubt that Greek (or Oriental – the author does not specify in the case of Bassit) *emporoi* lived in these ports and engaged, among other things, in international trade.[3] But these were not *emporia* in the Greek sense of the term. According to J.Y. Perreault, they were just 'ports of trade' based on the model of Polanyi. Is the distinction made by the author between *emporion* and 'port of trade' by specifying that "there is no doubt that in ancient times these sites [...] were real 'ports of trade'; strictly speaking, they did not *therefore* (italics mine) constitute Greek *emporia*" (p. 82) really convincing? According to Perreault, the Greek, Phoenician, Cypriot and North Syrian *emporoi* formed a mixed group. The Greeks did not live in separate, well-demarcated neighbourhoods as in Naucratis (regarding this see M. Gras, pp. 104-105 while A. Bresson, p. 185, is not as convincing). So the North Syrian ports cannot be called *emporia*. When we take into account the chronological difference between these sites dating back to the 6th century B.C. and Hellenistic Alexandria, does it not appear that there is a confusion between the term and the relevant function of the *emporion* (cf. P. Lévêque's remarks in

---

3. Mention must be made here of a description quoted by J.Y. Perreault of the Alexandrette port in the 18th century which was then considered as one of the ports of call in the Levant and one of the active centres of the Mediterranean trade: "a vile hamlet with five or six stores belonging to Francs or Europeans, the houses of the Aga and the customs officer, a few huts belonging to Greeks and Levantines" (p. 80). There are similar descriptions of the ports of Cyprus where the Ancients did not have any *emporion*. How any of the sites called *emporia* in ancient textes could be described in similar terms, especially the forty odd ports mentioned in the *Periplus of the Erythraean Sea*?

the book's conclusion on the sites in the kingdom of Pontus which served as *emporia* without being called so, p. 230) and an idealised oriental model of a big city with specialised districts and functions, although J.Y. Perreault's effort to reinstate the oriental character of the sites he is studying is perfectly justified? It is true that according to Strabo Alexandria was the largest *emporion* of *oikouménè*, but how many other *emporia* mentioned by the Ancients resembled Alexandrette in the 18th century A.D. or Bassit in the 6th century B.C.?

Pursuing the oriental connection, J. Teixidor (pp. 85-87) suggests that a Semitic term could have been the equivalent (and the predecessor: the Ougarit tablets dating back to the 14th century B.C.) of the Greek *emporion*. If his suggestion is admissible, it underlines the problem of taxes/customs duties which, paradoxically, the book hardly deals with. C. Zacagnini ("In margine all'*emporion*: modelli di scambio nelle economie del Vicino Oriente antico", pp. 127-143) draws attention to the theoretical debate on the economy of the ancient Middle East. He goes beyond the on-going quarrel between 'primitivists' and 'modernists'[4] and because the eastern trade is often accredited solely to the Phoenicians (who are associated with the double model of the classical *emporion* and the Polanyan 'port of trade' without any concrete proof of their involvement), he recalls the principal steps of the debate: the systematic distrust in the early stages about the theories of Polanyi is followed by the strong reaction of D.C. North who supports the theories of 'transaction costs' and M. Silver who tries to reinstate the notion of the predominance of the market in an ultra neo-liberal perspective. All of them look at the economic systems prevailing in the Middle East in ancient times from a 'modernistic' viewpoint which does not rely much on direct access to written sources and takes the easy way out by basing itself on overall linguistic changes covering three millennia without taking into account regional peculiarities and chronological changes. Although Zacagnini confines himself to the theoretical level, his arguments (backed by M. Liverani at other times) win our support. The author does not propose an alternate solution – literature on the economy of the Middle East in ancient times is so plentiful that there was no need to include a detailed analysis in this book. He just mentions a contract for the sale of wool during the 3rd millennium where it is quite clear that neither production costs, nor the notions of price and market and not even the immediate interest of the seller are taken into account. We are far from the concept of *emporion* which was totally unknown in the Middle East in ancient times. It would perhaps be useful if a specialist in Phoenician economy (do they exist?) could bridge the gap between the 'oriental' and 'Greek' outlooks on international trade.

M. Gras's paper ("Pour une Méditerranée des *emporia*", pp. 103-112), which analyses the notion of *emporion* in the Western Mediterranean region in

---

4. *Premières journées de Saint-Bertrand sur l'Économie Antique*, St Bertrand de Comminges, 6-7 May 1994.

ancient times by attempting to define a 'model', gives rise to reflections that go much beyond the historical and geographical scope of our study. From the Greek point of view, *emporion* could be the city's *epineion* or the boundary of its *chôra* (Sicily); it could also be the empirical starting point of what stories of the establishment of post-*emporion* ports will change into *poleis* (Alalia, Massalia, Ampurias). In a non-Greek Mediterranean more accessible to outsiders, it is the ethnic and cultural (and also economic) point of contact for peoples living on the borders of a much vaster zone than the *epineion* and the inhabitants of inland regions (cf. M. Gras's remarks on the Po delta, p. 108). But whenever the proposed model goes beyond the Western Mediterranean of Antiquity, the author insists on the notion of a "space for travelling" (p. 109) where the *emporion* becomes a *practice* (italics mine) which must take into account local conditions (native power, the proportion of different communities in the total population etc., p. 106). It is then difficult not to think of the numerous *emporia* in different regions of the Erythraean Sea (*Periplus of the Erythraean Sea = PME*) or in the Eastern Mediterranean mentioned by various authors. Against the Hellenistic notions of linear 'axes of trade' (P. Rouillard, p. 39) or of 'colonial' trade (R. Etienne, pp. 30-32) inspired by Strabo, I have defended elsewhere[5] the hypothesis of trade movements, during the Iron Age/Antiquity in the Eastern Mediterranean, that were more akin to a 'Brownian' movement than to strictly bilateral relations surmised on the basis of the 'import of Greek vases in the East'. Wouldn't the concept of linear trade movements inspired by Strabo and other writers be a simplified picture of a far more complex reality that justified the listing of several dozen *emporia* (otherwise unknown) by the Greek geographer and the anonymous author of the *PME*, where there was no 'colonial' or 'neo-capitalist' commercial activity but ordinary trade between producers of goods and merchants from distant lands?

R. Descat's paper (pp. 145-161) enquires into the actual effect of the Solonian law banning the export of goods, other than olive oil, from Attica. This gives the author an opportunity to make a detailed analysis of the social and economic conditions that gave rise to the 'commercial moral code' in Solon's time and of the different functions of the *agora* and the *emporion* in Athens and in other Greek cities during the classical period. At the risk of appearing too simplistic, it could be said that the *agora* was the place of Attican protectionism whereas, from the very beginning, the *emporion* was conceived as a place where foreigners were welcome. This difference did not fail to produce a lasting effect on the social structure (cf. A. Bresson, p. 165) and trade in Athens. A. Laronde (pp. 89-97) presents a convincing account of the historical geography of the

5. J.-F. SALLES, "Du blé, de l'huile et du vin. Notes sur les échanges commerciaux en Méditerranée orientale vers le milieu du 1er millénaire av. J.-C." (1st part), *Achaemenid History VI, Asia Minor and Egypt: Old Cultures in a New Empire*, ed. by H. Sancisi-Weerdenburg & A. Kuhrt, Leiden, 1991, pp. 207-236. The second part is being printed by the same publisher.

Cyrenian coast and its relations with inland trading centres. It is a pity that there is no map of the region. Y. Garlan (pp. 99-102) cannot give a satisfactory explanation for the inscription *eis emporion* found on the stamps on Chersonese amphoras. H. Duchêne (pp. 113-125) refers to the history and archaeology of the Delos *emporion* and provides interesting details about the port.

R. Etienne (pp. 23-34) and P. Rouillard (pp. 35-46) separately analyse the *emporia* mentioned by Strabo, but an average reader like me is incompetent to decide if the Veneti had an *emporion* (Rouillard, p. 37, n. 9) or they did not (Etienne, p. 23, n. 2) and if Strabo's lists contain 47 or 48 *emporia*. The two papers complement each other on several points and provide an exhaustive and subtle view of the *emporion* described by Greek geographers. They describe the location, hierarchy (?), various commercial and local functions, internal organisation, wealth and dynamism, regional variations, etc. We must take note of Rouillard's account of the technical means available to the *emporion* : a *limen* (and at times two), sometimes an *epineion* and in exceptional cases *néôria* (as in Alexandria). An apt concluding remark by Etienne: "Strabo's chain of *emporia* extols the advantages of peace during the Augustan age..." (p. 34) makes us wonder if the author, carried away by his urge to eulogize (certainly not overt, but nobody would deny Strabo's effort to promote Augustus in his works), does not have a tendency to present an idealised 'model' of the *emporion* – a symbol of the economic and commercial success of the new Roman Empire?

A. Bresson ("Les cités grecques et leurs *emporia*", pp. 163-226) gives a detailed analysis of the *emporion* concept without providing, as we have noted earlier, a simple definition. He does, however, give a summary of the different connotations of the word (pp. 223-225) based on the dual axis of commercial life (legal status : the *emporia* of Piraeus, Rhodes, etc., trading centre, a type of establishment where expatriate *emporoi* got together) together with that of a centre of political activity (link between *polis* and *emporion*). Two main ideas appear several times in Bresson's account. Contrary to a common cliché (which one?), the world of the *emporion* seems to be one of strict laws and controls imposed by the state or the city and not a world of licence. On the other hand, even if *emporion* is a Greek word, the concept is common to the entire Mediterranean region including Phoenicia, Etruria, Egypt and Carthage and even the Indian Ocean (*PME*). Perhaps an explanation of this double observation can be found in a brief remark made by the author where he says that the texts or inscriptions rarely allow us to really appreciate (quantitatively) that the "*emporion* is a place of profit" (p. 226).

It would take too long to list all the arguments advanced by A. Bresson, always supported by a rigorous interpretation of texts. However, the author points out that the meaning of the word *emporion* varies in the works of different ancient writers according to their point of view (pp. 215-216) and following the new interpretation of known inscriptions. Bresson reminds us that there was a concentration of foreign trade in the *emporion* and though it was sometimes monopolistic, it was always controlled. The *emporion* thus became the centre of a privileged and protected trading zone (examples mentioned are those of Thasos, Olynthus, Sinope, Carthage and Little Syrte and Marseille). It was also a business centre (e.g. Delos where the abundance of seals bears testimony to the volume of business carried out with distant lands, see H. Duchêne's paper). The author then goes on to distinguish ordinary *emporia* from 'local' or 'domestic' *emporia* straddling the native world and open only to merchants from the 'regional empire' (p. 217: discontinuous, subject or protected territories) entrusted with the task of tapping the wealth of the hinterland and drawing it to the main *emporion*. This gave rise to the notion of the 'factory' which was dependent on the central 'trading centre' (the author gives the example of Marseille, pp. 208-213). Bresson also stresses the notion of security which has to be maintained so that the necessary goods reach the *emporion*, the city's 'seat of energy', and so the city's merchants are welcomed in foreign *emporia*. This also gives rise to a series of texts and inscriptions regulating relations between cities and/or *emporia* (including competition, cf. Chios and Phocaea, p. 170) or supporting protectionism in cities and *emporia*. There are in addition the *symbola* or *eisagogè-exagogè* agreements governing international trade. It is clear, and a matter of sheer common sense, that although it ultimately depends on individual merchants, the optimisation of the *emporion*'s profit requires the state's or the city's intervention. But one must be careful not to look on it as a normal rule governing the working of the *emporion* in ancient times, of which Delos was one of the most obvious exceptions.[6]

On the other hand, I do not agree with A. Bresson when he tries to establish a parallel between the working of the *emporion* in the Hellenistic Mediterranean and what one learns about *emporia* in the Indian Ocean in the 1st century A.D. mentioned in the *Periplus of the Erythraean Sea*. The reading of the *Periplus* is often cursory. Thus Apologos is not "after" the Kalaios Islands (§ 35), it is at the end of the Persian Gulf and not near its entrance, about 1200 km from the Kalaios Islands. The *emporion* had trade relations with Omana and not with the southern coast of Arabia (p.193). It would be wrong to say that the western Arabian coast and the countries in the interior did not have any form of government (the Incense Kingdom often mentioned in the *Periplus* – cf. history of the kingdoms of Yemen (p. 197). The island of Dioskuridès (Socotra), which was the natural journey's end for ships taking advantage of the return monsoon (which explains its importance), always remained under the control of South Arabian kingdoms (p. 196).[7] There would be many other details worthy of note.

---

6. N.K. RAUH, *The Sacred Bonds of Commerce, Religion, Economy and Trade: Society at Hellenistic Roman Delos*, Gieben, Amsterdam, 1993.

7. Lastly, V. NAUMKIN, *Island of the Phoenix. An ethnographic study of the people of Socotra*, Ithaca Press, Reading, 1993.

It is difficult to say if the "legal" distinctions suggested by A. Bresson between *emporion apodedeigmenon, emporion nomimom, emporion enthesmon* and *emporion topikon* are relevant to the world of the *Periplus* and, consequently, the Mediterranean in the Hellenistic period.. The *emporia apodedeigmenon* like Myos Hormos, Bérénikè and Moscha were actually ports of loading/unloading for contracts signed elsewhere (in either Alexandria or Shabwa) and therefore "compulsory" transit points where it was possible to check if the cargo corresponded to the contract. The *emporia nomimom* were not "normal" ports as compared to the "wild" and "dangerous" ports as the author supposes. They were probably ports where the royal authority was exercised in a particular and ill-defined manner as suggested by J. Rougé. As for the *emporion enthesma,* is not the expression "*emporia* closed to external trade" on p. 194 a contradiction in itself? There is no doubt that the *emporia* of the *Periplus* merit a serious study, deeper than the ones undertaken by J. Rougé and L. Casson, but it should be approached from the viewpoint of the world of the *Periplus* and not just from the Greek viewpoint.

Trade in the Indian Ocean, as these sources indicate, was certainly well regulated but it was "divided into sectors".[8] Only Roman ships sailed on the direct route from Myos Hormos to Barygaza or Mouziris and they undoubtedly crossed a large number of Indian or Arab ships which covered the *internal* routes of the Indian Ocean. These sectors varied greatly at the human and political levels (African, Southern Arabs, Gulf Arabs, Persians, Baluchis, Indians, etc.) and came under vastly different economic and judicial systems. It is this variety that is described by the anonymous author of the *Periplus* while trying to find a Greek word to convey strictly local conditions (except for the general concept of the *emporion*) that were so extraordinary that they are found nowhere else in Graeco-Roman literature. These unique definitions try to transcribe in Greek the situations found in Arab, Indian, African and Persian ports of the Indian Ocean. They do not constitute a Greek view of the organisation of trade in this blatantly foreign area. At the most they can attempt a translation. But we are more likely to find an explanation of concepts like *emporion enthesmon* or *topikon* in Kautilya's *Arthaśàstra* than in a Greek analysis of *emporion*.

However, these reservations do not belittle either the significance of A. Bresson's contribution or the richness of the entire book which is indisputably an essential reference work on *emporion*. It is and will remain indispensable not only for all research on trade in Antiquity but also for those who are generally interested in the concepts that govern international trade and commerce. If there is one regret – and there is no doubt that it will be tackled by future seminars – it is that in the bountiful world of the *emporion*, as P. Lévêque puts it, the authors

8. See J.-F. SALLES, "*The Periplus of the Erythraean Sea* and the Arab-Persian Gulf", *Topoi* 3/2, 1993, pp. 493-524. L. Casson's excellent commentary on the *Periplus* often draws our attention to this division of the Indian Ocean trade into sectors more by omission than through a coherent analysis.

have dwelt solely on historical, economic and legal problems without paying much attention to the tireless activity of the *emporos* who contributed to the wealth of the *emporion*.

Jean-François SALLES
Institut F.-Courby, UMR 9969
Jean-Francois.Salles@mom.fr

Himanshu P. RAY, *The Winds of Change. Buddhism and the Maritime Links of Early South Asia*, Delhi, Oxford University Press, 1994.

Hinduism has always had reservations about sea voyages. After the colonisation of the Indian sub-continent by the British, the village became the basic unit of the administrative and political system as well as the revenue collection machinery based on the division of land. Maritime activities became the exclusive concern of Empire-builders, financiers and traders in the City. As a result, the Indian village became the archetype of modern economic thought, from Marx to Dumont, while the Indian coastline stretching over several thousand kilometres and trade with countries near and far faded into oblivion. The newly independent India concentrated all its attention on the development of its rural areas and cottage industries, further strengthening this view which could not but favour a policy of commercial self-sufficiency leading to a ban on imports. Indian historical thought, which has always been prolific, fitted easily into the prevailing mould and all research was focused on the development of social relationships in the context of agriculture, the birth of the upper classes, the creation of states, etc. or everything that scientific literature tends to put under the head "agrarian system".[1] Until recently, India was seen as a country that lived essentially in its villages, a country without a sea front, cut off from the external world, a country which had changed little since ancient times until its socio-economic castration during the colonial era.

One of the main virtues of H.P. Ray's book is that she presents a totally different picture of India as a country open to the outside world from very early times, maintaining close and uninterrupted links with the lands bordering the Indian Ocean and with even more distant lands like China and the Mediterranean countries. Though there is enough evidence in support of the maritime links dating back to the 3rd millennium, it is the historical period (*c.* 300 B.C. to 300 A.D.) that witnessed the most significant changes, at least the best documented changes, which constitute the book's chronological framework. The book is crammed with information, adequately supported by arguments, though sometimes repetitive (which is inevitable). The presentation is excellent with a detailed bibliography (pp. 203-222) and it is abundantly illustrated with maps. It is not possible to give a step-by-step analysis of this complex work but we may point out three major traits:

the re-evaluation of historical and archaeological data relating to India's maritime links during the historical period;

---

1. Readers, who are not very familiar with this literature, will find an analytical summary of the development of Indian historical thought in the past and in more recent times in *Recent Perspectives of Early Indian History*, ed. by R. THAPAR Popular Prakashan, Bombay, 1995. The book is a collection of eight essays containing the latest research findings dating from the Harappan age to the 14th century A.D.

a central theory on the role of Buddhism in the development of these maritime links;

an overview of research perspectives on maritime archaeology that could give a new orientation to Indian historiography.[2]

The author's main aim is to establish the antiquity of trading networks linking different regions of India and some of these regions with the outside world (2. *The Evolution of Trading Networks).* The urban settlements in the Gangetic plain in the middle of the 1st millennium B.C., which gradually spread throughout the peninsula during the post-Mauryan period (2nd century B.C.-2nd century A.D.), provided the backdrop for this trade. Other factors like the expansion of communications by land and sea (the earliest Buddhist texts mention the merchants of Bharuch and coastal navigation) and political centralisation as a consequence of the proper organization of states (the Magadha kingdom as early as the 4th century B.C. and later the Mauryan Empire served as a model for the Kushans in the North, the Ksatrapas in Gujerat, the Satavahanas in the Deccan, and the Cholas, Cheras and Pandyas in the South) were favourable to the development of this dynamic movement. Finally, some of the earliest inscriptions relating to donations to monasteries reveal the existence of a class of professional businessmen and traders. These same inscriptions testify to the general growth of wealth and the spread of this prosperity among different sections of the population (especially craftsmen) in addition to the elite.

Ray demonstrates the existence of domestic trading networks going back to the pre-Mauryan era in Gujerat (an indication of the antiquity and the continuing importance of Bharuch as a trading centre) and in the Gangetic plain possibly extending towards Bengal.[3] The author deals at length with the networks of the megalithic period in South India where the mining of minerals like copper and iron and precious stones like diamond and beryl and pearl-fishery contributed to the development of inland sites (high valleys and plateaux) as well as those on the coast (estuaries). These claims have been confirmed by archaeological excavations extending from Banbhore in Makran to Kodumanal in Tamilnadu as well as those in Andhra (Amaravati) and Orissa (Sisupalgarh). However, nothing is known about equivalent periods in coastal Bengal. Further, the spread across the entire peninsula of some important categories of Indian pottery (Black-and-Red, Northern Black Polished, Red Polished and Rouletted ware with excellent maps showing their distribution) bears witness to the southward movement during the post-Mauryan period of networks established in the Gangetic plain during the Mauryan period. The texts themselves refer to the new quest for

2. For the definition of epistemological bases and a rapid appraisal of research see H.P. RAY, "Trade and Contacts", *Recent Perspectives...* , 1995, pp. 142-175.

3. See pp. 21 & 23 for interesting observations on "Buddha's routes" and the spread of the known area (*Madhyadesa*) towards the East during the historical period.

precious commodities like gold, gems and pearls. Other texts describe in detail the organization of this trade.

The demonstration is convincing. However, it seems to me that there is one major weakness because the sources are not properly dated. Specialists have been discussing for a long time, without reaching a plausible conclusion, the dates of the great ancient Indian works like the *Mahabharata,* the *Arthasastra,* the *Puranas* and even the *Jatakas* often believed to belong to a later period. Pali literature appears to predate the period under consideration and the historical value of a work like the *Milindapanha* is strongly disputed. Ray uses many of these works with great felicity, but we can question their validity in relation to a well-defined period much older than the time of their writing. This does not imply that these proofs should be rejected but it would be better to use them more prudently, without giving them the stamp of authority. The same applies to archaeological data, very few of which come from sites that have been properly dated[4] and documented (convergence of several chronological elements), and the division of a site into different periods often enters into conflict with similar cultural contexts in other sites. As a matter of fact, it is more than likely that Ray's thesis is correct, but its demonstration requires fewer arguments than those marshalled by the author.

It would have been better if the author had developed in more detail two points of his thesis. Reminding us that most of India's coastal plains are narrow and hardly self-sufficient, except of course the Gangetic plain (see n. 13 below), Ray suggests that a major portion of the interregional trade networks were interested in trading in essential commodities and objects of daily use. In this book, the author seems to be concerned only in "prestige goods" or mining products. Similarly (*ibid.*), Ray stresses that in ancient India the port was not the seat of political power or of the affluent classes (the "elite" as she prefers to call them), but only a centre for collecting tax on the fruits of maritime trade. Thus the location of a port was determined in most cases by the richness of the hinterland and not by the ease with which it could be approached from the sea. Perhaps, the author should have given more concrete examples of ports in Gujerat or on the western coast of the Indian peninsula.

I will refer more briefly to Ray's review of India's relations with Rome already discussed in this issue (*Topoi*, 3/2, 1993, pp. 455-491). The author gives a summary of the principal theories on this subject — stemming from the research of European scholars — which still dominate historical thought in India. A recent writer (1987) ascribes the urban decline in the peninsula during the 3rd and 4th century A.D. to the interruption of trade with the West. The author too declares forcefully that the prosperity mentioned earlier existed before the

4. It often happens that the exact date of a particular period in an Indian archaeological site depends on a single radio-carbon dating. See Sandrine Elaigne's comments in *Topoi*, 6/2, 1996, pp. 627-640, and also her equally pertinent observations about the quantification of archaeological finds.

establishment of direct trade links between Rome and India, whose antecedents are yet to be discovered. Ray finds them in the old and uninterrupted contacts between the Persian Gulf and the Indian sub-continent[5] and what he considers as Hellenistic influences in India. The examples she has given are those of etched pottery and the technique of rouletted ware, bowls and dishes with the *omphalos* motif on the inner bottom and some moulded potteries. If these exchanges are confirmed (more detailed analyses are needed, especially of the exact chronological context of the archaeological finds in the Gulf and in India), it will be possible to revise B. Begley's observations[6] which recognize the Hellenistic influence (2nd century B.C. at the latest) on these types of objects, but without pinpointing the route. Archaeological evidence seems to indicate that this route passed through the Persian Gulf till the 2nd century B.C. Ray bases her arguments on these findings to underline the segmentation of trade networks in the Indian Ocean, often concealed behind the predominance of the direct relations between the Red Sea and India (*e.g.* Warmington and Casson recently), a topic to which she comes back later (p. 188).

The critical analysis of wine amphoras, fragments of Roman sigillated pottery, bronze or glass objects, Roman resins and intaglios and finally coins, enables the author to reduce the actual share of imports to its correct — and minimal — proportion. She is in a position to judge the actual volume of the trade between Rome and India, which was smaller than it was touted to be, and its impact on the development of Indian communities involved in this trade. Nevertheless, we remain somewhat dissatisfied. The Wheeler model of a regular and abundant flow (which ate into the Roman treasury according to Pliny) is knocked down as also the claim of a permanent Roman presence in India. But she does not furnish any new theory or model. If it is not what we believed it to be, what was the true nature of Indo-Roman trade? Were they just personal adventures undertaken with the support of the imperial coterie in Rome (A. Tchernia)? Or were they organised networks with local correspondants that were operated on an irregular basis? If the old theory needs to be revised, then there is a lot to understand about the relations between Rome and India and the organisation of this trade, i.e. the machinery set up by the merchants themselves in order to avoid strictly 'anecdotal' interpretations of Roman artefacts found in India.

Finally, Ray gives a very detailed account of the trade relations between India and Southeast Asia (4. *Early Contacts between South and Southeast Asia*). It must be noted that this topic is coloured by a nationalistic view which sees

5. There are some inaccuracies regarding the interpretation of recent archaeological finds in the Gulf (pp. 52-57), but no real errors.

6. V. BEGLEY, "Ceramic Evidence for pre-*Periplus* Trade on the Indian Coasts", *Rome and India. The Ancient Sea Trade*, ed. by R.D. de Puma & V. Begley, Oxford University Press, Delhi, 1992, pp. 157-196.

traces of a brahmanical influence dating from the 5th century A.D. in the temples, sculptures, royal titles and legends of Southeast Asia. This "Hinduisation" of Asia is said to have been effected by kings (?), colonies (?) and merchants. This theory has now come under severe criticism and the author presents numerous archaeological remains as proof of the ancient and continuous links between India and Asia, extending from the Bay of Bengal to Vietnam and the Moluccas Islands. They seem to have traded mainly in perishable goods (herbs and spices [cinnamon, cassia and camphor], different kinds of wood, textiles, sugar-cane, etc.), although Southeast Asia was India's only source of tin. The author adds a list of Roman finds in Southeast Asia which were often Indian imitations of Roman goods. Numerous inscriptions provide valuable information about those who were engaged in this exchange of goods. One wonders whether it was trade in the real sense or political exchanges (tributes, gifts and return gifts, etc.) of an "imperialist" nature. The lack of literary data has given rise to many anthropological interpretations which minimise the impact of Hinduism on the development of Southeast Asia in ancient times (1st century B.C.-5th/6th century A.D.) when Buddhism and Brahmanism coexisted and sometimes influenced each other (see also pp. 154-161 on the spread of Buddhism and its influence in Southeast Asia).

This relationship between the two religious communities and the development of trade is the main focus of the book (5. *Buddhism and Trade*). The theory (considered very important in India) is that there was a correlation between the spread of Buddhism and the expansion of trade in India from the pre-Mauryan period. Buddhism, which developed in urban surroundings as a reaction (?) to Brahmanism having its roots in rural areas, recognises the "dignity" of the trading profession (some of the Buddha's earliest disciples were merchants) unlike Brahmanism which divides society into four distinct *varnas* organised on hierarchical lines. It is true that Jainism too transgressed the Brahmanical doctrine and played a significant role in the development of India's social structure in the post-Mauryan era.[7] However, according to Ray, Jainism does not have a monastic order similar to the Buddhist order which was one of the major driving forces behind the expansion of trade. The traditional "retreat" of sages during the rainy season soon became a permanent establishment housing Buddhist monks and nuns and created a new dynamic relationship between the clergy and the ordinary folk. At the same time, monasteries became the guardians of knowledge and skills, especially writing and medicine[8] as stressed by the author.

---

7. The author has been criticised by some of her Indian colleagues for having failed to devote sufficient attention to the influence of Jaịnism.

8. Ray lays much stress on the spread of writing through trade by studying the numerous seals bearing inscriptions in the *kharoshti* script found all over India. In other places, she takes great pains to point out the abundance and the informative or symbolic value of the iconography of these seals (which often have pictures of

The monastery was the principal recipient of gifts and donations (one of the basic tenets of the Buddhist faith) from lay followers who acquired a high social status as indicated by inscriptions praising their generosity. The most prestigious givers of gifts were the royal families whose liberal patronage is evident in Gujerat, in the Deccan and in Southeast Asia.[9] Apart from large land-holdings, the monasteries had enormous reserves of wealth which were partly reinvested in trade by the laity or by the monks themselves, cf. p. 149, this extract from the *Jataka* : *The Elder Ananda once received a present of a thousand robes. The king on hearing this thought: "The Supreme Buddha allows only three robes. Ananda is doing a little trade in cloth, I suppose".*[10] Finally, the laity's participation in the rites conducted by the monks (*e.g.* the monthly *uposatha* ceremony) is an indication of the laity's awareness of its Buddhist identity which also made it more cohesive as a community as seen in the merchant diasporas.[11]

To support his thesis, the author describes in detail the location of monasteries along the main trade routes crossing the peninsula: the route across the Gangetic plain, the Deccan route, the southern route through the Krishna valley and the concentration of Buddhist establishments at crucial points along these routes at Mathura, Junnar, Nasik, etc. Drawing attention to the establishment of monasteries in the vicinity of coastal sites (ports), Ray stresses that Buddhism claimed to protect its followers from the perils of the sea, *e.g.* Boddhisattva Avalokitesvara is considered to be the protector of sailors. Finally, the author analyses the construction process of the monasteries and the sculptures ornamenting them.

Ray winds up his arguments in the *Concluding Reflections* (pp. 189-201). He attributes the decline of this flourishing trade after the 3rd-4th century A.D. to the resurgence of Hinduism following the break-up of Buddhism into rival sects both in India and in Southeast Asia. One would have nevertheless expected an answer to a problem which has not even been mentioned. Ray rightly insists on the diversion of the western trade (with Rome [?], Egypt, Southern Arabia)

---

boats). Is the area covered by these seals an indication of the geographical spread of Buddhist trade as claimed by the author?

9. According to the author, the absence of powerful and generous dynasties explains why the monastic institution did not spread in Tamilnadu and Bengal. Perhaps, this hypothesis should be toned down in the case of Tamilnadu where there were powerful dynasties and in the case of Bengal the date of the earliest Buddhist monasteries should be defined.

10. For relations between monasteries and merchants' guilds, see H.P. RAY's earlier book, *Monastery and Guild, Commerce under the Satavahanas*, Delhi, Oxford University Press, 1986. In the present book, the author has refuted, like other authors, the hypothesis that monasteries played the role of caravanserais for merchants' caravans.

11. The author draws her inspiration from the anthropological models proposed by C. Meillassoux.

towards Sri Lanka in the 4th century A.D. when trade with the West stopped completely. Was this not the period when Buddhism was in its full glory in Sri Lanka, thus providing another proof of the close association of Buddhism and trade? And if this is not true, does the thesis remain valid?

The author ends up by opening a new field of historical research called "maritime archaeology".[12] It covers not only ancient remains but also includes wind systems and navigation calendars side-by-side with ship-building techniques and planning of ports. But the name is quite explicit and the subject is new to India.[13] Ray stresses the need to undertake technological, historical or ethnographical studies, particularly the last as ethnography has recently gained importance in India. Indian texts are silent about ship-building. All we know is that carpenters from Varanasi, plagued by debts, built a boat by cutting trees in the forest and sailed down the Ganges to the Bay of Bengal and went to another country. Other sources mention several types of boats and navigation techniques (pp. 179-181: Buddhist literature, incidentally in Tamil) but there is no real description of ships. We do find ancient pictures of boats (on seals, coins and especially on "memorial steles" as in Gujerat — see the works of J. Deloche[14]) but they are usually stereotyped and not very informative. On the contrary, traditional ship- and boat-building techniques are still seen in India, particularly the technique of sewn boats.

Ray is interested in ancient Graeco-Roman and Arabian ship-building techniques.[15] She is probably right to draw attention to the extraordinary nature of the ships having a capacity of 1000 tonnes mentioned by L. Casson and he often wonders about the frequent claim about the "superiority" of Roman ships.

---

12. The author makes practically no allusions to undersea archaeology as practised in Europe. It is true that this discipline is almost unknown in India. Ray refers in passing to experimental archaeology (maritime) without going deeper into the subject.

13. The author repeats some of her ideas in "An Interpretative Essay on Maritime History", *Journal of Indian Ocean Studies*, vol. 3/2, 1996, New Delhi (Society for Indian Ocean Studies), pp. 167-176. In addition to what is given above, the author rightly stresses the role played by *Hajj* (the pilgrimage to Mecca) in the greater religious, cultural and social cohesion in the Indian Ocean, although she examines with caution Wink's recent theories on the triptych of 'trade-spread of Islam-birth of states': A. WINK, *Al Hind. The Making of the Indo-Islamic World*. Oxford University Press, New Delhi, 1990, which holds that Islam totally dominated trade in the Indian Ocean during the medieval period.

14. J. DELOCHE, "Iconographic Evidence on the Development of Boat and Ship Structures in India (2nd century B.C.-15th century A.D.), *Tradition and Archaeology, Early Maritime Contacts in the Indian Ocean*, ed. by H.P. RAY & J.-F. SALLES, New Delhi (1996), pp. 199-224, with bibliography.

15. As regards Arabia, the author is right to refute the theory which locates Solomon's Ophir in India (p.168) and which wrongly believes that the Gerrheans engaged in maritime trade in the Red Sea.

One point which intrigues her is the data in our possession about the ship-building tradition in the Red Sea area which is totally devoid of forests, especially because the texts do not mention any import of wood for ship-building purposes as in the case of the Persian Gulf. Without neglecting the possibility of dismantled boats being transported on the Nile to the Red Sea (considering that the link with the Amer Lakes was not built before Trajan's time), the author expresses doubts. Was the trade between Rome and India really carried out with Roman ships (never mentioned in the *Periplus*, nor by Strabo who is quite vague about the 120 ships leaving for India) or was it carried out with the help of Arab and Indian ships? Frankly speaking, there is no convincing answer to this question.

L. Casson has proposed a sailing schedule for ships according to which ships leaving the Red Sea in July[16] reached the Indian coast in early September. Ray (pp. 187-188 partially repeating pp. 85-86) points out that this means that the sailors would cross the sea at the height of the north-west monsoon and such a dangerous crossing would be possible only because of the "superiority" of Roman ships. If Casson's suggestion appears impractical, the author should have suggested another alternative. The solution may lie in J. Rougé's suggestion[17] that the ships probably sailed down the Red Sea in July, then stopped in the South-Arabian ports for trade when the monsoon was at its height and completed their journey in late August or early September. This delayed their arrival in India by barely two to three weeks as compared to Casson's schedule and gave them enough time to engage in trade before setting off for the Red Sea in November with the onset of the south-west monsoon.

An important aspect of maritime archaeology is the research on ports (see pp. 170-171 for ports on the Red Sea, explained in detail in a special report published in the present issue). Ray reminds us that the Indian peninsula does not have any natural harbours and that it is difficult to approach the coast almost everywhere. This explains why many ports are located in the estuaries of rivers. It is very unlikely that these ports were built in ancient times![18] What has often been interpreted in this manner (pp.185-186 and the author's doubts) should certainly be re-examined in the light of the new facts being discovered about the frequent shifting of river estuaries generally due to siltation of the coast.

---

16. Regarding navigation conditions in the Red Sea, read A. GIL-ARTAGNAN's recent essay *Expédition Pount (Autour de l'Afrique sur la route des Phéniciens). Essai de reconstitution d'un navire et d'une navigation antiques* (1975-1991), L'Harmattan, Paris, 1994.

17. J. ROUGÉ, "La navigation en mer Érythrée dans l'Antiquité", *L'Arabie et ses mers bordières. 1. Itiniraires et voisinages*, ed. by J.-F. Salles, TMO 16, Lyon, 1988, pp. 59-74.

18. In a related field, the author wrongly mentions the construction of a port in Delos in 8th century B.C. (p. 185).

The new avenues of research opened by Ray are full of promise. Although we have dwelt longer in this article on the author's new way of approaching problems related to the links between the West and India, we must point out that she has not neglected Southeast Asia. Ray reviews in detail the archaeological excavations and historical data which enable us to get a better idea of the maritime activities in this region during Antiquity.[19] It becomes clear that the generally accepted division of the Indian Ocean into two parts, the western part covering Africa, Arabia and India and the eastern part extending from the Bay of Bengal to Southeast Asia, is largely artificial and future research should look at both these parts together. This is one of the innovative aspects of Ray's work. Another significant trait of the rapidly growing field of maritime archaeology, although it tends to overshadow conventional archaeology, is the determination to go beyond the Indo-Gangetic plain and dissertations on the "Indian village" and open new avenues of research leading to the maritime domain where India occupied an important place. Though it is possible that merchants who had embraced Buddhism were not the only ones to sail to these distant lands, it is to Ray's credit that she has exposed Indian historiography to the "winds of change".

Jean-François SALLES
Institut F.-Courby, UMR 5649
Jean-Francois.Salles@mom.fr

19. We must mention in particular the work done by P.-Y. MANGUIN, *e g.* "Southeast Asian Shipping in the Indian Ocean during the First Millennium A.D.", in *Tradition and Archaeology...*, pp. 181-198.

LIST OF ILLUSTRATIONS*

---

* We use bold to note the number of the pages.